OF THE IMMORTAL

Blood of a Thousand

publisher
Mike Richardson

series editor
Dave Chipps

collection editor
Lynn Adair

collection designer
Harald Graham

**English-language version produced by
Studio Proteus for Dark Horse Comics, Inc.**

This book collects issues one through six
of the Dark Horse comic-book series,
Blade of the Immortal.

Published by
Dark Horse Comics, Inc.
10956 SE Main Street
Milwaukie, OR 97222

www.darkhorse.com

To find a comics shop in your area, call the
Comic Shop Locator Service toll-free at 1-888-266-4226.

First edition: March 1997
ISBN: 1-56971-239-5

7 9 10 8 6

Printed in Canada

OF THE IMMORTAL

art and story
HIROAKI SAMURA

translation
Dana Lewis & Toren Smith

lettering and retouch
Wayne Truman

Blood of a Thousand

DARK HORSE COMICS®

ABOUT THE TRANSLATION

The Swastika

The main character in *Blade of the Immortal*, Manji, has taken the "crux gammata" as both his name and his personal symbol. This symbol is also known as the *swastika*, a name derived from the Sanskrit *svastika* (meaning "welfare," from su — "well" + asti "he is"). As a symbol of prosperity and good fortune, the swastika was widely used throughout the ancient world (for example, appearing often on Mesopotamian coinage), including North and South America and has been used in Japan as a symbol of Buddhism since ancient times. To be precise, the symbol generally used by Japanese Buddhists is the *sauvastika*, which moves in a counterclockwise direction, and is called the *manji* in Japanese. The arms of the swastika, which point in a clockwise direction, are generally considered a solar symbol. It was this version (the *hakenkreuz*) that was perverted by the Nazis. The *sauvastika* generally stands for night and often for magical practices. It is important that readers understand that the *swastika* has ancient and honorable origins, and it is those that apply to this story, which takes place in the 18th century [ca. 1782-3]. *There is no anti-Semitic or pro-Nazi meaning behind the use of the symbol in this story. Those meanings did not exist until after 1910.*

The Artwork

The creator of *Blade of the Immortal* requested that we make an effort to avoid mirror-imaging his artwork. Normally, all of our manga are first copied in a mirror-image in order to facilitate the left-to-right reading of the pages. However, Mr. Samura decided that he would rather see his pages reversed via the technique of cutting up the panels and re-pasting them in reverse order. While we feel that this often leads to problems in panel-to-panel continuity, we place primary importance on the wishes of the creator. Therefore, most of *Blade of the Immortal* has been produced using the "cut and paste" technique. There are, of course, some sequences where it was impossible to do this, and mirror-imaged panels or pages were used.

The Sound Effects & Dialogue

Since some of Mr. Samura's sound effects are integral parts of the artwork, we decided to leave those in their original Japanese. When it was crucial to the understanding of the panel that the sound effect be in English, however, Mr. Samura chose to redraw the panel. We hope readers will view the un-retouched sound effects as essential portions of Mr. Samura's extraordinary artwork. In addition, Mr. Samura's treatment of dialogue is quite different from that featured in average samurai manga and is considered to be one of the things that has made *Blade* such a hit in Japan. Mr. Samura has mixed a variety of linguistic styles in this fantasy story where some characters speak in the mannered style of old Japan while others speak as if they were street-corner punks from a bad area of modern-day Tokyo. The anachronistic slang used by some of the characters in the English translation reflects the unusual mix of speech patterns from the original, Japanese text.

GLOSSARY

Daimyō: the lords of provincial feudal fiefs known as *han*

Daruma: a Japanese doll without arms or legs, modeled on a Buddhist priest who meditated so long his limbs atrophied

Dōjō: a hall for martial arts training

Edo: capital of pre-modern Japan; later renamed Tokyo

Hatamoto: the inner circle of *daimyō*, or feudal lords

Heian: the period of the Heian Court (800 A.D. - 1200 A.D.), the golden age of Japanese poetry

Honsho: an artisans' district in central Edo

Ittō-ryū: the radical sword school of Anotsu Kagehisa

Kasai: a district in Edo

Kengō: a highly accomplished swordsman

Kessen-chū: the "sacred bloodworms"; a person infected with them cannot die but feels pain like a mortal

Mount Takeo: temple mountains on the western outskirts of Edo, famous for its colony of macaque monkeys

Mutenichi-ryū: the sword school led by Rin's father

Oibara: when followers of a departed lord commit a ritual suicide to follow him in death

Onmitsu: a ninja of the Edo Shōgunate; performed secret missions and spying as well as assassinations

Ryo: a gold piece

Sensei: an honorific term for a teacher or artist

Seppuku: ritual suicide; also, *harakiri*

Shinobi-metsuke: "ninja censor"; an intelligence officer, both administrator and field agent

Yōjimbō: bodyguard

Yomi: the land of the dead

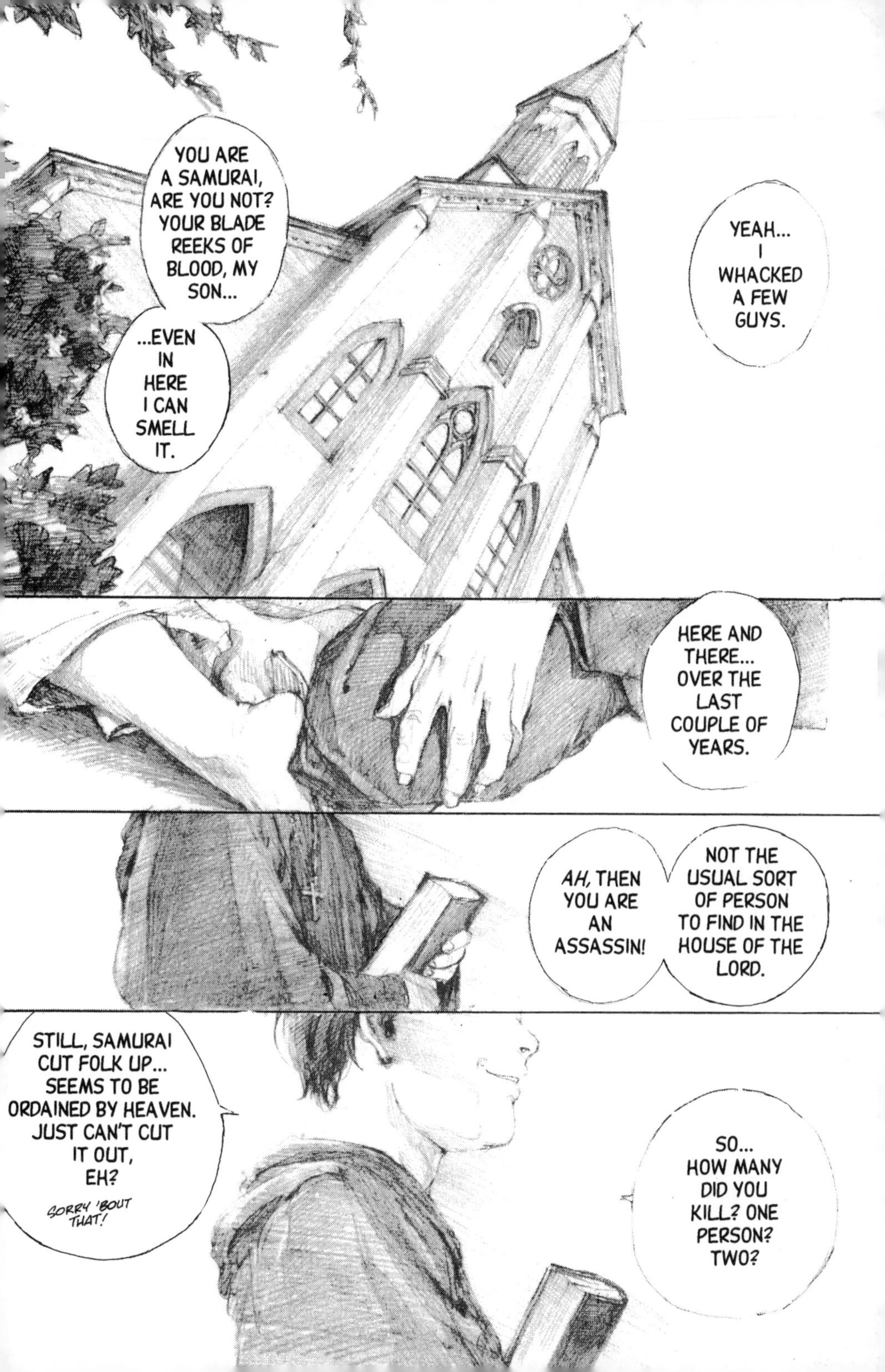
YOU ARE A SAMURAI, ARE YOU NOT? YOUR BLADE REEKS OF BLOOD, MY SON...
...EVEN IN HERE I CAN SMELL IT.
YEAH... I WHACKED A FEW GUYS.
HERE AND THERE... OVER THE LAST COUPLE OF YEARS.
AH, THEN YOU ARE AN ASSASSIN!
NOT THE USUAL SORT OF PERSON TO FIND IN THE HOUSE OF THE LORD.
STILL, SAMURAI CUT FOLK UP... SEEMS TO BE ORDAINED BY HEAVEN. JUST CAN'T CUT IT OUT, EH?
SORRY 'BOUT THAT!
SO... HOW MANY DID YOU KILL? ONE PERSON? TWO?

PROLOGUE: CRIMINAL

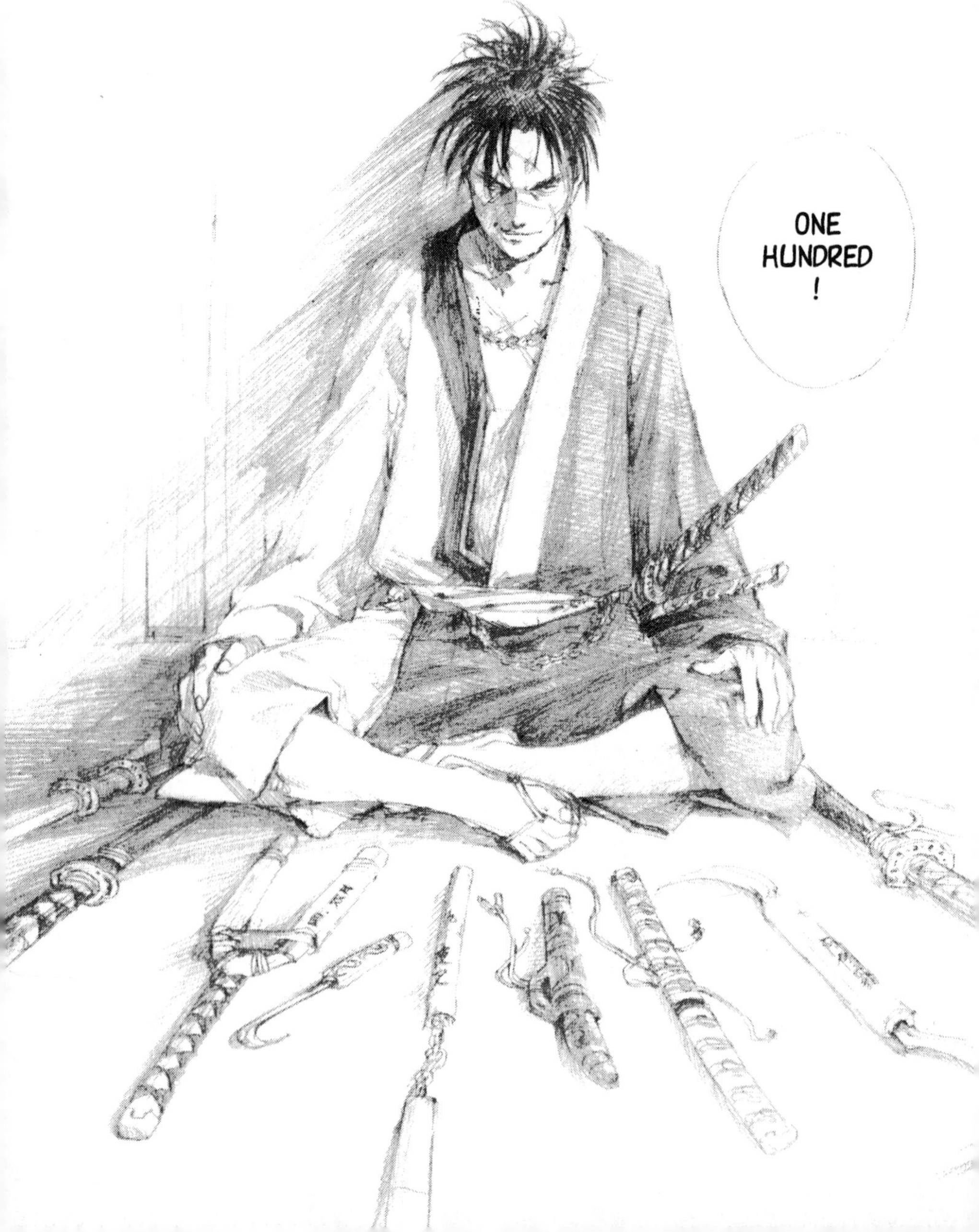
ONE HUNDRED !

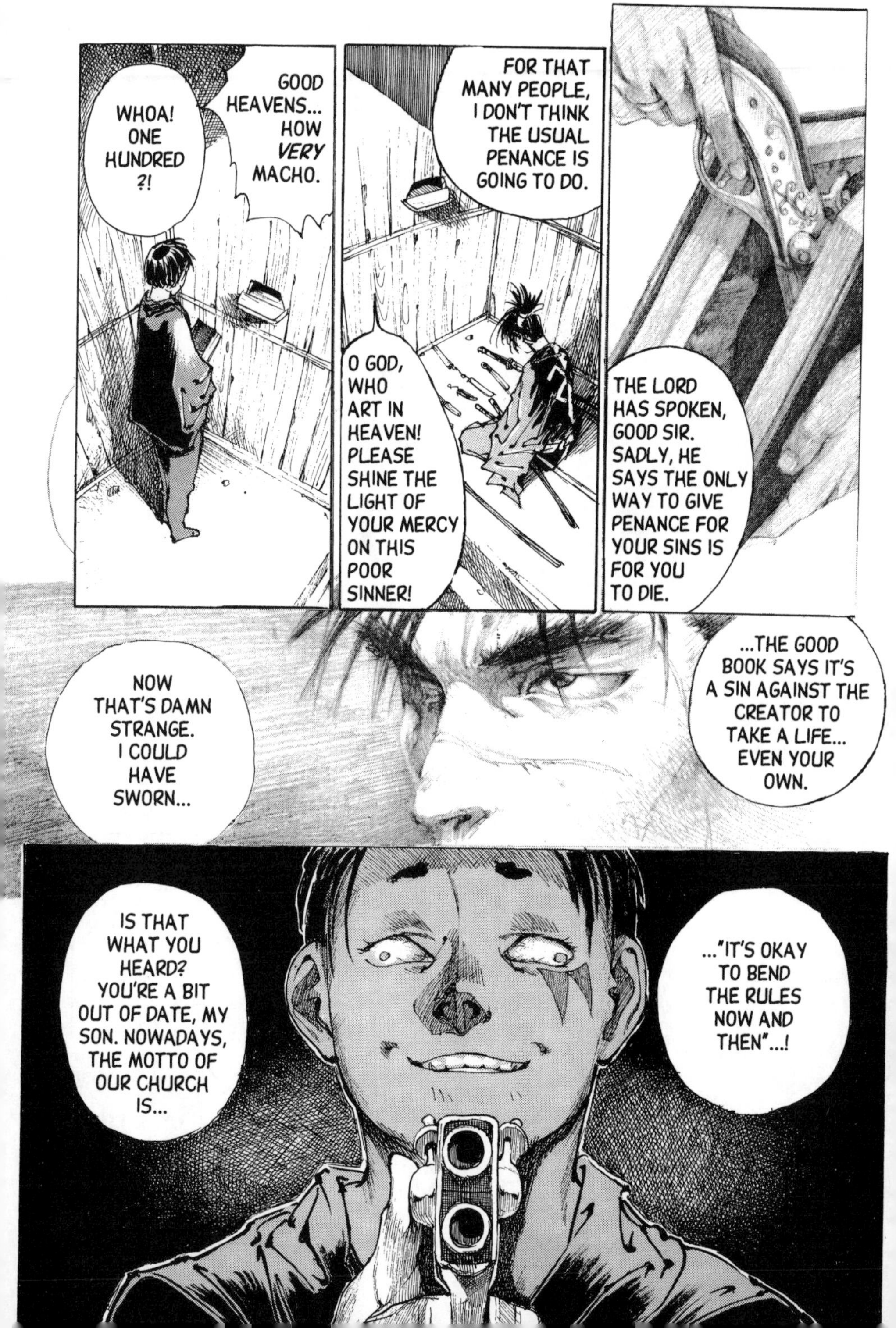
WHOA! ONE HUNDRED ?!
GOOD HEAVENS... HOW *VERY* MACHO.
FOR THAT MANY PEOPLE, I DON'T THINK THE USUAL PENANCE IS GOING TO DO.
O GOD, WHO ART IN HEAVEN! PLEASE SHINE THE LIGHT OF YOUR MERCY ON THIS POOR SINNER!
THE LORD HAS SPOKEN, GOOD SIR. SADLY, HE SAYS THE ONLY WAY TO GIVE PENANCE FOR YOUR SINS IS FOR YOU TO DIE.
NOW THAT'S DAMN STRANGE. I COULD HAVE SWORN...
...THE GOOD BOOK SAYS IT'S A SIN AGAINST THE CREATOR TO TAKE A LIFE... EVEN YOUR OWN.
IS THAT WHAT YOU HEARD? YOU'RE A BIT OUT OF DATE, MY SON. NOWADAYS, THE MOTTO OF OUR CHURCH IS...
..."IT'S OKAY TO BEND THE RULES NOW AND THEN"...!

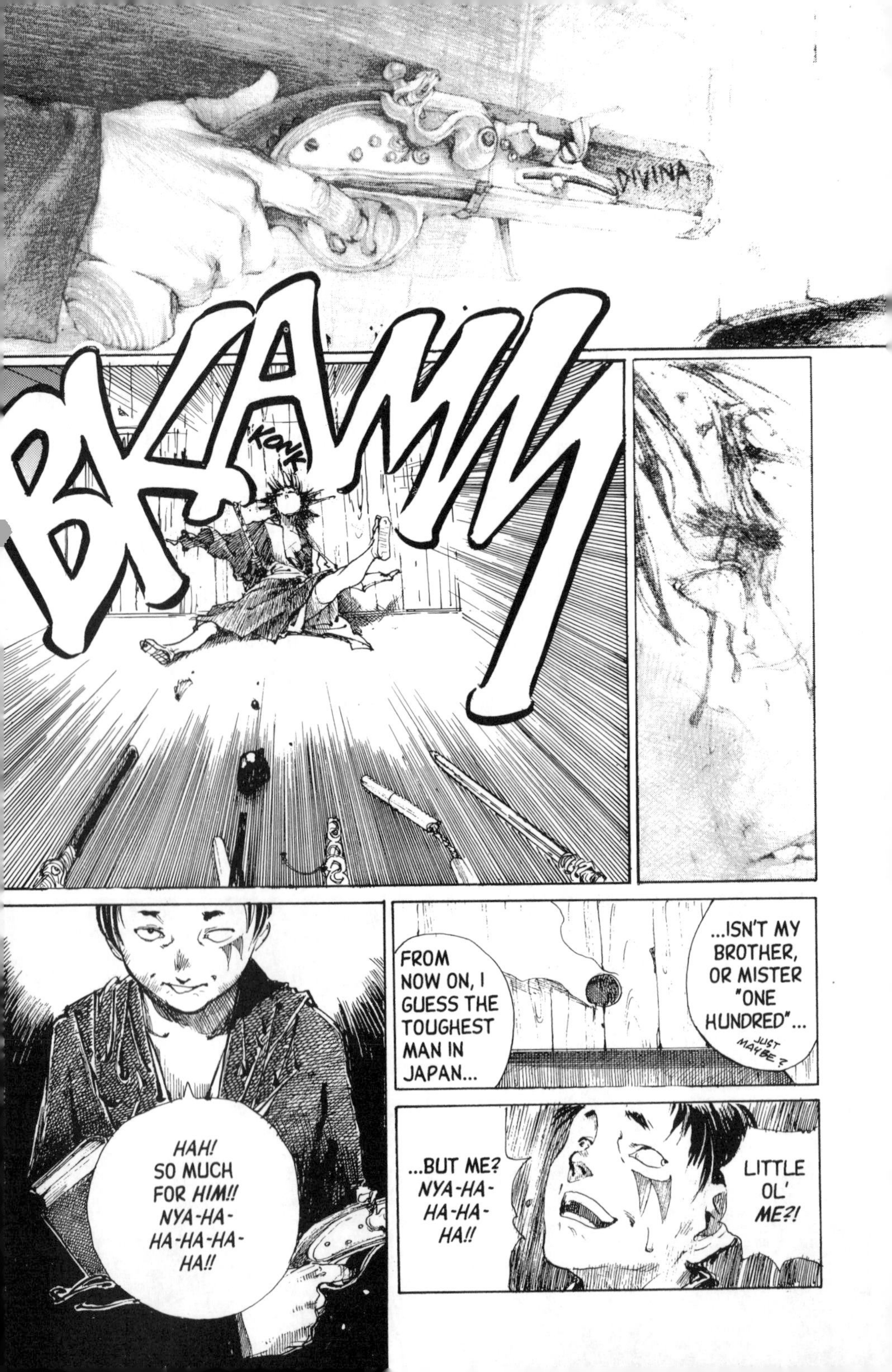
DIVINA
BLAMM
KONK
HAH! SO MUCH FOR HIM!! NYA-HA-HA-HA-HA-HA!!
FROM NOW ON, I GUESS THE TOUGHEST MAN IN JAPAN...
...ISN'T MY BROTHER, OR MISTER "ONE HUNDRED"...
JUST MAYBE?
...BUT ME? NYA-HA-HA-HA-HA!!
LITTLE OL' ME?!

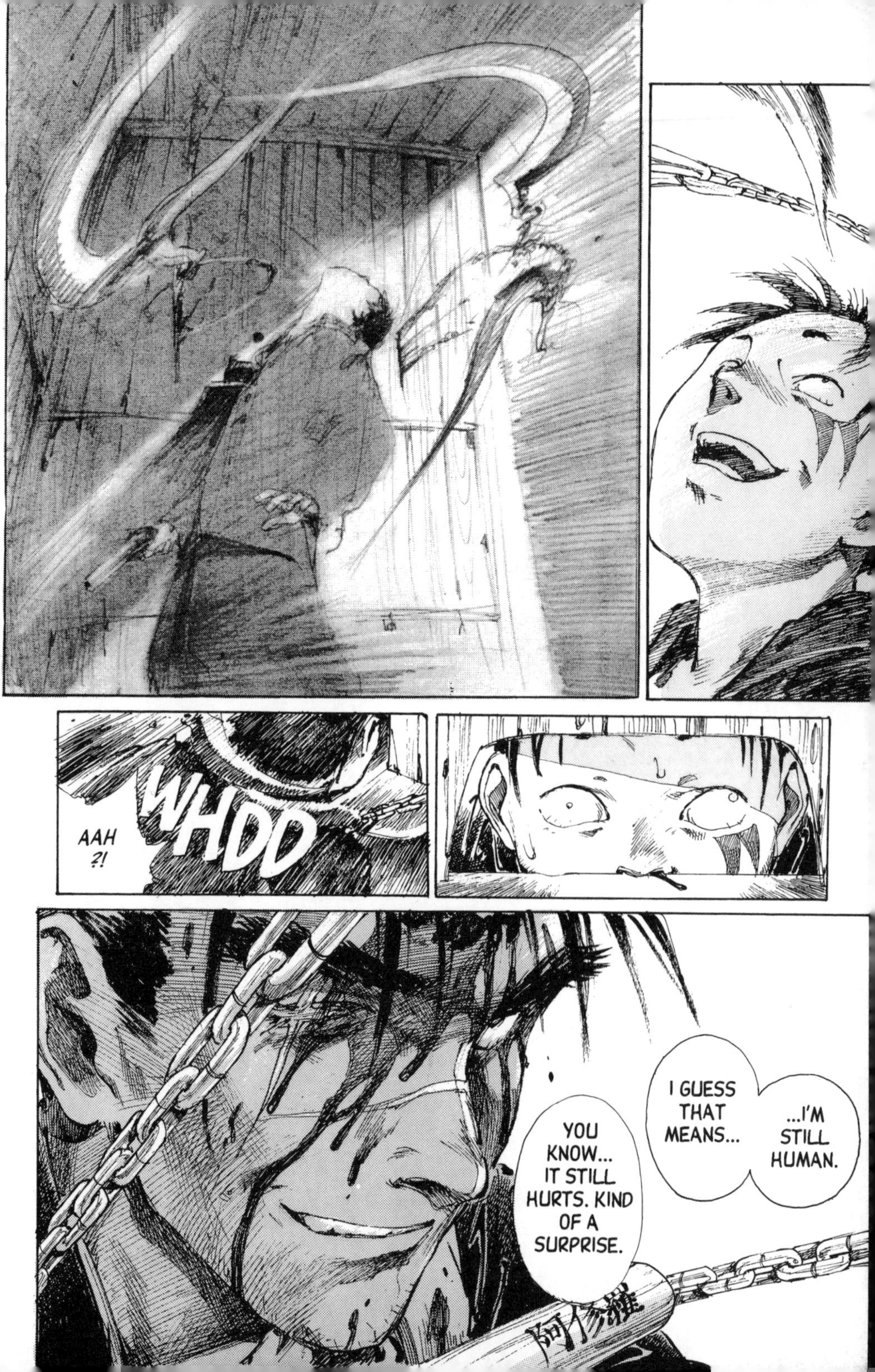
AAH ?!
WHDD
YOU KNOW... IT STILL HURTS. KIND OF A SURPRISE.
I GUESS THAT MEANS...
...I'M STILL HUMAN.

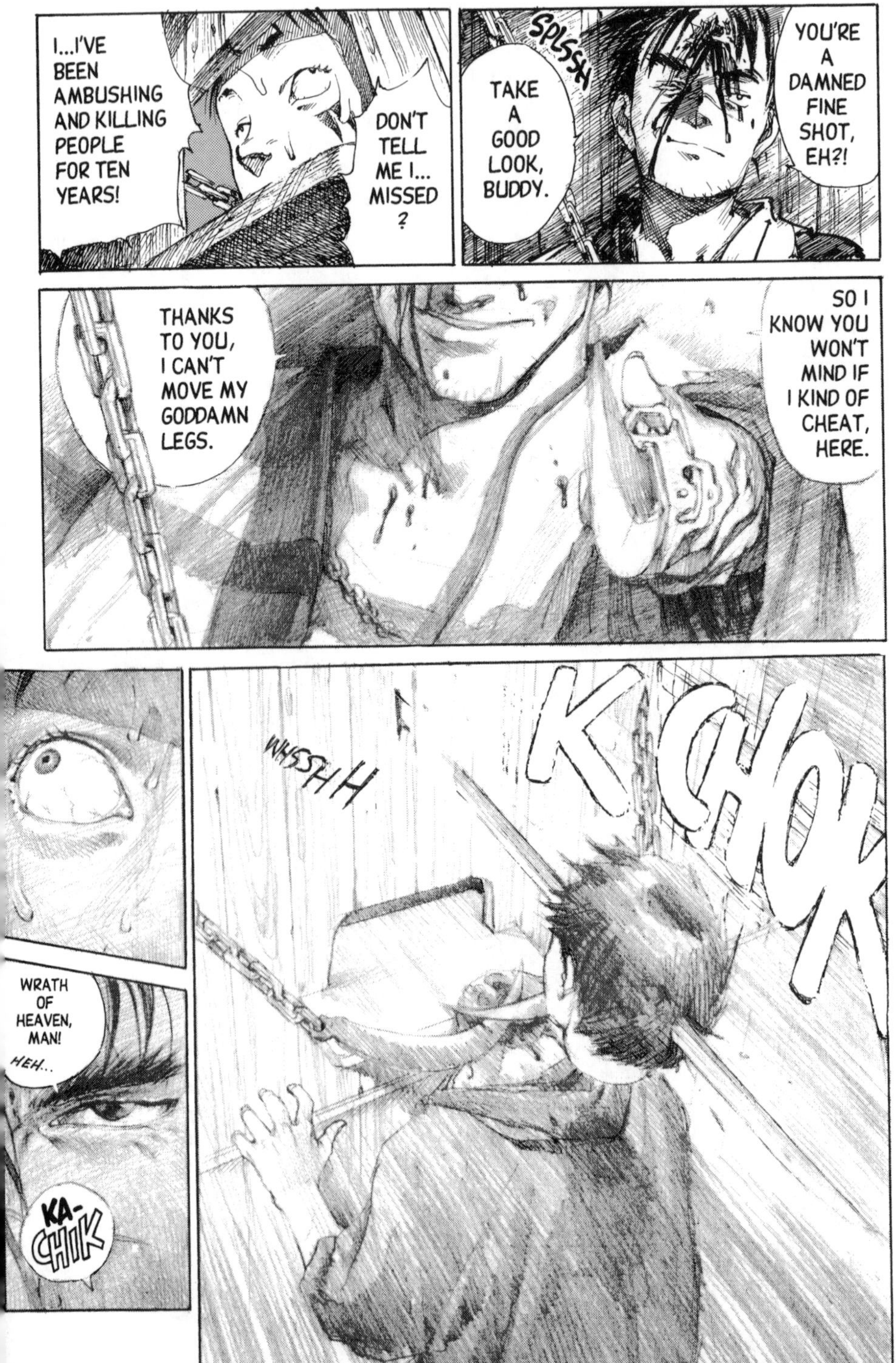
I...I'VE BEEN AMBUSHING AND KILLING PEOPLE FOR TEN YEARS!
DON'T TELL ME I... MISSED?
SPLSSH
TAKE A GOOD LOOK, BUDDY.
YOU'RE A DAMNED FINE SHOT, EH?!
THANKS TO YOU, I CAN'T MOVE MY GODDAMN LEGS.
SO I KNOW YOU WON'T MIND IF I KIND OF CHEAT, HERE.
WRATH OF HEAVEN, MAN!
HEH...
KA-CHIK
WHSSHH
KCHOK

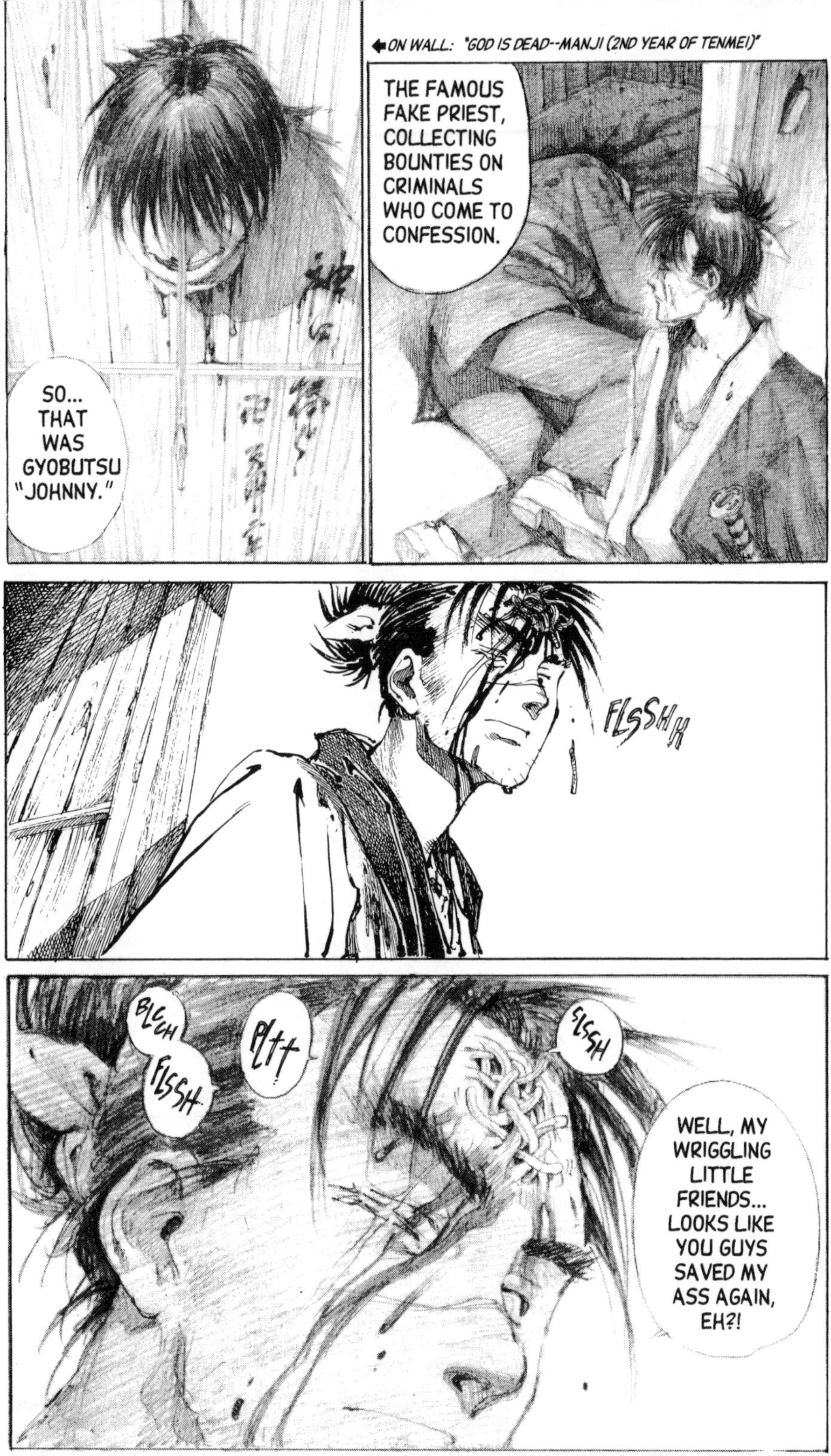
ON WALL: "GOD IS DEAD--MANJI (2ND YEAR OF TENMEI)"
SO... THAT WAS GYOBUTSU "JOHNNY."
THE FAMOUS FAKE PRIEST, COLLECTING BOUNTIES ON CRIMINALS WHO COME TO CONFESSION.
FLSSHK
BLCCH
FLSSH
PLTT!
SLSSH
WELL, MY WRIGGLING LITTLE FRIENDS... LOOKS LIKE YOU GUYS SAVED MY ASS AGAIN, EH?!

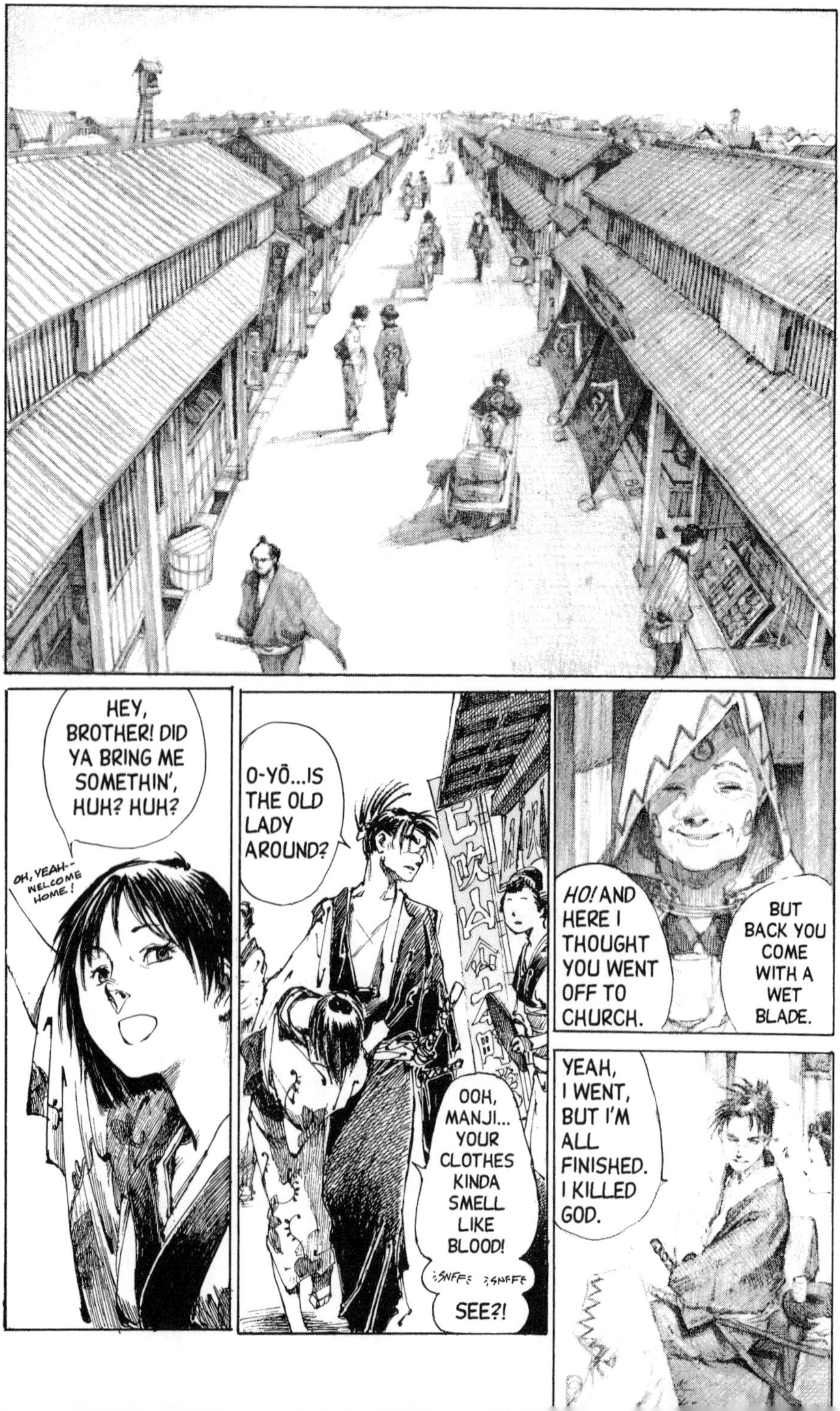
HEY, BROTHER! DID YA BRING ME SOMETHIN', HUH? HUH?
OH, YEAH-- WELCOME HOME!
O-YŌ...IS THE OLD LADY AROUND?
OOH, MANJI... YOUR CLOTHES KINDA SMELL LIKE BLOOD!
SNFF SNFF
SEE?!
HO! AND HERE I THOUGHT YOU WENT OFF TO CHURCH.
BUT BACK YOU COME WITH A WET BLADE.
YEAH, I WENT, BUT I'M ALL FINISHED. I KILLED GOD.

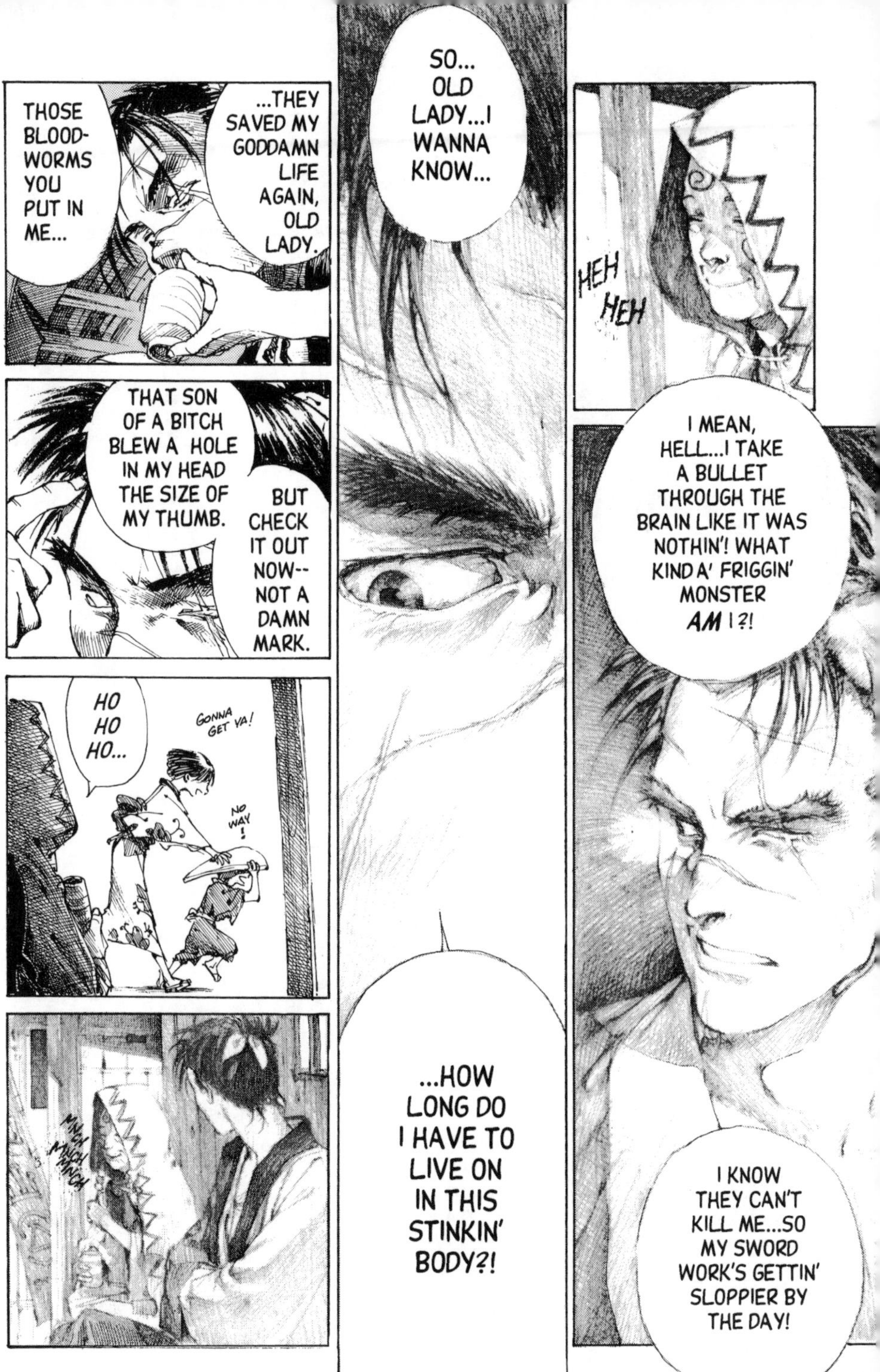
THOSE BLOOD-WORMS YOU PUT IN ME...
...THEY SAVED MY GODDAMN LIFE AGAIN, OLD LADY.
THAT SON OF A BITCH BLEW A HOLE IN MY HEAD THE SIZE OF MY THUMB.
BUT CHECK IT OUT NOW-- NOT A DAMN MARK.
HO HO HO...
GONNA GET YA!
NO WAY!
MNCH MNCH MNCH
SO... OLD LADY...I WANNA KNOW...
...HOW LONG DO I HAVE TO LIVE ON IN THIS STINKIN' BODY?!
HEH HEH
I MEAN, HELL...I TAKE A BULLET THROUGH THE BRAIN LIKE IT WAS NOTHIN'! WHAT KIND A' FRIGGIN' MONSTER AM I?!
I KNOW THEY CAN'T KILL ME...SO MY SWORD WORK'S GETTIN' SLOPPIER BY THE DAY!

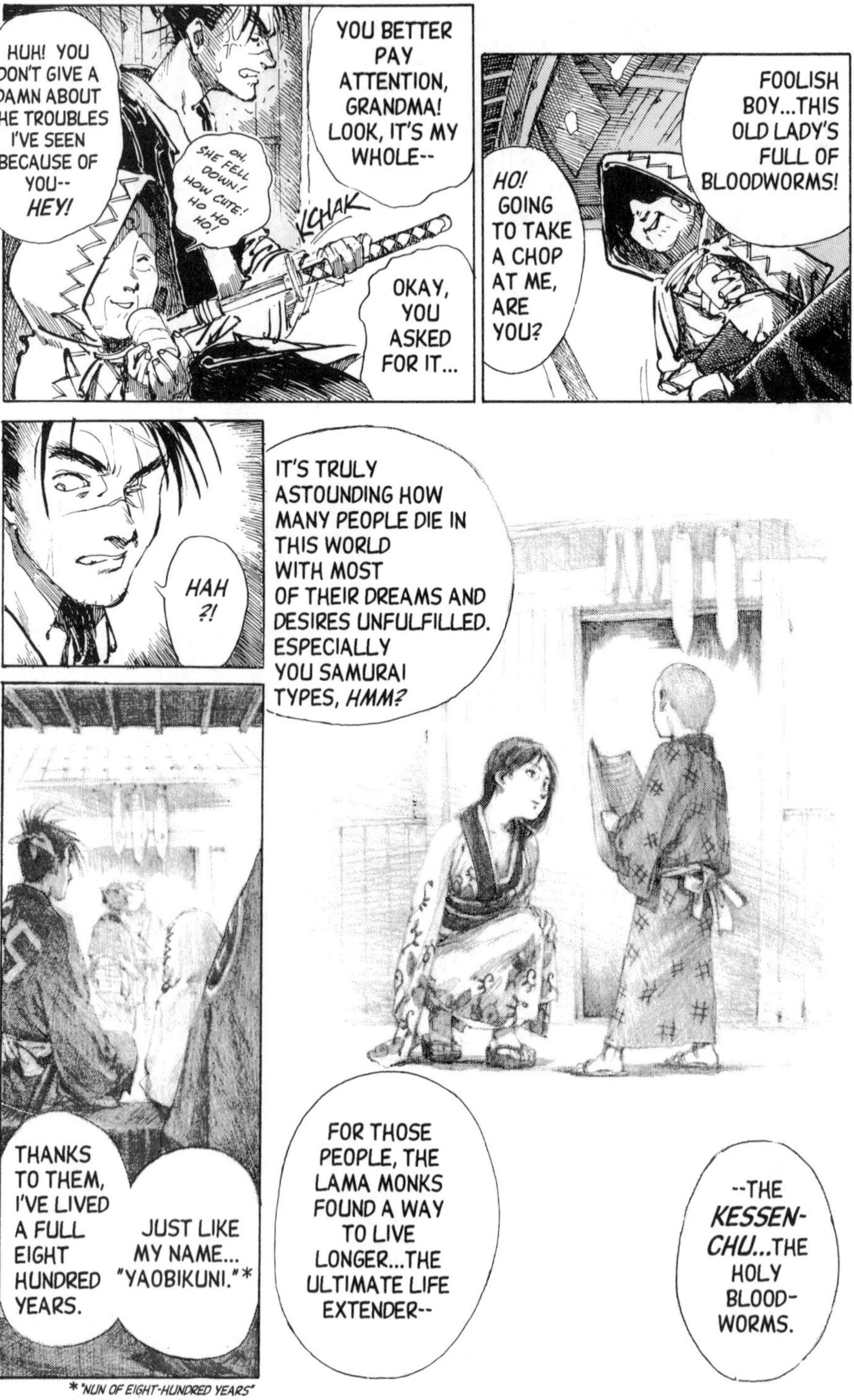
HUH! YOU DON'T GIVE A DAMN ABOUT THE TROUBLES I'VE SEEN BECAUSE OF YOU-- *HEY!*
OH, SHE FELL DOWN! HOW CUTE! HO HO HO!
YOU BETTER PAY ATTENTION, GRANDMA! LOOK, IT'S MY WHOLE--
KCHAK
OKAY, YOU ASKED FOR IT...
HO! GOING TO TAKE A CHOP AT ME, ARE YOU?
FOOLISH BOY...THIS OLD LADY'S FULL OF BLOODWORMS!
HAH ?!
IT'S TRULY ASTOUNDING HOW MANY PEOPLE DIE IN THIS WORLD WITH MOST OF THEIR DREAMS AND DESIRES UNFULFILLED. ESPECIALLY YOU SAMURAI TYPES, *HMM?*
THANKS TO THEM, I'VE LIVED A FULL EIGHT HUNDRED YEARS.
JUST LIKE MY NAME... "YAOBIKUNI."*
FOR THOSE PEOPLE, THE LAMA MONKS FOUND A WAY TO LIVE LONGER...THE ULTIMATE LIFE EXTENDER--
--THE *KESSEN-CHU*...THE HOLY BLOOD-WORMS.

* "NUN OF EIGHT-HUNDRED YEARS"

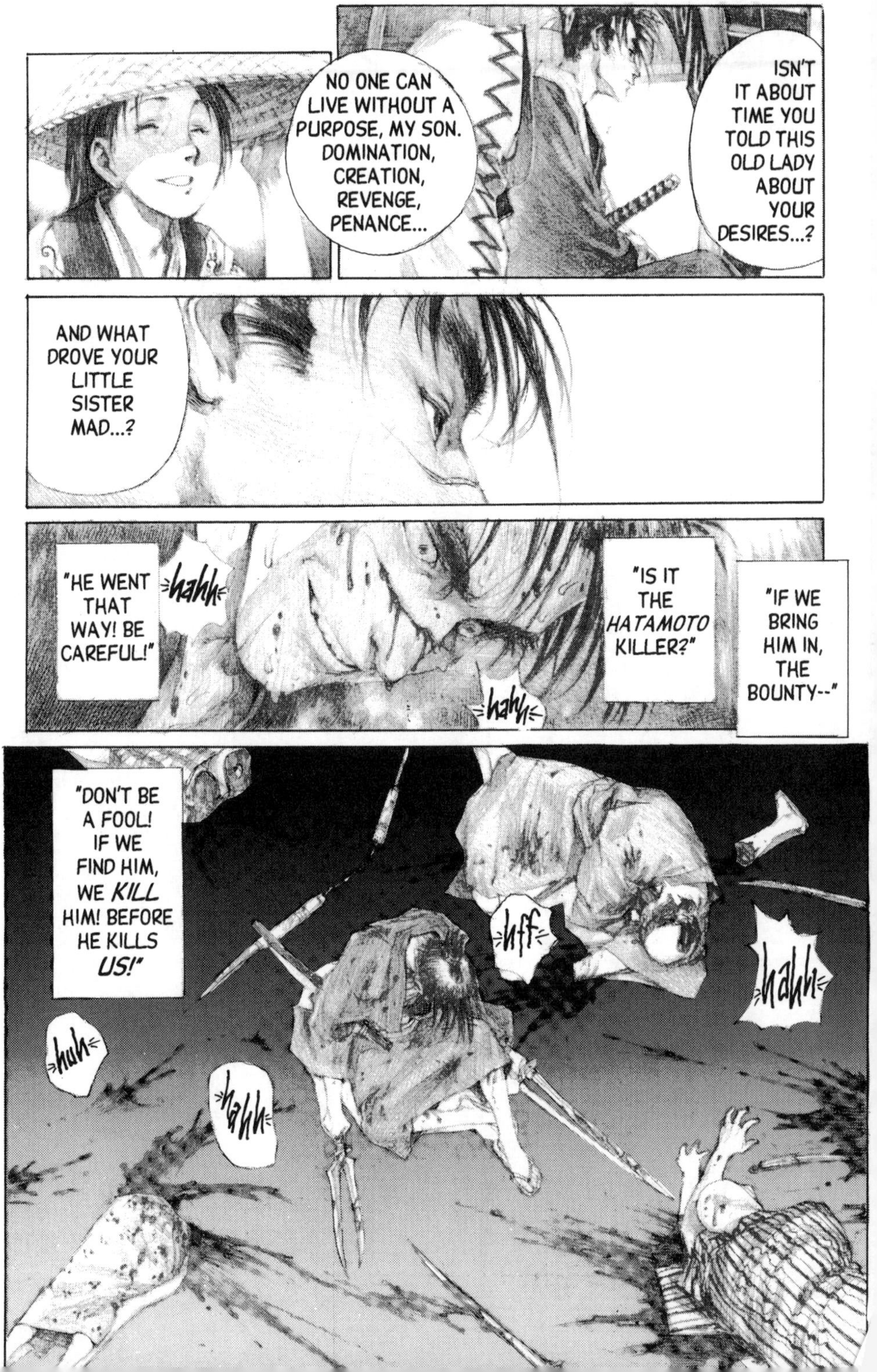
NO ONE CAN LIVE WITHOUT A PURPOSE, MY SON. DOMINATION, CREATION, REVENGE, PENANCE...
ISN'T IT ABOUT TIME YOU TOLD THIS OLD LADY ABOUT YOUR DESIRES...?
AND WHAT DROVE YOUR LITTLE SISTER MAD...?
"HE WENT THAT WAY! BE CAREFUL!"
hahh
"IS IT THE *HATAMOTO* KILLER?"
hahh
"IF WE BRING HIM IN, THE BOUNTY--"
"DON'T BE A FOOL! IF WE FIND HIM, WE *KILL* HIM! BEFORE HE KILLS *US!*"
hff
hahh
huh
hahh

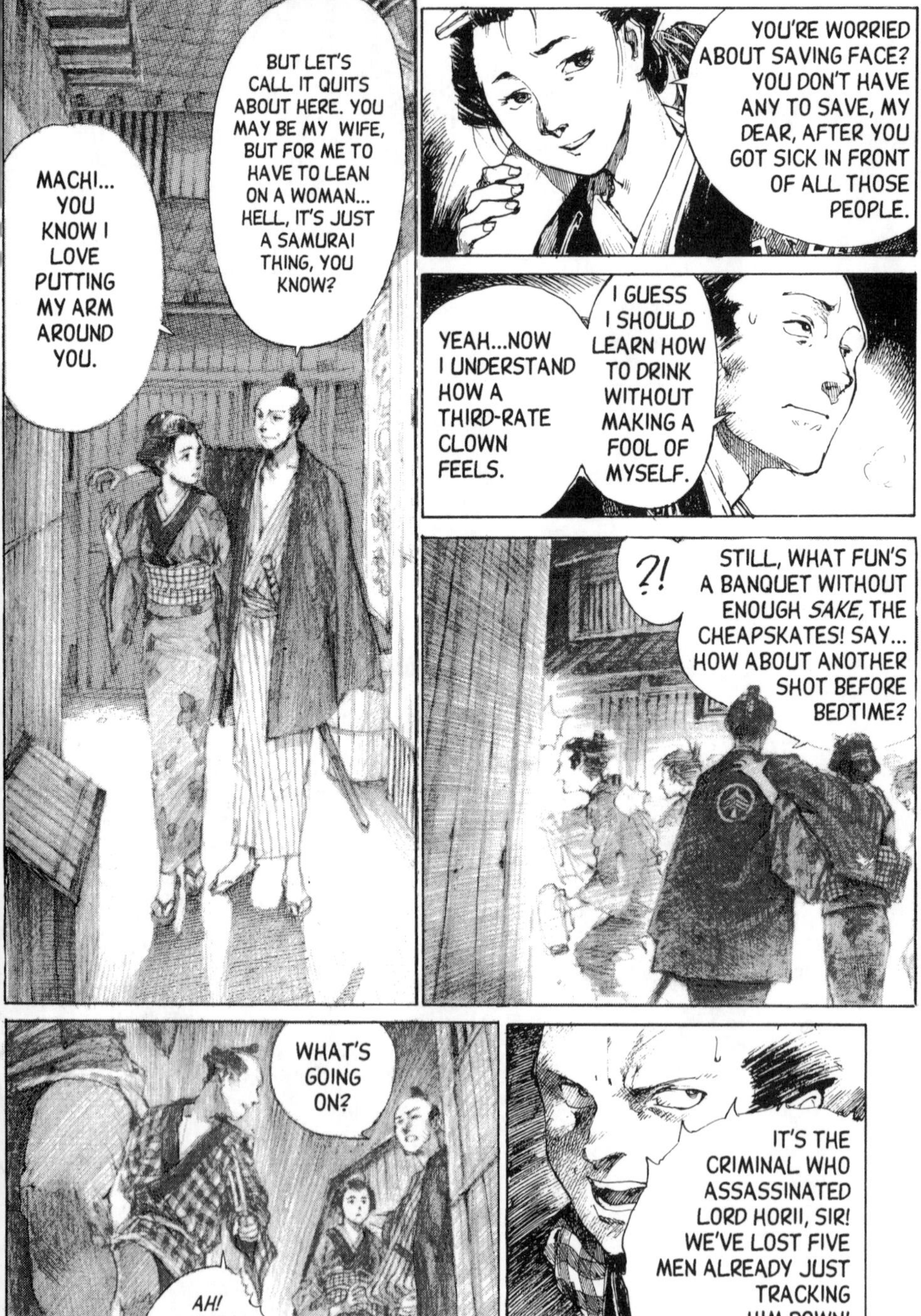
MACHI... YOU KNOW I LOVE PUTTING MY ARM AROUND YOU.
BUT LET'S CALL IT QUITS ABOUT HERE. YOU MAY BE MY WIFE, BUT FOR ME TO HAVE TO LEAN ON A WOMAN... HELL, IT'S JUST A SAMURAI THING, YOU KNOW?
YOU'RE WORRIED ABOUT SAVING FACE? YOU DON'T HAVE ANY TO SAVE, MY DEAR, AFTER YOU GOT SICK IN FRONT OF ALL THOSE PEOPLE.
YEAH...NOW I UNDERSTAND HOW A THIRD-RATE CLOWN FEELS.
I GUESS I SHOULD LEARN HOW TO DRINK WITHOUT MAKING A FOOL OF MYSELF.
?!
STILL, WHAT FUN'S A BANQUET WITHOUT ENOUGH *SAKE,* THE CHEAPSKATES! SAY... HOW ABOUT ANOTHER SHOT BEFORE BEDTIME?
WHAT'S GOING ON?
AH! OFFICER TATSUMASA!
IT'S THE CRIMINAL WHO ASSASSINATED LORD HORII, SIR! WE'VE LOST FIVE MEN ALREADY JUST TRACKING HIM DOWN!

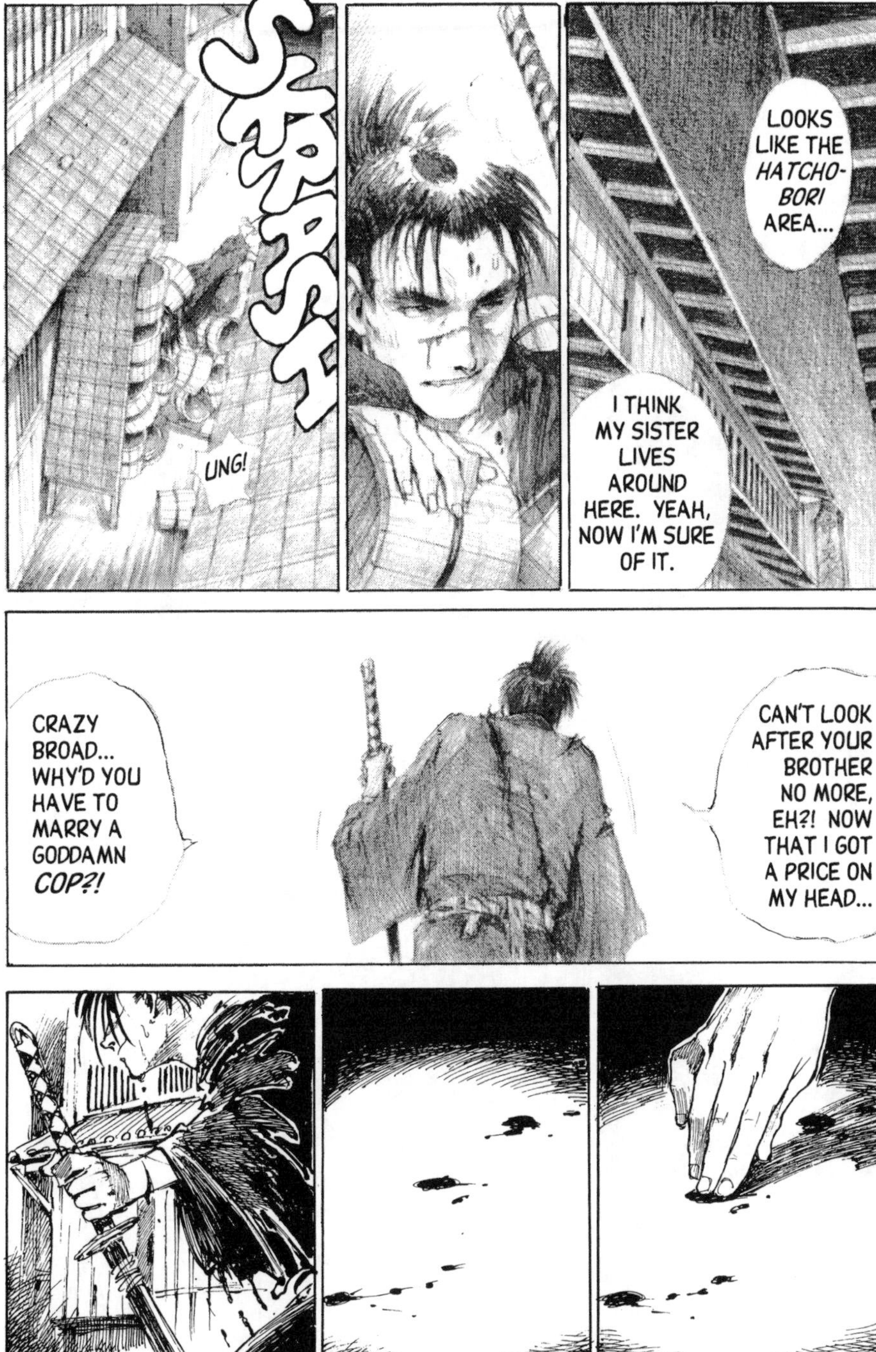
SKRASH
UNG!
LOOKS LIKE THE HATCHO-BORI AREA...
I THINK MY SISTER LIVES AROUND HERE. YEAH, NOW I'M SURE OF IT.
CRAZY BROAD... WHY'D YOU HAVE TO MARRY A GODDAMN COP?!
CAN'T LOOK AFTER YOUR BROTHER NO MORE, EH?! NOW THAT I GOT A PRICE ON MY HEAD...

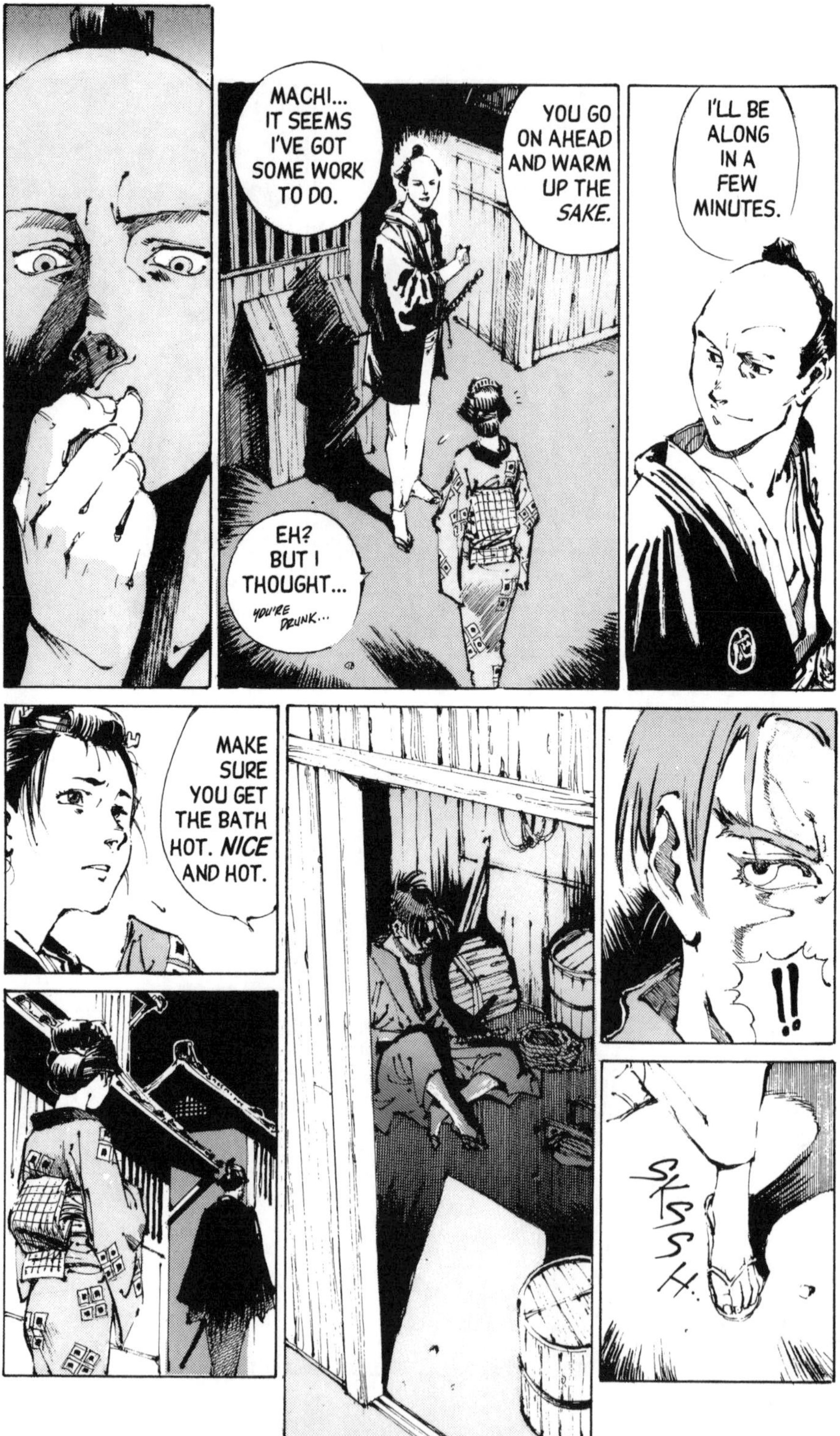
MACHI... IT SEEMS I'VE GOT SOME WORK TO DO.
YOU GO ON AHEAD AND WARM UP THE *SAKE.*
EH? BUT I THOUGHT...
YOU'RE DRUNK...
I'LL BE ALONG IN A FEW MINUTES.
MAKE SURE YOU GET THE BATH HOT. *NICE* AND HOT.
!!
SKSSH...

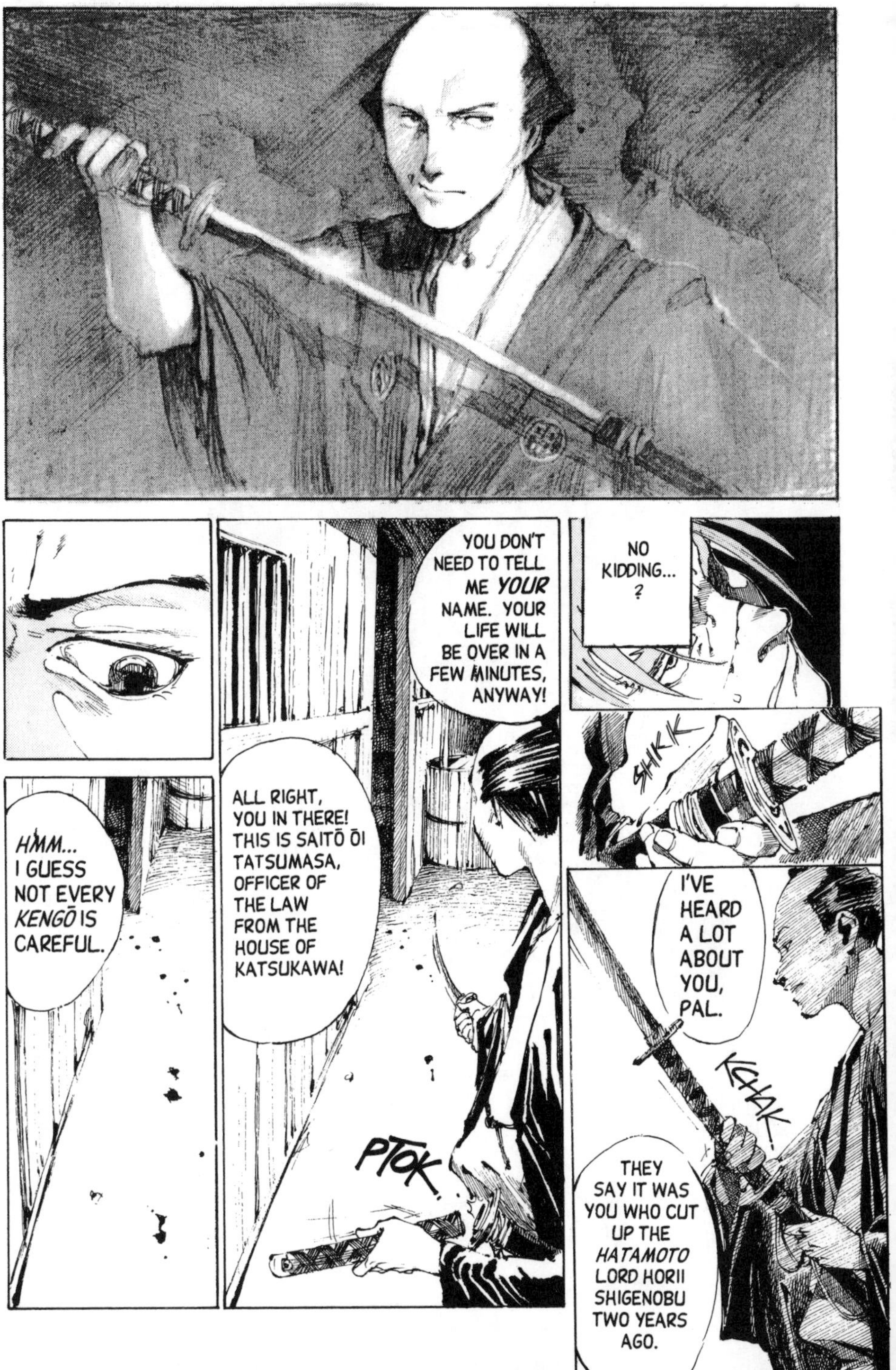
HMM... I GUESS NOT EVERY *KENGŌ* IS CAREFUL.
YOU DON'T NEED TO TELL ME *YOUR* NAME. YOUR LIFE WILL BE OVER IN A FEW MINUTES, ANYWAY!
ALL RIGHT, YOU IN THERE! THIS IS SAITŌ ŌI TATSUMASA, OFFICER OF THE LAW FROM THE HOUSE OF KATSUKAWA!
PTOK!
NO KIDDING...?
SHKK
I'VE HEARD A LOT ABOUT YOU, PAL.
KCHAK
THEY SAY IT WAS YOU WHO CUT UP THE *HATAMOTO* LORD HORII SHIGENOBU TWO YEARS AGO.

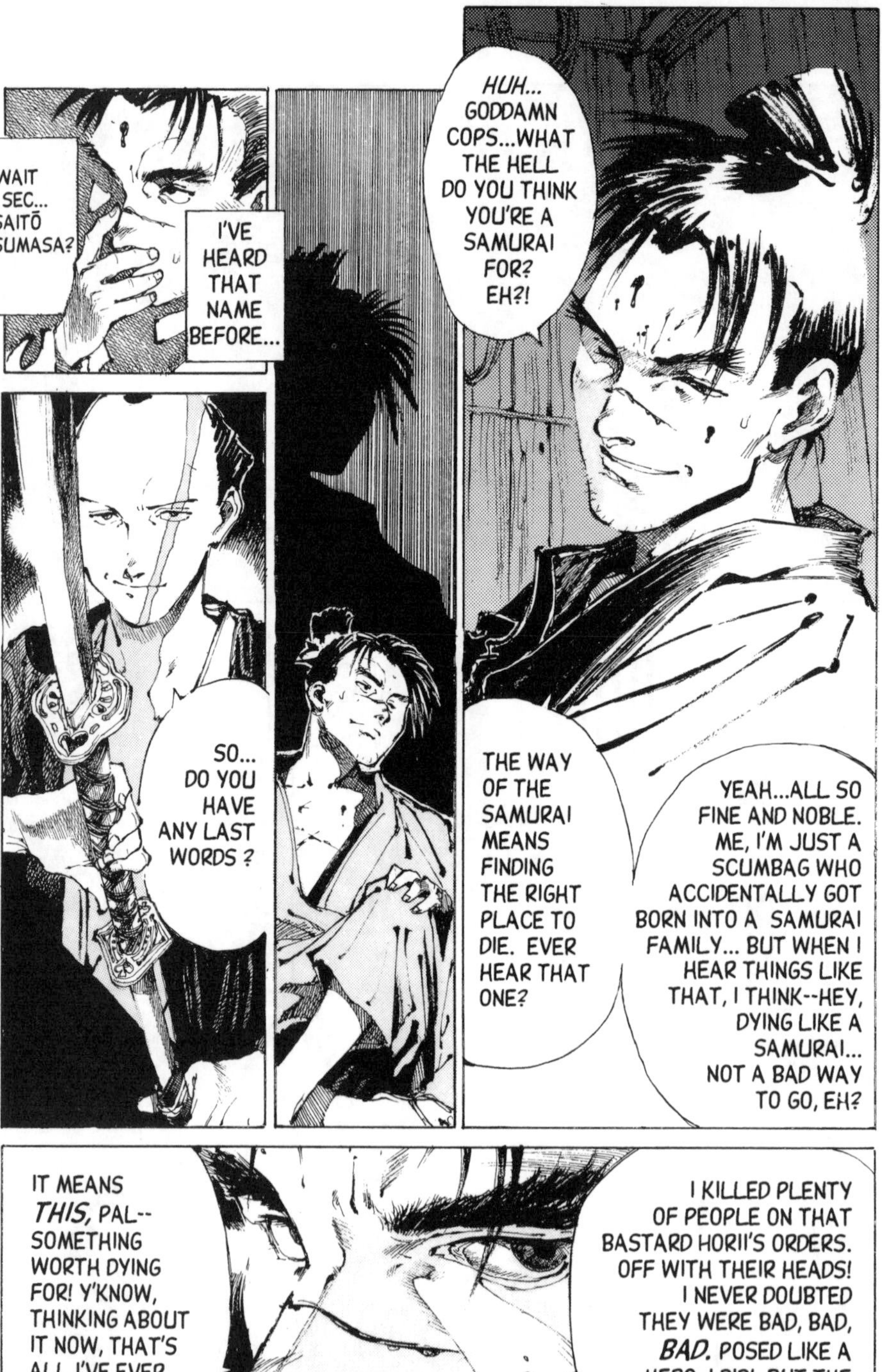
WAIT A SEC... SAITŌ TATSUMASA?
I'VE HEARD THAT NAME BEFORE...
HUH... GODDAMN COPS...WHAT THE HELL DO YOU THINK YOU'RE A SAMURAI FOR? EH?!
SO... DO YOU HAVE ANY LAST WORDS ?
THE WAY OF THE SAMURAI MEANS FINDING THE RIGHT PLACE TO DIE. EVER HEAR THAT ONE?
YEAH...ALL SO FINE AND NOBLE. ME, I'M JUST A SCUMBAG WHO ACCIDENTALLY GOT BORN INTO A SAMURAI FAMILY... BUT WHEN I HEAR THINGS LIKE THAT, I THINK--HEY, DYING LIKE A SAMURAI... NOT A BAD WAY TO GO, EH?
IT MEANS THIS, PAL--SOMETHING WORTH DYING FOR! Y'KNOW, THINKING ABOUT IT NOW, THAT'S ALL I'VE EVER WANTED.
I KILLED PLENTY OF PEOPLE ON THAT BASTARD HORII'S ORDERS. OFF WITH THEIR HEADS! I NEVER DOUBTED THEY WERE BAD, BAD, BAD. POSED LIKE A HERO, I DID! BUT THE REAL BAD GUYS...

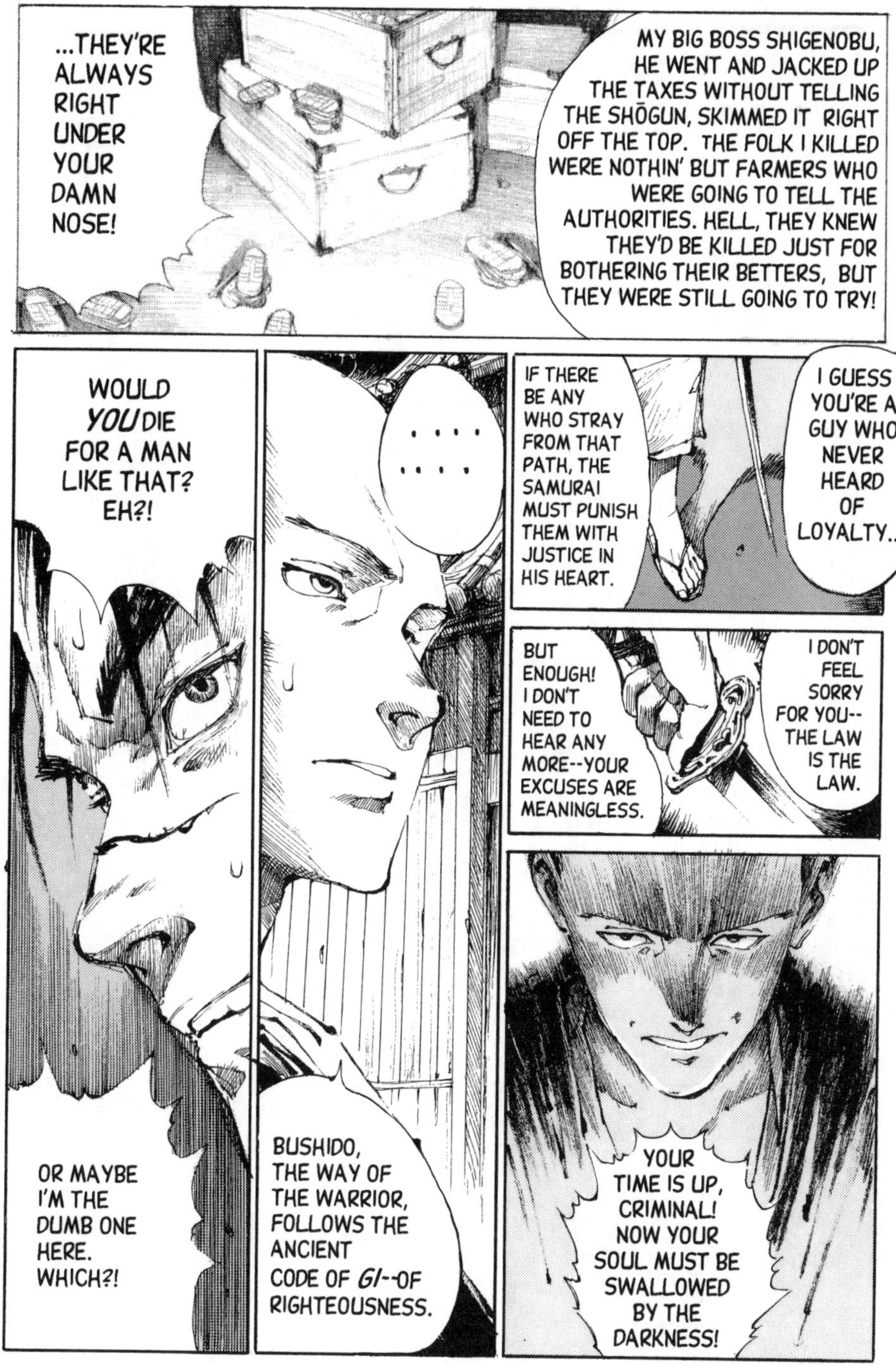
...THEY'RE ALWAYS RIGHT UNDER YOUR DAMN NOSE!
MY BIG BOSS SHIGENOBU, HE WENT AND JACKED UP THE TAXES WITHOUT TELLING THE SHŌGUN, SKIMMED IT RIGHT OFF THE TOP. THE FOLK I KILLED WERE NOTHIN' BUT FARMERS WHO WERE GOING TO TELL THE AUTHORITIES. HELL, THEY KNEW THEY'D BE KILLED JUST FOR BOTHERING THEIR BETTERS, BUT THEY WERE STILL GOING TO TRY!
WOULD *YOU* DIE FOR A MAN LIKE THAT? EH?!
OR MAYBE I'M THE DUMB ONE HERE. WHICH?!
....
BUSHIDO, THE WAY OF THE WARRIOR, FOLLOWS THE ANCIENT CODE OF *GI*--OF RIGHTEOUSNESS.
IF THERE BE ANY WHO STRAY FROM THAT PATH, THE SAMURAI MUST PUNISH THEM WITH JUSTICE IN HIS HEART.
I GUESS YOU'RE A GUY WHO NEVER HEARD OF LOYALTY...
BUT ENOUGH! I DON'T NEED TO HEAR ANY MORE--YOUR EXCUSES ARE MEANINGLESS.
I DON'T FEEL SORRY FOR YOU-- THE LAW IS THE LAW.
YOUR TIME IS UP, CRIMINAL! NOW YOUR SOUL MUST BE SWALLOWED BY THE DARKNESS!

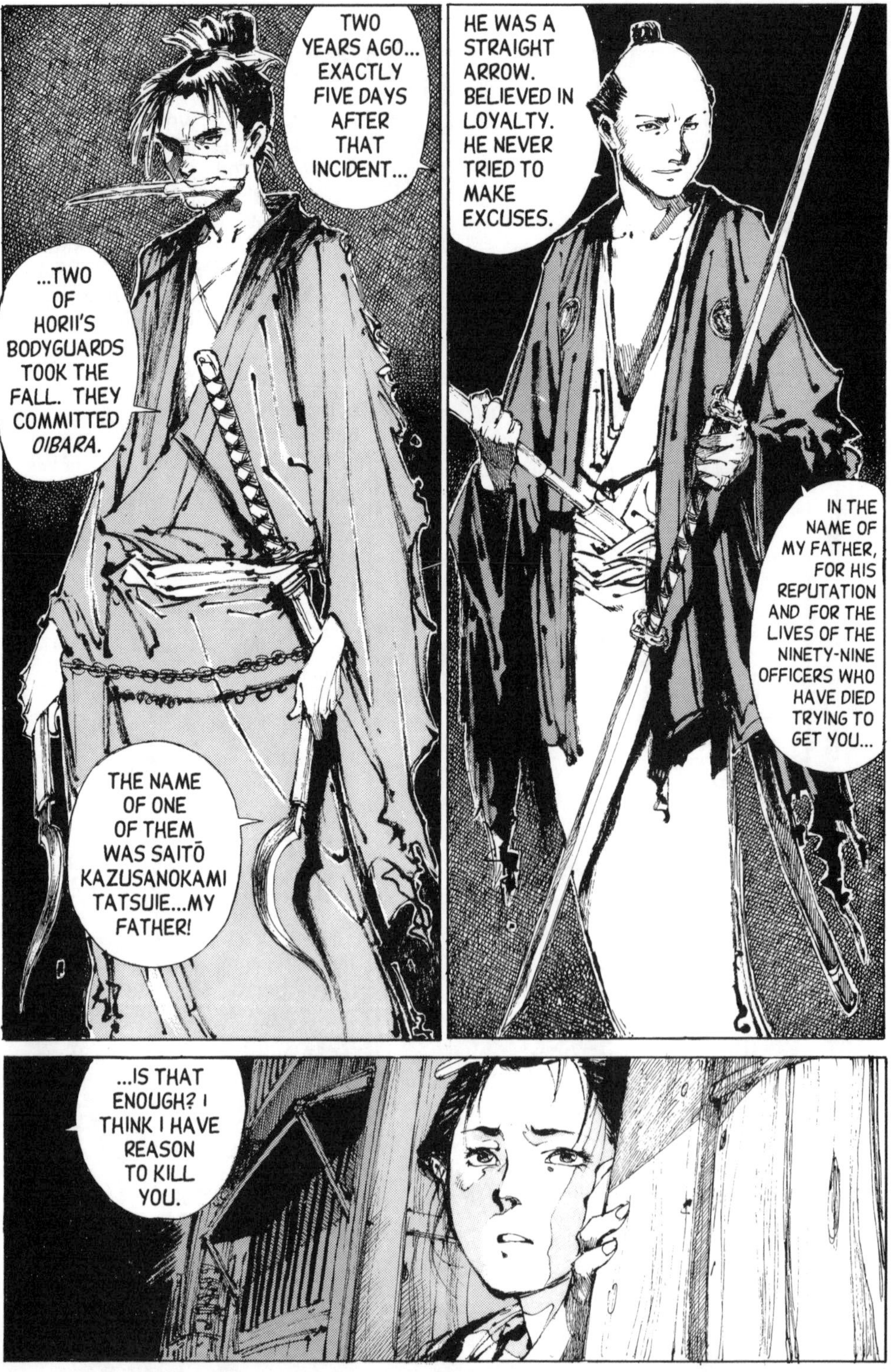
TWO YEARS AGO... EXACTLY FIVE DAYS AFTER THAT INCIDENT...
...TWO OF HORII'S BODYGUARDS TOOK THE FALL. THEY COMMITTED *OIBARA.*
THE NAME OF ONE OF THEM WAS SAITŌ KAZUSANOKAMI TATSUIE...MY FATHER!
HE WAS A STRAIGHT ARROW. BELIEVED IN LOYALTY. HE NEVER TRIED TO MAKE EXCUSES.
IN THE NAME OF MY FATHER, FOR HIS REPUTATION AND FOR THE LIVES OF THE NINETY-NINE OFFICERS WHO HAVE DIED TRYING TO GET YOU...
...IS THAT ENOUGH? I THINK I HAVE REASON TO KILL YOU.

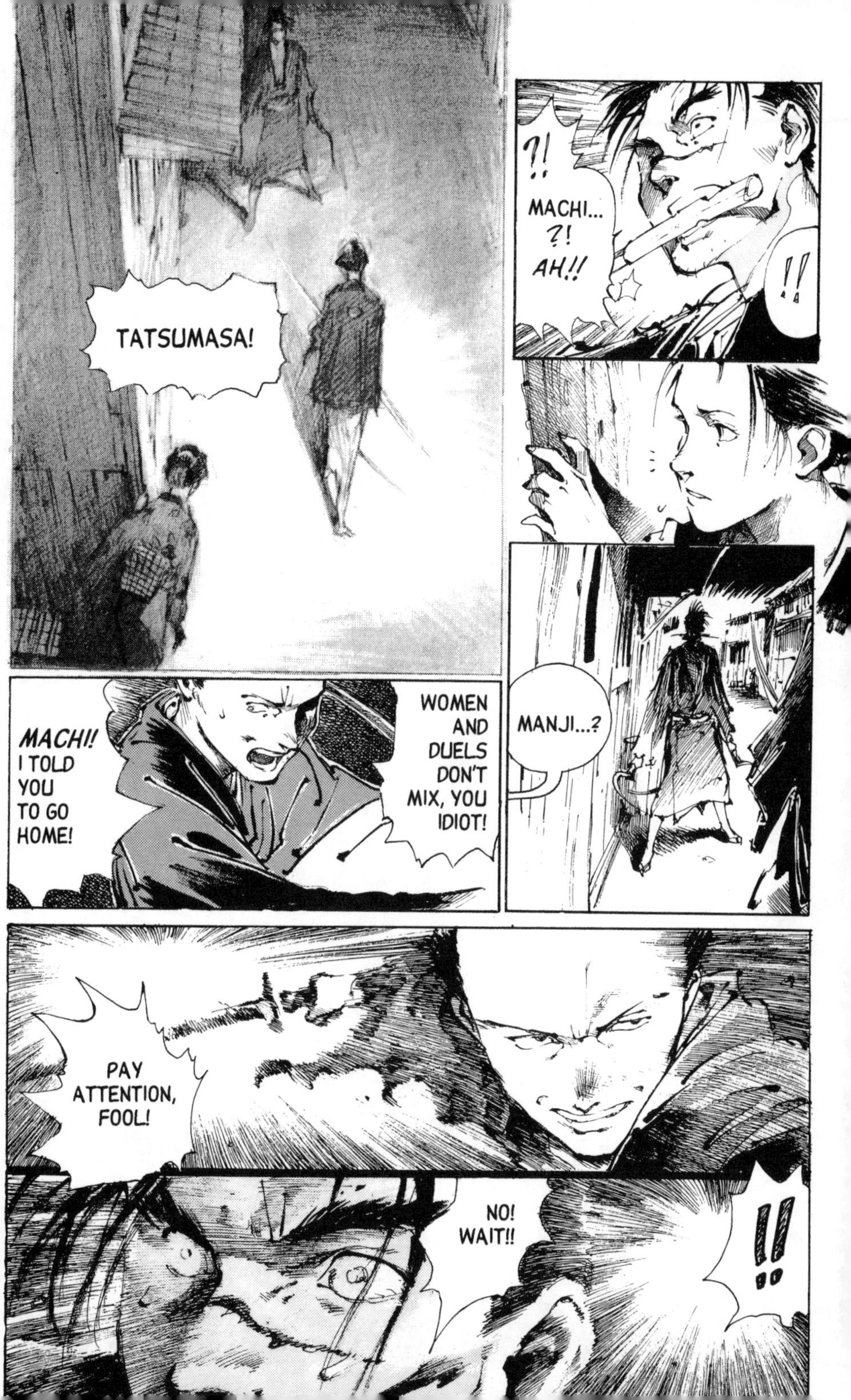

TATSUMASA!
?!
MACHI... ?! AH!!
!!
MACHI!! I TOLD YOU TO GO HOME!
WOMEN AND DUELS DON'T MIX, YOU IDIOT!
MANJI...?
PAY ATTENTION, FOOL!
NO! WAIT!!
!!

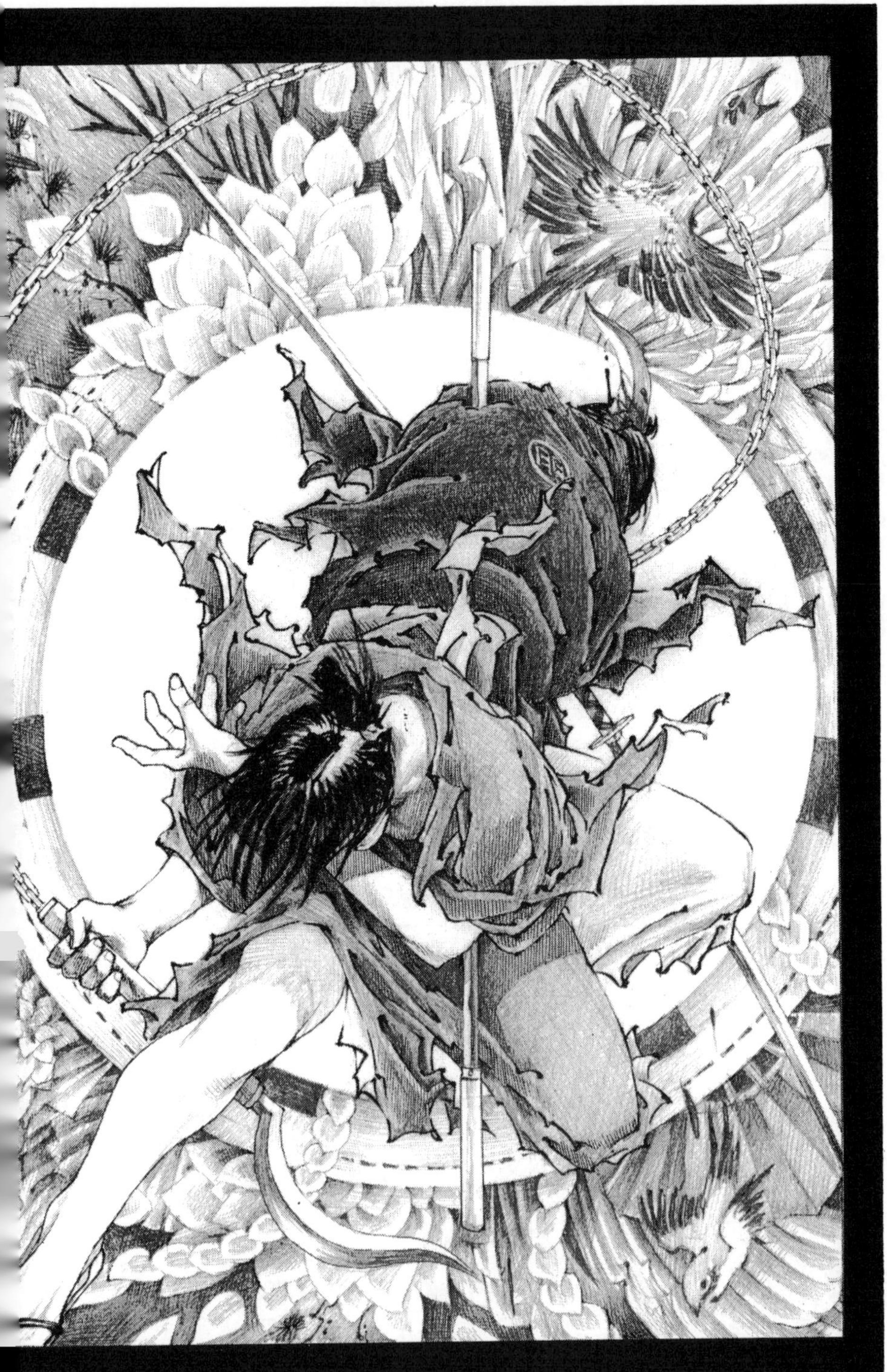

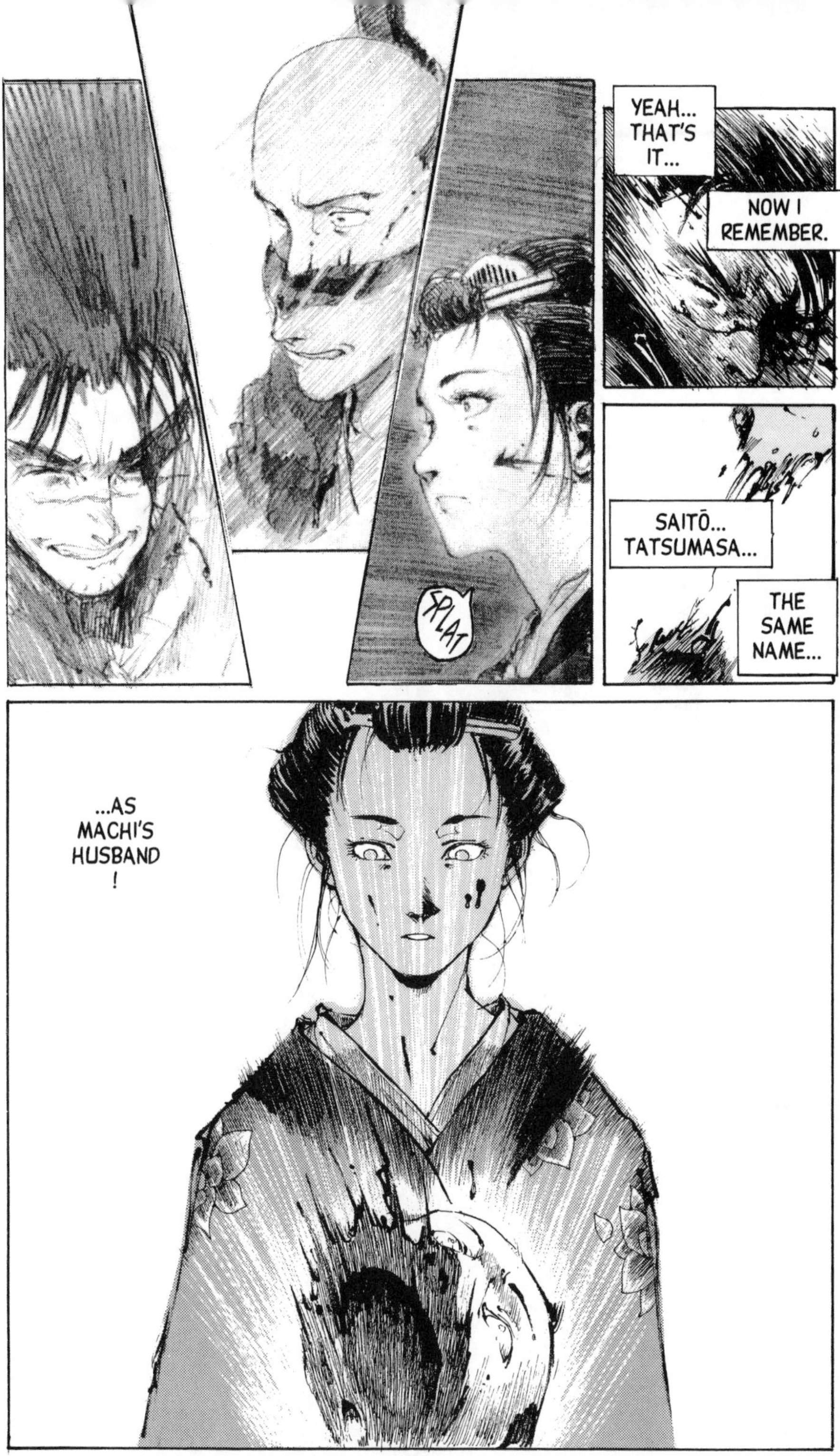
SPLAT
YEAH... THAT'S IT...
NOW I REMEMBER.
SAITŌ... TATSUMASA...
THE SAME NAME...
...AS MACHI'S HUSBAND!

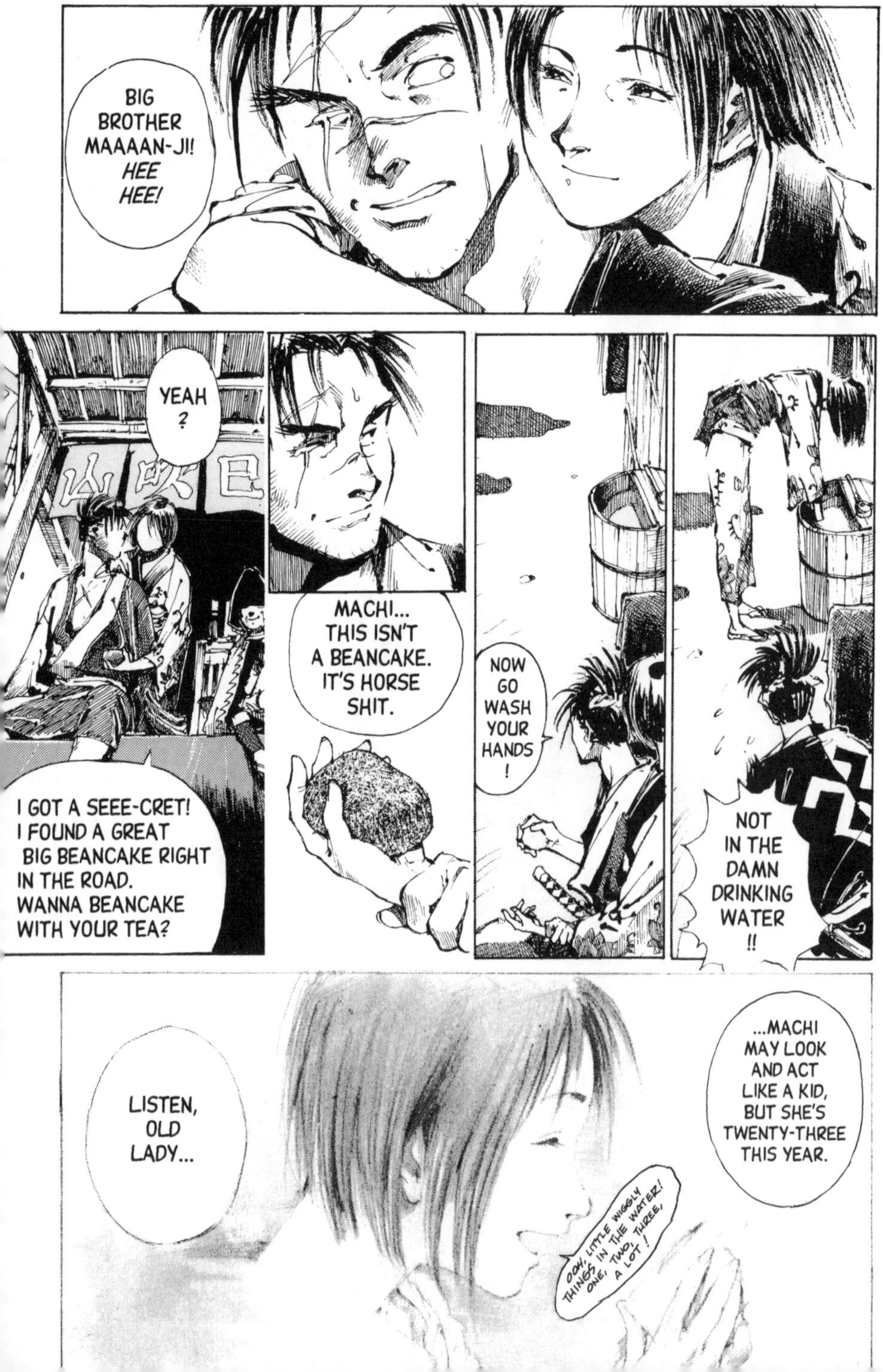

BIG BROTHER MAAAAN-JI! *HEE HEE!*
YEAH ?
I GOT A SEEE-CRET! I FOUND A GREAT BIG BEANCAKE RIGHT IN THE ROAD. WANNA BEANCAKE WITH YOUR TEA?
MACHI... THIS ISN'T A BEANCAKE. IT'S HORSE SHIT.
NOW GO WASH YOUR HANDS !
NOT IN THE DAMN DRINKING WATER !!
LISTEN, OLD LADY...
OOH, LITTLE WIGGLY THINGS IN THE WATER! ONE, TWO, THREE, A LOT!
...MACHI MAY LOOK AND ACT LIKE A KID, BUT SHE'S TWENTY-THREE THIS YEAR.

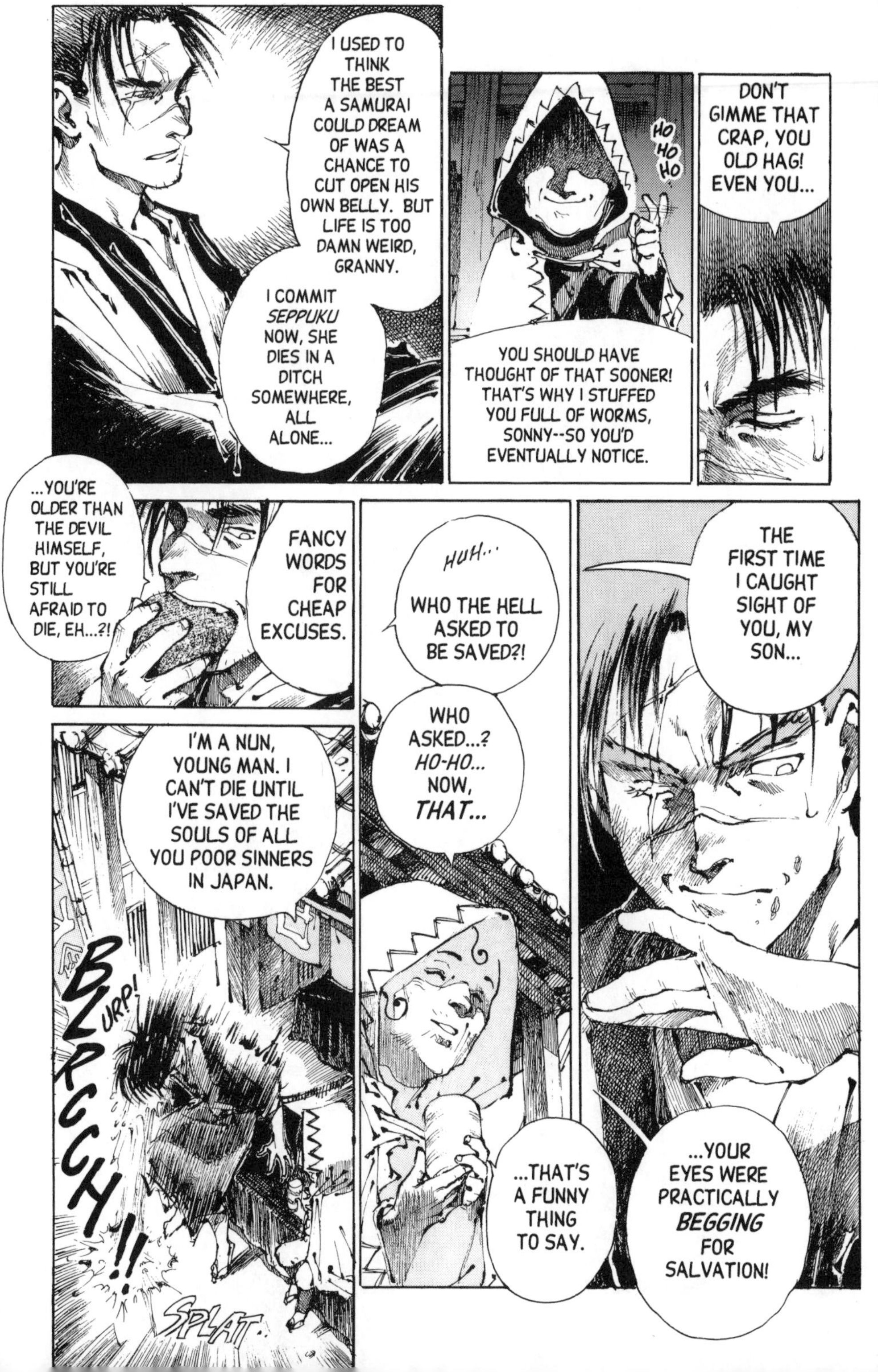
I USED TO THINK THE BEST A SAMURAI COULD DREAM OF WAS A CHANCE TO CUT OPEN HIS OWN BELLY. BUT LIFE IS TOO DAMN WEIRD, GRANNY.
I COMMIT *SEPPUKU* NOW, SHE DIES IN A DITCH SOMEWHERE, ALL ALONE...
HO HO HO
YOU SHOULD HAVE THOUGHT OF THAT SOONER! THAT'S WHY I STUFFED YOU FULL OF WORMS, SONNY--SO YOU'D EVENTUALLY NOTICE.
DON'T GIMME THAT CRAP, YOU OLD HAG! EVEN YOU...
...YOU'RE OLDER THAN THE DEVIL HIMSELF, BUT YOU'RE STILL AFRAID TO DIE, EH...?!
FANCY WORDS FOR CHEAP EXCUSES.
I'M A NUN, YOUNG MAN. I CAN'T DIE UNTIL I'VE SAVED THE SOULS OF ALL YOU POOR SINNERS IN JAPAN.
BLRRCCH!!
URP!
SPLAT.
HUH...
WHO THE HELL ASKED TO BE SAVED?!
WHO ASKED...? *HO-HO...* NOW, *THAT...*
...THAT'S A FUNNY THING TO SAY.
THE FIRST TIME I CAUGHT SIGHT OF YOU, MY SON...
...YOUR EYES WERE PRACTICALLY *BEGGING* FOR SALVATION!

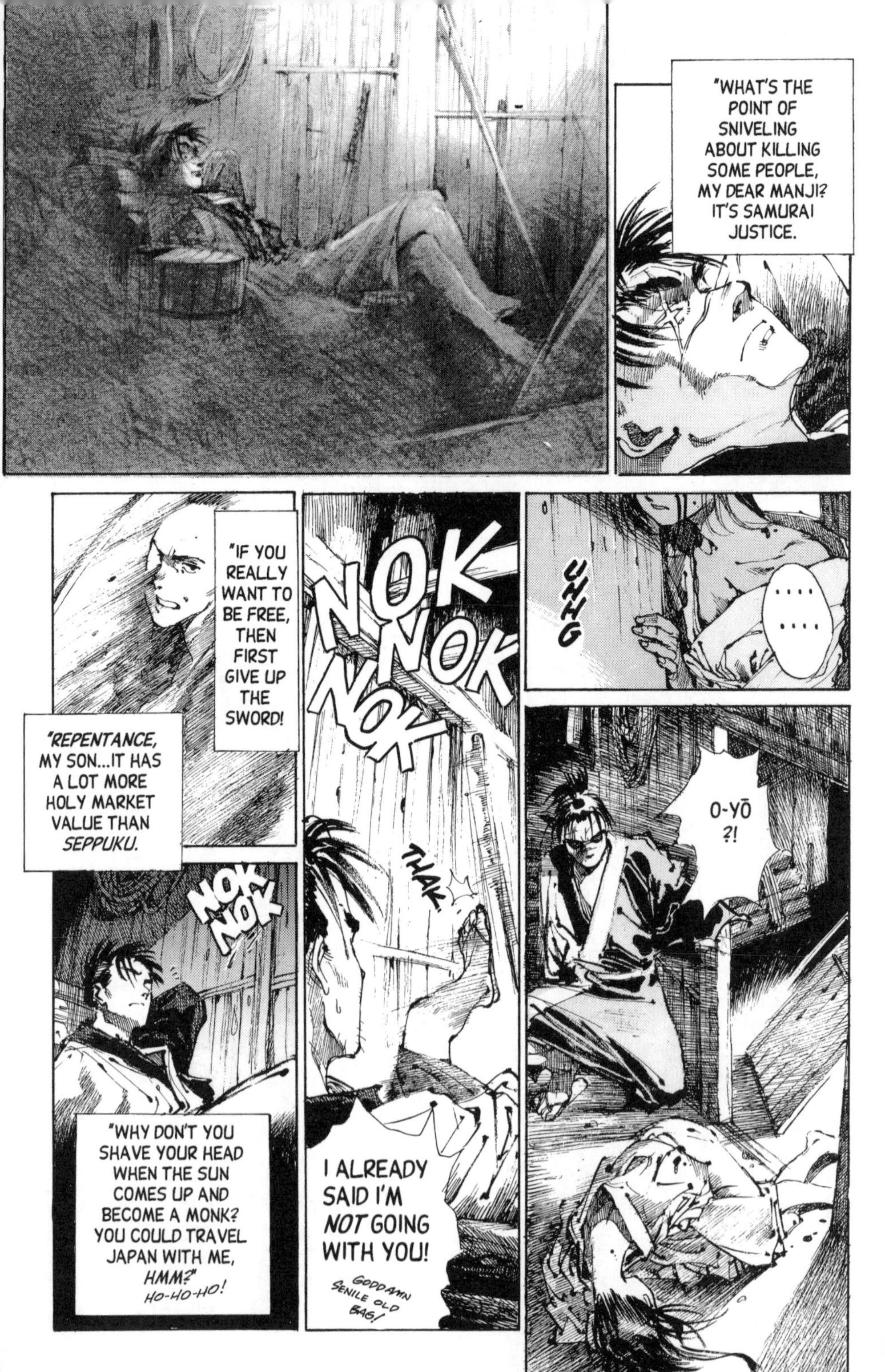
"WHAT'S THE POINT OF SNIVELING ABOUT KILLING SOME PEOPLE, MY DEAR MANJI? IT'S SAMURAI JUSTICE.
"IF YOU REALLY WANT TO BE FREE, THEN FIRST GIVE UP THE SWORD!
"REPENTANCE, MY SON...IT HAS A LOT MORE HOLY MARKET VALUE THAN SEPPUKU.
NOK NOK
"WHY DON'T YOU SHAVE YOUR HEAD WHEN THE SUN COMES UP AND BECOME A MONK? YOU COULD TRAVEL JAPAN WITH ME, HMM?"
HO-HO-HO!
NOK NOK NOK
THAK!
I ALREADY SAID I'M NOT GOING WITH YOU!
GODDAMN SENILE OLD BAG!
UHHG
....
....
O-YŌ ?!

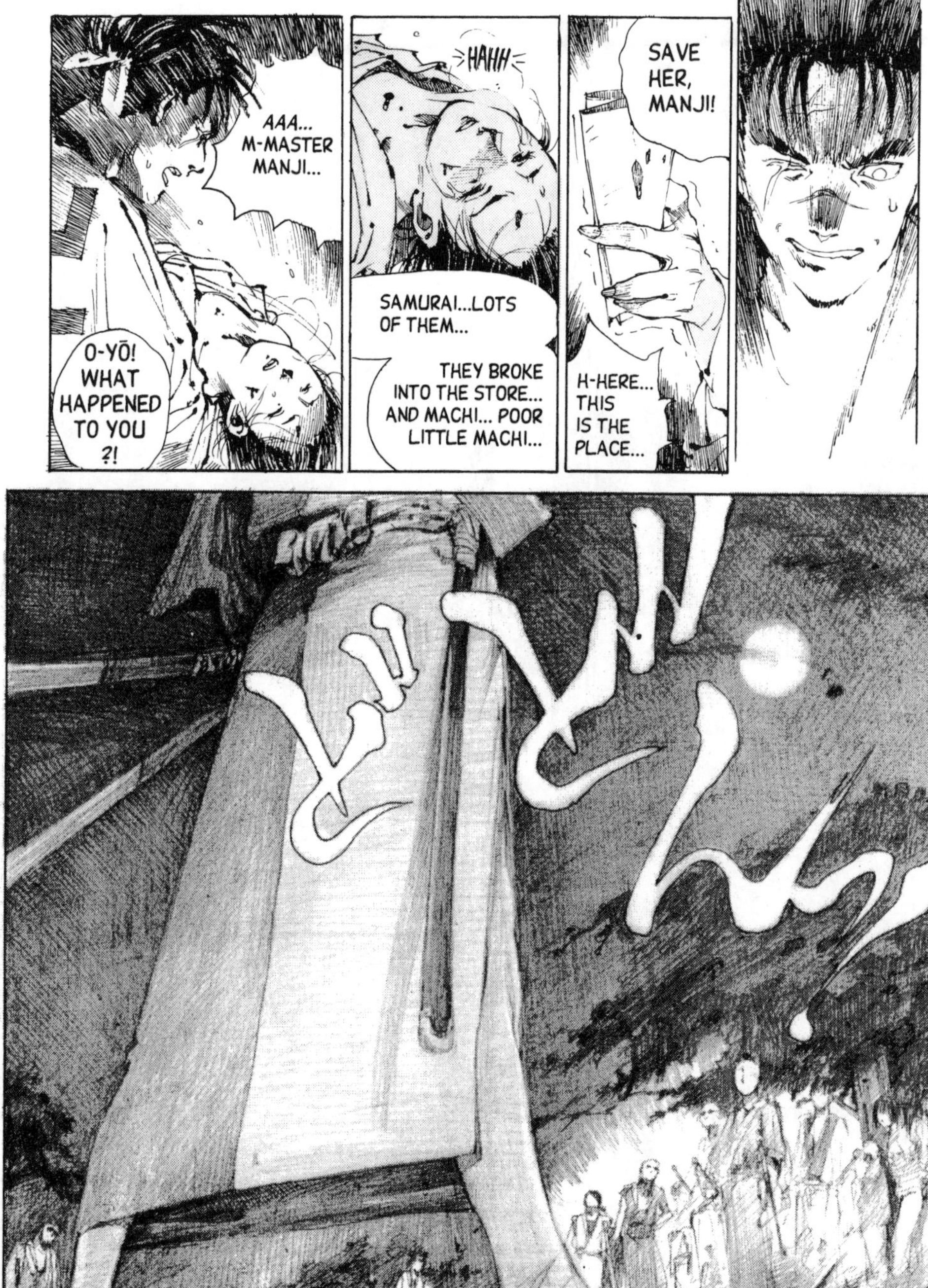
AAA...
M-MASTER MANJI...
O-YŌ! WHAT HAPPENED TO YOU ?!
HAHH
SAMURAI...LOTS OF THEM...
THEY BROKE INTO THE STORE... AND MACHI... POOR LITTLE MACHI...
SAVE HER, MANJI!
H-HERE... THIS IS THE PLACE...
どどん

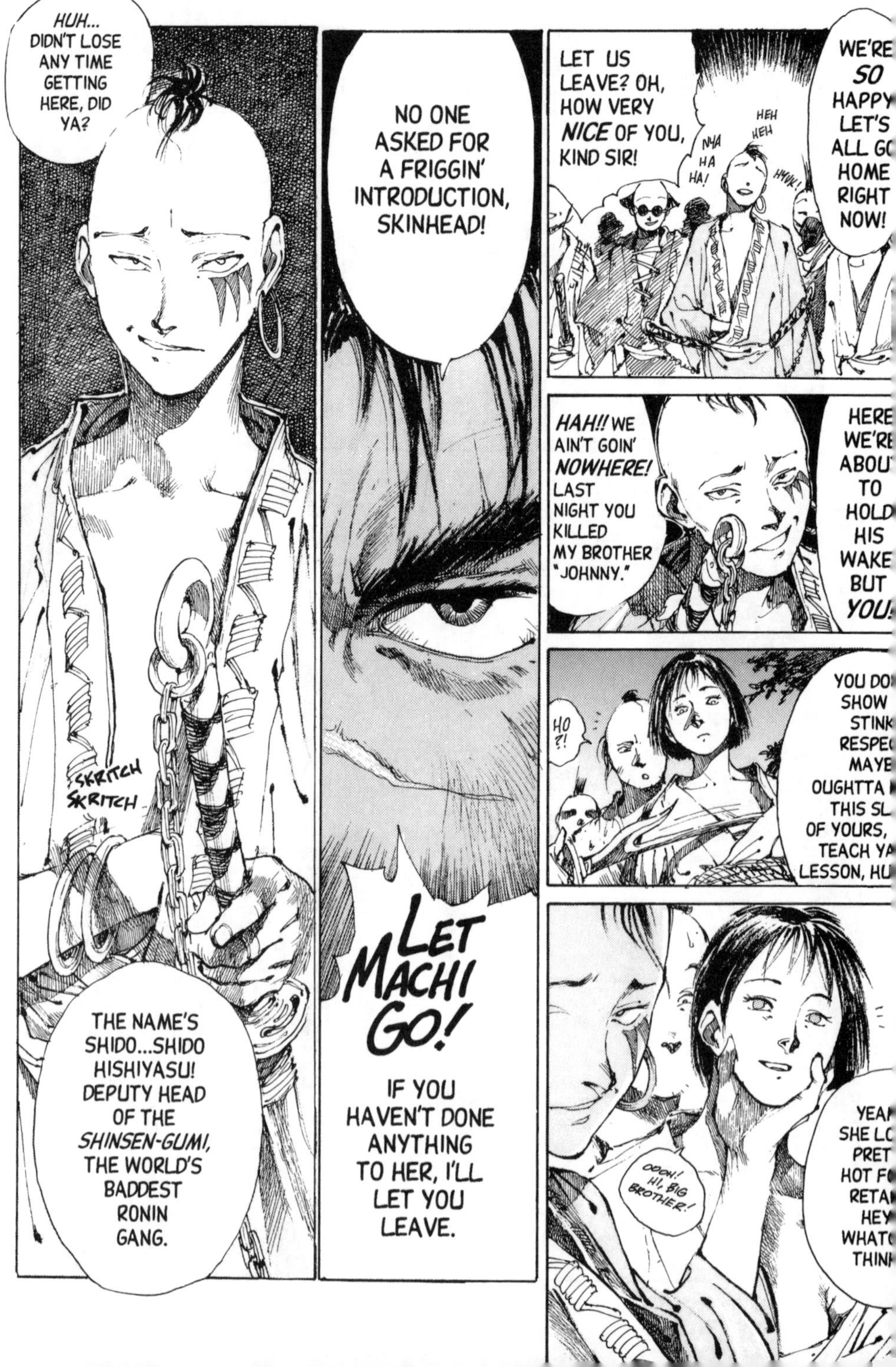
HUH... DIDN'T LOSE ANY TIME GETTING HERE, DID YA?
SKRITCH SKRITCH
THE NAME'S SHIDO...SHIDO HISHIYASU! DEPUTY HEAD OF THE SHINSEN-GUMI, THE WORLD'S BADDEST RONIN GANG.
NO ONE ASKED FOR A FRIGGIN' INTRODUCTION, SKINHEAD!
LET MACHI GO!
IF YOU HAVEN'T DONE ANYTHING TO HER, I'LL LET YOU LEAVE.
LET US LEAVE? OH, HOW VERY NICE OF YOU, KIND SIR!
HEH HEH
NYA HA HA!
HYUK!
WE'RE SO HAPPY LET'S ALL GC HOME RIGHT NOW!
HAH!! WE AIN'T GOIN' NOWHERE! LAST NIGHT YOU KILLED MY BROTHER "JOHNNY."
HERE WE'RE ABOU TO HOLD HIS WAKE BUT YOU
HO ?!
YOU DO SHOW STINK RESPE MAYE OUGHTTA THIS SL OF YOURS, TEACH YA LESSON, HU
OOOH! HI, BIG BROTHER!
YEA SHE LO PRET HOT F RETA HEY WHAT THINK

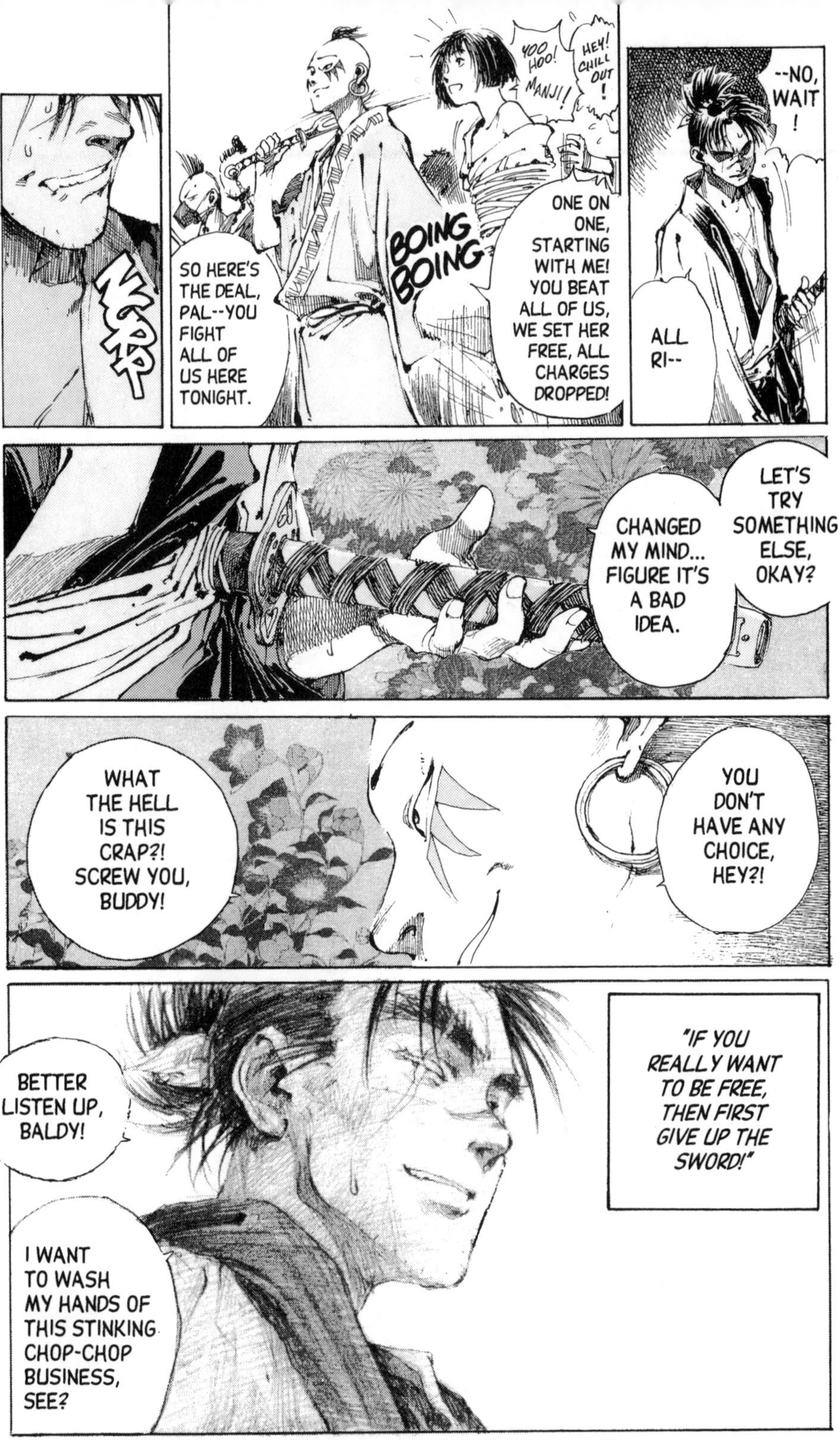
NGRR
YOO HOO!
MANJI!
HEY! CHILL OUT!
SO HERE'S THE DEAL, PAL--YOU FIGHT ALL OF US HERE TONIGHT.
BOING BOING
ONE ON ONE, STARTING WITH ME! YOU BEAT ALL OF US, WE SET HER FREE, ALL CHARGES DROPPED!
--NO, WAIT!
ALL RI--
CHANGED MY MIND... FIGURE IT'S A BAD IDEA.
LET'S TRY SOMETHING ELSE, OKAY?
WHAT THE HELL IS THIS CRAP?! SCREW YOU, BUDDY!
YOU DON'T HAVE ANY CHOICE, HEY?!
BETTER LISTEN UP, BALDY!
I WANT TO WASH MY HANDS OF THIS STINKING CHOP-CHOP BUSINESS, SEE?
"IF YOU REALLY WANT TO BE FREE, THEN FIRST GIVE UP THE SWORD!"

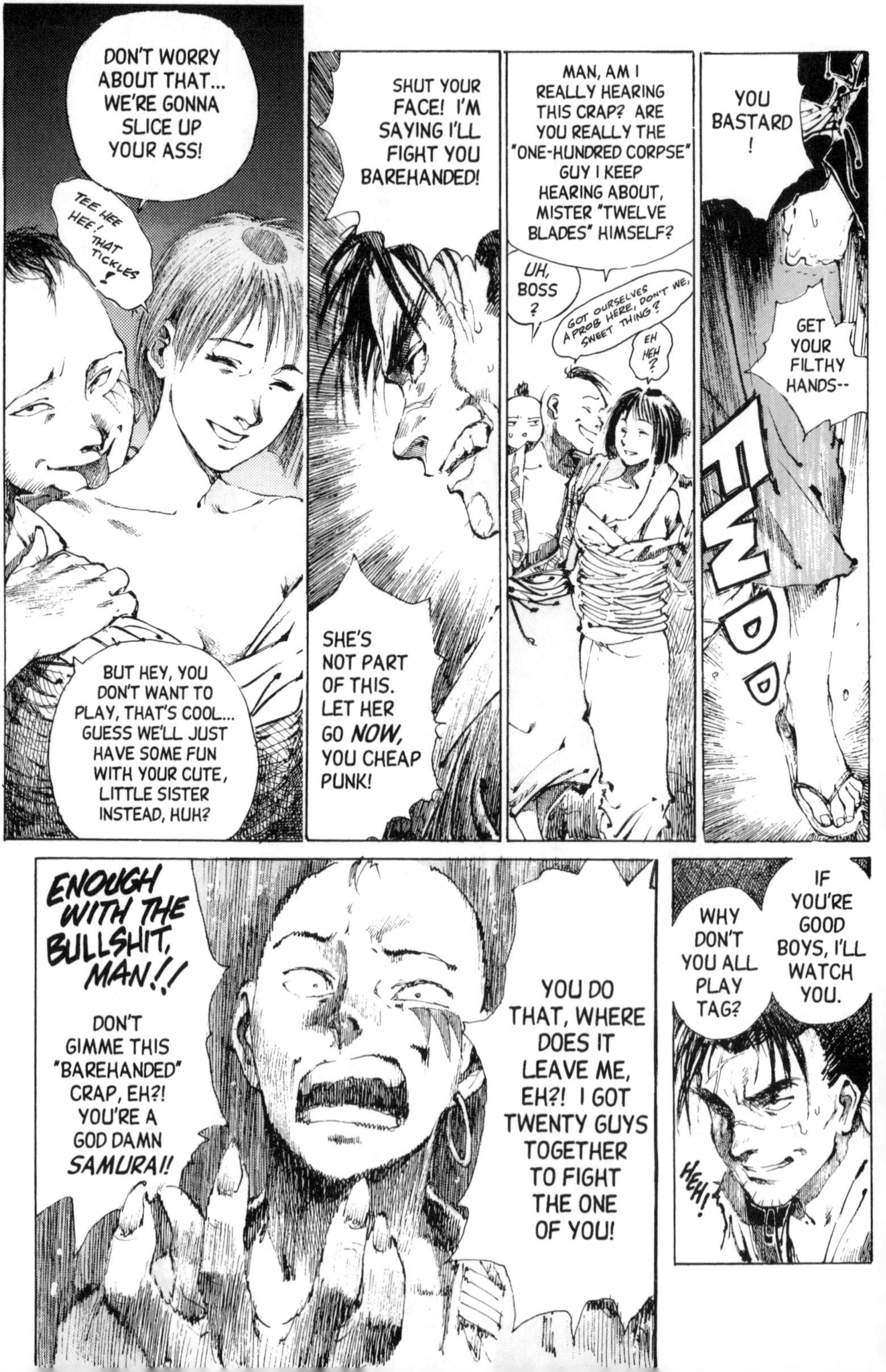
DON'T WORRY ABOUT THAT... WE'RE GONNA SLICE UP YOUR ASS!
TEE HEE HEE! THAT TICKLES!
BUT HEY, YOU DON'T WANT TO PLAY, THAT'S COOL... GUESS WE'LL JUST HAVE SOME FUN WITH YOUR CUTE, LITTLE SISTER INSTEAD, HUH?
SHUT YOUR FACE! I'M SAYING I'LL FIGHT YOU BAREHANDED!
SHE'S NOT PART OF THIS. LET HER GO NOW, YOU CHEAP PUNK!
MAN, AM I REALLY HEARING THIS CRAP? ARE YOU REALLY THE "ONE-HUNDRED CORPSE" GUY I KEEP HEARING ABOUT, MISTER "TWELVE BLADES" HIMSELF?
UH, BOSS?
GOT OURSELVES A PROB HERE, DON'T WE, SWEET THING?
EH HEH?
YOU BASTARD!
GET YOUR FILTHY HANDS--
FWDDD
ENOUGH WITH THE BULLSHIT, MAN!!
DON'T GIMME THIS "BAREHANDED" CRAP, EH?! YOU'RE A GOD DAMN SAMURAI!
YOU DO THAT, WHERE DOES IT LEAVE ME, EH?! I GOT TWENTY GUYS TOGETHER TO FIGHT THE ONE OF YOU!
WHY DON'T YOU ALL PLAY TAG?
IF YOU'RE GOOD BOYS, I'LL WATCH YOU.
HEH!

WHY YOU!! I OUGHTTA--!

SO... UH, BOSS?

WHATCHA GONNA DO?

OKAY... LET THE GIRL GO.

HUH ?!

THE HELL WITH IT. I OVERESTIMATED THE GUY. I DON'T WASTE TIME ON TRASH LIKE HIM.

MANJI !!

WELL, THERE YA ARE. HE SAID YOU CAN GO.

HOPE IT WASN'T TOO TIGHT.

SEE YA! ♡

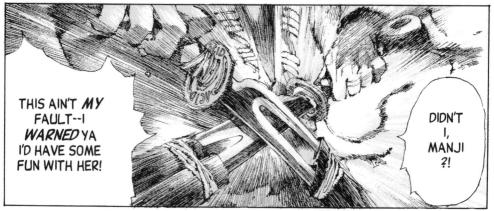

THIS AIN'T MY FAULT--I WARNED YA I'D HAVE SOME FUN WITH HER!

DIDN'T I, MANJI ?!

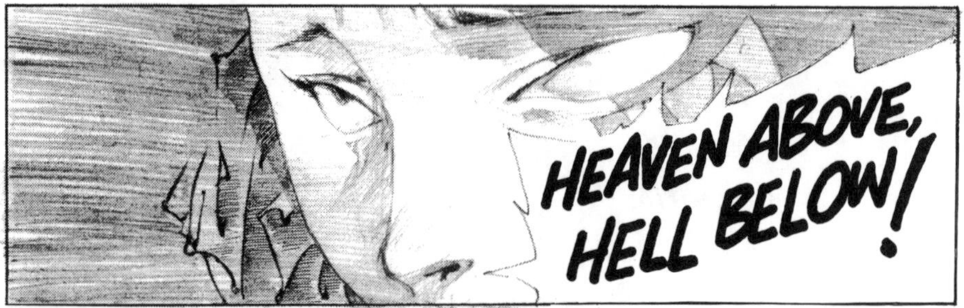
HEAVEN ABOVE, HELL BELOW!
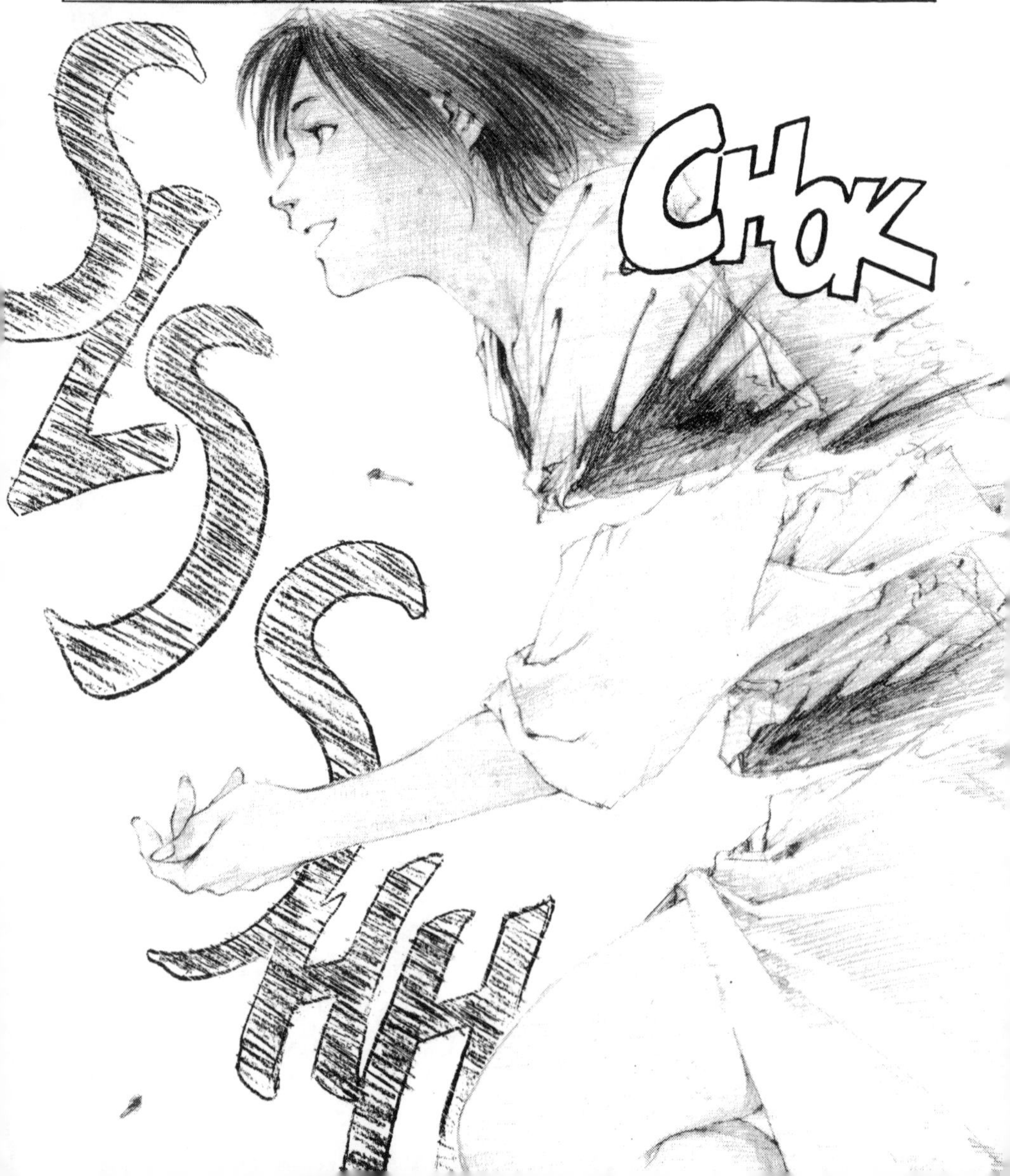
SSSHH
CHOK

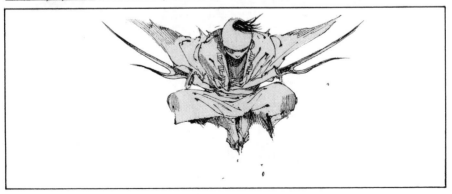

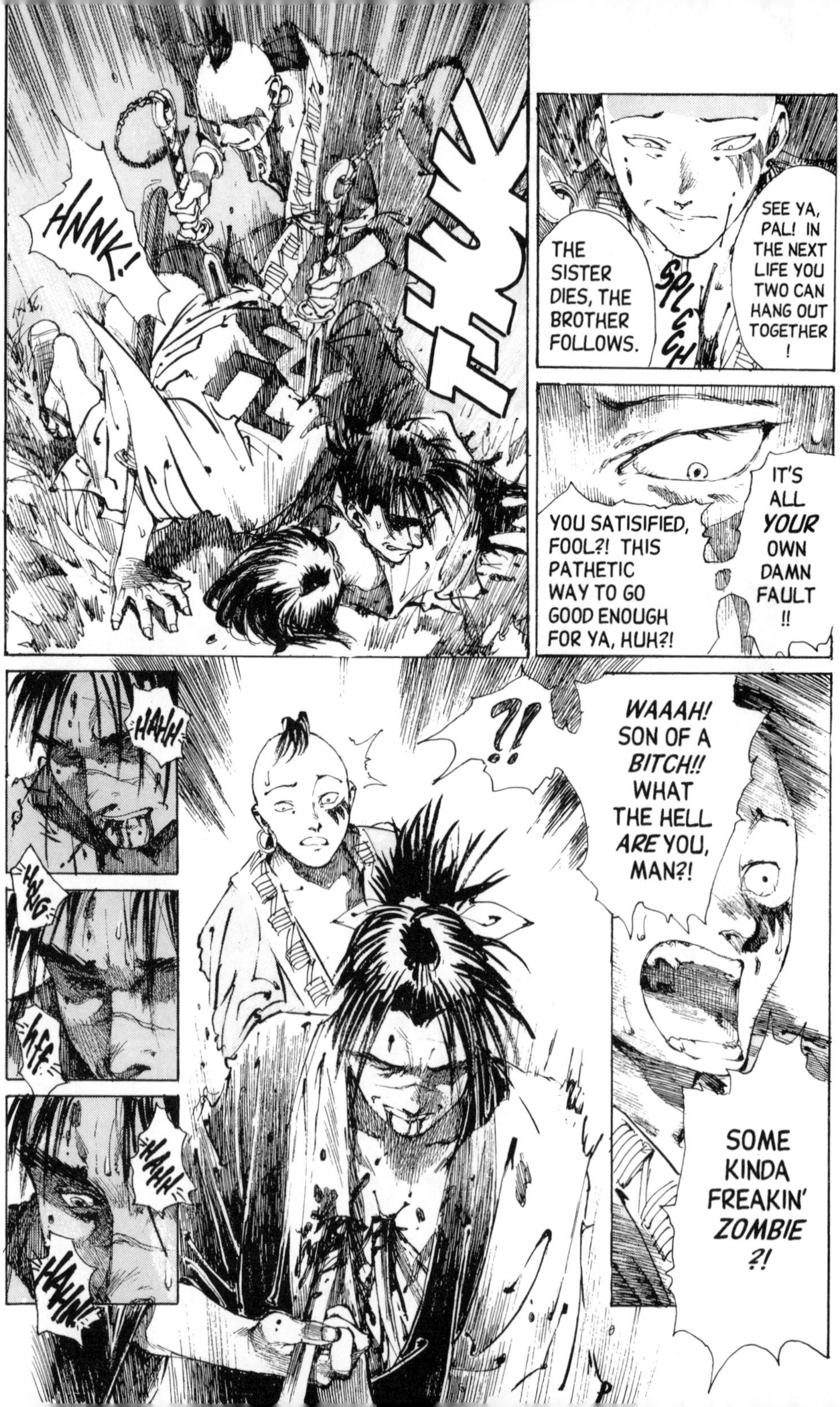
HNNK!
THUNK
THE SISTER DIES, THE BROTHER FOLLOWS.
SPLECH
SEE YA, PAL! IN THE NEXT LIFE YOU TWO CAN HANG OUT TOGETHER!
YOU SATISIFIED, FOOL?! THIS PATHETIC WAY TO GO GOOD ENOUGH FOR YA, HUH?!
IT'S ALL YOUR OWN DAMN FAULT!!
HAHH
HANG
HFF
HAHH
HAHH
?!
WAAAH! SON OF A BITCH!! WHAT THE HELL ARE YOU, MAN?!
SOME KINDA FREAKIN' ZOMBIE?!

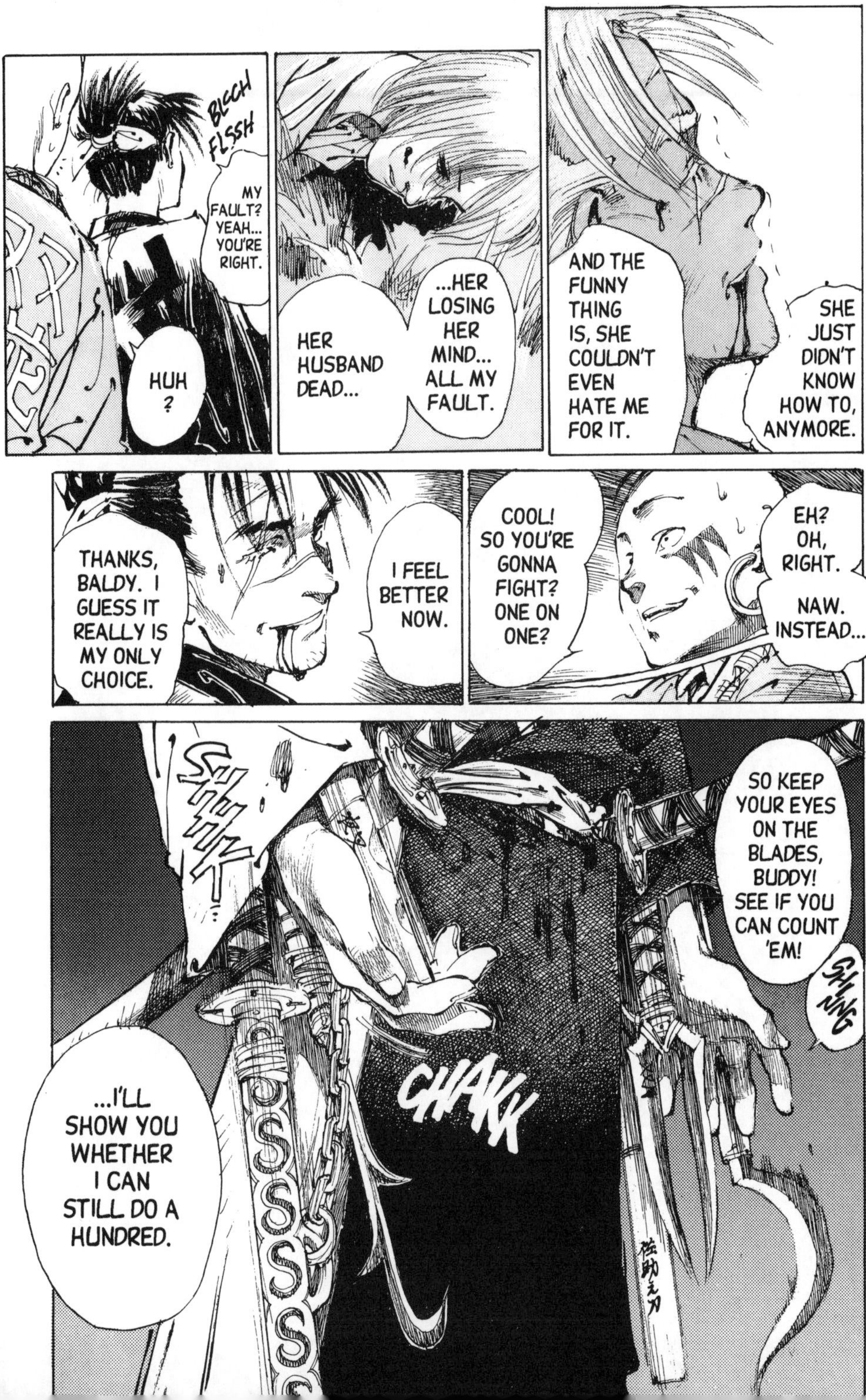
BLCCH
FLSSH
MY FAULT? YEAH... YOU'RE RIGHT.
HUH ?
HER HUSBAND DEAD...
...HER LOSING HER MIND... ALL MY FAULT.
AND THE FUNNY THING IS, SHE COULDN'T EVEN HATE ME FOR IT.
SHE JUST DIDN'T KNOW HOW TO, ANYMORE.
THANKS, BALDY. I GUESS IT REALLY IS MY ONLY CHOICE.
I FEEL BETTER NOW.
COOL! SO YOU'RE GONNA FIGHT? ONE ON ONE?
EH? OH, RIGHT.
NAW. INSTEAD...
...I'LL SHOW YOU WHETHER I CAN STILL DO A HUNDRED.
SO KEEP YOUR EYES ON THE BLADES, BUDDY! SEE IF YOU CAN COUNT 'EM!
CHAKK

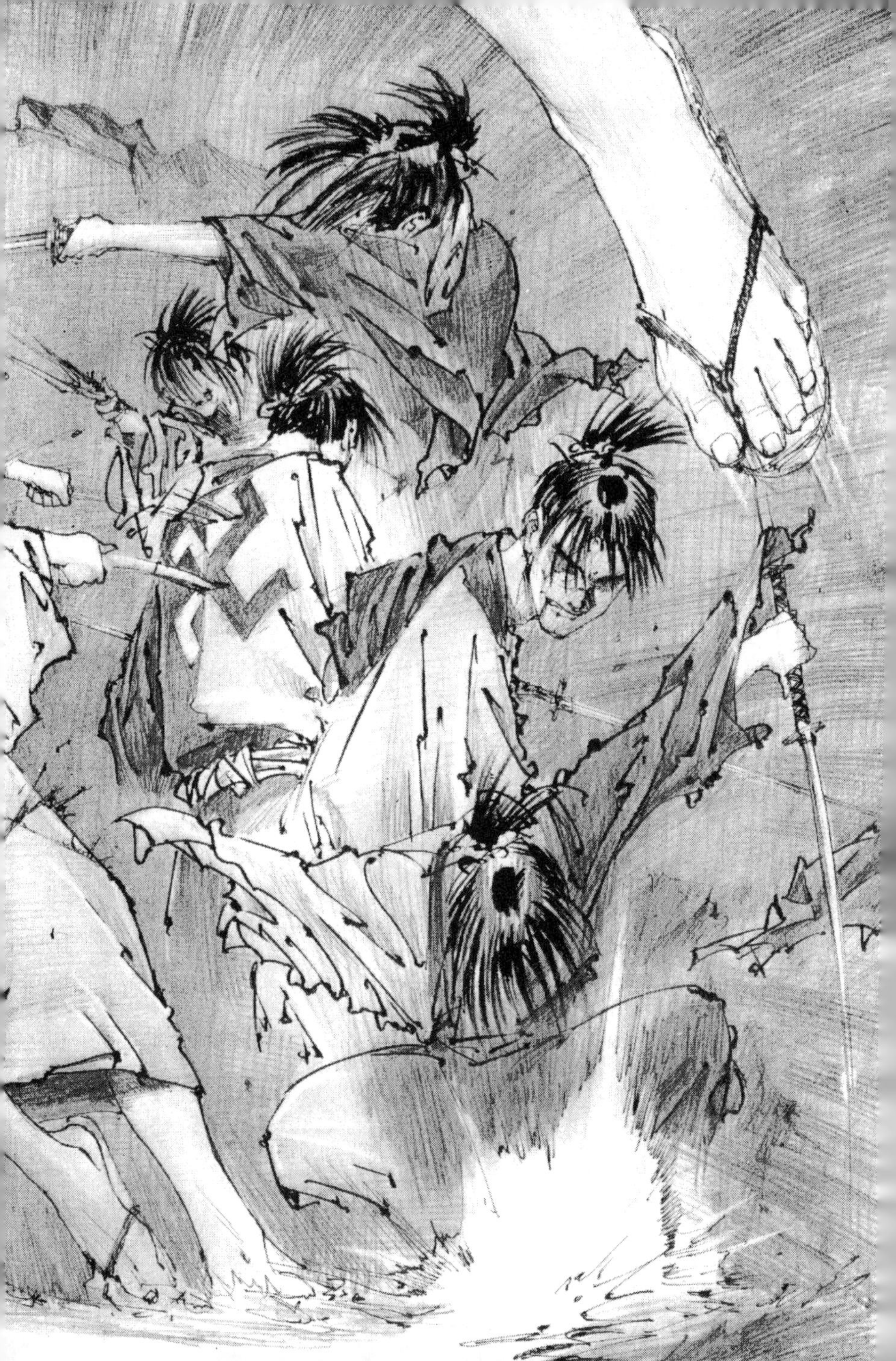

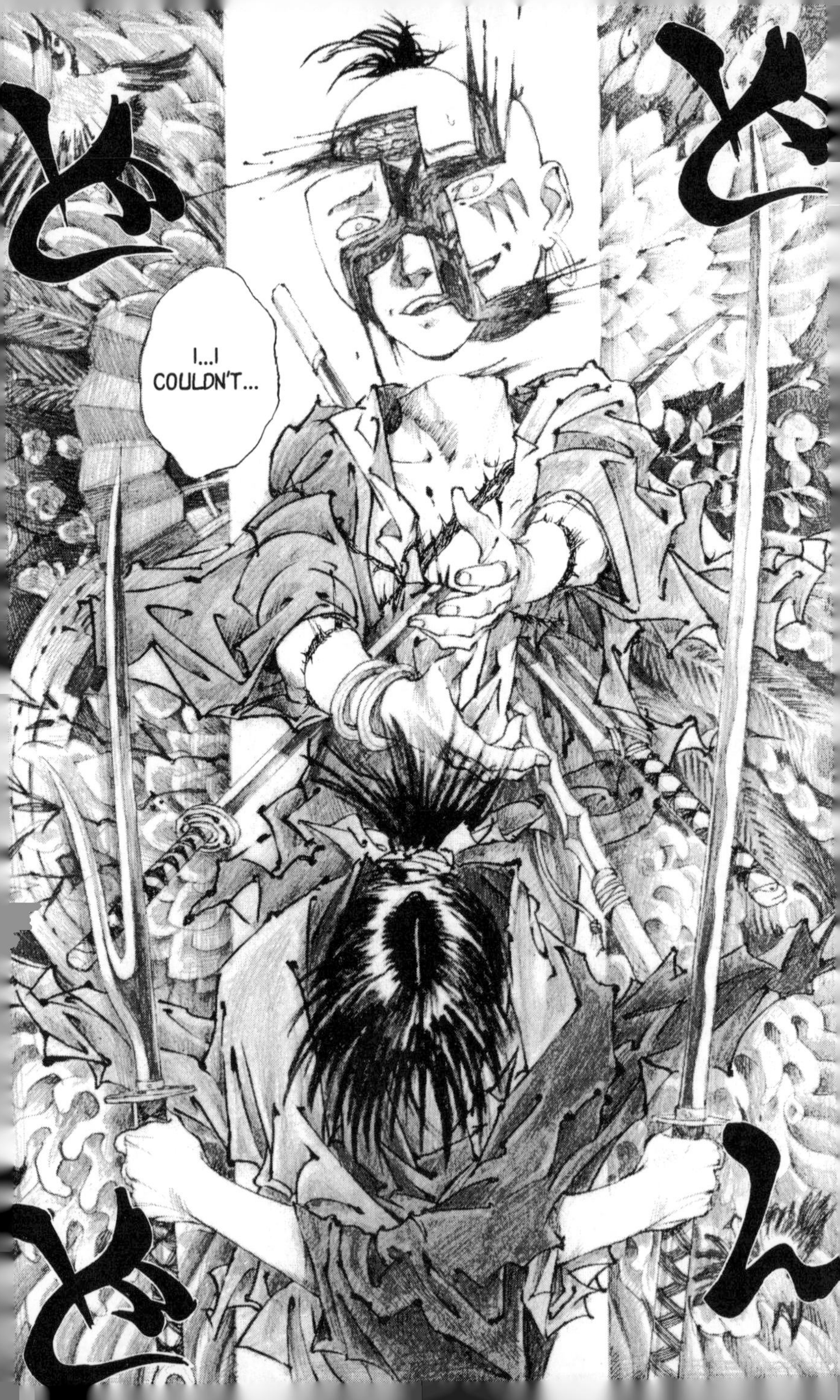
I...I COULDN'T...
どどどん

UH--OH!

MACHI... .....

IT'S LIKE SKINHEAD HERE SAID. HELL, IF I COULD, I'D LOVE TO LET THEM KILL ME.

BUT I DON'T EVEN HAVE THAT CHOICE!

CHECK IT OUT--HERE'S MY DAMN BODY, ALL FIXED UP AGAIN. AND SO...!

OH, MAN!

M-MOMMY!

SHUT UP, FOOL!

A WORD TO ALL THE NEW FRIENDS I'VE MADE HERE TODAY! I'M HERE TO HELP YOU JOIN YOUR BOSS ON THE OTHER SIDE!

WHEN YOU GET THERE, GIVE HIM A COUPLE A' FLOWERS FOR ME, OKAY?!

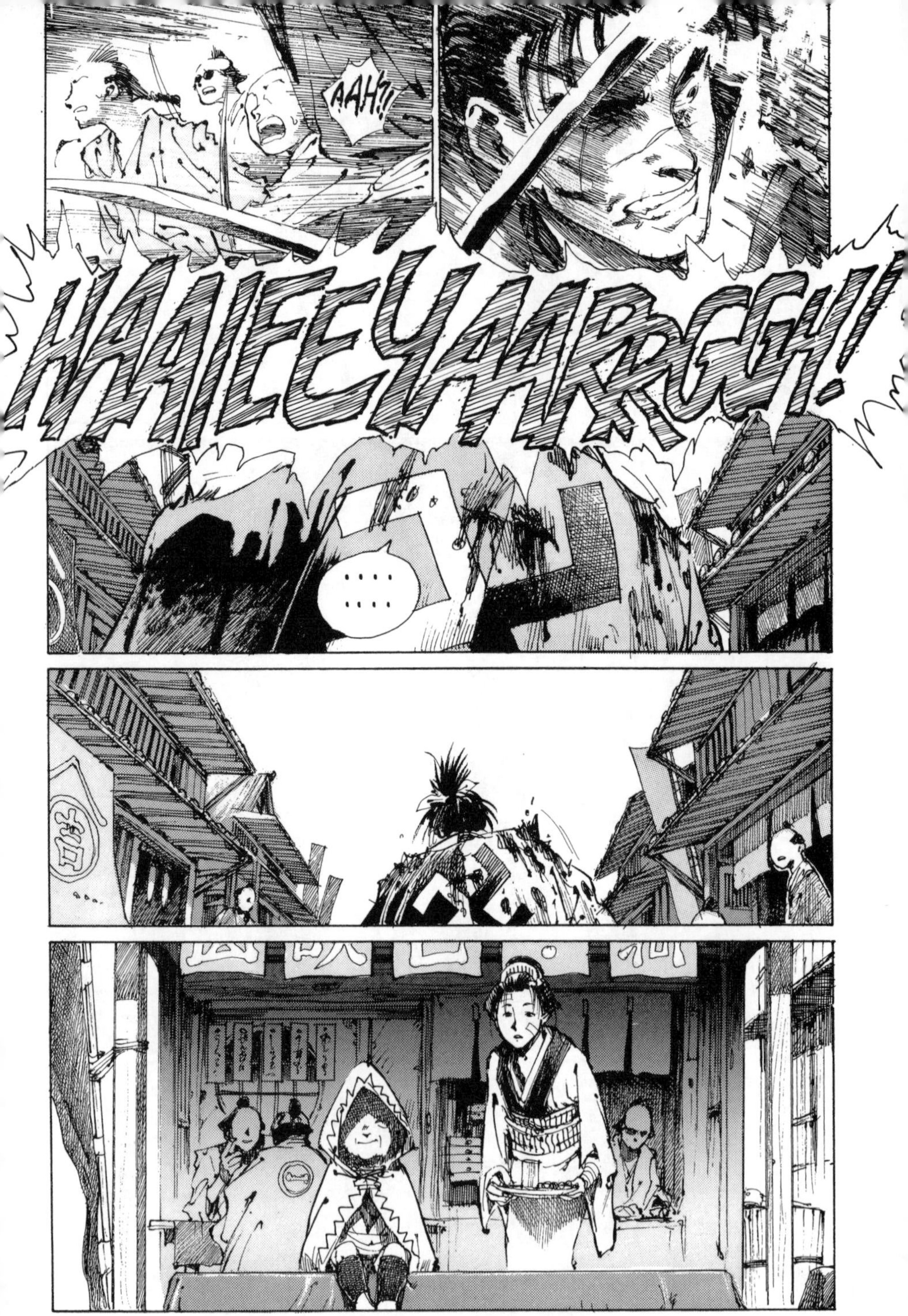
AAH!!
HAAIEEYAARRGGH!
....
...

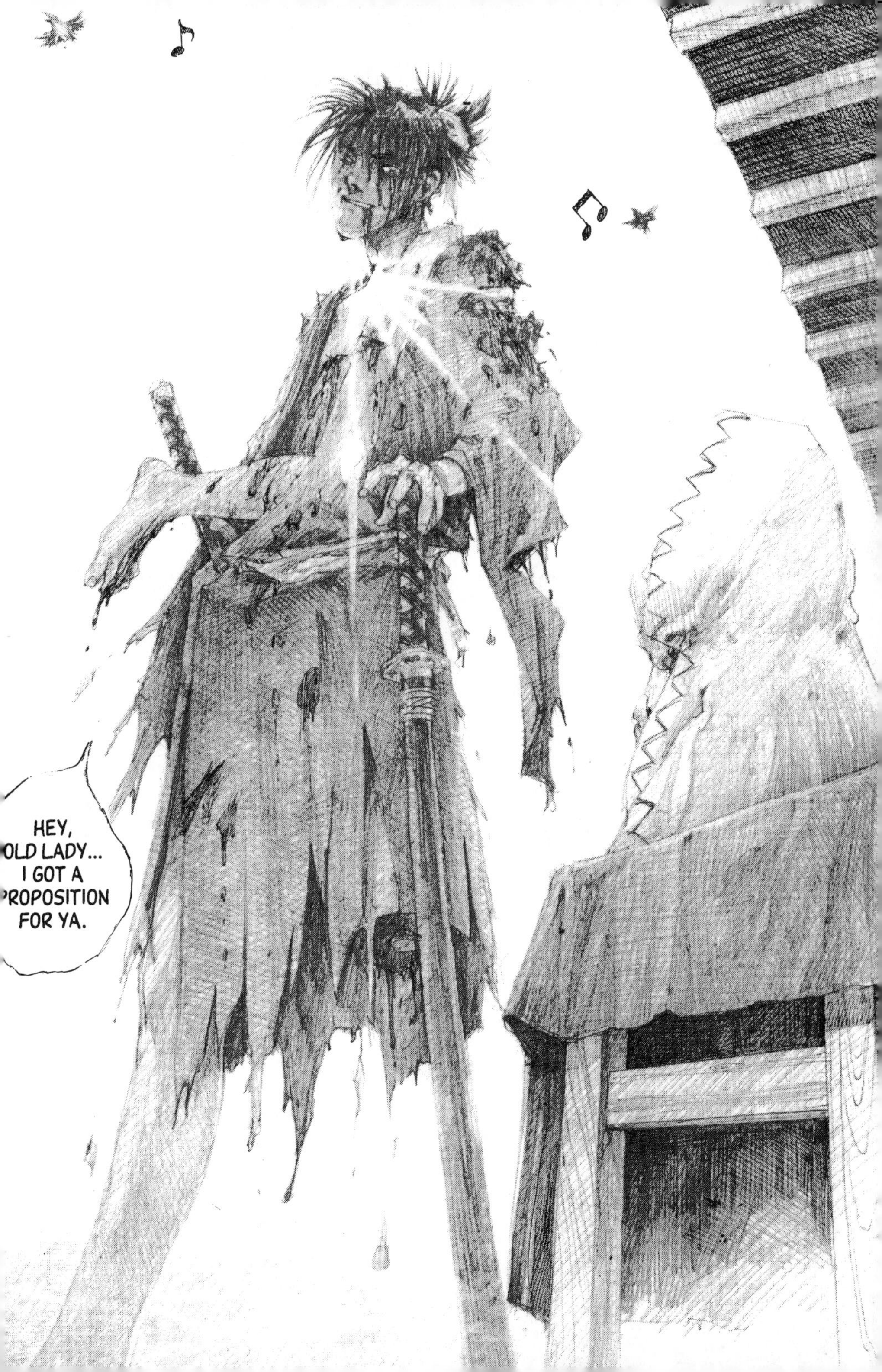
HEY, OLD LADY... I GOT A PROPOSITION FOR YA.

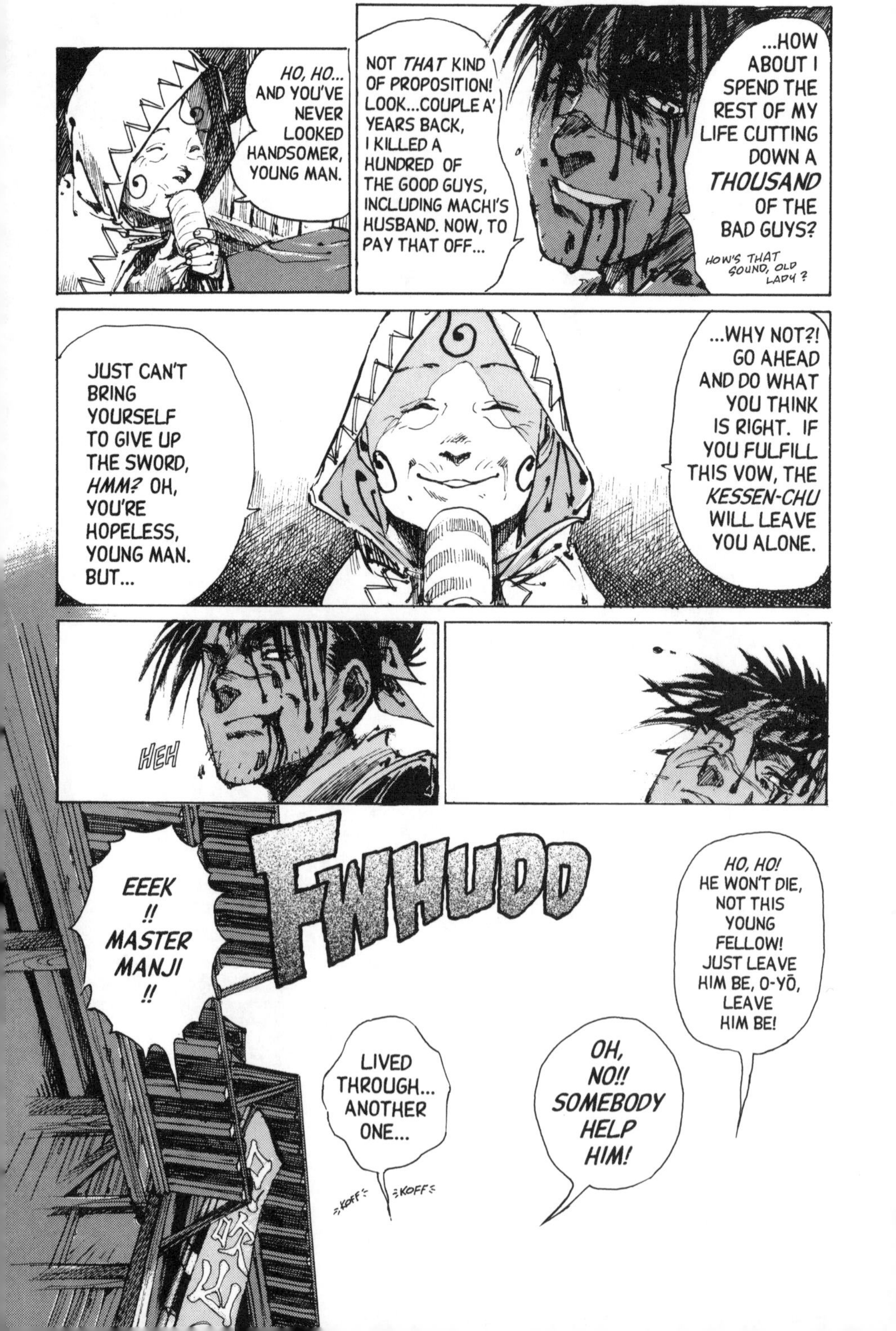
HO, HO... AND YOU'VE NEVER LOOKED HANDSOMER, YOUNG MAN.
NOT THAT KIND OF PROPOSITION! LOOK...COUPLE A' YEARS BACK, I KILLED A HUNDRED OF THE GOOD GUYS, INCLUDING MACHI'S HUSBAND. NOW, TO PAY THAT OFF...
...HOW ABOUT I SPEND THE REST OF MY LIFE CUTTING DOWN A THOUSAND OF THE BAD GUYS?
HOW'S THAT SOUND, OLD LADY?
JUST CAN'T BRING YOURSELF TO GIVE UP THE SWORD, HMM? OH, YOU'RE HOPELESS, YOUNG MAN. BUT...
...WHY NOT?! GO AHEAD AND DO WHAT YOU THINK IS RIGHT. IF YOU FULFILL THIS VOW, THE KESSEN-CHU WILL LEAVE YOU ALONE.
HEH
EEEK !! MASTER MANJI !!
FWHUDD
HO, HO! HE WON'T DIE, NOT THIS YOUNG FELLOW! JUST LEAVE HIM BE, O-YŌ, LEAVE HIM BE!
LIVED THROUGH... ANOTHER ONE...
KOFF KOFF
OH, NO!! SOMEBODY HELP HIM!

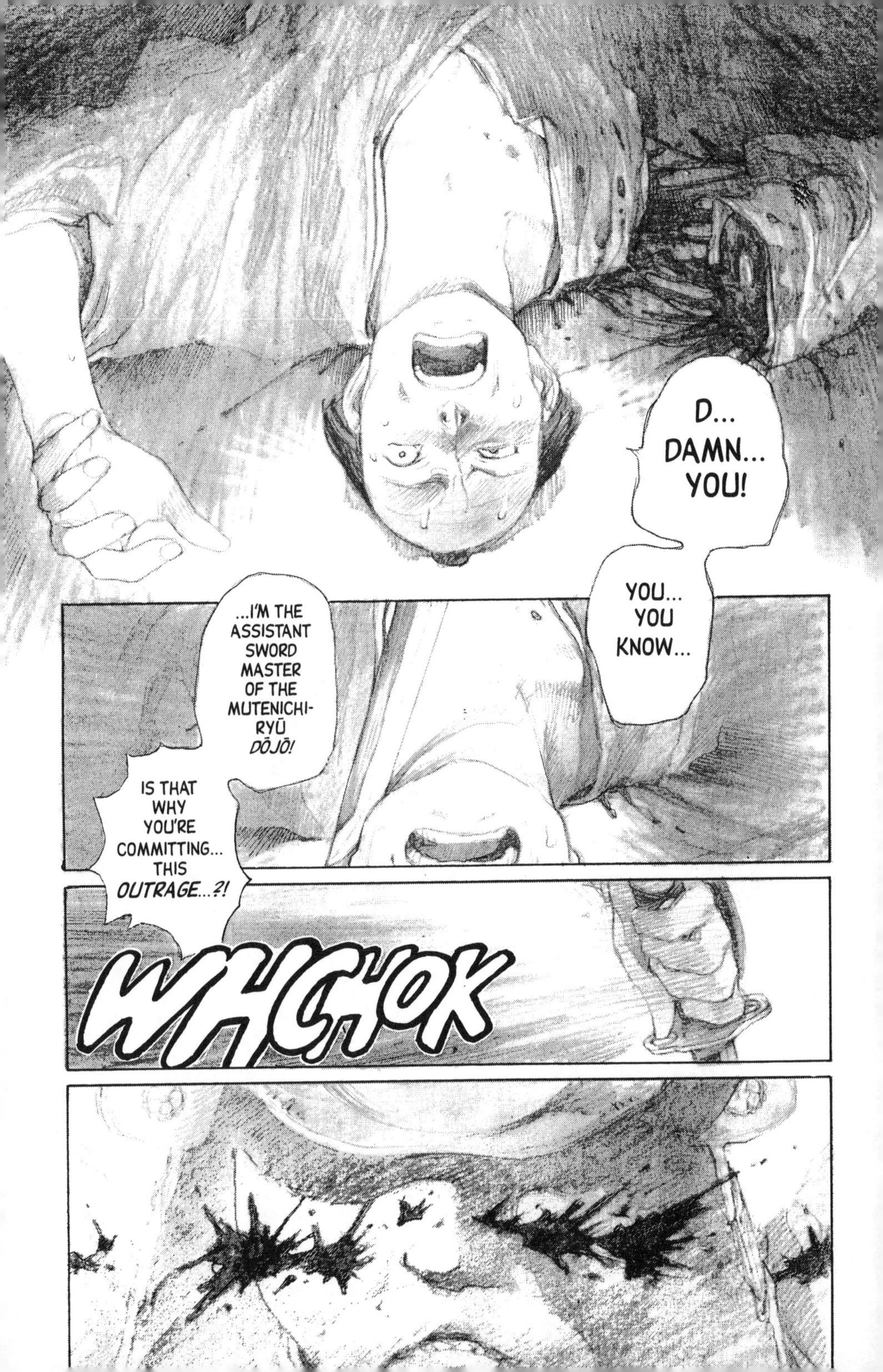
D... DAMN... YOU!
YOU... YOU KNOW...
...I'M THE ASSISTANT SWORD MASTER OF THE MUTENICHI-RYŪ *DŌJŌ!*
IS THAT WHY YOU'RE COMMITTING... THIS *OUTRAGE...?!*
WHCHOK

CONQUEST

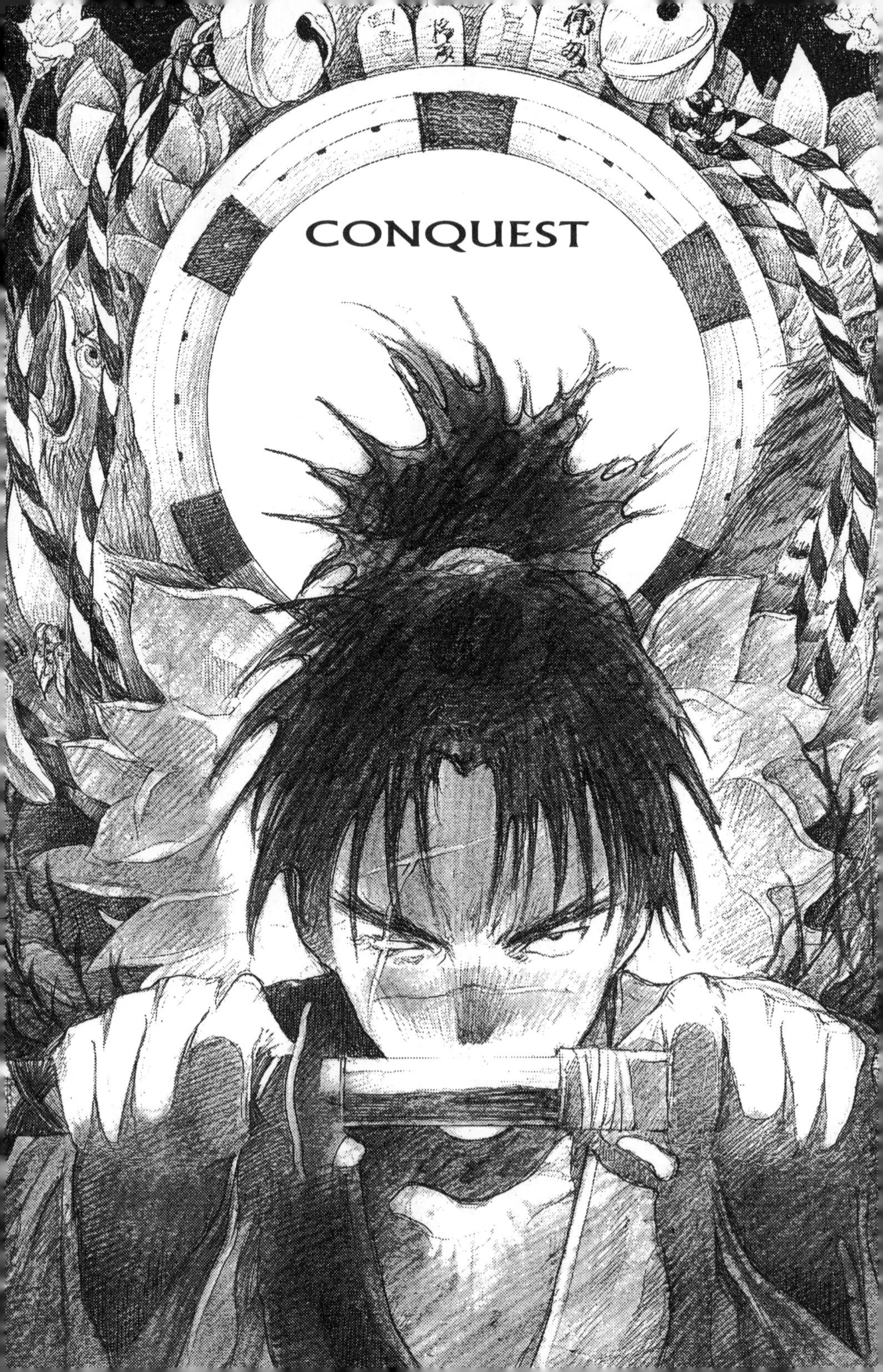

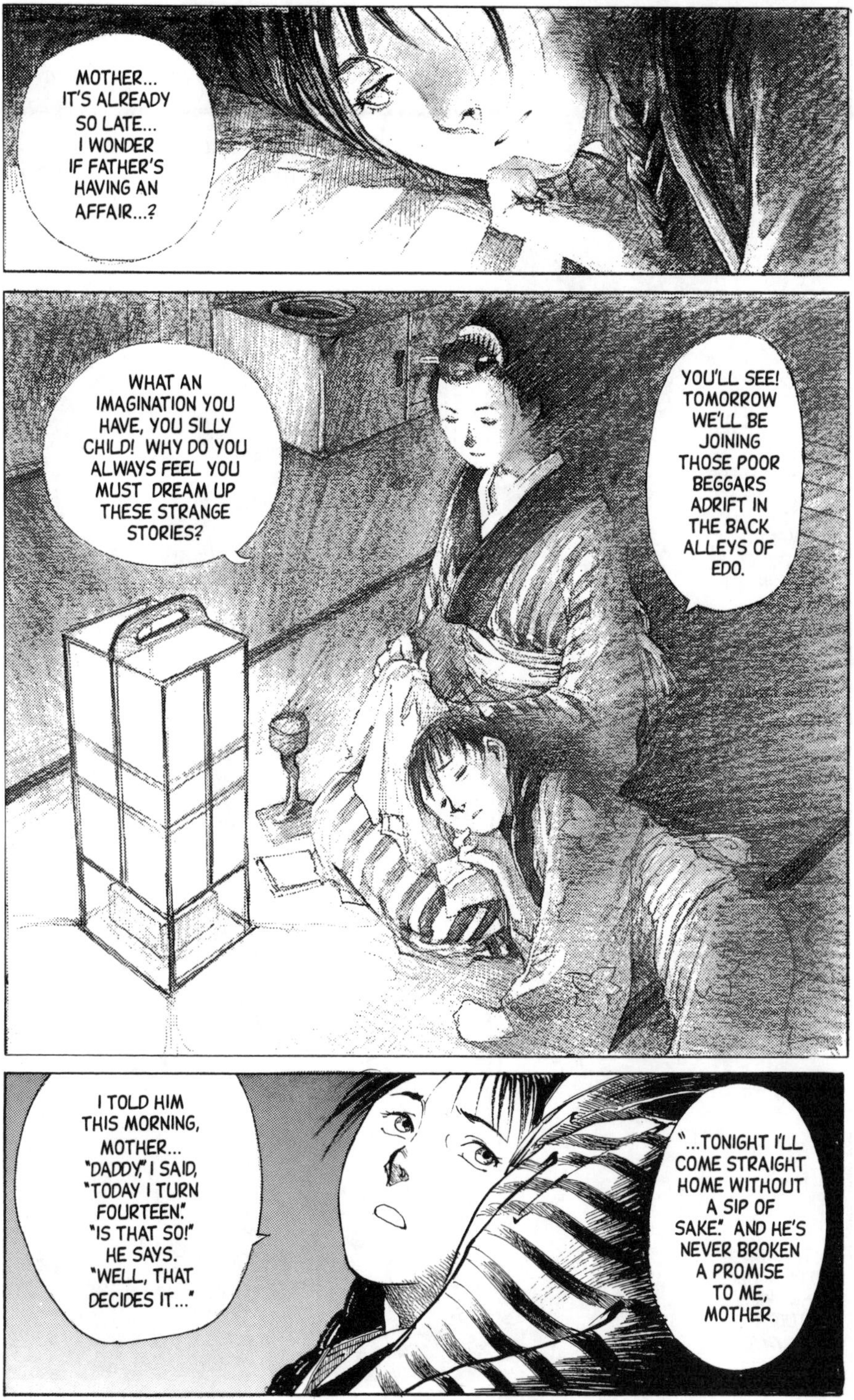
MOTHER... IT'S ALREADY SO LATE... I WONDER IF FATHER'S HAVING AN AFFAIR...?
WHAT AN IMAGINATION YOU HAVE, YOU SILLY CHILD! WHY DO YOU ALWAYS FEEL YOU MUST DREAM UP THESE STRANGE STORIES?
YOU'LL SEE! TOMORROW WE'LL BE JOINING THOSE POOR BEGGARS ADRIFT IN THE BACK ALLEYS OF EDO.
I TOLD HIM THIS MORNING, MOTHER... "DADDY," I SAID, "TODAY I TURN FOURTEEN." "IS THAT SO!" HE SAYS. "WELL, THAT DECIDES IT..."
"...TONIGHT I'LL COME STRAIGHT HOME WITHOUT A SIP OF SAKE." AND HE'S NEVER BROKEN A PROMISE TO ME, MOTHER.

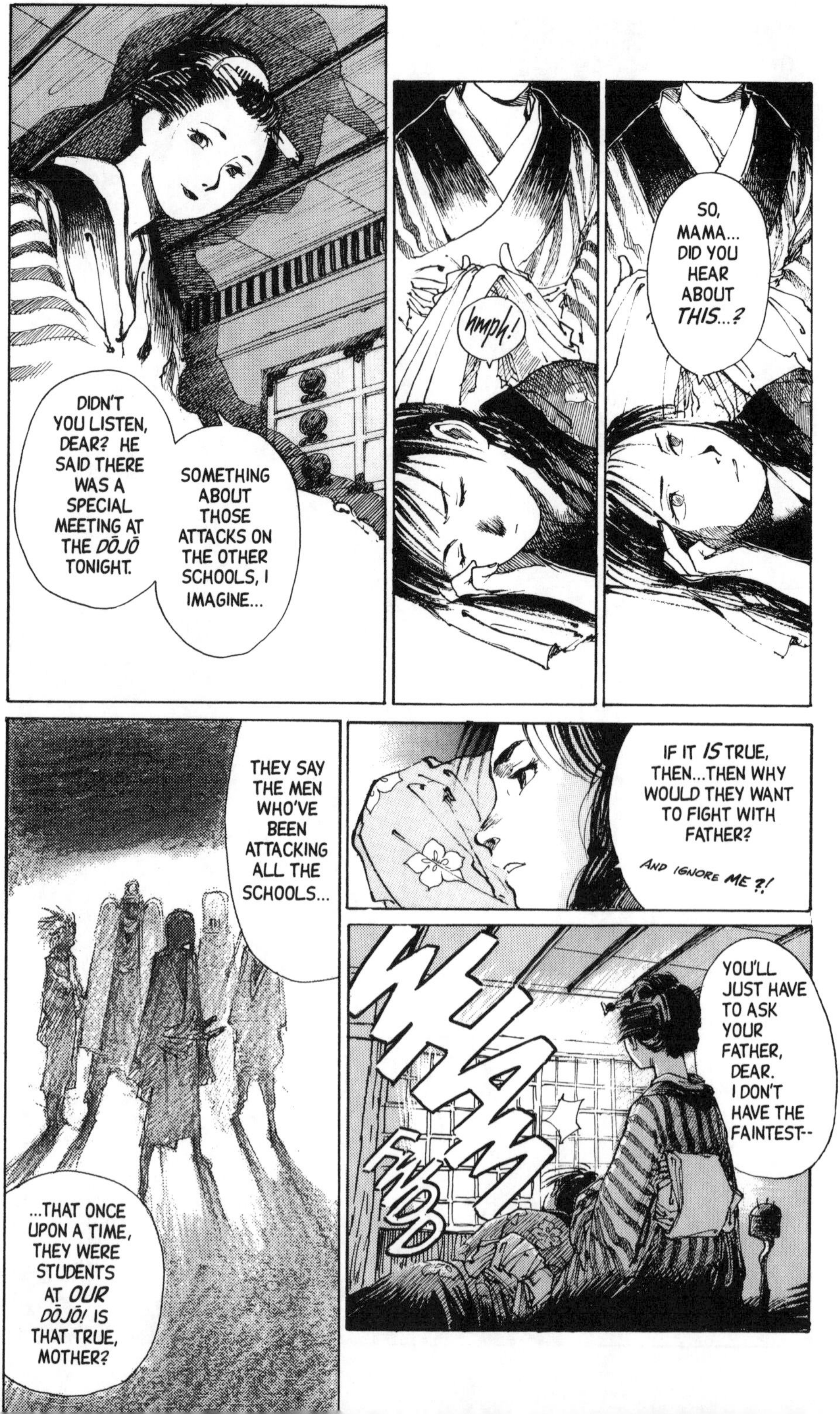
DIDN'T YOU LISTEN, DEAR? HE SAID THERE WAS A SPECIAL MEETING AT THE *DŌJŌ* TONIGHT.
SOMETHING ABOUT THOSE ATTACKS ON THE OTHER SCHOOLS, I IMAGINE...
hmph!
SO, MAMA... DID YOU HEAR ABOUT *THIS*...?
THEY SAY THE MEN WHO'VE BEEN ATTACKING ALL THE SCHOOLS...
...THAT ONCE UPON A TIME, THEY WERE STUDENTS AT *OUR DŌJŌ!* IS THAT TRUE, MOTHER?
IF IT *IS* TRUE, THEN...THEN WHY WOULD THEY WANT TO FIGHT WITH FATHER?
AND IGNORE ME ?!
WHAM
FWOOD
YOU'LL JUST HAVE TO ASK YOUR FATHER, DEAR. I DON'T HAVE THE FAINTEST--

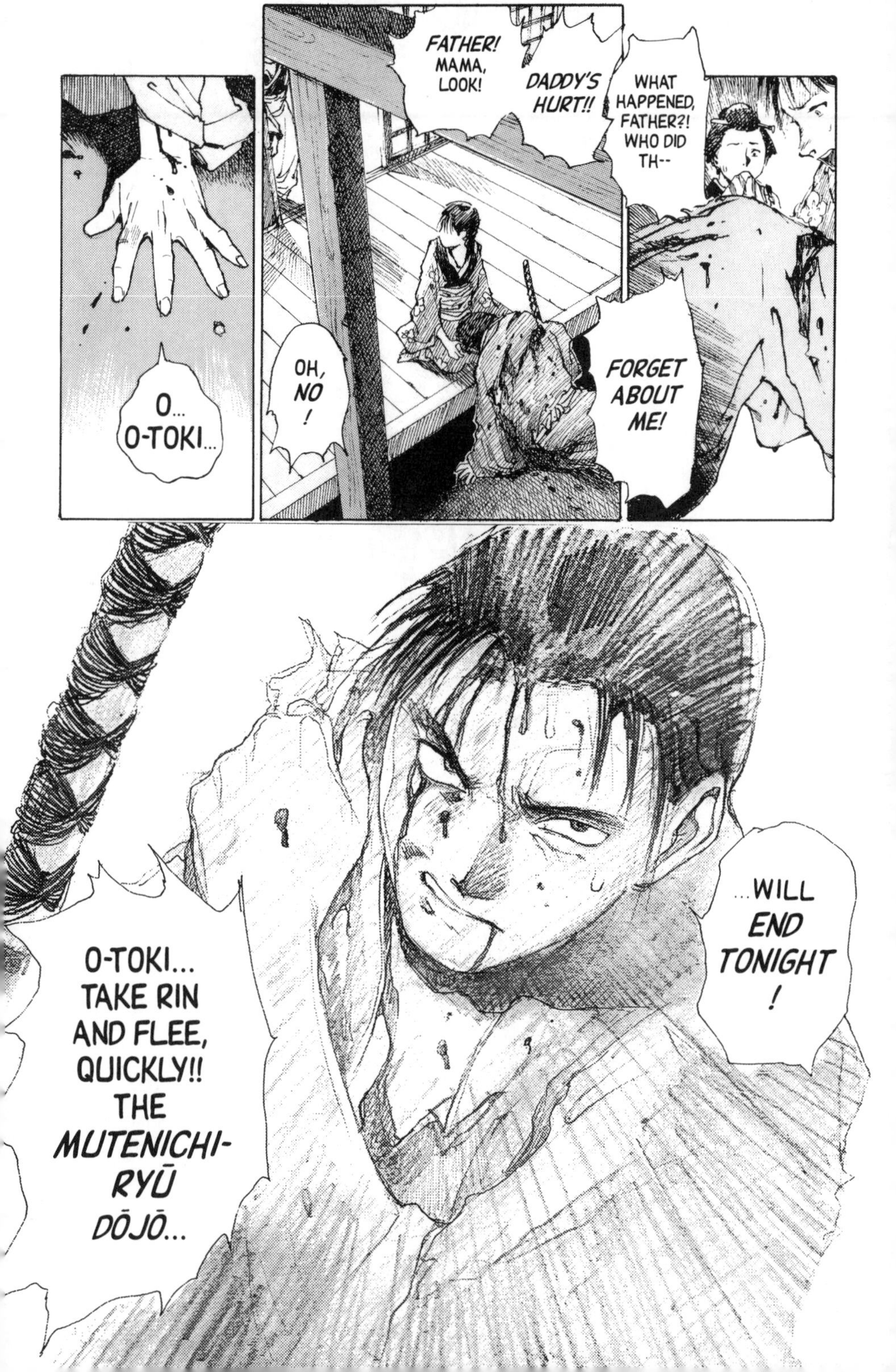
O... O-TOKI...
FATHER! MAMA, LOOK!
DADDY'S HURT!!
OH, NO!
WHAT HAPPENED, FATHER?! WHO DID TH--
FORGET ABOUT ME!
O-TOKI... TAKE RIN AND FLEE, QUICKLY!! THE MUTENICHI-RYŪ DŌJŌ...
...WILL END TONIGHT!

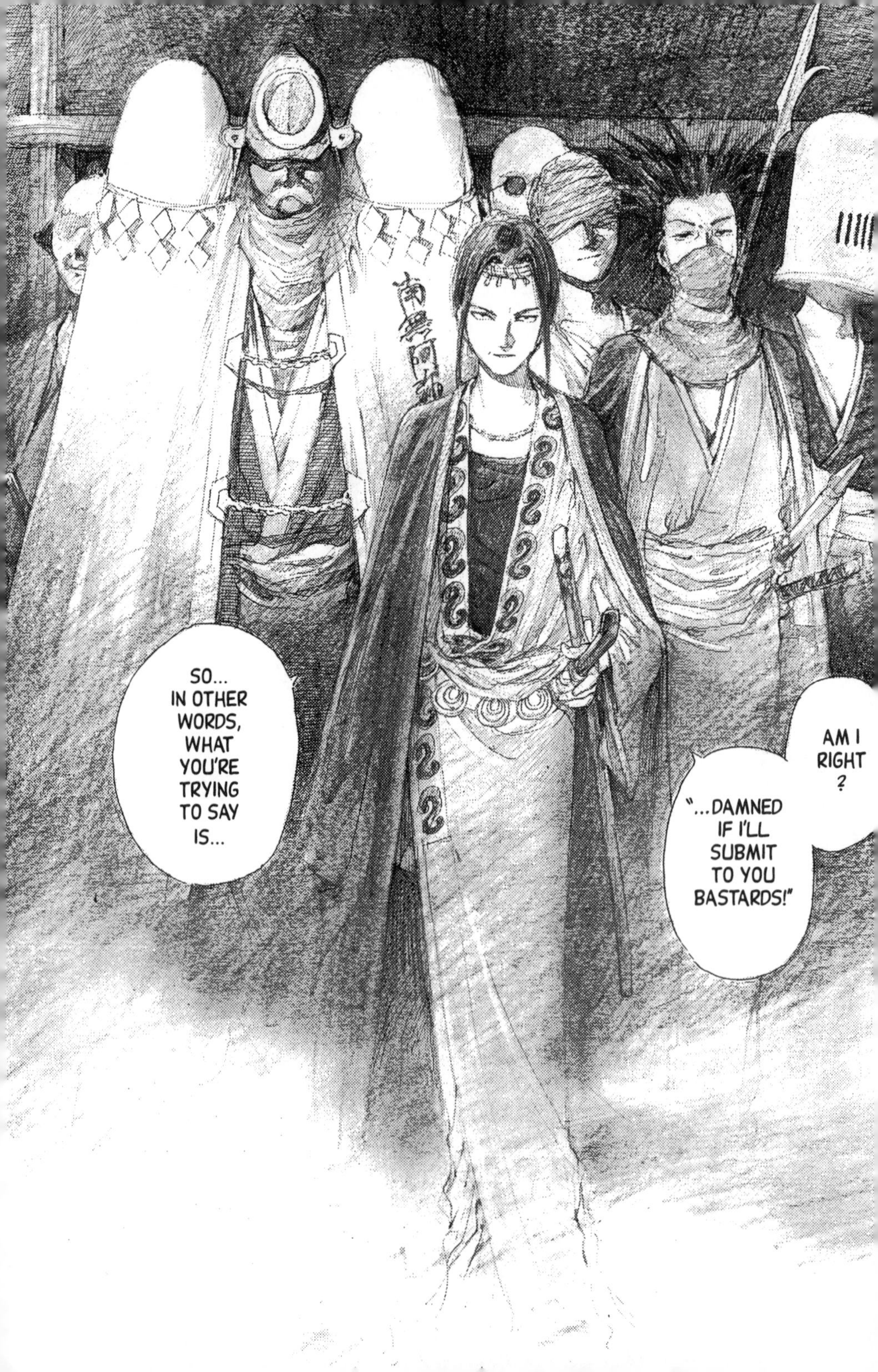
SO... IN OTHER WORDS, WHAT YOU'RE TRYING TO SAY IS...
"...DAMNED IF I'LL SUBMIT TO YOU BASTARDS!"
AM I RIGHT?

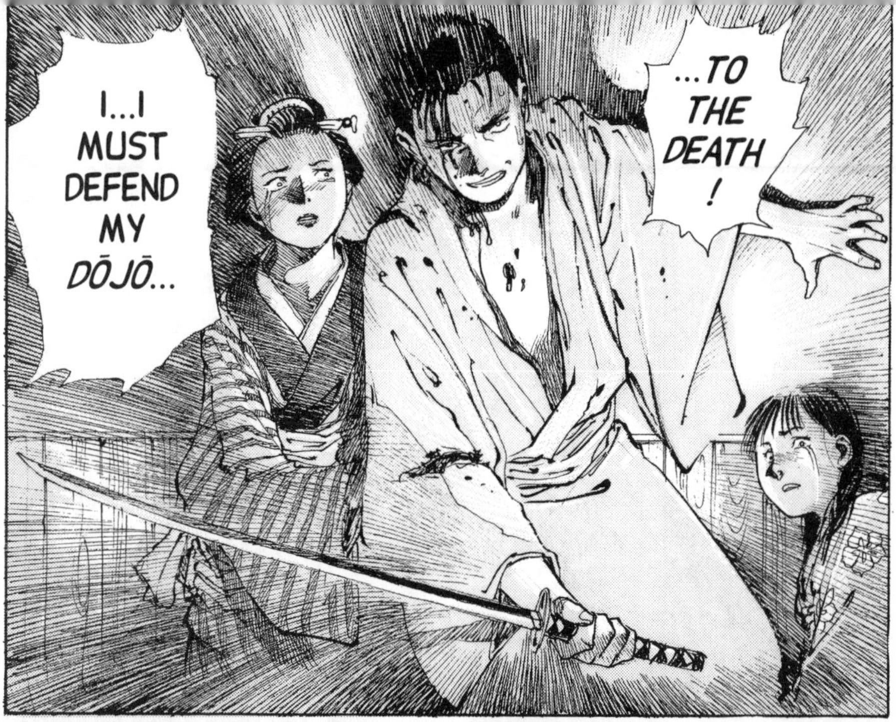
I...I MUST DEFEND MY *DŌJŌ*...
...TO THE DEATH!
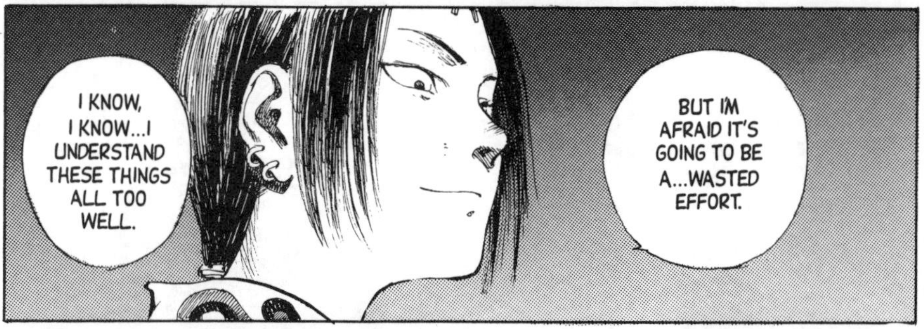
I KNOW, I KNOW...I UNDERSTAND THESE THINGS ALL TOO WELL.
BUT I'M AFRAID IT'S GOING TO BE A...WASTED EFFORT.
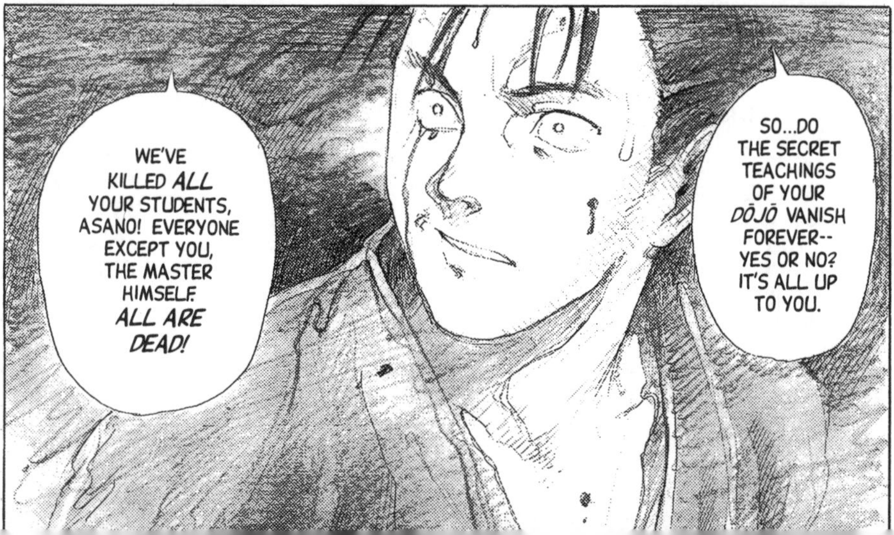
WE'VE KILLED *ALL* YOUR STUDENTS, ASANO! EVERYONE EXCEPT YOU, THE MASTER HIMSELF. *ALL ARE DEAD!*
SO...DO THE SECRET TEACHINGS OF YOUR *DŌJŌ* VANISH FOREVER--YES OR NO? IT'S ALL UP TO YOU.

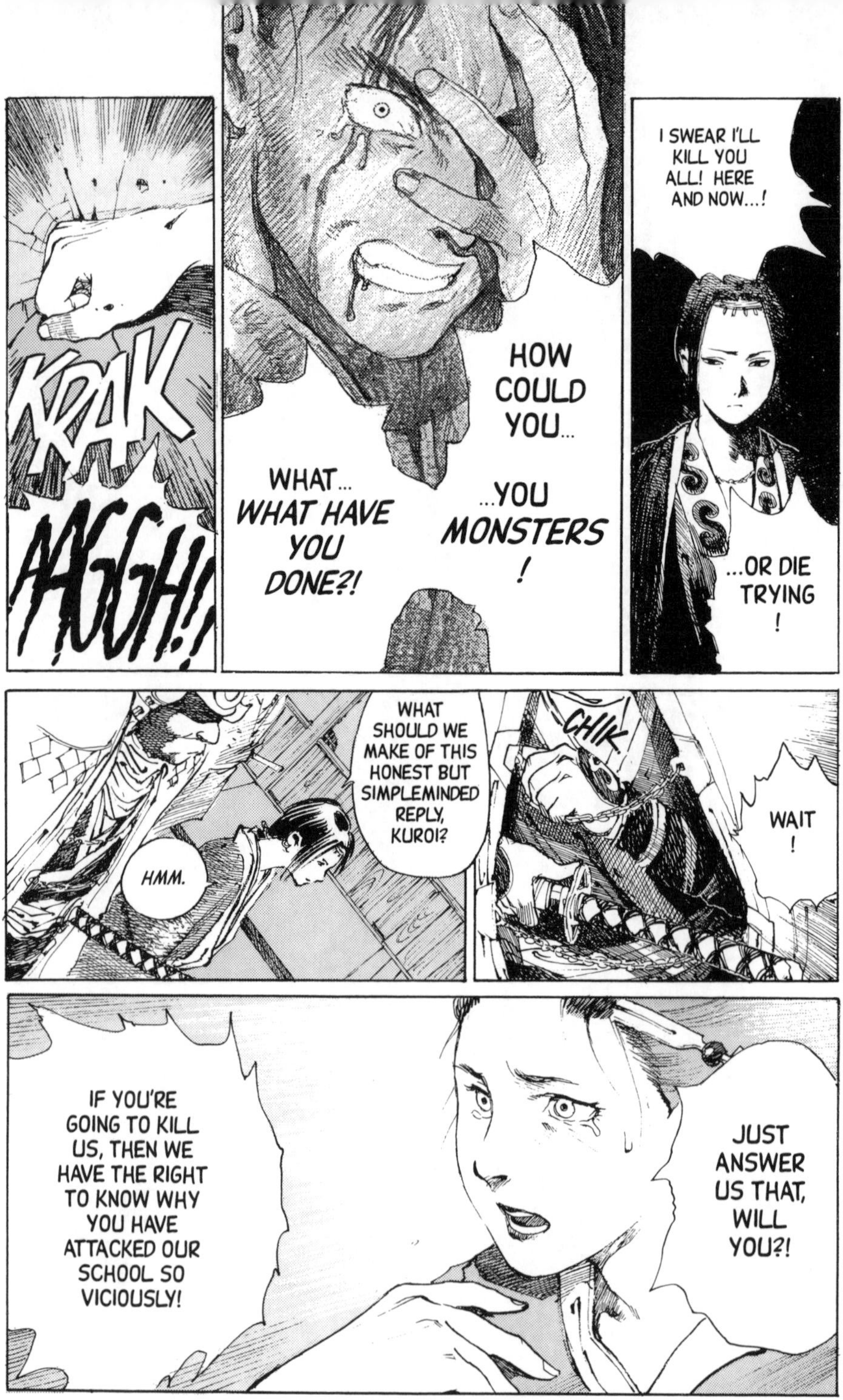
KRAK
AAGGH!!
WHAT... WHAT HAVE YOU DONE?!
HOW COULD YOU...
...YOU MONSTERS!
I SWEAR I'LL KILL YOU ALL! HERE AND NOW...!
...OR DIE TRYING!
HMM.
WHAT SHOULD WE MAKE OF THIS HONEST BUT SIMPLEMINDED REPLY, KUROI?
CHIK
WAIT!
IF YOU'RE GOING TO KILL US, THEN WE HAVE THE RIGHT TO KNOW WHY YOU HAVE ATTACKED OUR SCHOOL SO VICIOUSLY!
JUST ANSWER US THAT, WILL YOU?!

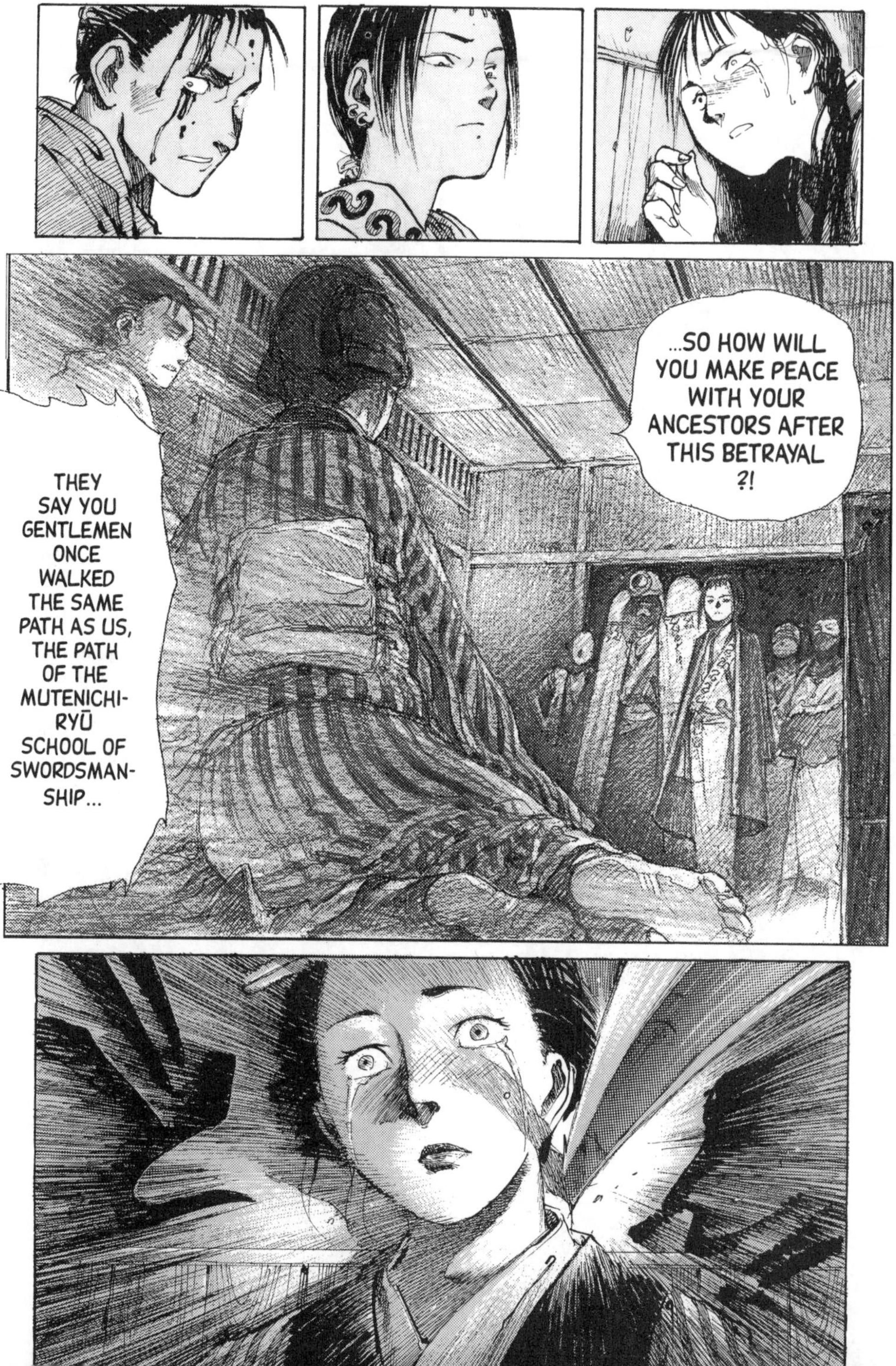
THEY SAY YOU GENTLEMEN ONCE WALKED THE SAME PATH AS US, THE PATH OF THE MUTENICHI-RYŪ SCHOOL OF SWORDSMAN-SHIP...
...SO HOW WILL YOU MAKE PEACE WITH YOUR ANCESTORS AFTER THIS BETRAYAL ?!

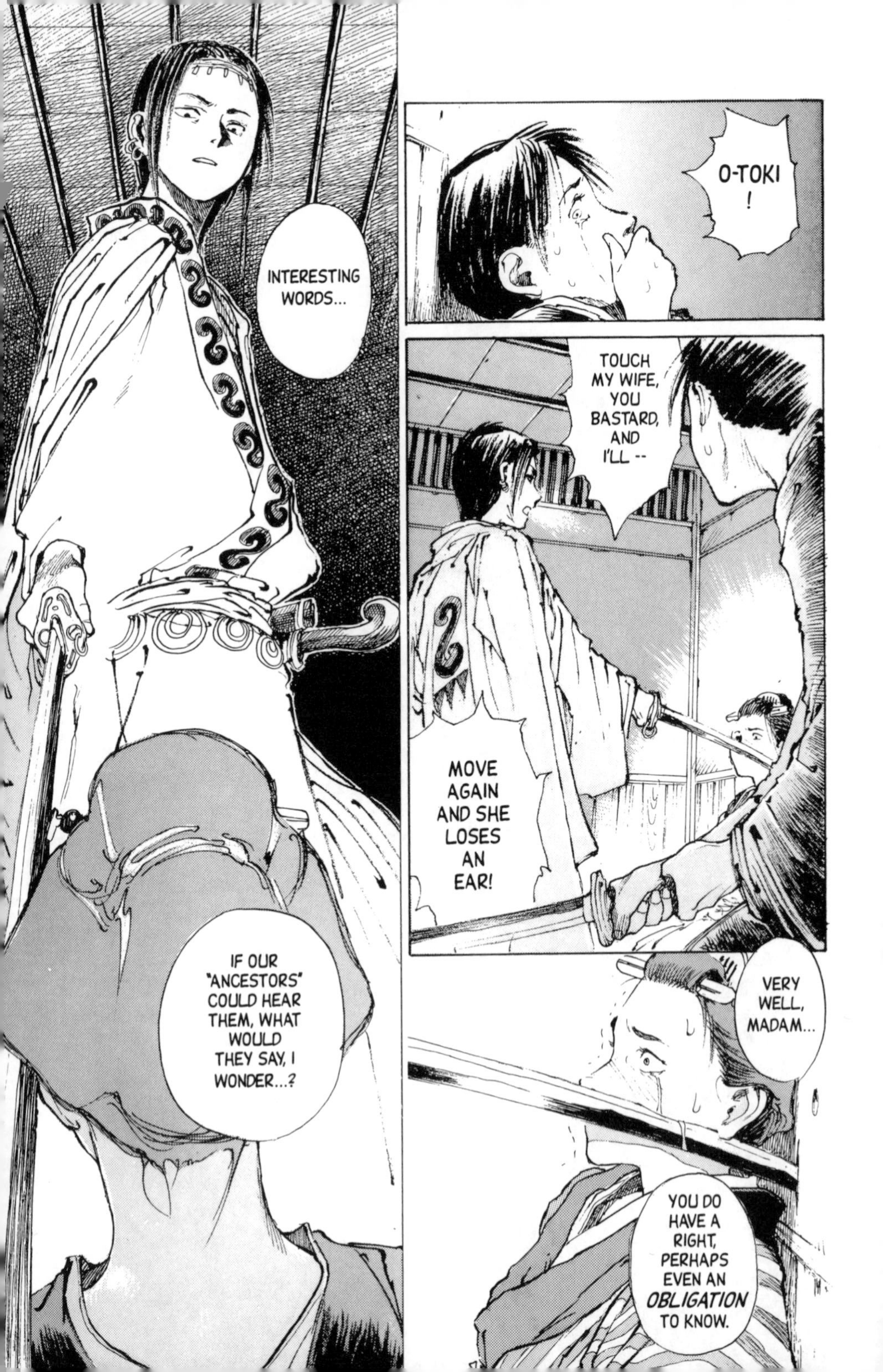
INTERESTING WORDS...
IF OUR "ANCESTORS" COULD HEAR THEM, WHAT WOULD THEY SAY, I WONDER...?
O-TOKI !
TOUCH MY WIFE, YOU BASTARD, AND I'LL --
MOVE AGAIN AND SHE LOSES AN EAR!
VERY WELL, MADAM...
YOU DO HAVE A RIGHT, PERHAPS EVEN AN *OBLIGATION* TO KNOW.

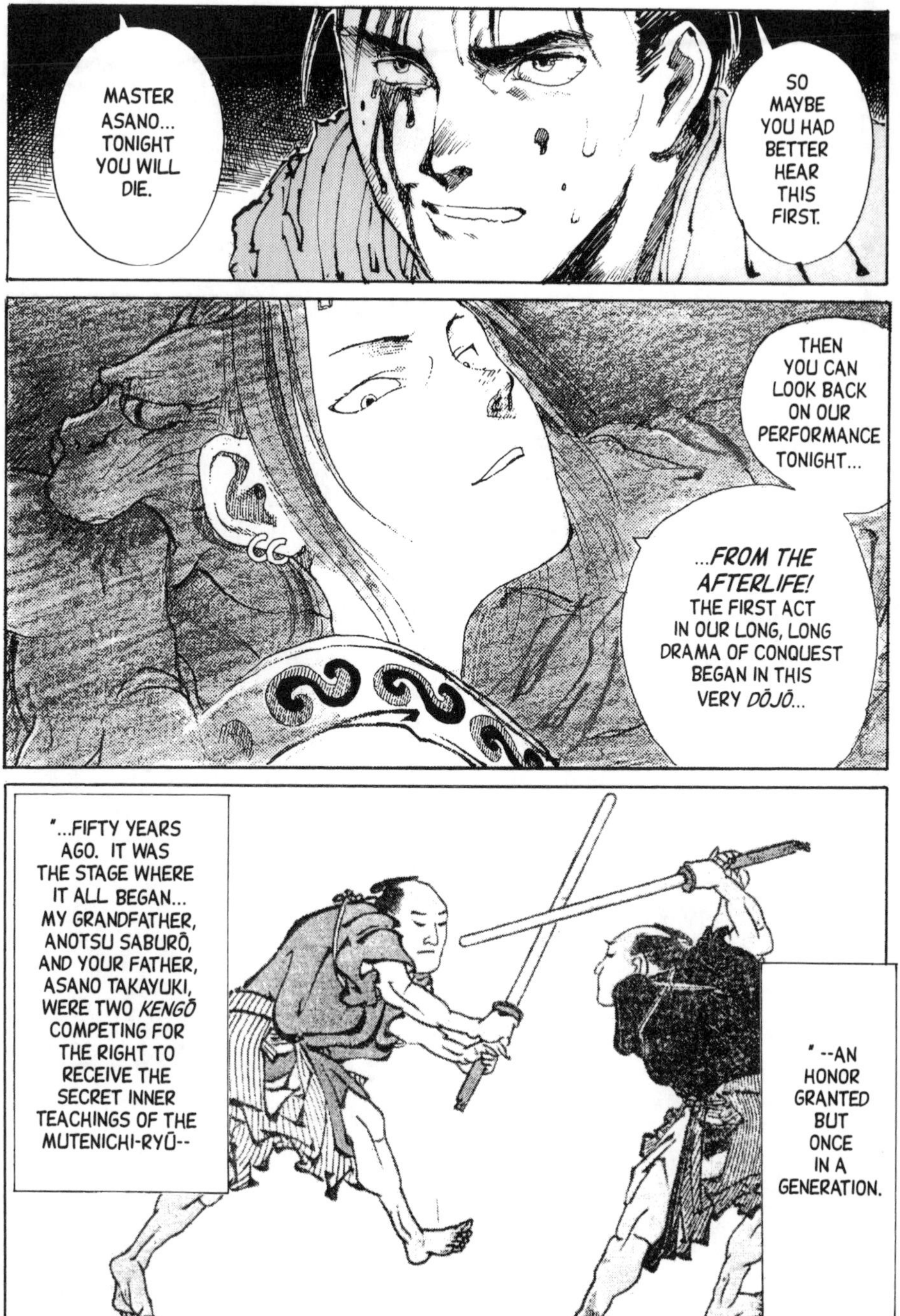
MASTER ASANO... TONIGHT YOU WILL DIE.
SO MAYBE YOU HAD BETTER HEAR THIS FIRST.
THEN YOU CAN LOOK BACK ON OUR PERFORMANCE TONIGHT...
...*FROM THE AFTERLIFE!* THE FIRST ACT IN OUR LONG, LONG DRAMA OF CONQUEST BEGAN IN THIS VERY *DŌJŌ*...
"...FIFTY YEARS AGO. IT WAS THE STAGE WHERE IT ALL BEGAN... MY GRANDFATHER, ANOTSU SABURŌ, AND YOUR FATHER, ASANO TAKAYUKI, WERE TWO *KENGŌ* COMPETING FOR THE RIGHT TO RECEIVE THE SECRET INNER TEACHINGS OF THE MUTENICHI-RYŪ--
" --AN HONOR GRANTED BUT ONCE IN A GENERATION.
FROM HOKUSAI'S "HOKUSAI MANGA"

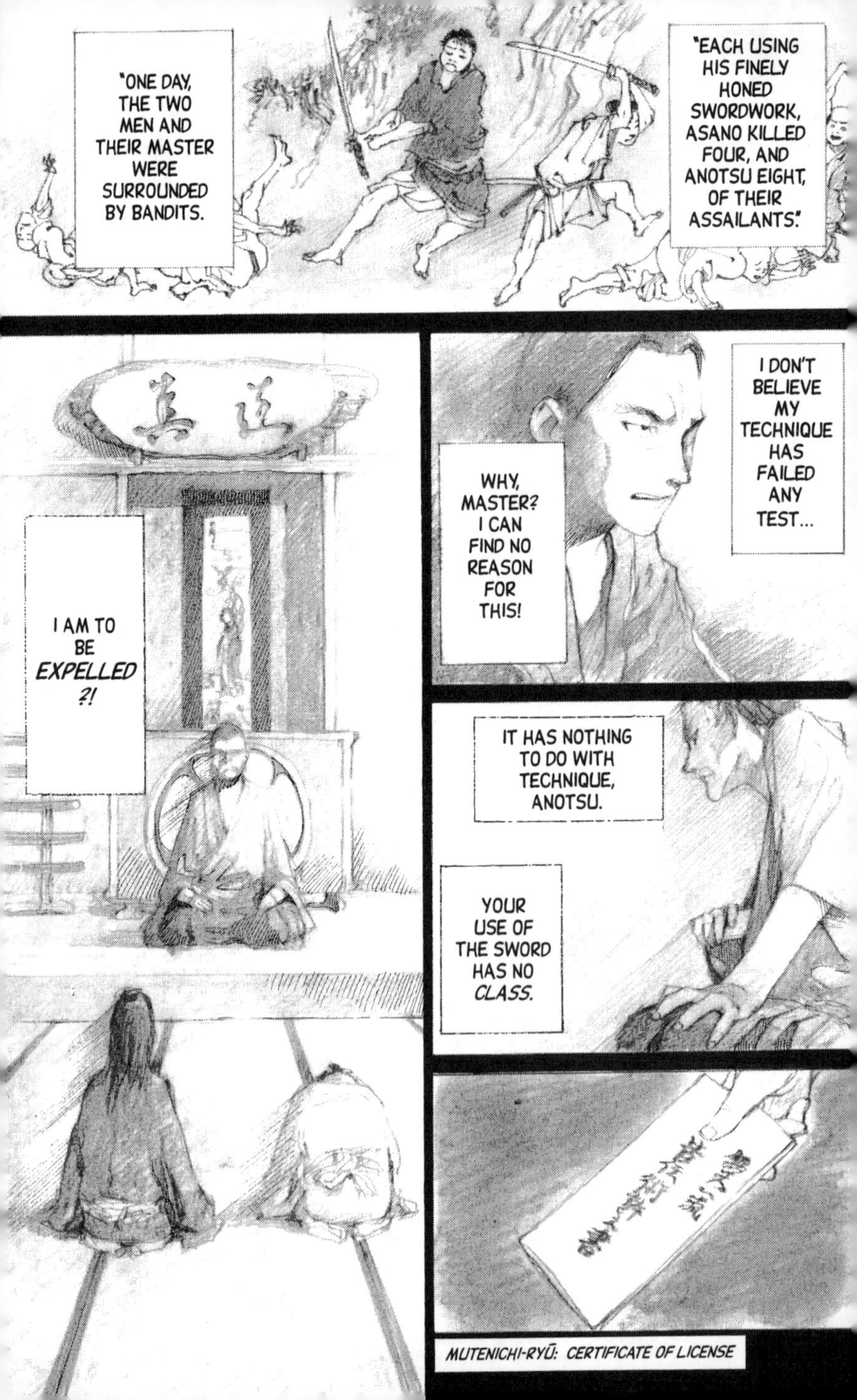
"ONE DAY, THE TWO MEN AND THEIR MASTER WERE SURROUNDED BY BANDITS.
"EACH USING HIS FINELY HONED SWORDWORK, ASANO KILLED FOUR, AND ANOTSU EIGHT, OF THEIR ASSAILANTS."
I AM TO BE *EXPELLED* ?!
WHY, MASTER? I CAN FIND NO REASON FOR THIS!
I DON'T BELIEVE MY TECHNIQUE HAS FAILED ANY TEST...
IT HAS NOTHING TO DO WITH TECHNIQUE, ANOTSU.
YOUR USE OF THE SWORD HAS NO *CLASS.*
MUTENICHI-RYŪ: CERTIFICATE OF LICENSE

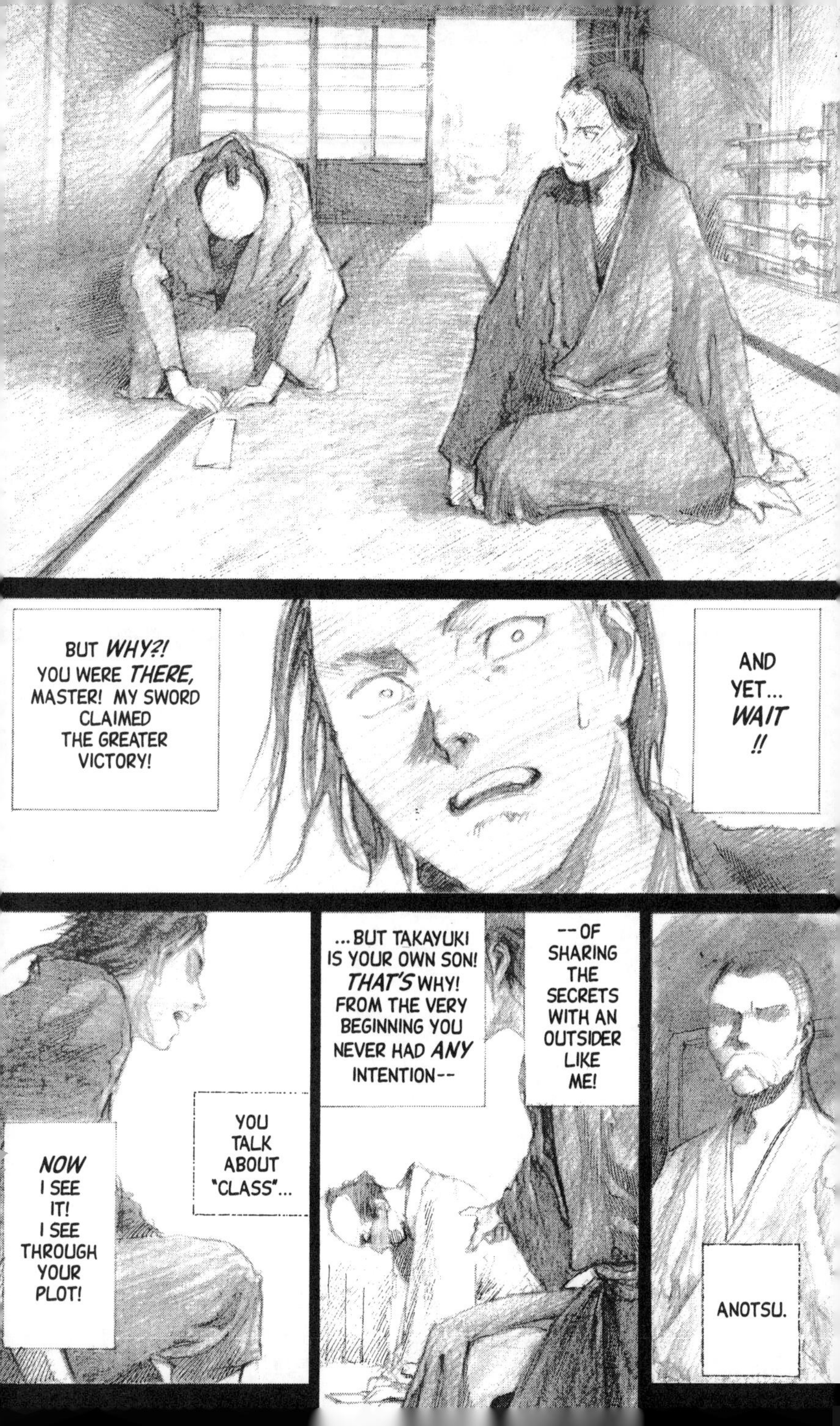
BUT WHY?! YOU WERE THERE, MASTER! MY SWORD CLAIMED THE GREATER VICTORY!
AND YET... WAIT !!
NOW I SEE IT! I SEE THROUGH YOUR PLOT!
YOU TALK ABOUT "CLASS"...
...BUT TAKAYUKI IS YOUR OWN SON! THAT'S WHY! FROM THE VERY BEGINNING YOU NEVER HAD ANY INTENTION--
--OF SHARING THE SECRETS WITH AN OUTSIDER LIKE ME!
ANOTSU.

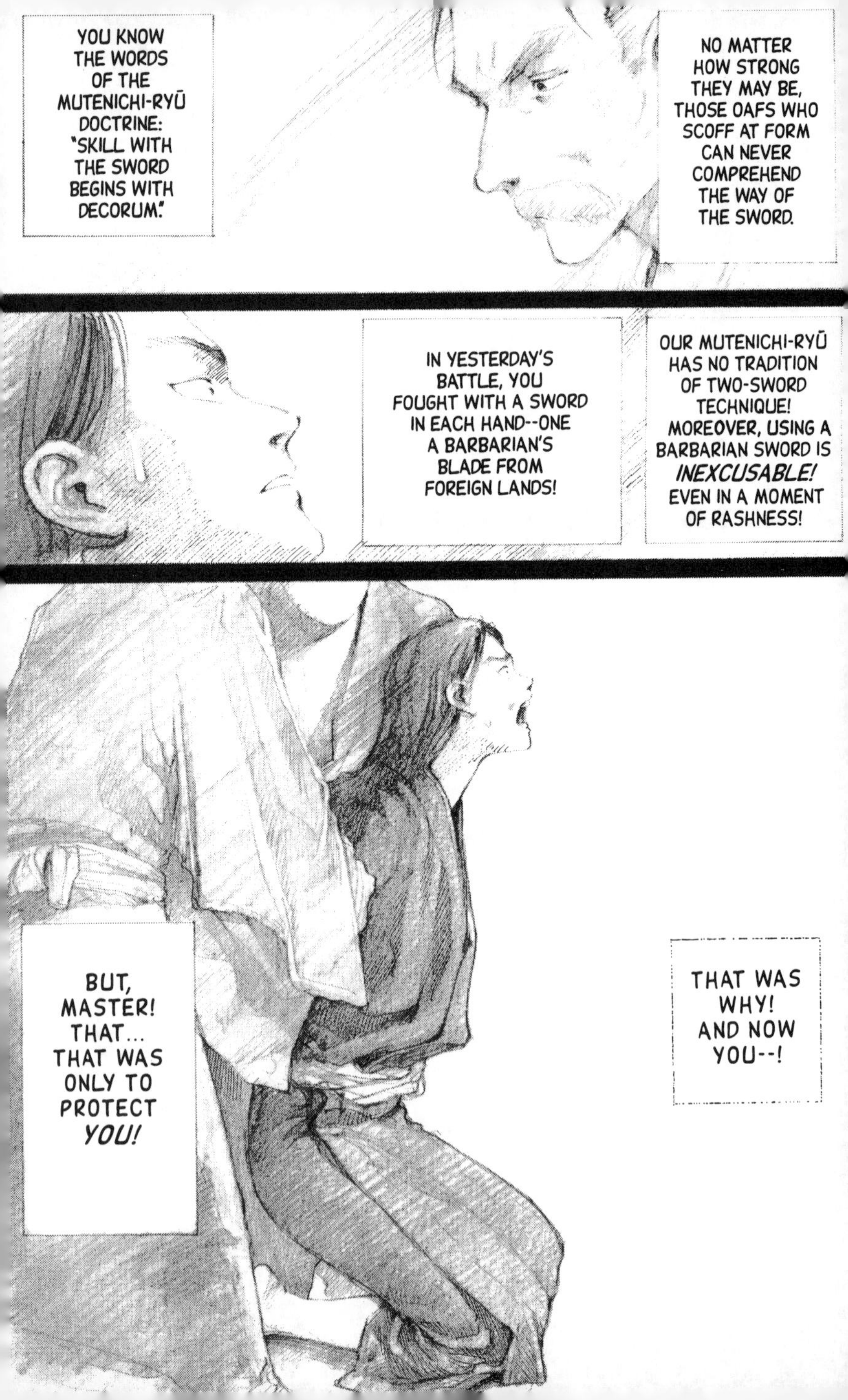
YOU KNOW THE WORDS OF THE MUTENICHI-RYŪ DOCTRINE: "SKILL WITH THE SWORD BEGINS WITH DECORUM."
NO MATTER HOW STRONG THEY MAY BE, THOSE OAFS WHO SCOFF AT FORM CAN NEVER COMPREHEND THE WAY OF THE SWORD.
IN YESTERDAY'S BATTLE, YOU FOUGHT WITH A SWORD IN EACH HAND--ONE A BARBARIAN'S BLADE FROM FOREIGN LANDS!
OUR MUTENICHI-RYŪ HAS NO TRADITION OF TWO-SWORD TECHNIQUE! MOREOVER, USING A BARBARIAN SWORD IS *INEXCUSABLE!* EVEN IN A MOMENT OF RASHNESS!
BUT, MASTER! THAT... THAT WAS ONLY TO PROTECT *YOU!*
THAT WAS WHY! AND NOW YOU--!

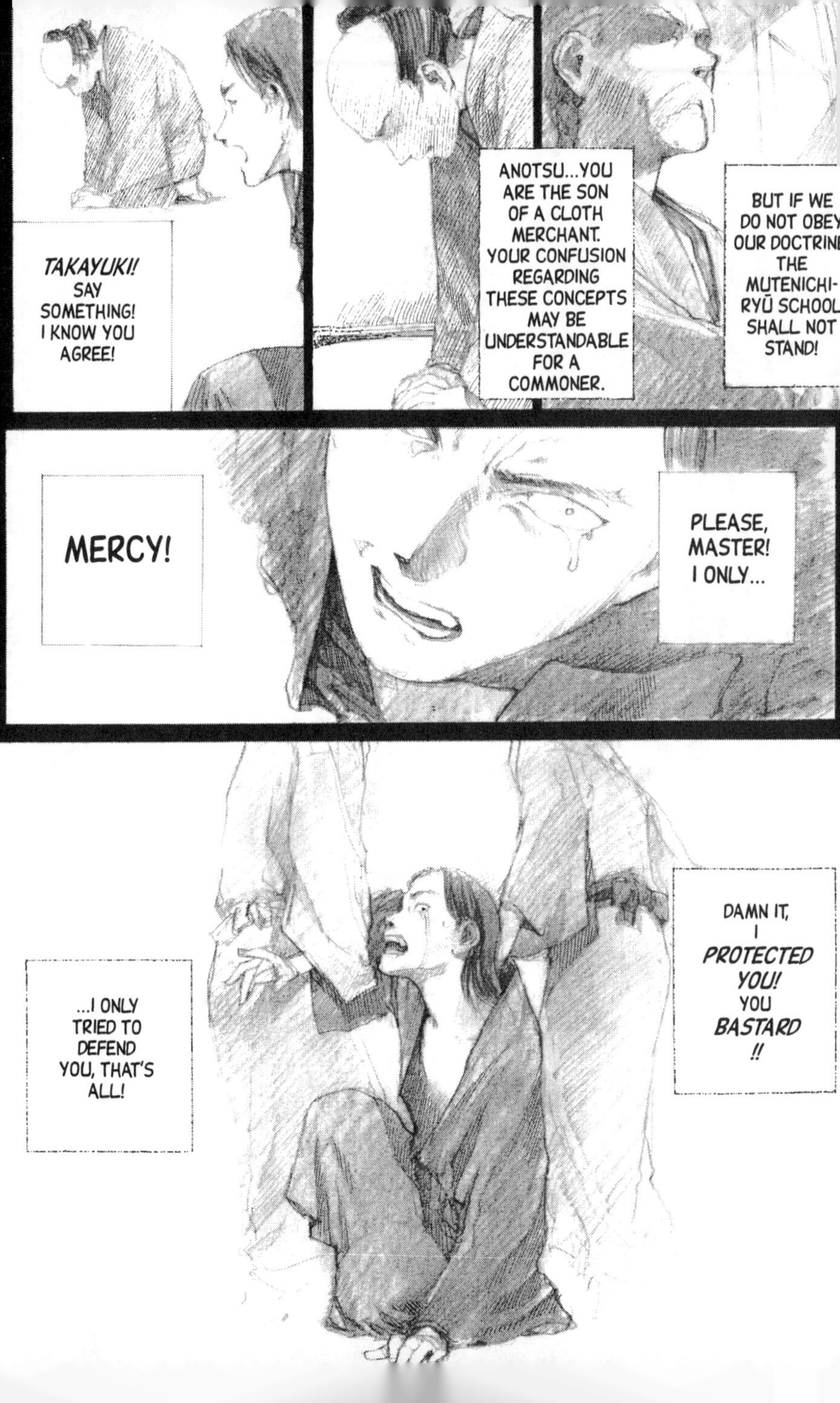
TAKAYUKI! SAY SOMETHING! I KNOW YOU AGREE!
ANOTSU...YOU ARE THE SON OF A CLOTH MERCHANT. YOUR CONFUSION REGARDING THESE CONCEPTS MAY BE UNDERSTANDABLE FOR A COMMONER.
BUT IF WE DO NOT OBEY OUR DOCTRINE, THE MUTENICHI-RYŪ SCHOOL SHALL NOT STAND!
MERCY!
PLEASE, MASTER! I ONLY...
...I ONLY TRIED TO DEFEND YOU, THAT'S ALL!
DAMN IT, I PROTECTED YOU! YOU BASTARD!!

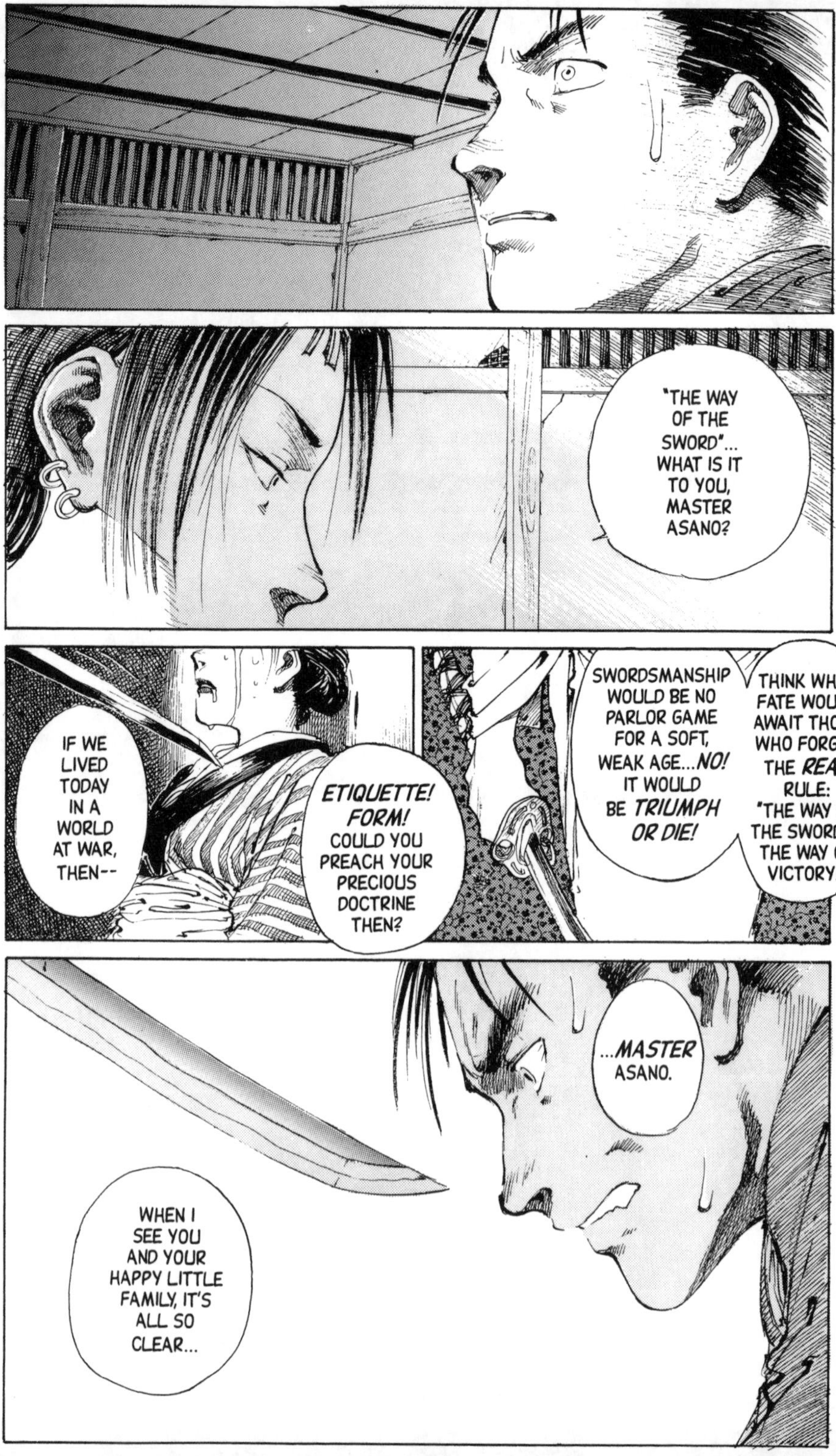
"THE WAY OF THE SWORD"... WHAT IS IT TO YOU, MASTER ASANO?
IF WE LIVED TODAY IN A WORLD AT WAR, THEN--
ETIQUETTE! FORM! COULD YOU PREACH YOUR PRECIOUS DOCTRINE THEN?
SWORDSMANSHIP WOULD BE NO PARLOR GAME FOR A SOFT, WEAK AGE...NO! IT WOULD BE TRIUMPH OR DIE!
THINK WHAT FATE WOULD AWAIT THOSE WHO FORGOT THE REAL RULE: "THE WAY OF THE SWORD IS THE WAY OF VICTORY!"
...MASTER ASANO.
WHEN I SEE YOU AND YOUR HAPPY LITTLE FAMILY, IT'S ALL SO CLEAR...

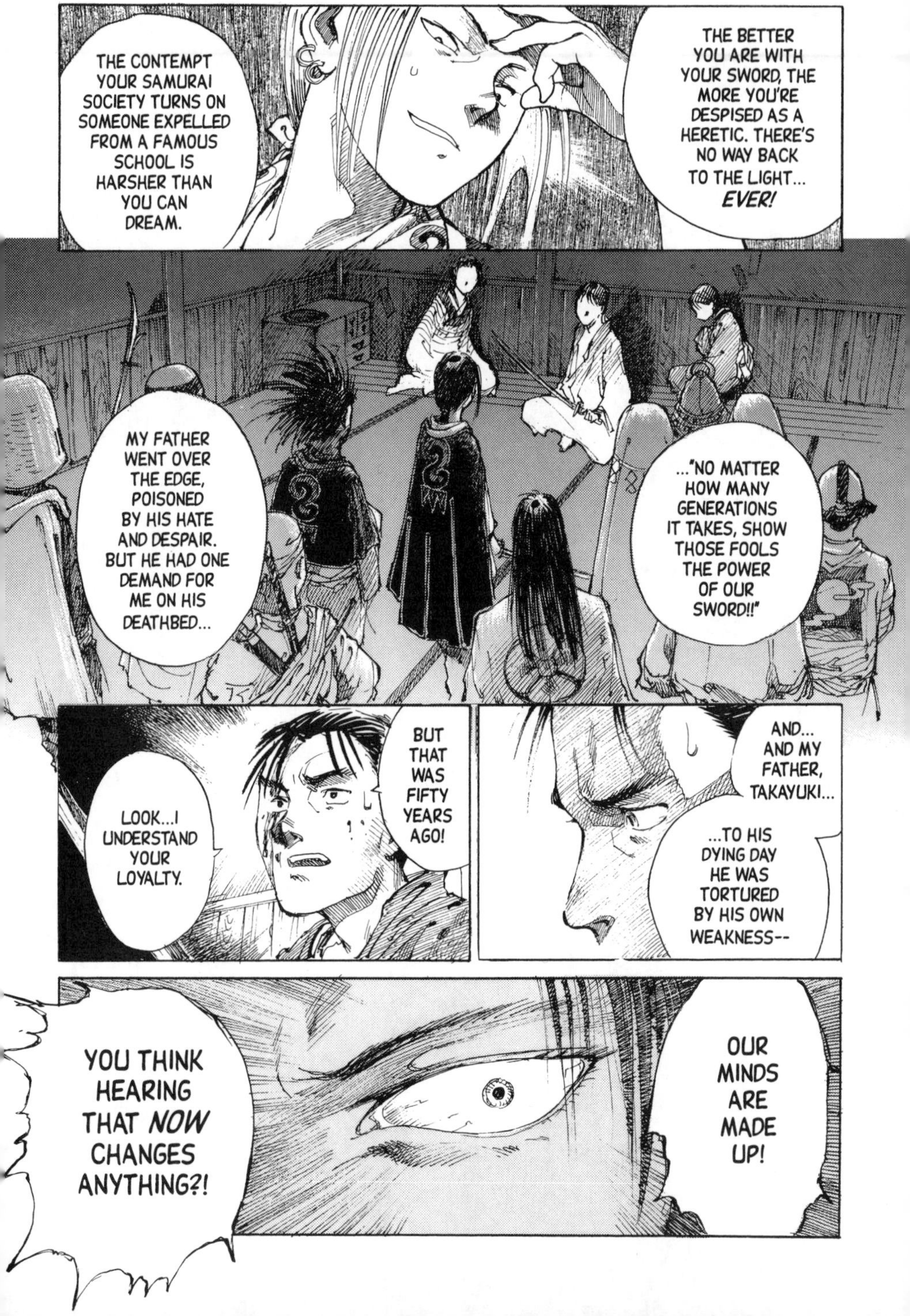

THE CONTEMPT YOUR SAMURAI SOCIETY TURNS ON SOMEONE EXPELLED FROM A FAMOUS SCHOOL IS HARSHER THAN YOU CAN DREAM.
THE BETTER YOU ARE WITH YOUR SWORD, THE MORE YOU'RE DESPISED AS A HERETIC. THERE'S NO WAY BACK TO THE LIGHT... *EVER!*
MY FATHER WENT OVER THE EDGE, POISONED BY HIS HATE AND DESPAIR. BUT HE HAD ONE DEMAND FOR ME ON HIS DEATHBED...
..."NO MATTER HOW MANY GENERATIONS IT TAKES, SHOW THOSE FOOLS THE POWER OF OUR SWORD!!"
LOOK...I UNDERSTAND YOUR LOYALTY.
BUT THAT WAS FIFTY YEARS AGO!
AND... AND MY FATHER, TAKAYUKI...
...TO HIS DYING DAY HE WAS TORTURED BY HIS OWN WEAKNESS--
YOU THINK HEARING THAT *NOW* CHANGES ANYTHING?!
OUR MINDS ARE MADE UP!

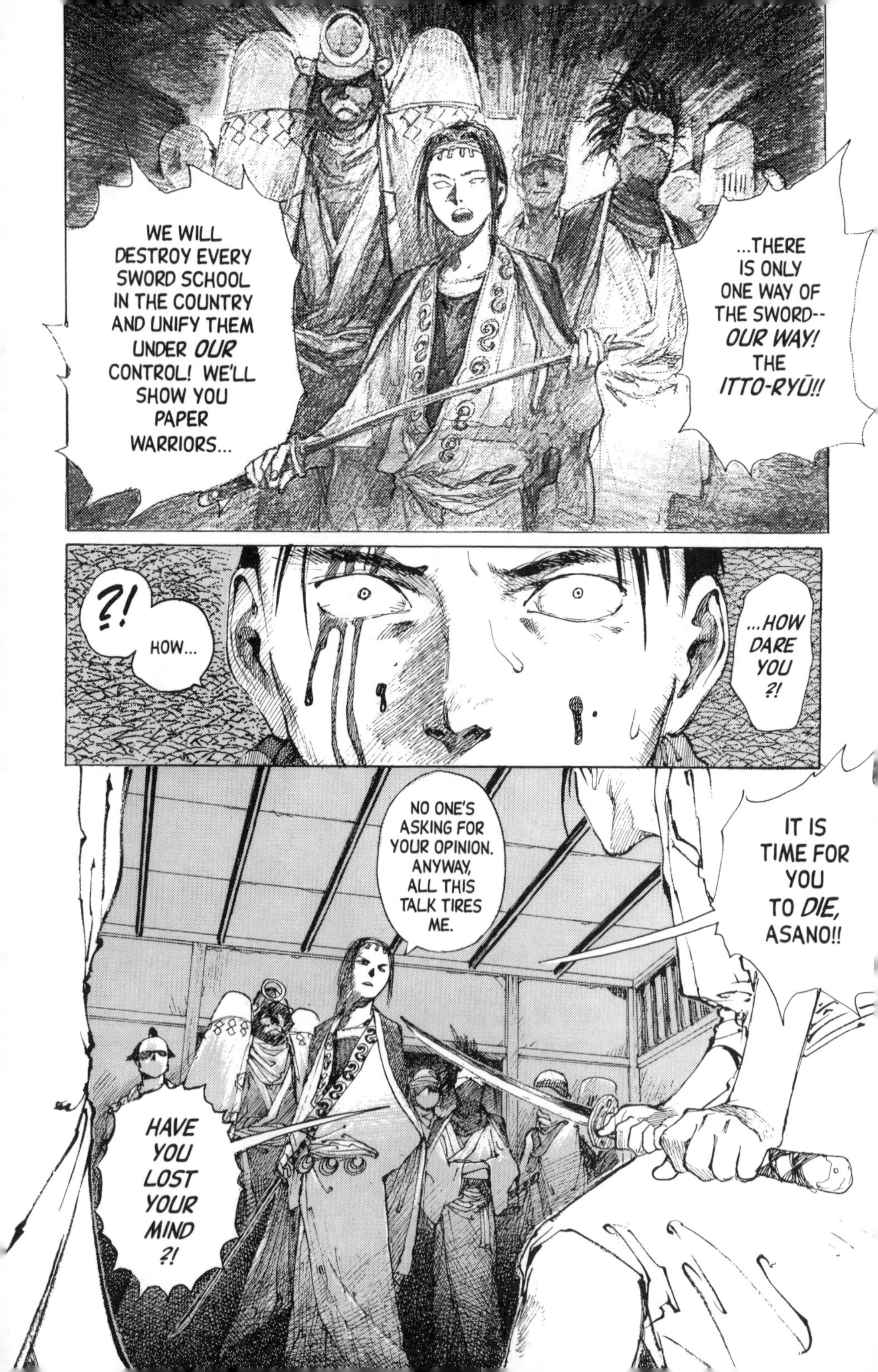

WE WILL DESTROY EVERY SWORD SCHOOL IN THE COUNTRY AND UNIFY THEM UNDER *OUR* CONTROL! WE'LL SHOW YOU PAPER WARRIORS...
...THERE IS ONLY ONE WAY OF THE SWORD-- *OUR WAY!* THE *ITTO-RYŪ!!*
?!
HOW...
...*HOW DARE YOU ?!*
NO ONE'S ASKING FOR YOUR OPINION. ANYWAY, ALL THIS TALK TIRES ME.
IT IS TIME FOR YOU TO *DIE,* ASANO!!
HAVE YOU LOST YOUR MIND ?!

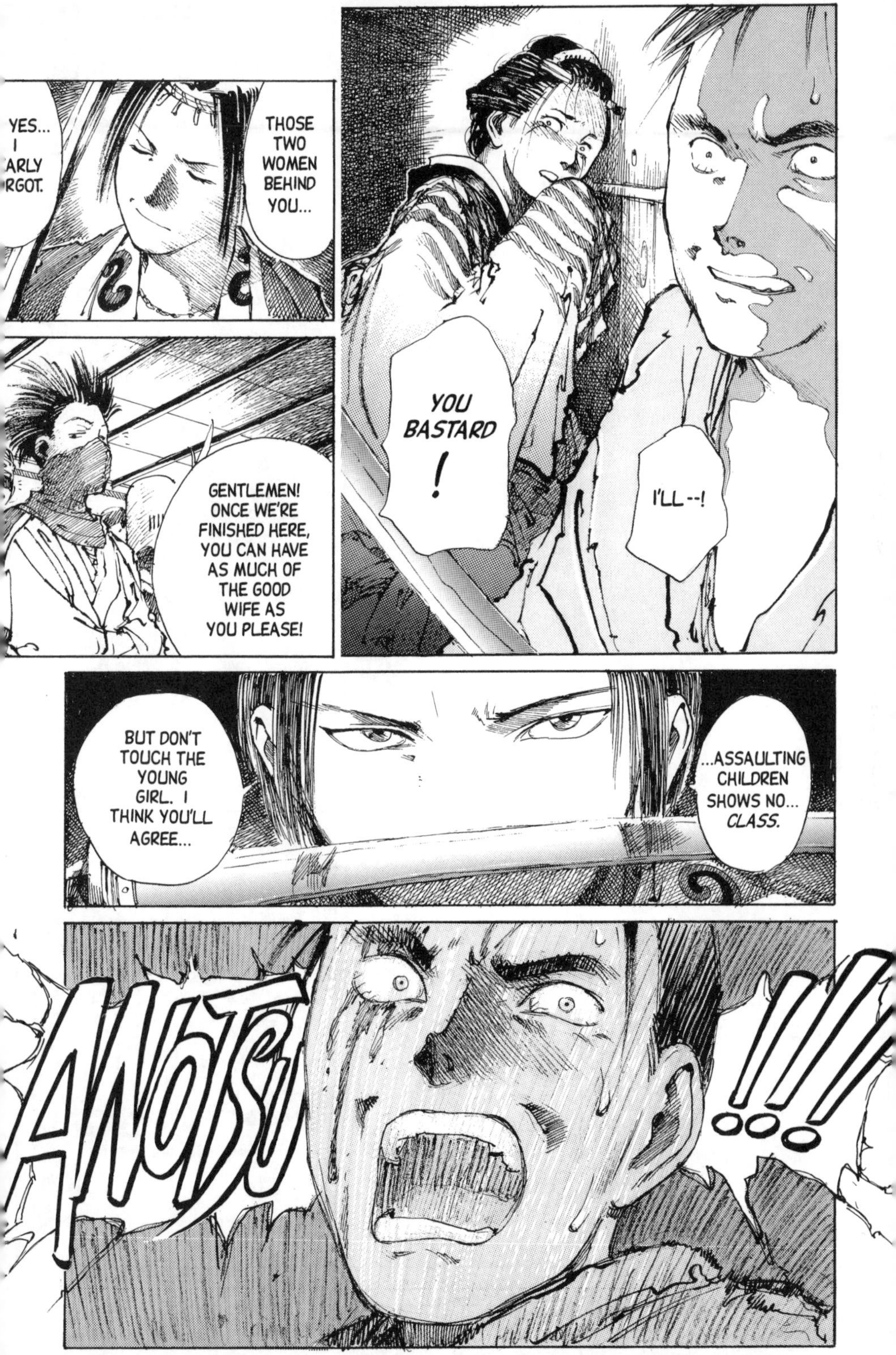
YES... I ARLY RGOT.
THOSE TWO WOMEN BEHIND YOU...
GENTLEMEN! ONCE WE'RE FINISHED HERE, YOU CAN HAVE AS MUCH OF THE GOOD WIFE AS YOU PLEASE!
YOU BASTARD !
I'LL --!
BUT DON'T TOUCH THE YOUNG GIRL. I THINK YOU'LL AGREE...
...ASSAULTING CHILDREN SHOWS NO... CLASS.
ANOTSU!!!

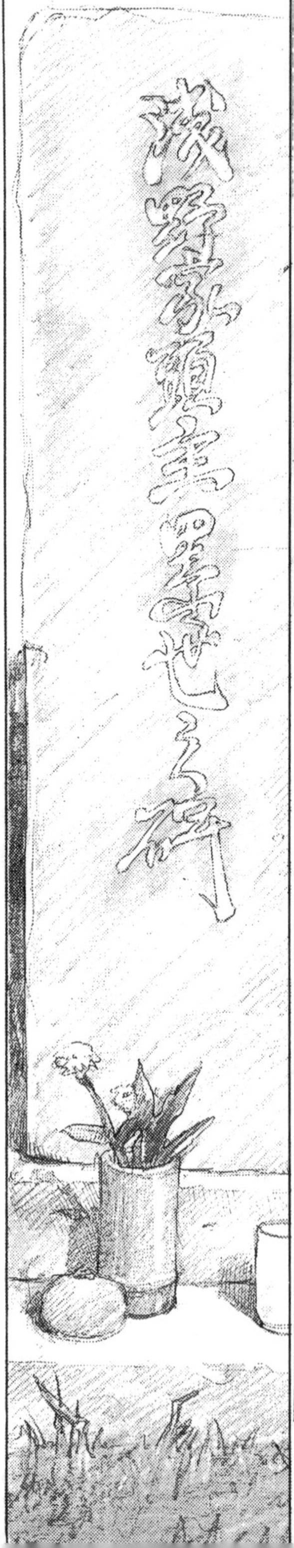

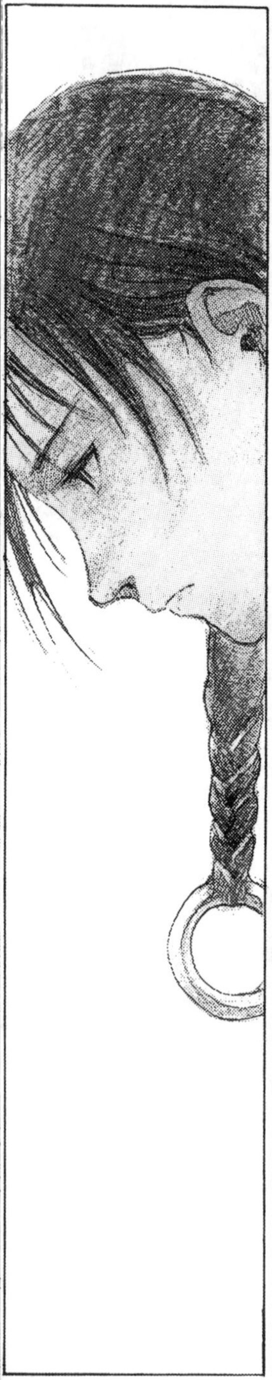

HEADSTONE: KUROSE, HEAD
OF THE HOUSE OF ASANO

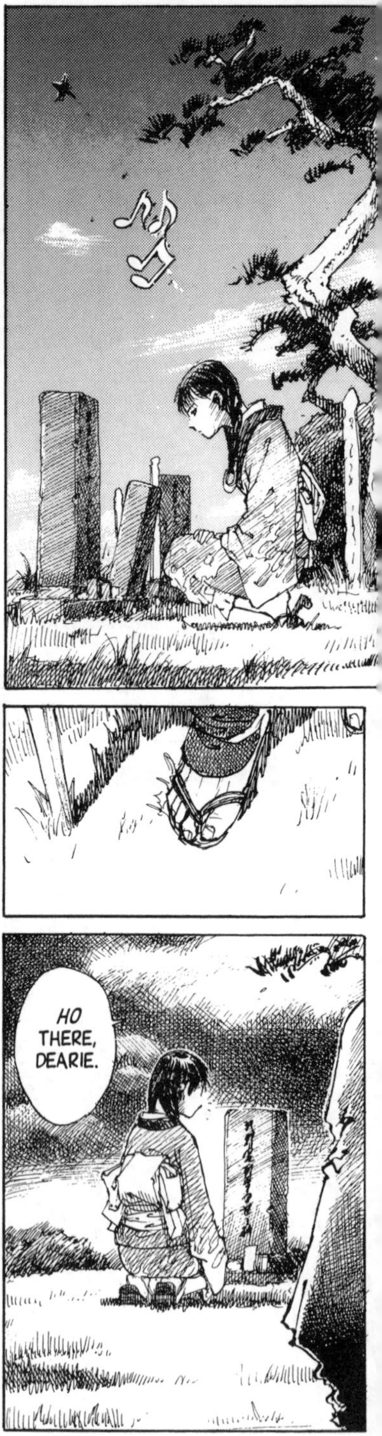
HO THERE, DEARIE.

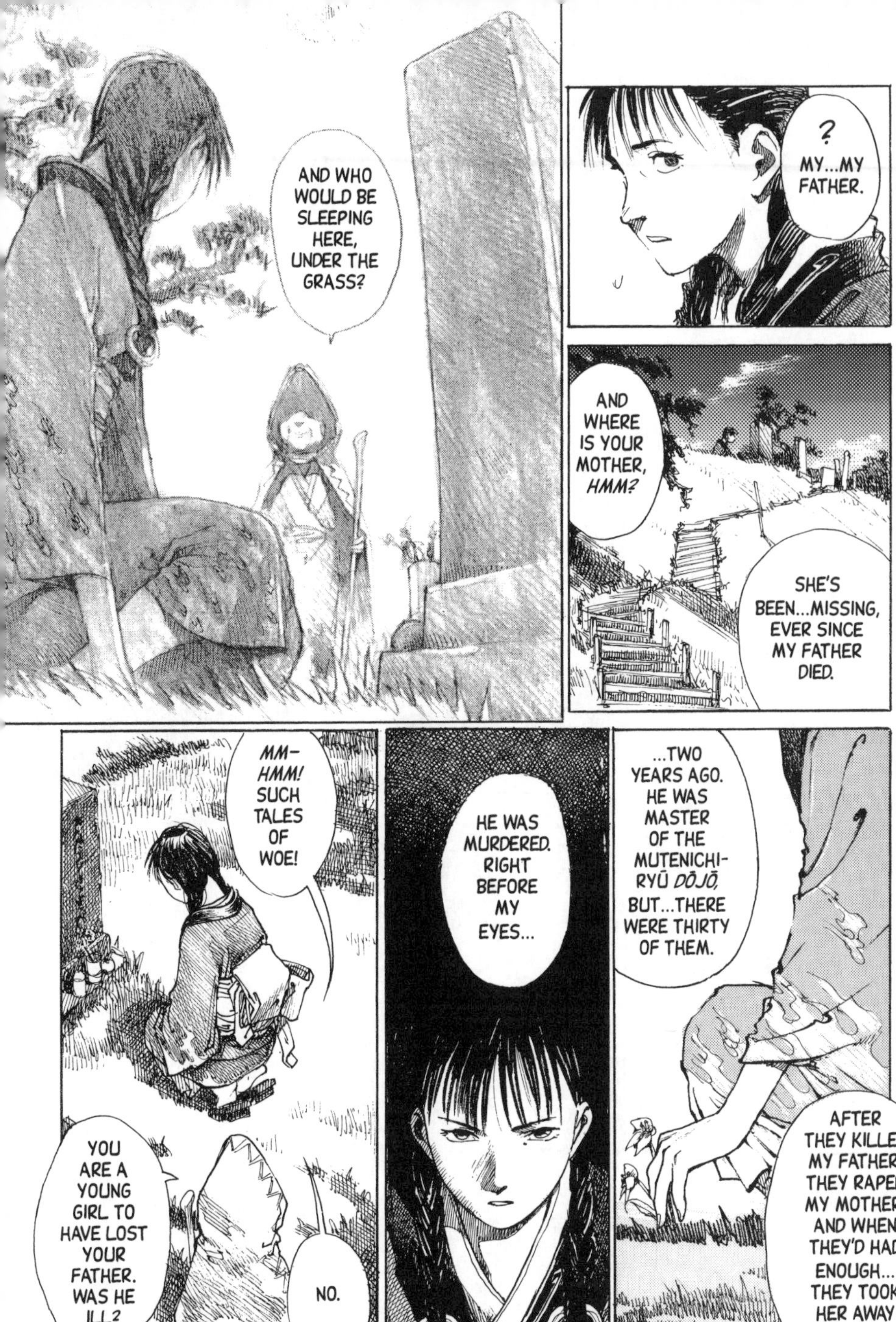
AND WHO WOULD BE SLEEPING HERE, UNDER THE GRASS?
?
MY...MY FATHER.
AND WHERE IS YOUR MOTHER, *HMM?*
SHE'S BEEN...MISSING, EVER SINCE MY FATHER DIED.
MM-HMM! SUCH TALES OF WOE!
YOU ARE A YOUNG GIRL TO HAVE LOST YOUR FATHER. WAS HE ILL?
NO.
HE WAS MURDERED. RIGHT BEFORE MY EYES...
...TWO YEARS AGO. HE WAS MASTER OF THE MUTENICHI-RYŪ *DŌJŌ,* BUT...THERE WERE THIRTY OF THEM.
AFTER THEY KILLED MY FATHER, THEY RAPED MY MOTHER. AND WHEN THEY'D HAD ENOUGH... THEY TOOK HER AWAY WITH THEM.

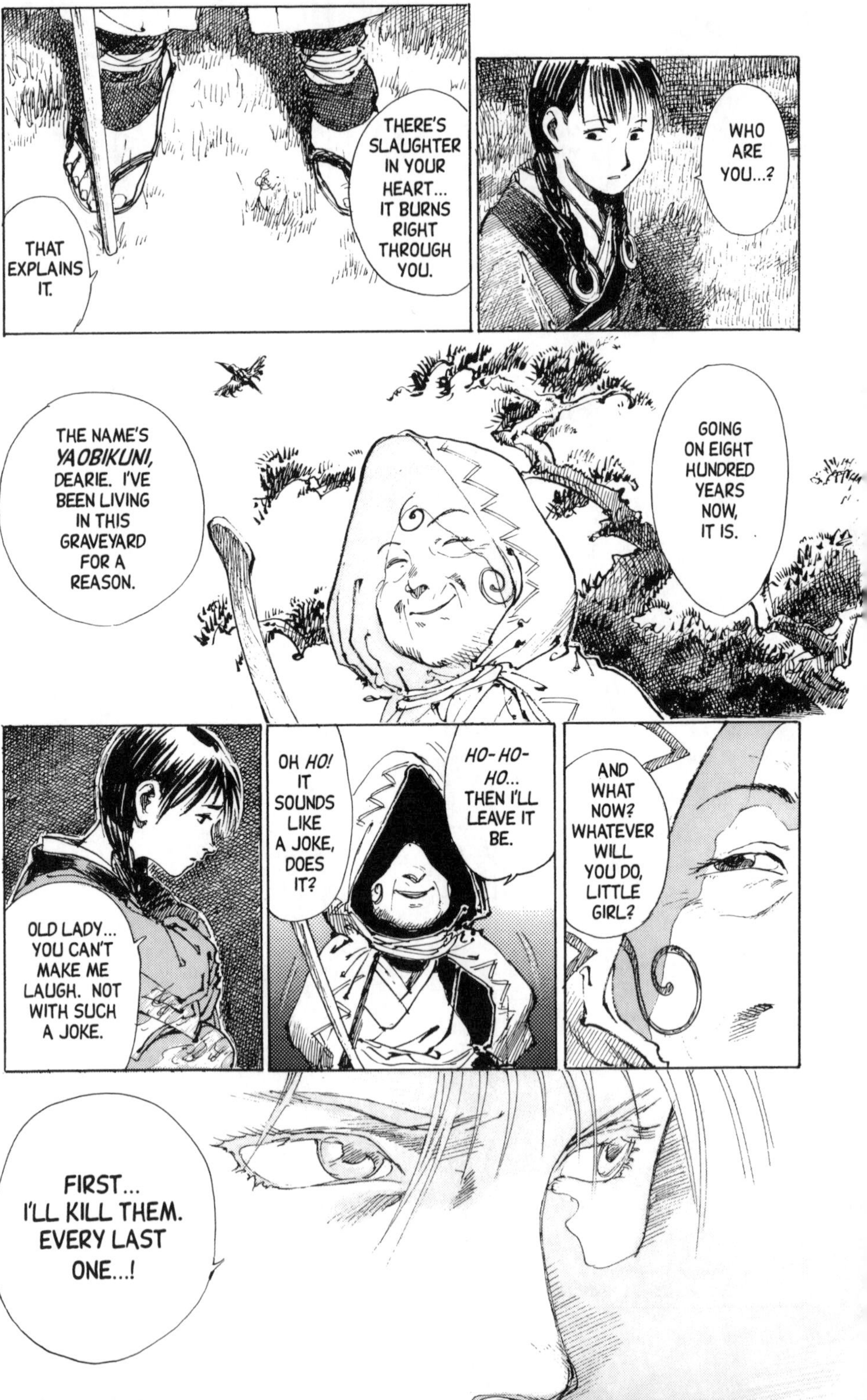
THAT EXPLAINS IT.
THERE'S SLAUGHTER IN YOUR HEART... IT BURNS RIGHT THROUGH YOU.
WHO ARE YOU...?
THE NAME'S *YAOBIKUNI,* DEARIE. I'VE BEEN LIVING IN THIS GRAVEYARD FOR A REASON.
GOING ON EIGHT HUNDRED YEARS NOW, IT IS.
OLD LADY... YOU CAN'T MAKE ME LAUGH. NOT WITH SUCH A JOKE.
OH *HO!* IT SOUNDS LIKE A JOKE, DOES IT?
HO-HO-HO... THEN I'LL LEAVE IT BE.
AND WHAT NOW? WHATEVER WILL YOU DO, LITTLE GIRL?
FIRST... I'LL KILL THEM. EVERY LAST ONE...!

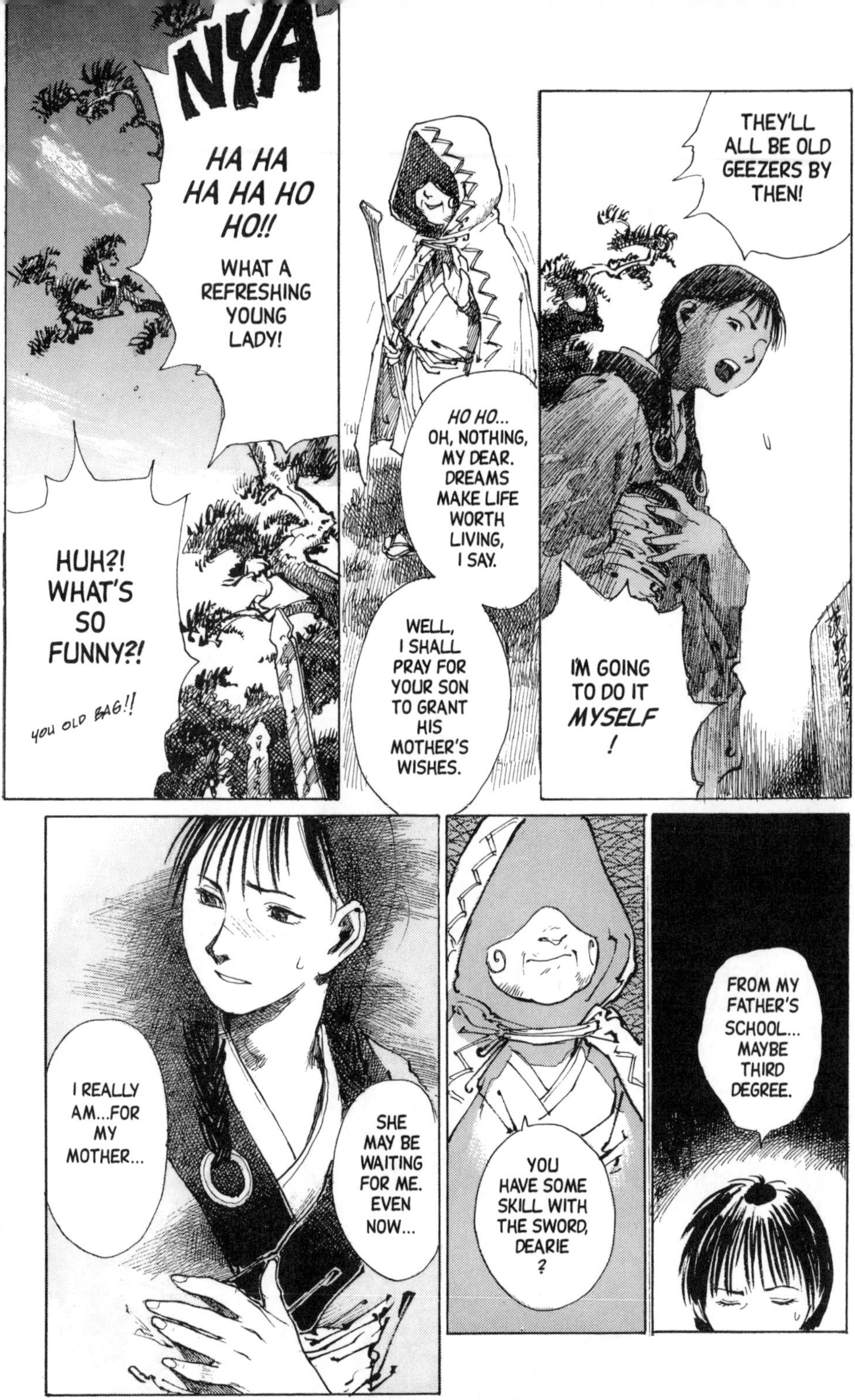
NYA
HA HA HA HA HO HO!!
WHAT A REFRESHING YOUNG LADY!
HUH?! WHAT'S SO FUNNY?!
YOU OLD BAG!!
HO HO... OH, NOTHING, MY DEAR. DREAMS MAKE LIFE WORTH LIVING, I SAY.
WELL, I SHALL PRAY FOR YOUR SON TO GRANT HIS MOTHER'S WISHES.
THEY'LL ALL BE OLD GEEZERS BY THEN!
I'M GOING TO DO IT MYSELF!
I REALLY AM...FOR MY MOTHER...
SHE MAY BE WAITING FOR ME. EVEN NOW...
YOU HAVE SOME SKILL WITH THE SWORD, DEARIE?
FROM MY FATHER'S SCHOOL... MAYBE THIRD DEGREE.

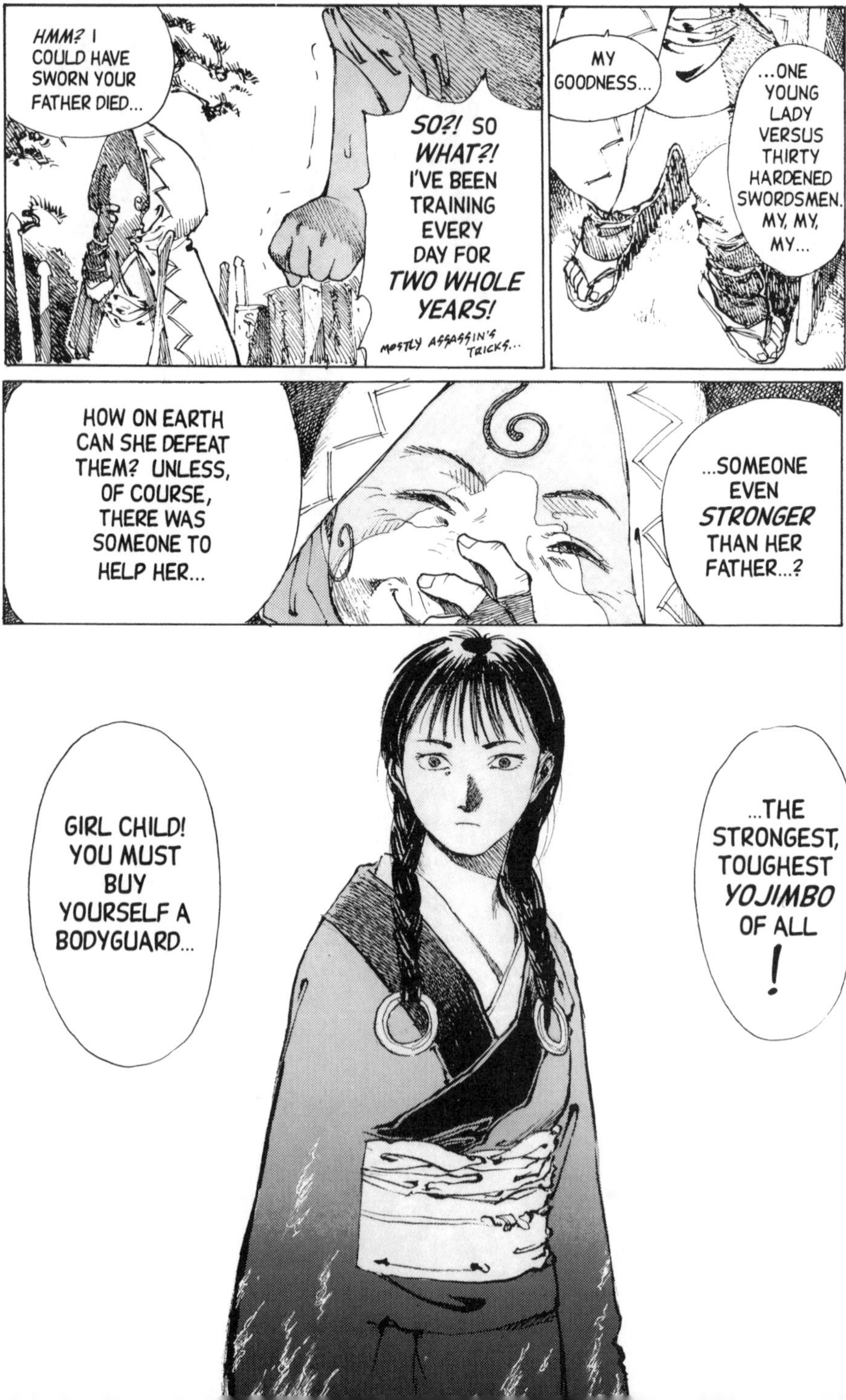
HMM? I COULD HAVE SWORN YOUR FATHER DIED...
SO?! SO WHAT?! I'VE BEEN TRAINING EVERY DAY FOR TWO WHOLE YEARS!
MOSTLY ASSASSIN'S TRICKS...
MY GOODNESS...
...ONE YOUNG LADY VERSUS THIRTY HARDENED SWORDSMEN. MY, MY, MY...
HOW ON EARTH CAN SHE DEFEAT THEM? UNLESS, OF COURSE, THERE WAS SOMEONE TO HELP HER...
...SOMEONE EVEN STRONGER THAN HER FATHER...?
GIRL CHILD! YOU MUST BUY YOURSELF A BODYGUARD...
...THE STRONGEST, TOUGHEST YOJIMBO OF ALL !

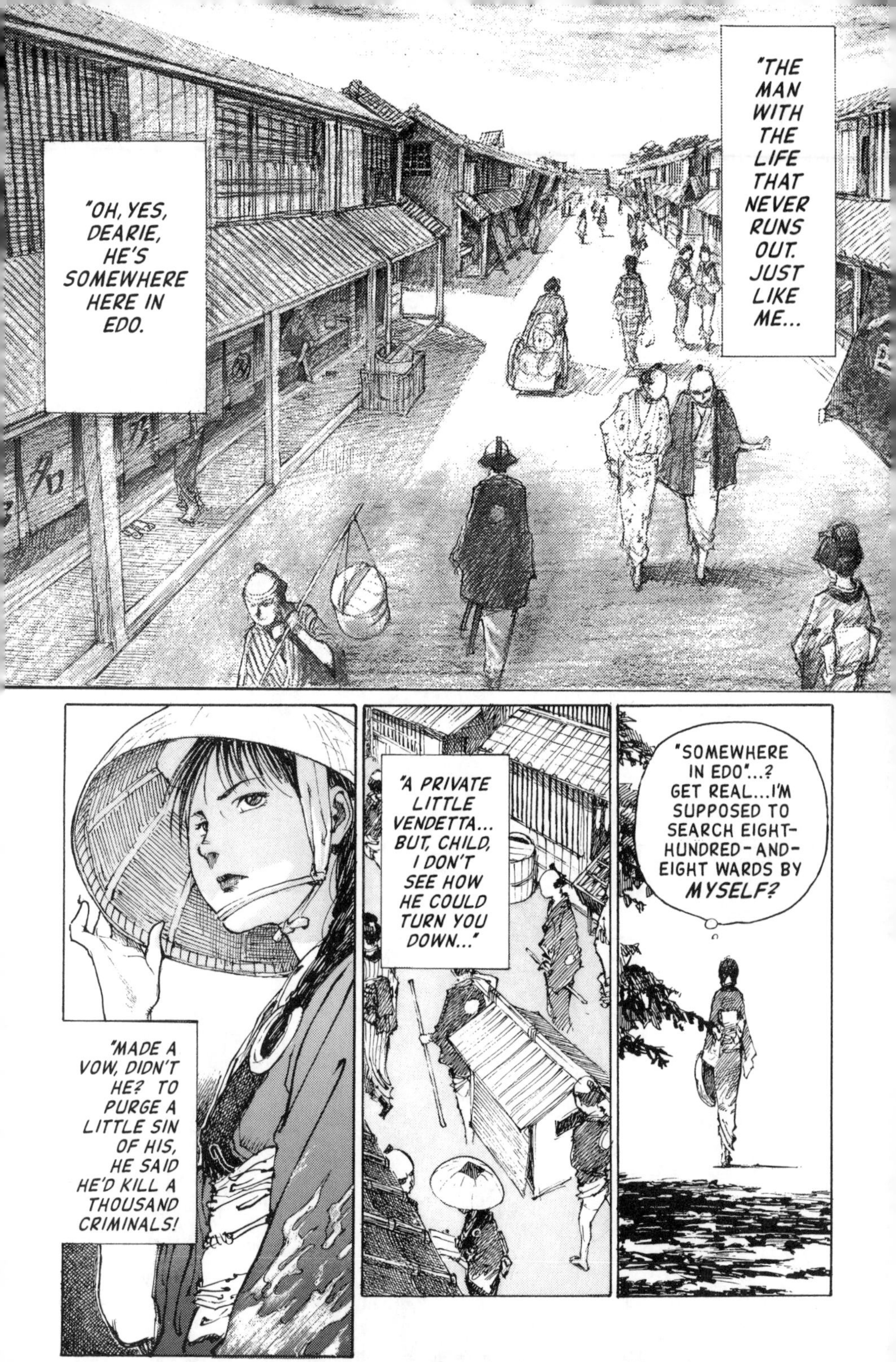
"OH, YES, DEARIE, HE'S SOMEWHERE HERE IN EDO.
"THE MAN WITH THE LIFE THAT NEVER RUNS OUT. JUST LIKE ME...
"MADE A VOW, DIDN'T HE? TO PURGE A LITTLE SIN OF HIS, HE SAID HE'D KILL A THOUSAND CRIMINALS!
"A PRIVATE LITTLE VENDETTA... BUT, CHILD, I DON'T SEE HOW HE COULD TURN YOU DOWN..."
"SOMEWHERE IN EDO"...? GET REAL...I'M SUPPOSED TO SEARCH EIGHT-HUNDRED-AND-EIGHT WARDS BY MYSELF?

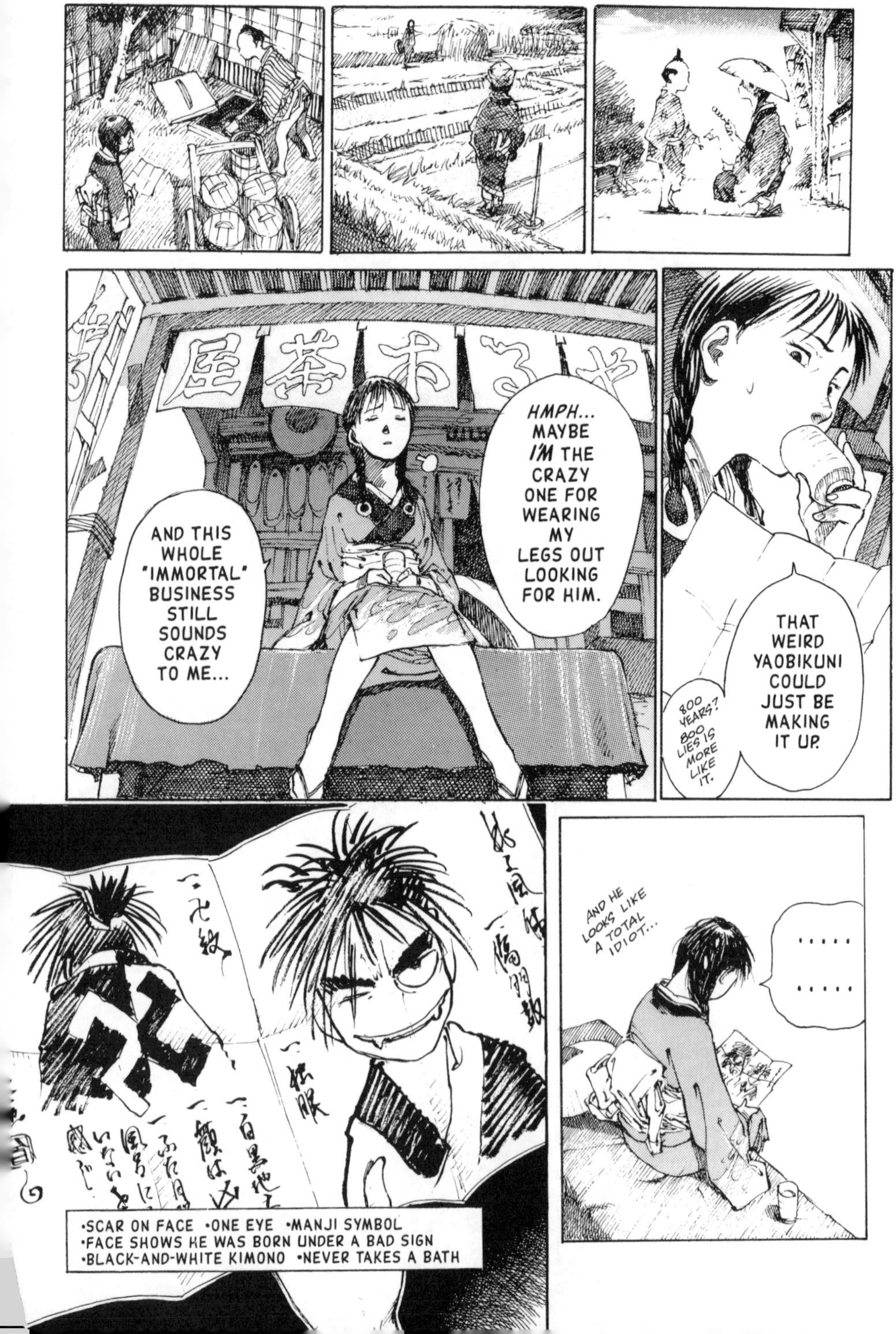
AND THIS WHOLE "IMMORTAL" BUSINESS STILL SOUNDS CRAZY TO ME...
HMPH... MAYBE I'M THE CRAZY ONE FOR WEARING MY LEGS OUT LOOKING FOR HIM.
THAT WEIRD YAOBIKUNI COULD JUST BE MAKING IT UP.
800 YEARS? 800 LIES IS MORE LIKE IT.
•SCAR ON FACE •ONE EYE •MANJI SYMBOL
•FACE SHOWS HE WAS BORN UNDER A BAD SIGN
•BLACK-AND-WHITE KIMONO •NEVER TAKES A BATH
AND HE LOOKS LIKE A TOTAL IDIOT...
....

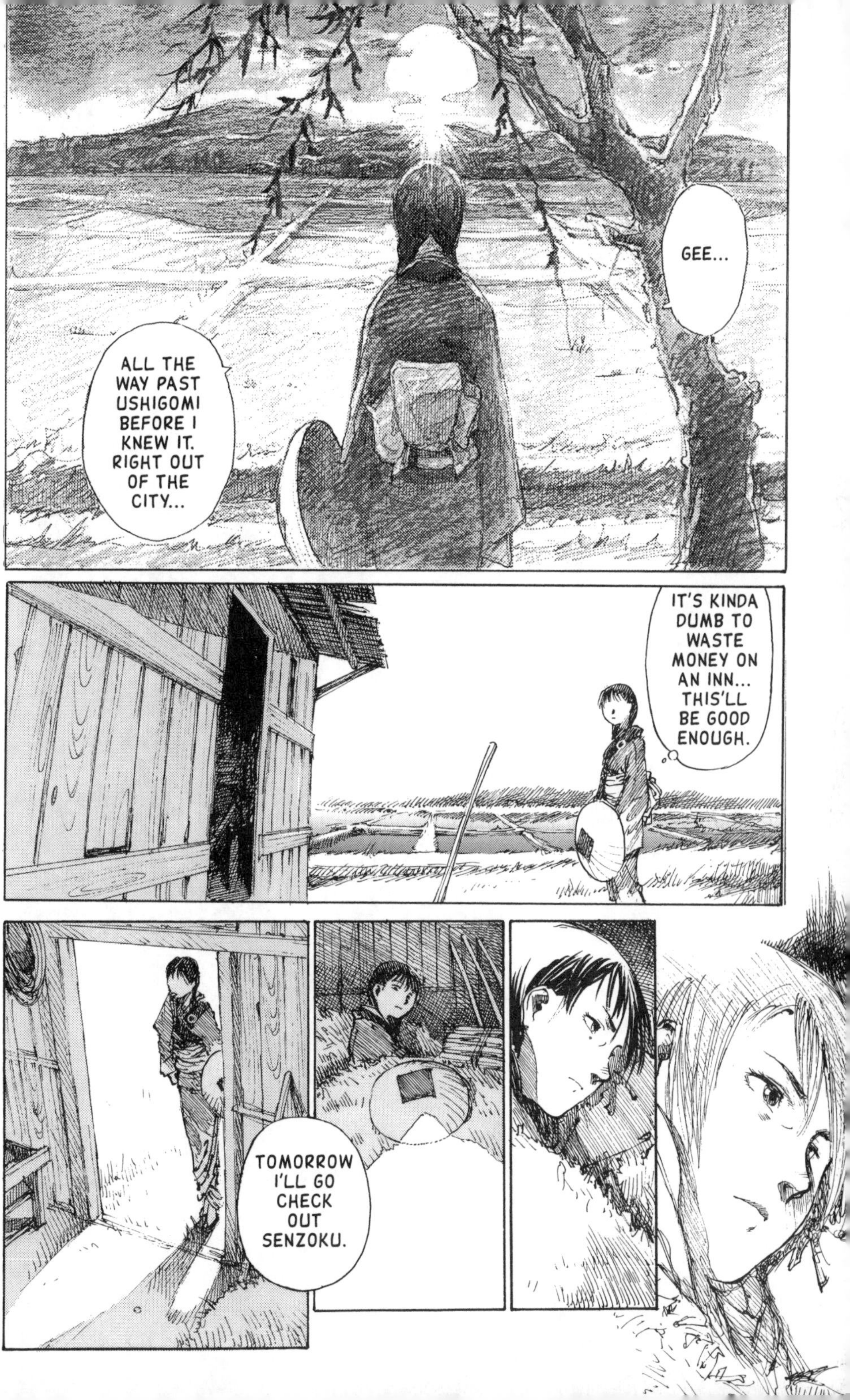
ALL THE WAY PAST USHIGOMI BEFORE I KNEW IT. RIGHT OUT OF THE CITY...
GEE...
IT'S KINDA DUMB TO WASTE MONEY ON AN INN... THIS'LL BE GOOD ENOUGH.
TOMORROW I'LL GO CHECK OUT SENZOKU.

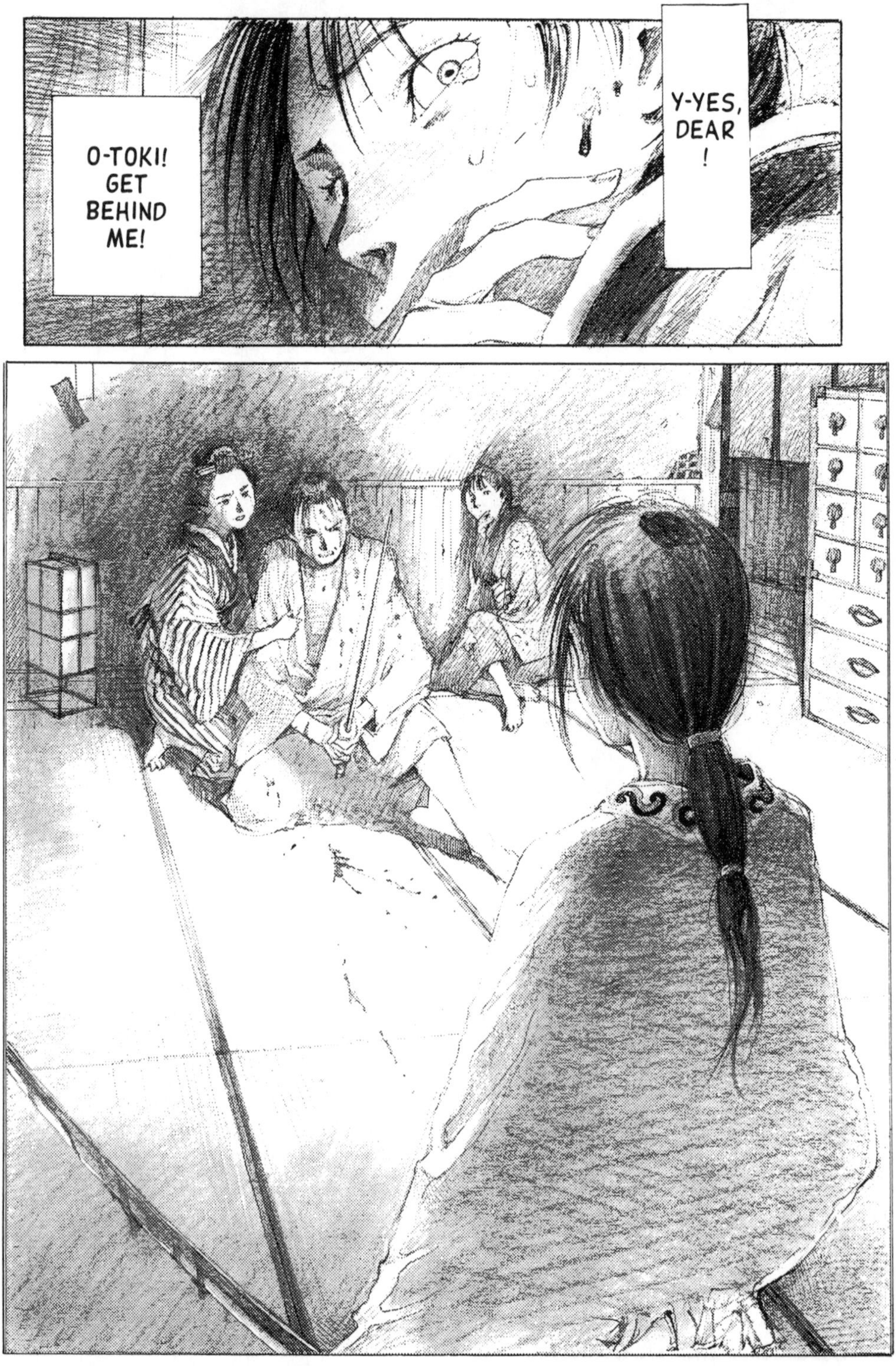
O-TOKI! GET BEHIND ME!
Y-YES, DEAR!

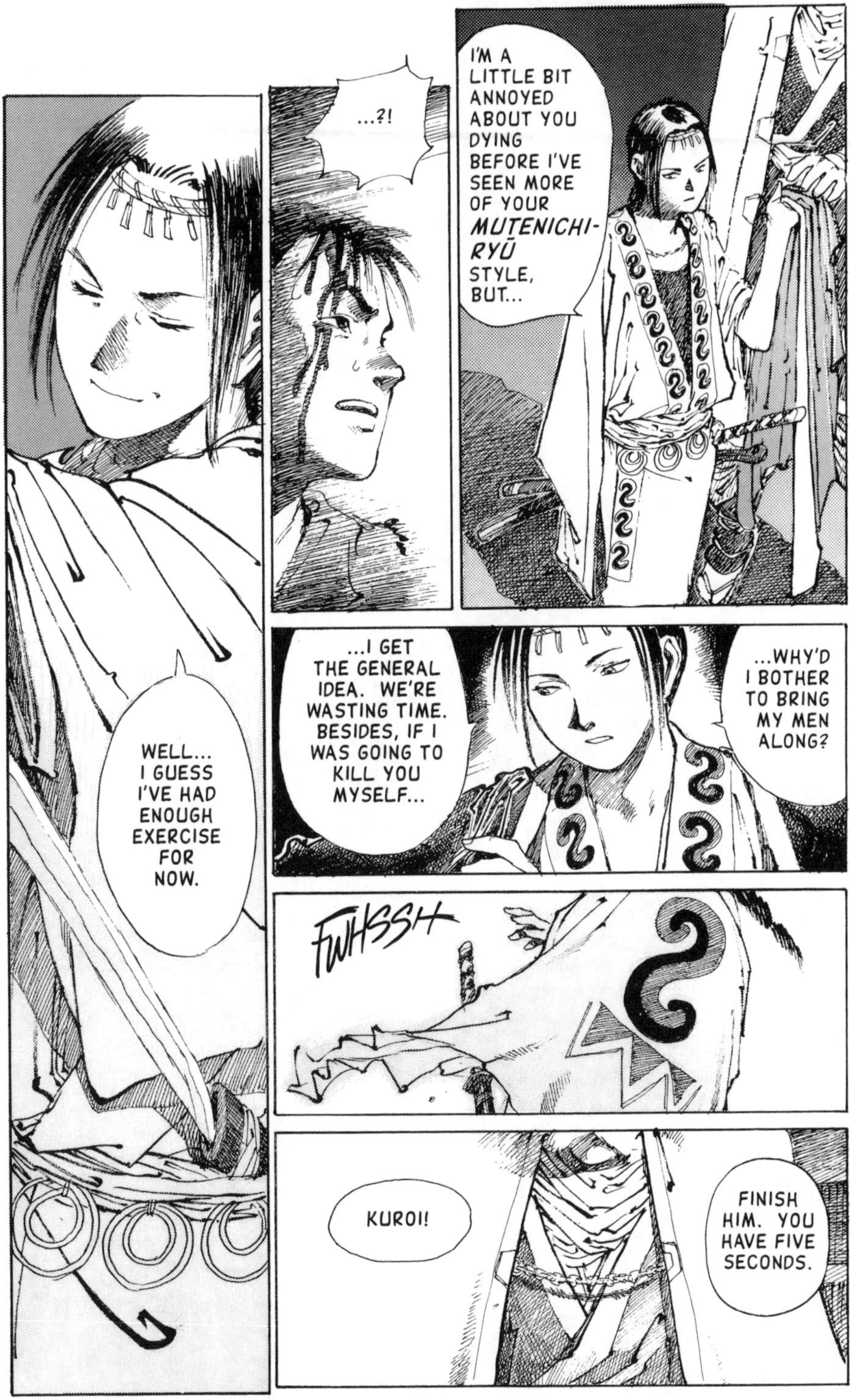
WELL... I GUESS I'VE HAD ENOUGH EXERCISE FOR NOW.
...?!
I'M A LITTLE BIT ANNOYED ABOUT YOU DYING BEFORE I'VE SEEN MORE OF YOUR *MUTENICHI-RYŪ* STYLE, BUT...
...I GET THE GENERAL IDEA. WE'RE WASTING TIME. BESIDES, IF I WAS GOING TO KILL YOU MYSELF...
...WHY'D I BOTHER TO BRING MY MEN ALONG?
FWHSSH
KUROI!
FINISH HIM. YOU HAVE FIVE SECONDS.

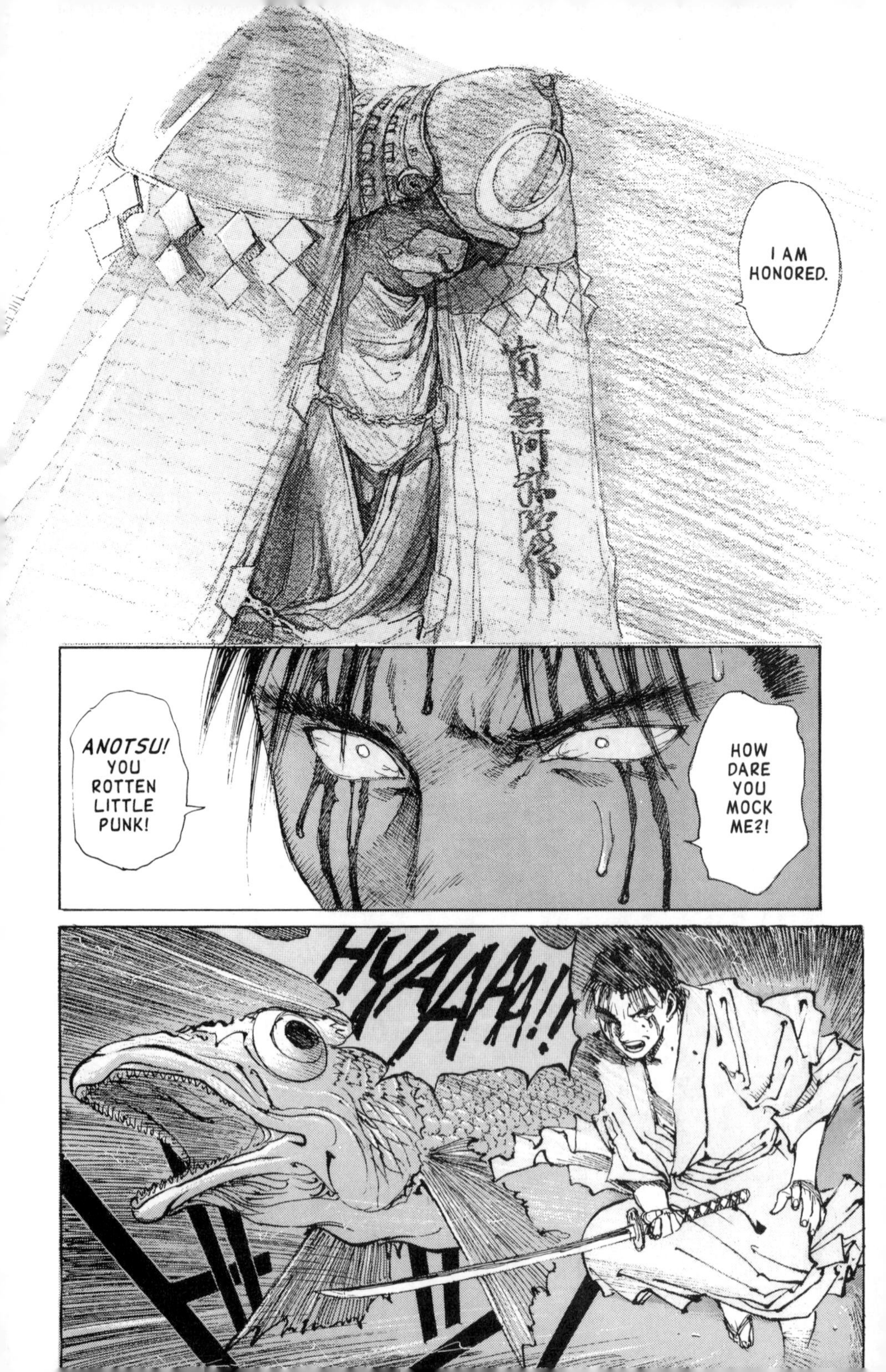
I AM HONORED.
ANOTSU! YOU ROTTEN LITTLE PUNK!
HOW DARE YOU MOCK ME?!
HYAAA!!

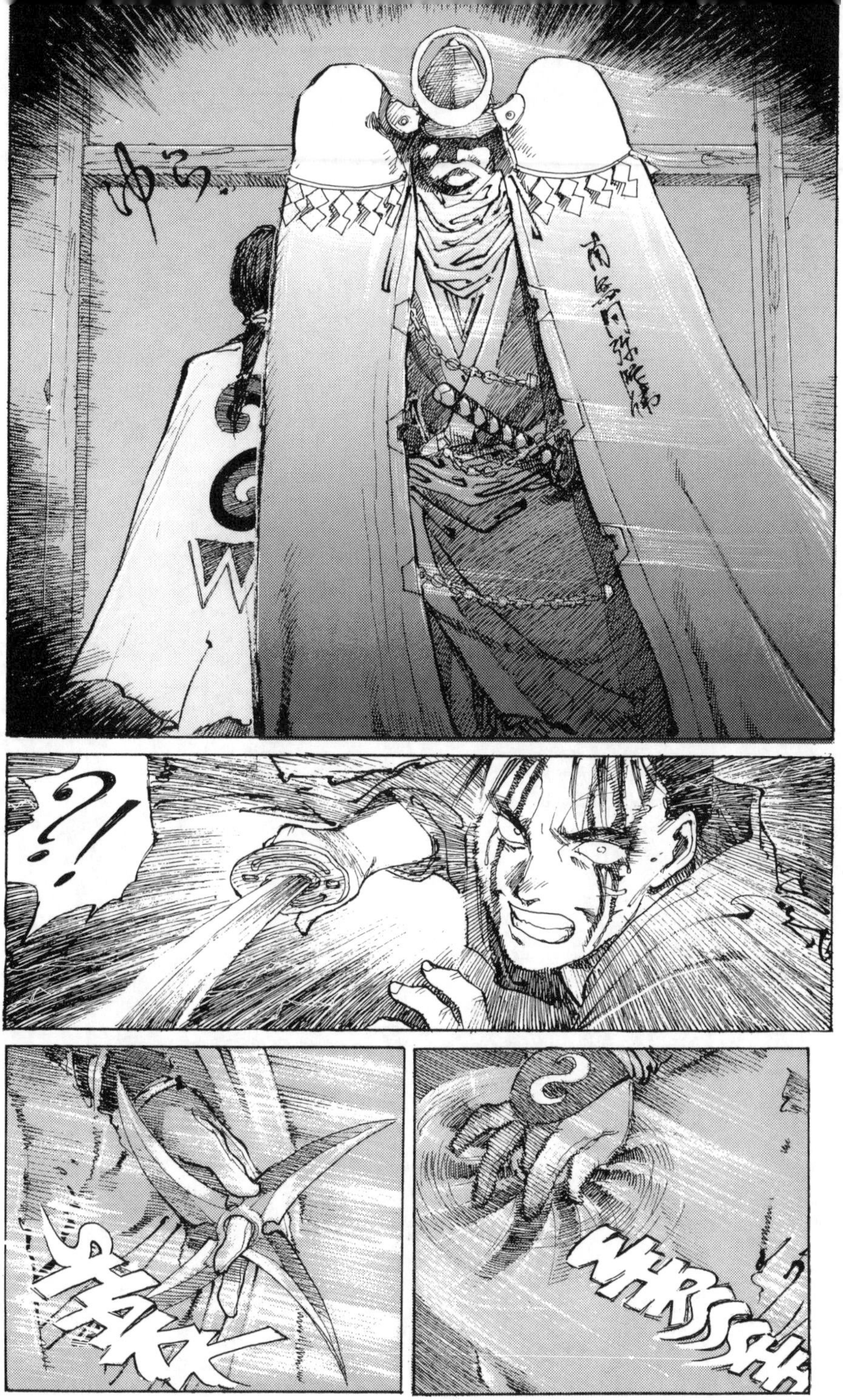

?!
SHAKK
WHRSSHH

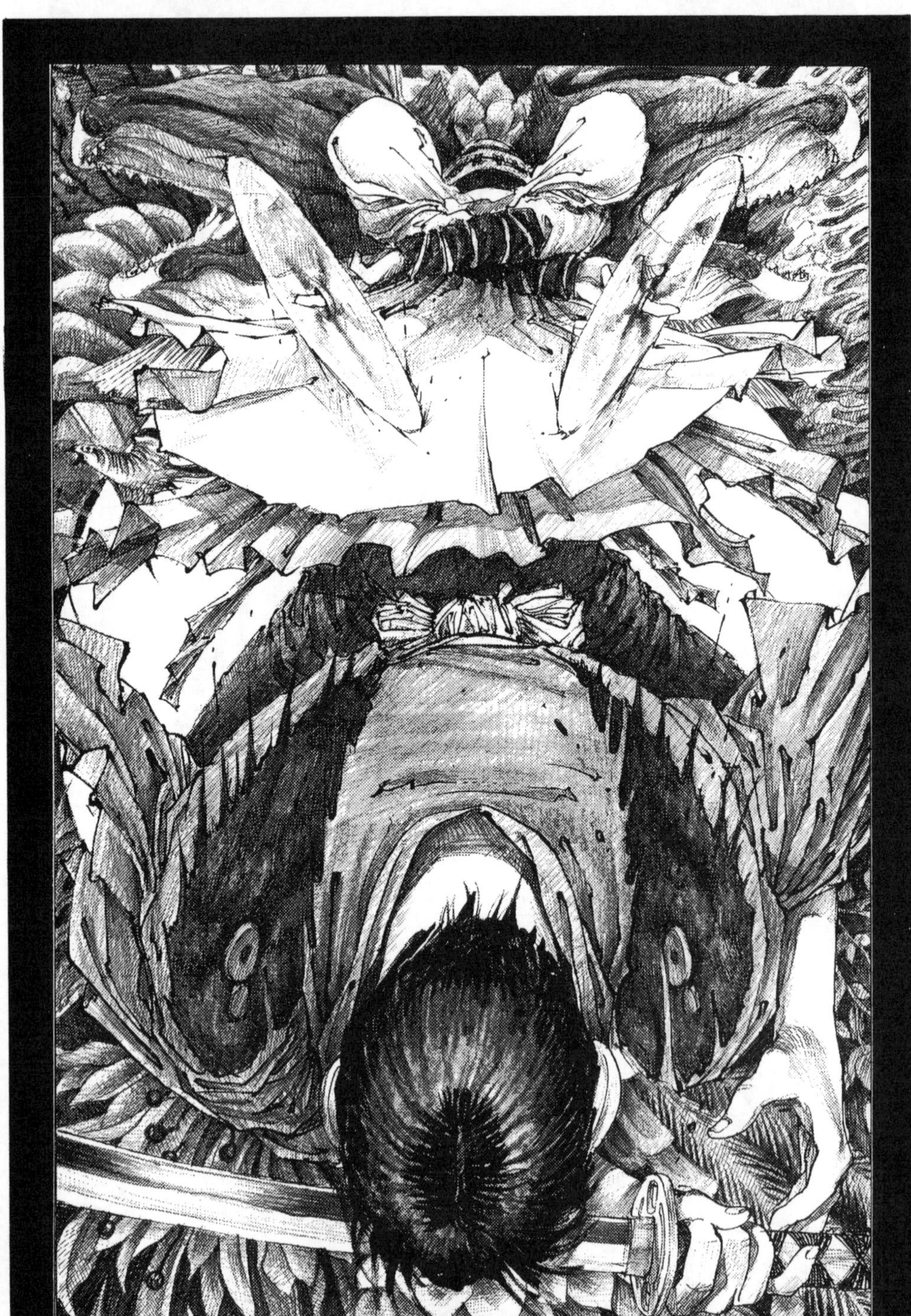

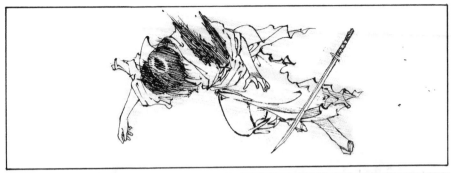

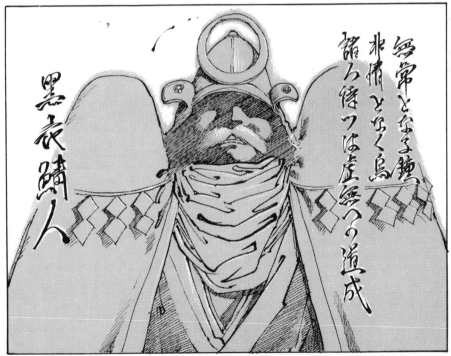

黒衣鯖人

無常となる鐘、
非情となく鳥、
錯乱待つは虚無への道成

"THE BELL RINGS AGAINST A HOLLOW SKY; THE RAVEN CAWS--NO MERCY!
ALL SAMURAI WALK THE PATH TO NOTHINGNESS." *KUROI SABATO*

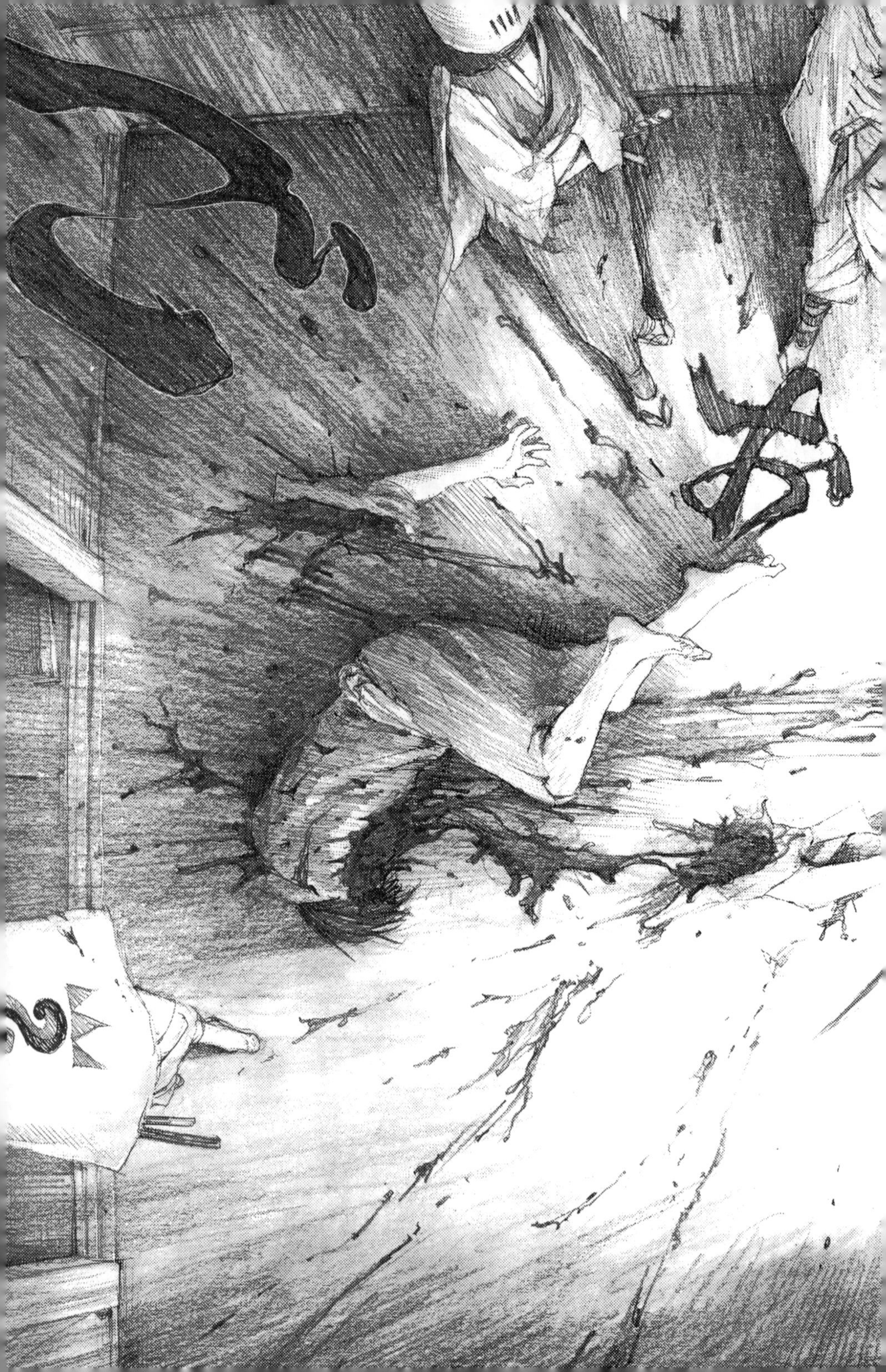

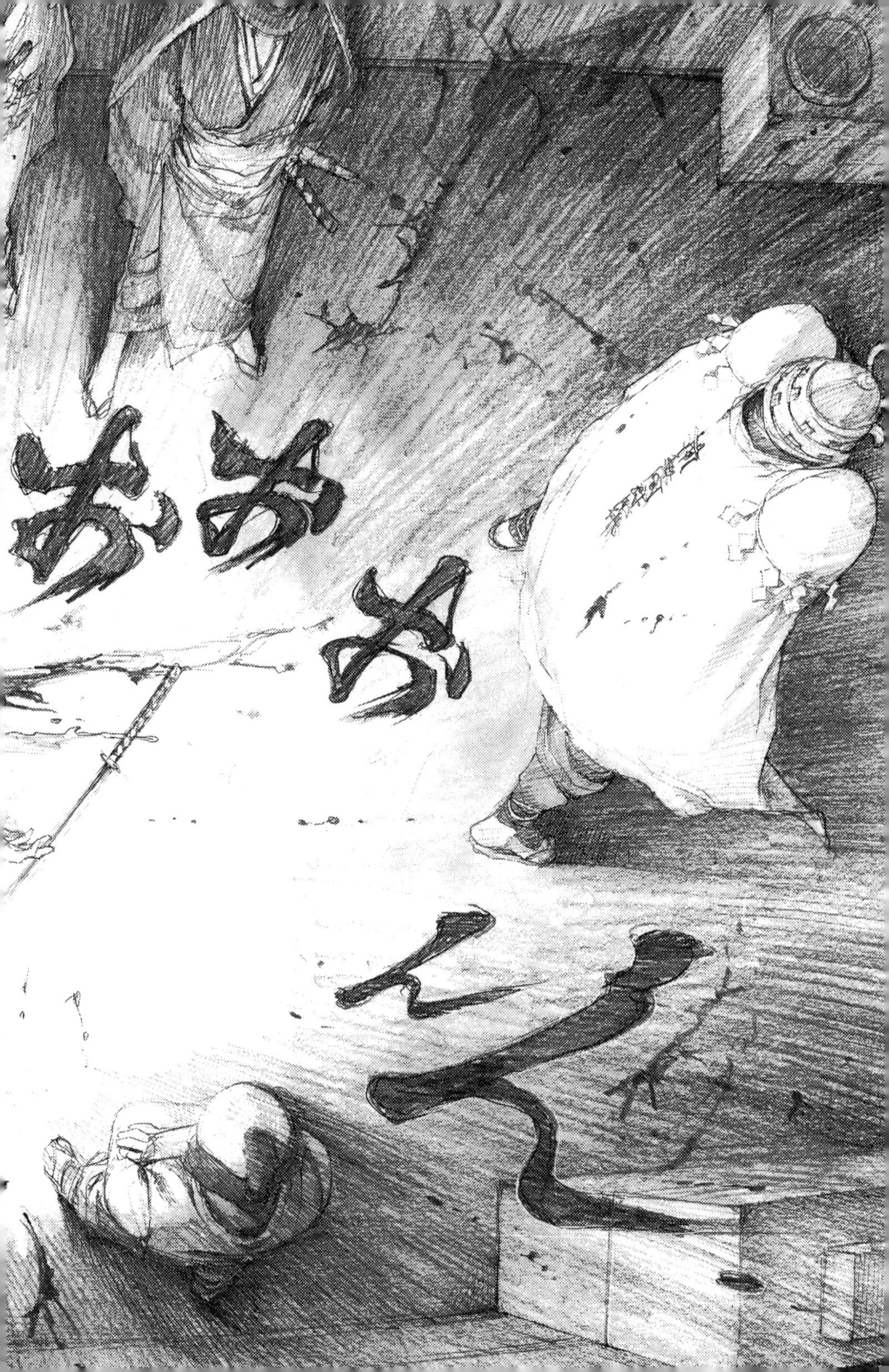
おおおん

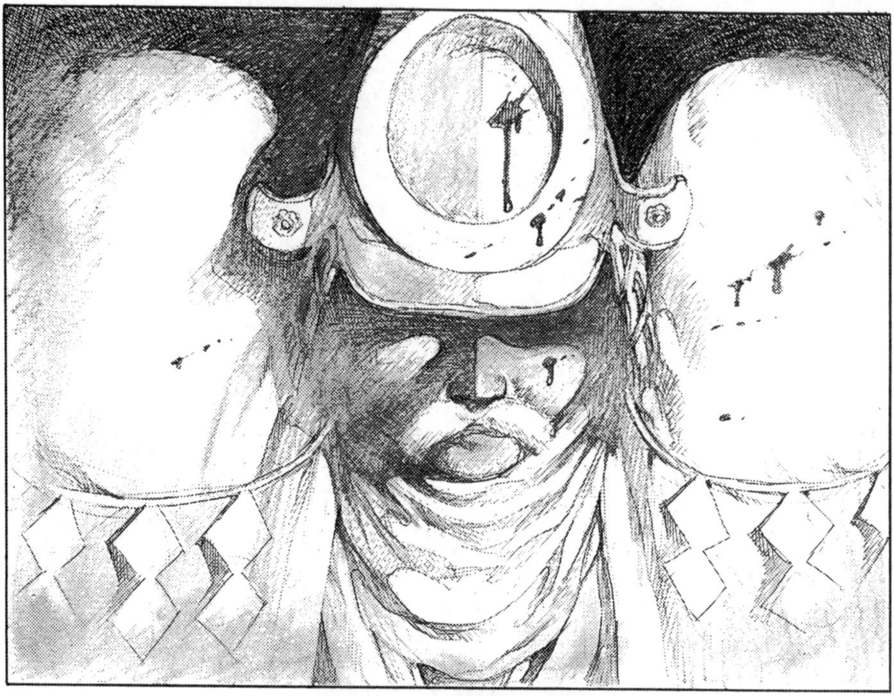
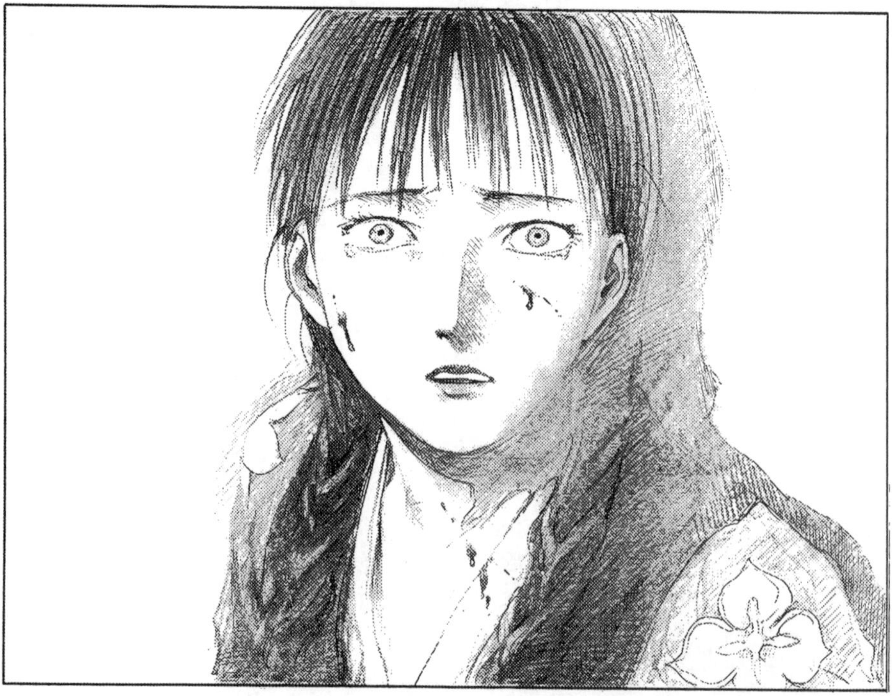

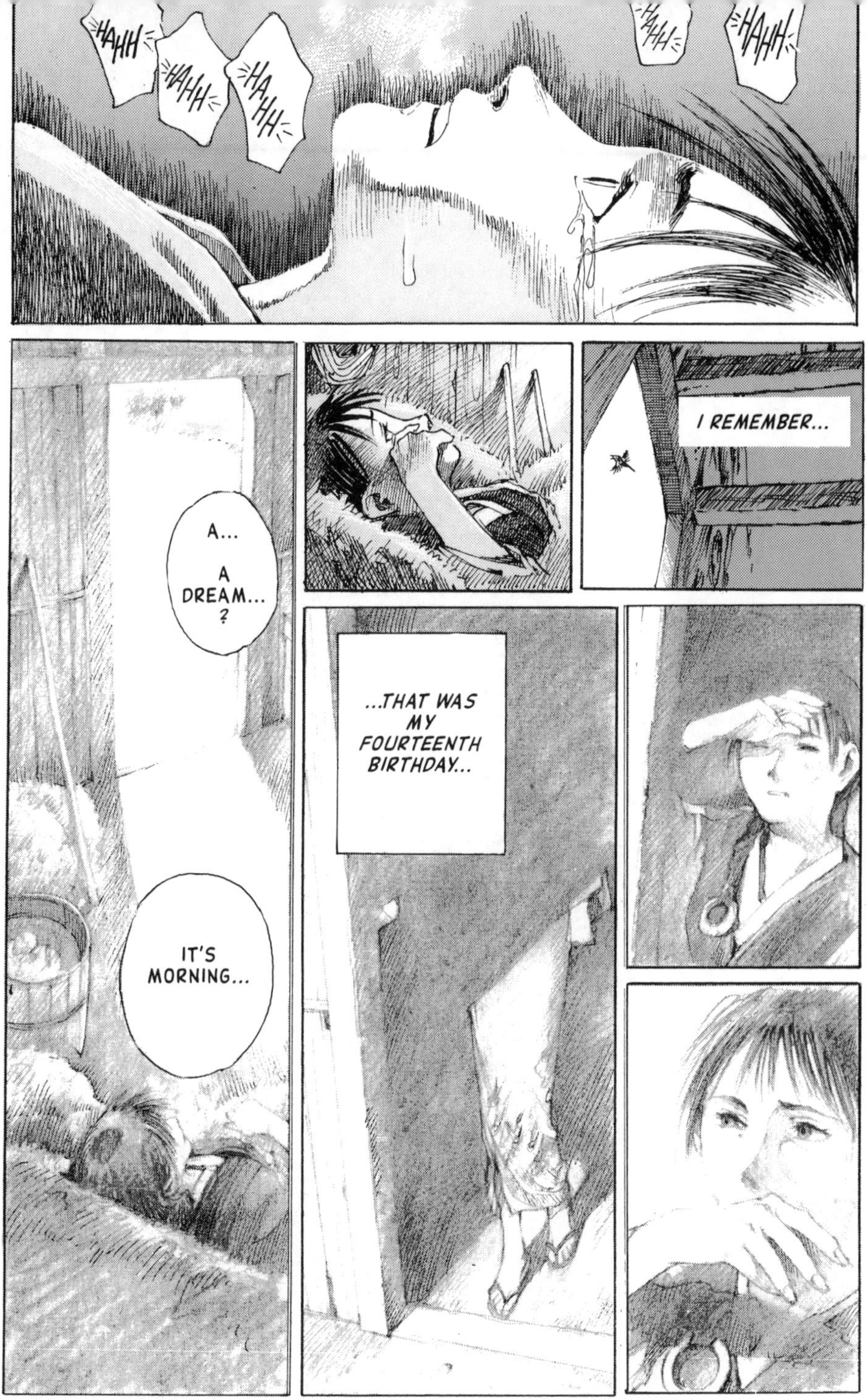
HAHH
HAHH
HAHH
HAHH
HAHH
A... A DREAM...?
IT'S MORNING...
I REMEMBER...
...THAT WAS MY FOURTEENTH BIRTHDAY...

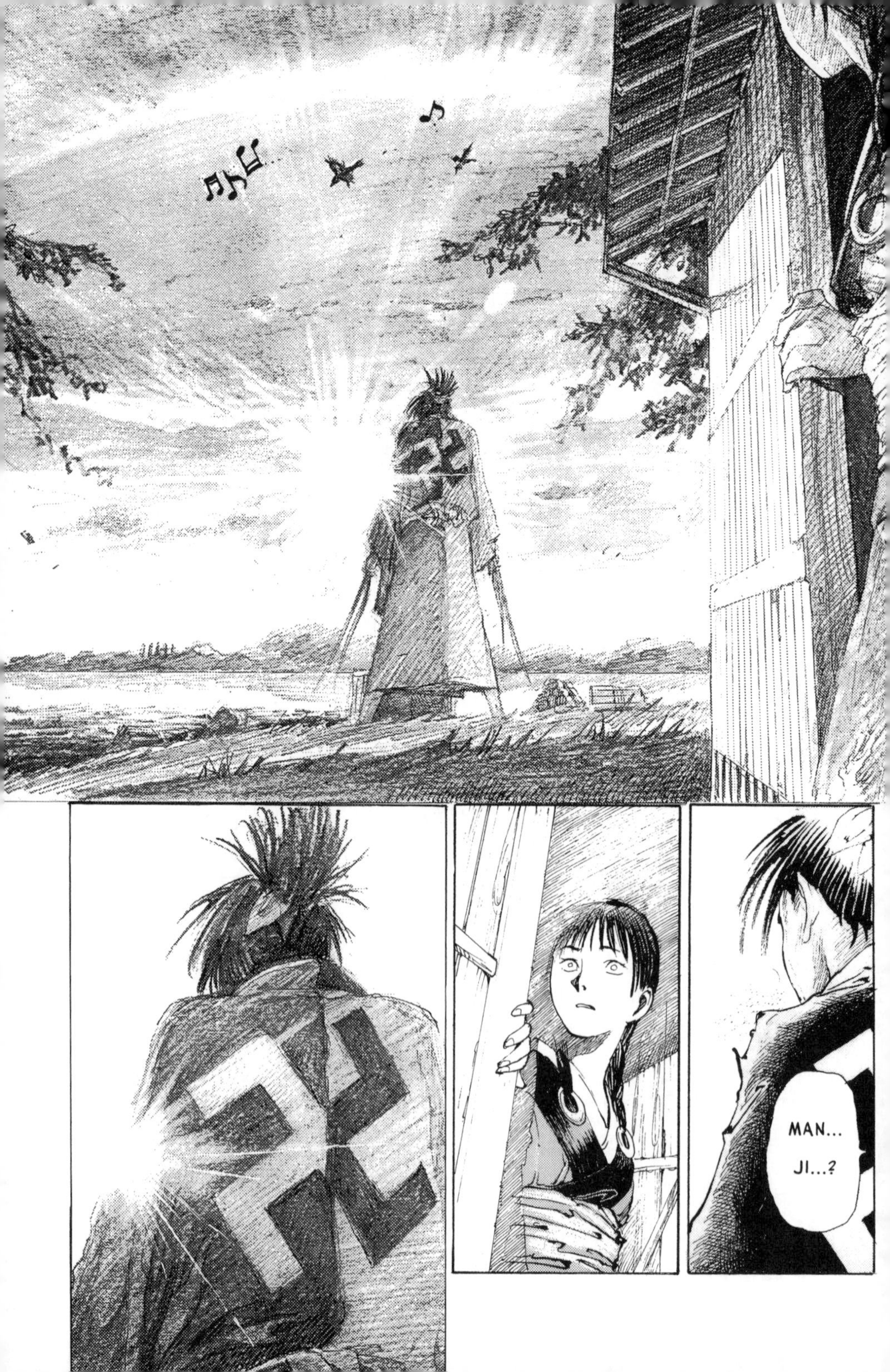
MAN...
JI...?

YOU'RE FINALLY UP, ARE YOU? TOO BAD.

DON'T COME OUT YET OR YOU'LL GET STUCK FULL OF SPLINTERS.

...?

=HAHH= =HFFF=

=HAHH= ...

HUH? UM, OKAY!

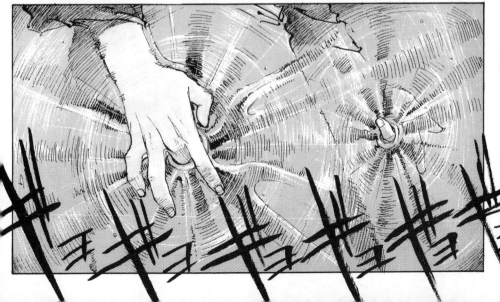

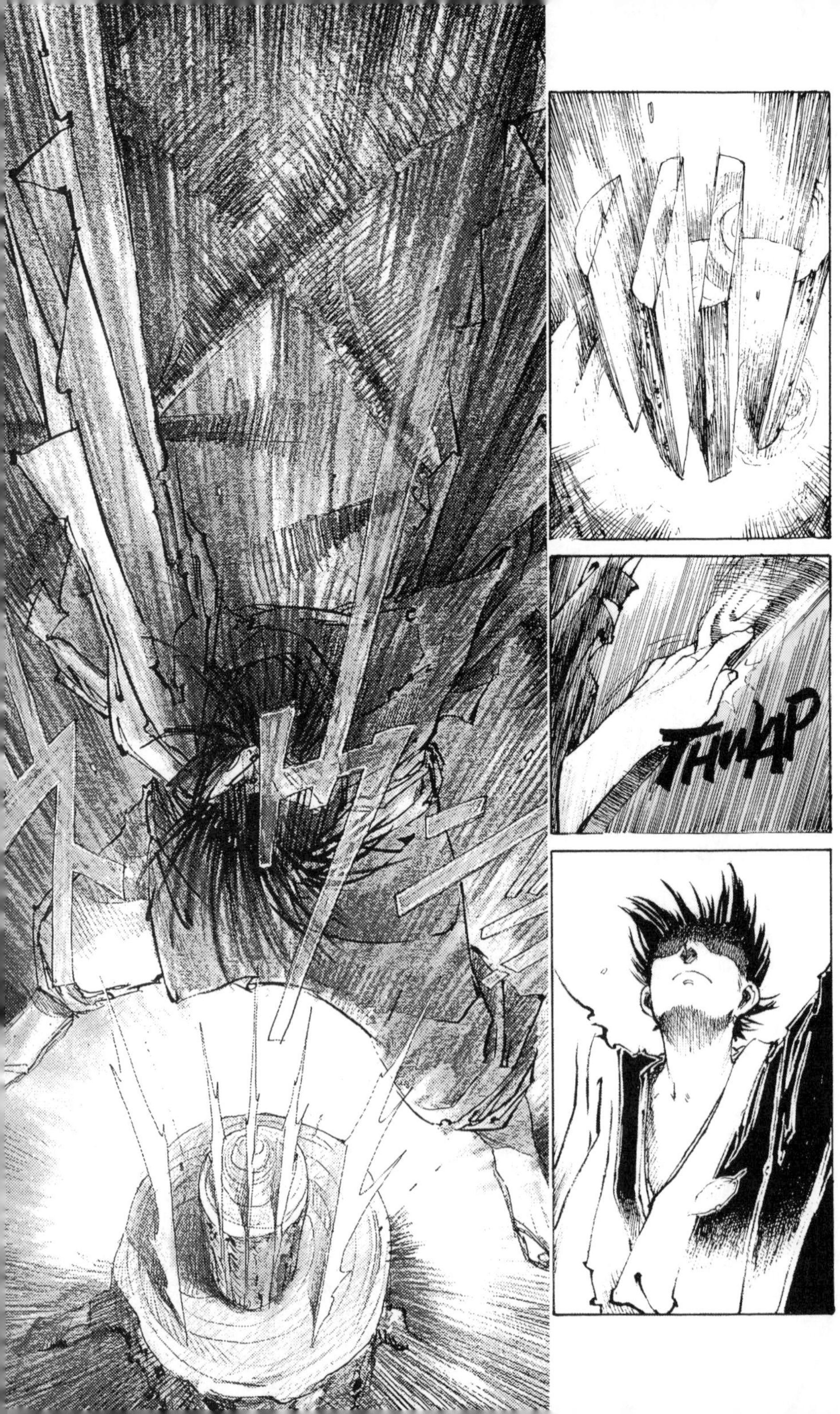
THWAP

HRMM.

WELL, THE OUTSIDE SURFACES ARE A BIT RAGGED, BUT...

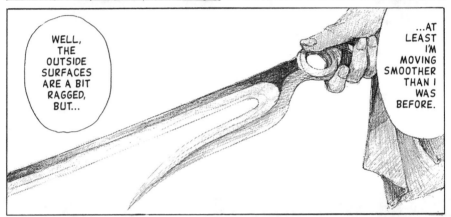

...AT LEAST I'M MOVING SMOOTHER THAN I WAS BEFORE.

WOW. DO YOU, *UM*, DO ALL YOUR FIREWOOD THAT WAY?

• • •

HELL, NO! YOU THINK I'M *NUTS*, KID?

GEE, SORRY... *HEH*, *HEH*, *HEH*...

SILLY OL' ME...

WHENN... I'M TIRED...

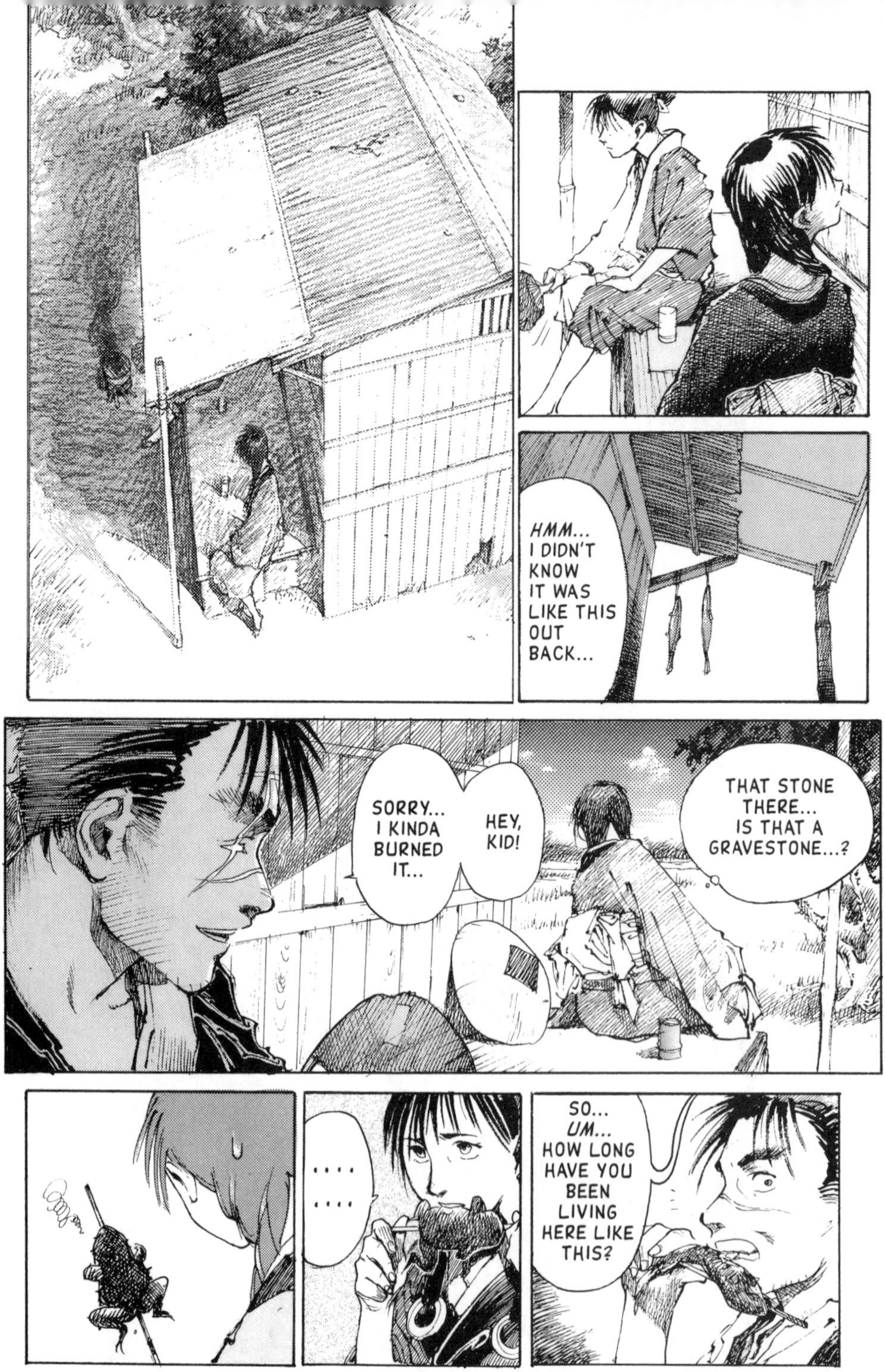
HMM... I DIDN'T KNOW IT WAS LIKE THIS OUT BACK...
SORRY... I KINDA BURNED IT...
HEY, KID!
THAT STONE THERE... IS THAT A GRAVESTONE...?
....
SO... *UM*... HOW LONG HAVE YOU BEEN LIVING HERE LIKE THIS?

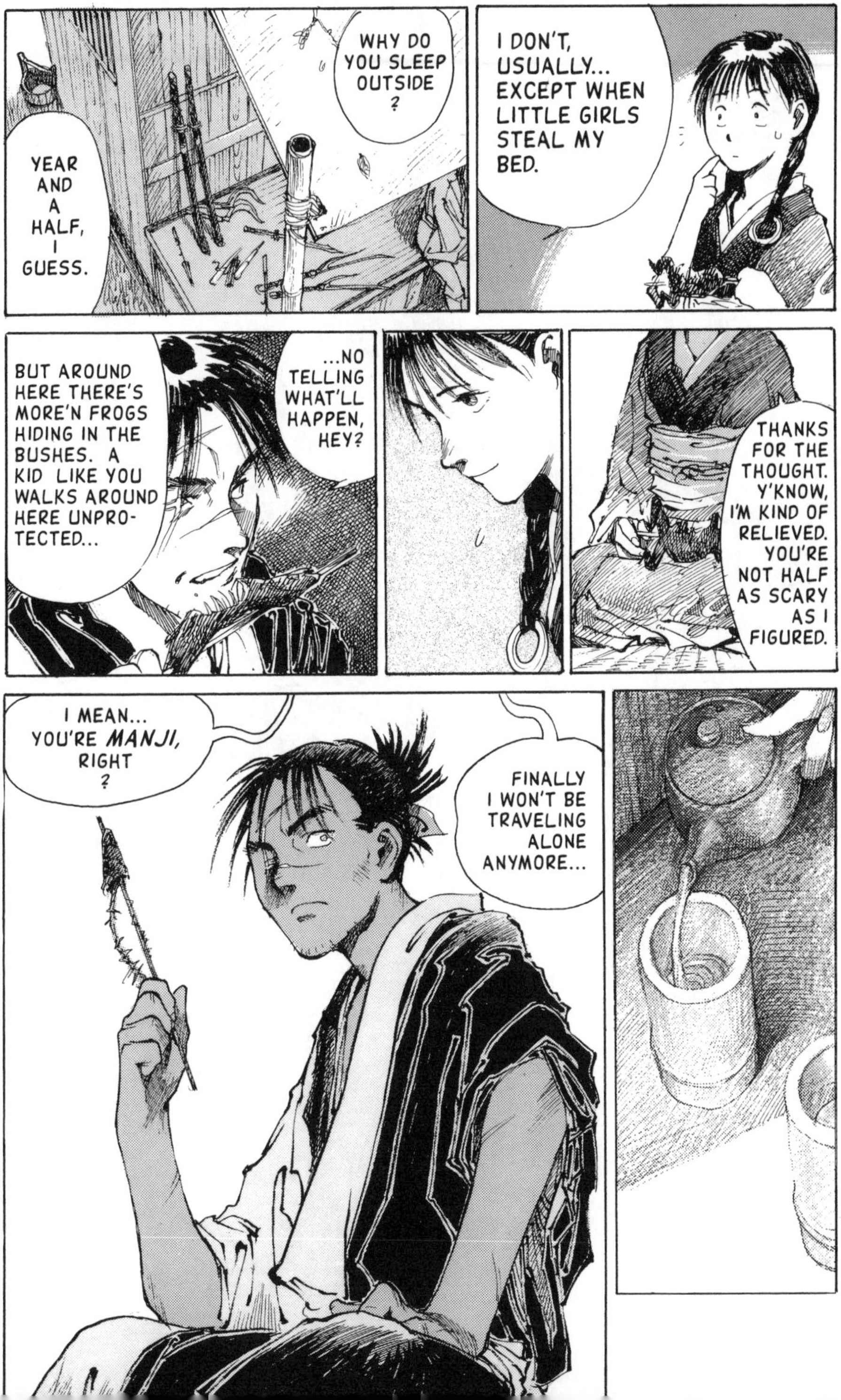
YEAR AND A HALF, I GUESS.
WHY DO YOU SLEEP OUTSIDE?
I DON'T, USUALLY... EXCEPT WHEN LITTLE GIRLS STEAL MY BED.
BUT AROUND HERE THERE'S MORE'N FROGS HIDING IN THE BUSHES. A KID LIKE YOU WALKS AROUND HERE UNPROTECTED...
...NO TELLING WHAT'LL HAPPEN, HEY?
THANKS FOR THE THOUGHT. Y'KNOW, I'M KIND OF RELIEVED. YOU'RE NOT HALF AS SCARY AS I FIGURED.
I MEAN... YOU'RE *MANJI*, RIGHT?
FINALLY I WON'T BE TRAVELING ALONE ANYMORE...

HUH. BIG JOB, KID. I'M IMPRESSED.

...HMM. I SEE-- YOU WANT TO GET YOUR PARENTS' KILLERS.

PHFFitt

WELL, TO BE HONEST... I HAVE NO IDEA WHERE ANOTSU'S ITTO-RYŪ IS BASED.

SORRY... THERE WEREN'T ANY TEA LEAVES.

BUT THEY SAID THEY WERE GOING TO CONQUER AND UNIFY ALL THE SWORD SCHOOLS.

SO...SO THAT MEANS IF WE HIT EVERY FAMOUS DŌJŌ, GO DOOR TO DOOR, THEN SOMETIME WE'LL--

PLEASE! I BEG YOU! HELP ME!

WITH OUR SWORD SKILLS AND YOUR IMMORTAL BODY, WE CAN--

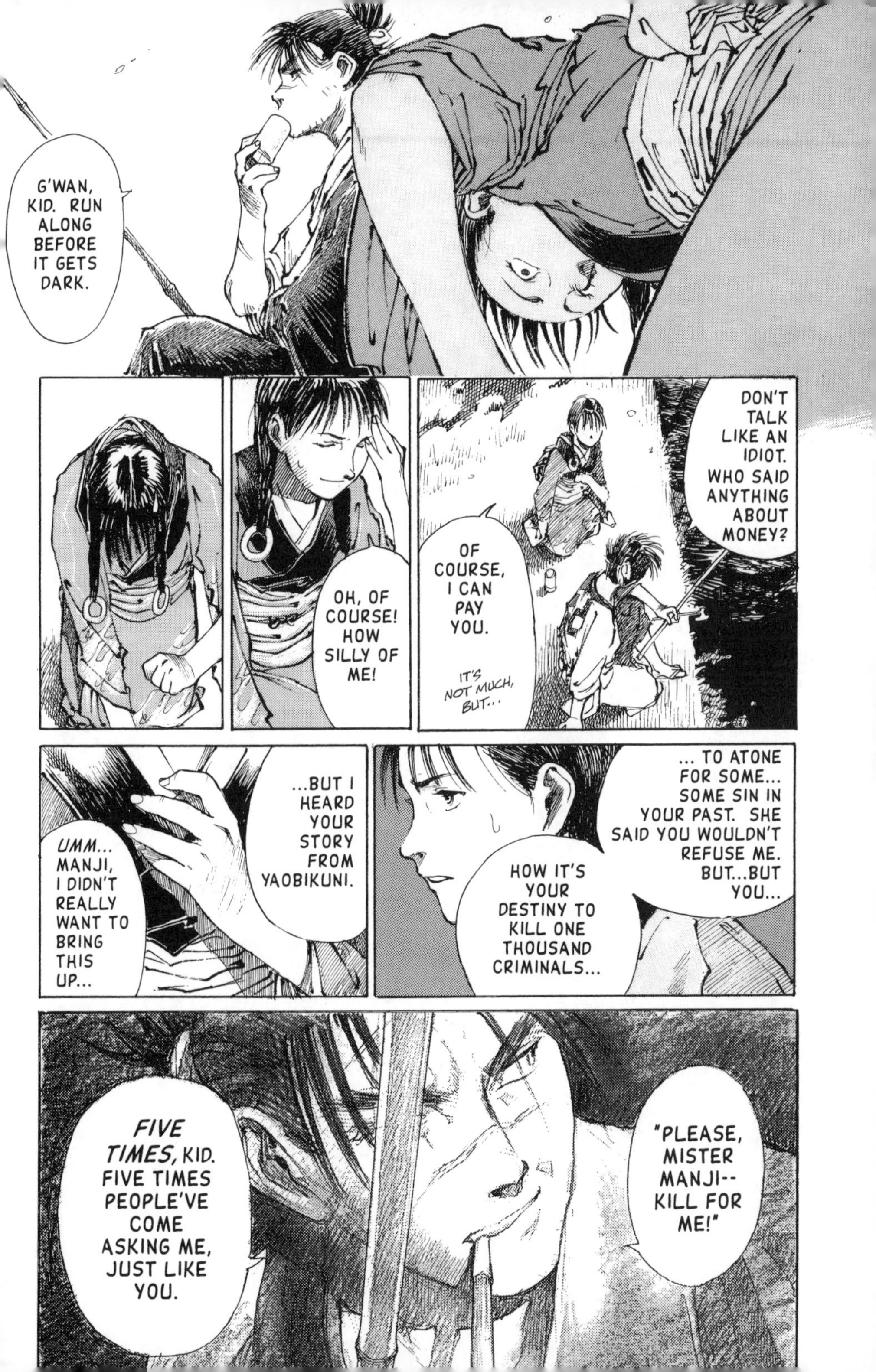
G'WAN, KID. RUN ALONG BEFORE IT GETS DARK.
OH, OF COURSE! HOW SILLY OF ME!
OF COURSE, I CAN PAY YOU.
IT'S NOT MUCH, BUT...
DON'T TALK LIKE AN IDIOT. WHO SAID ANYTHING ABOUT MONEY?
UMM... MANJI, I DIDN'T REALLY WANT TO BRING THIS UP...
...BUT I HEARD YOUR STORY FROM YAOBIKUNI.
HOW IT'S YOUR DESTINY TO KILL ONE THOUSAND CRIMINALS...
... TO ATONE FOR SOME... SOME SIN IN YOUR PAST. SHE SAID YOU WOULDN'T REFUSE ME. BUT...BUT YOU...
FIVE TIMES, KID. FIVE TIMES PEOPLE'VE COME ASKING ME, JUST LIKE YOU.
"PLEASE, MISTER MANJI-- KILL FOR ME!"

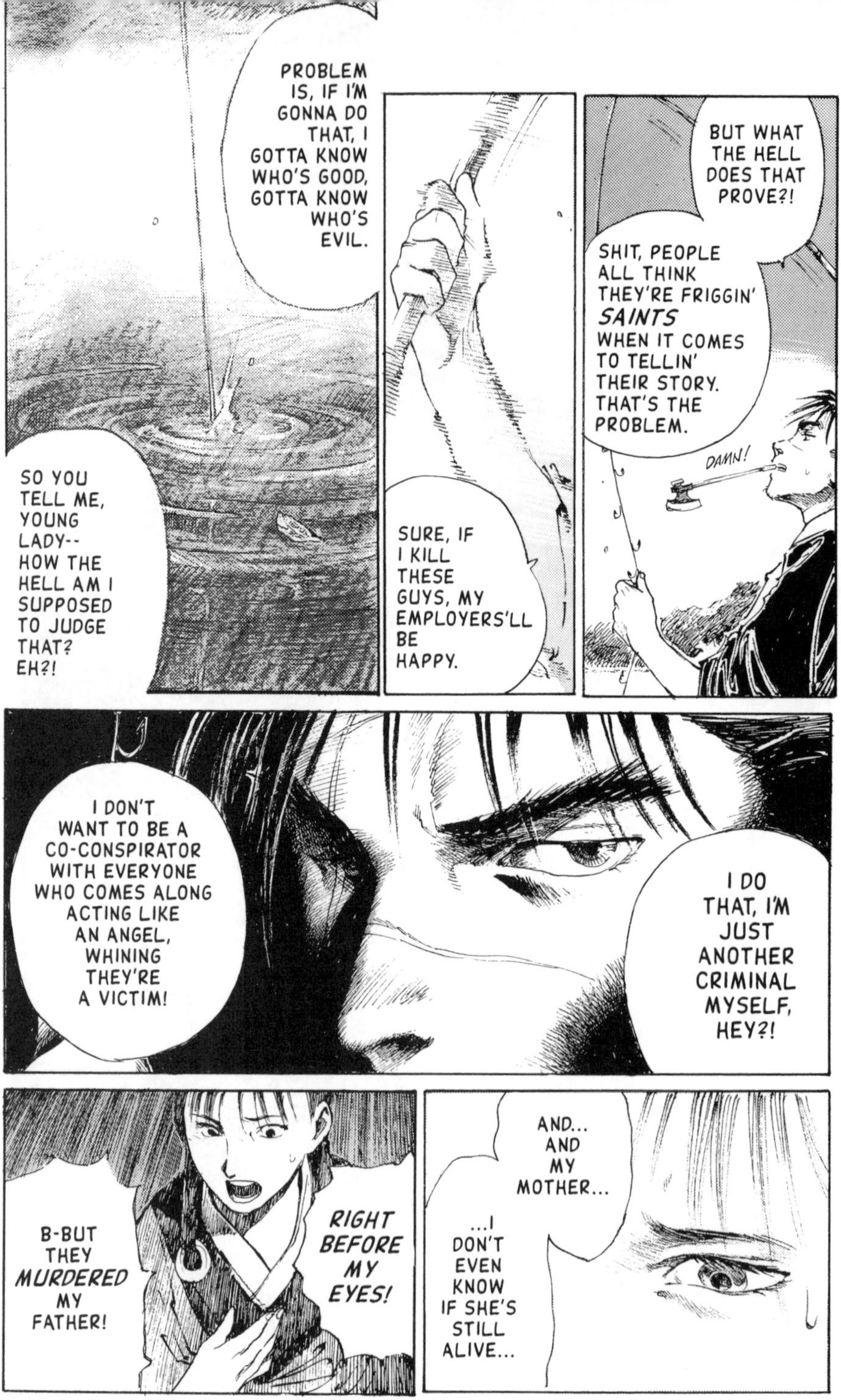
PROBLEM IS, IF I'M GONNA DO THAT, I GOTTA KNOW WHO'S GOOD, GOTTA KNOW WHO'S EVIL.
SO YOU TELL ME, YOUNG LADY-- HOW THE HELL AM I SUPPOSED TO JUDGE THAT? EH?!
SURE, IF I KILL THESE GUYS, MY EMPLOYERS'LL BE HAPPY.
BUT WHAT THE HELL DOES THAT PROVE?!
SHIT, PEOPLE ALL THINK THEY'RE FRIGGIN' *SAINTS* WHEN IT COMES TO TELLIN' THEIR STORY. THAT'S THE PROBLEM.
DAMN!
I DON'T WANT TO BE A CO-CONSPIRATOR WITH EVERYONE WHO COMES ALONG ACTING LIKE AN ANGEL, WHINING THEY'RE A VICTIM!
I DO THAT, I'M JUST ANOTHER CRIMINAL MYSELF, HEY?!
B-BUT THEY *MURDERED* MY FATHER!
RIGHT BEFORE MY EYES!
AND... AND MY MOTHER...
...I DON'T EVEN KNOW IF SHE'S STILL ALIVE...

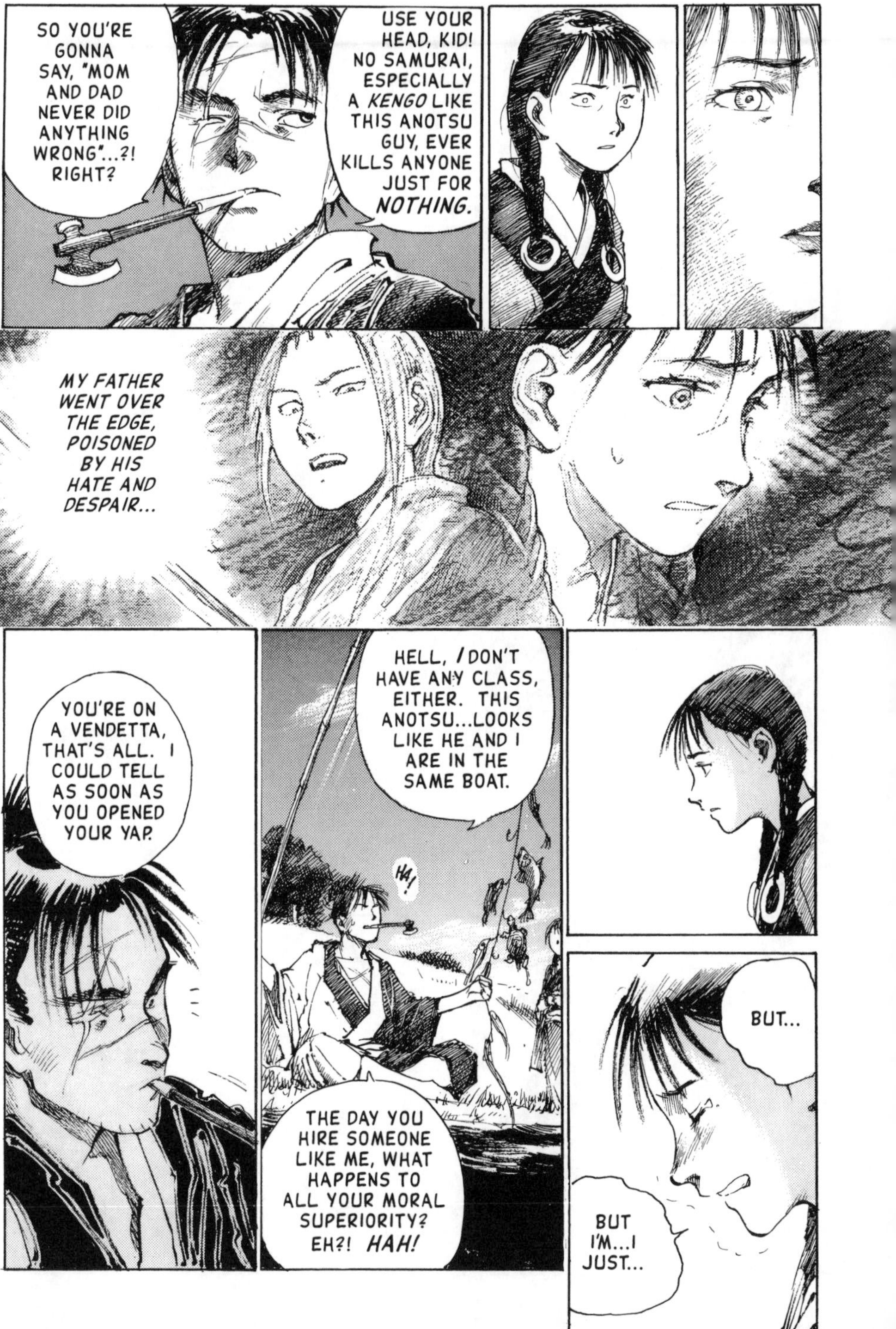
SO YOU'RE GONNA SAY, "MOM AND DAD NEVER DID ANYTHING WRONG"...?! RIGHT?
USE YOUR HEAD, KID! NO SAMURAI, ESPECIALLY A *KENGO* LIKE THIS ANOTSU GUY, EVER KILLS ANYONE JUST FOR *NOTHING.*
MY FATHER WENT OVER THE EDGE, POISONED BY HIS HATE AND DESPAIR...
YOU'RE ON A VENDETTA, THAT'S ALL. I COULD TELL AS SOON AS YOU OPENED YOUR YAP.
HELL, *I* DON'T HAVE ANY CLASS, EITHER. THIS ANOTSU...LOOKS LIKE HE AND I ARE IN THE SAME BOAT.
HA!
THE DAY YOU HIRE SOMEONE LIKE ME, WHAT HAPPENS TO ALL YOUR MORAL SUPERIORITY? EH?! *HAH!*
BUT...
BUT I'M...I JUST...

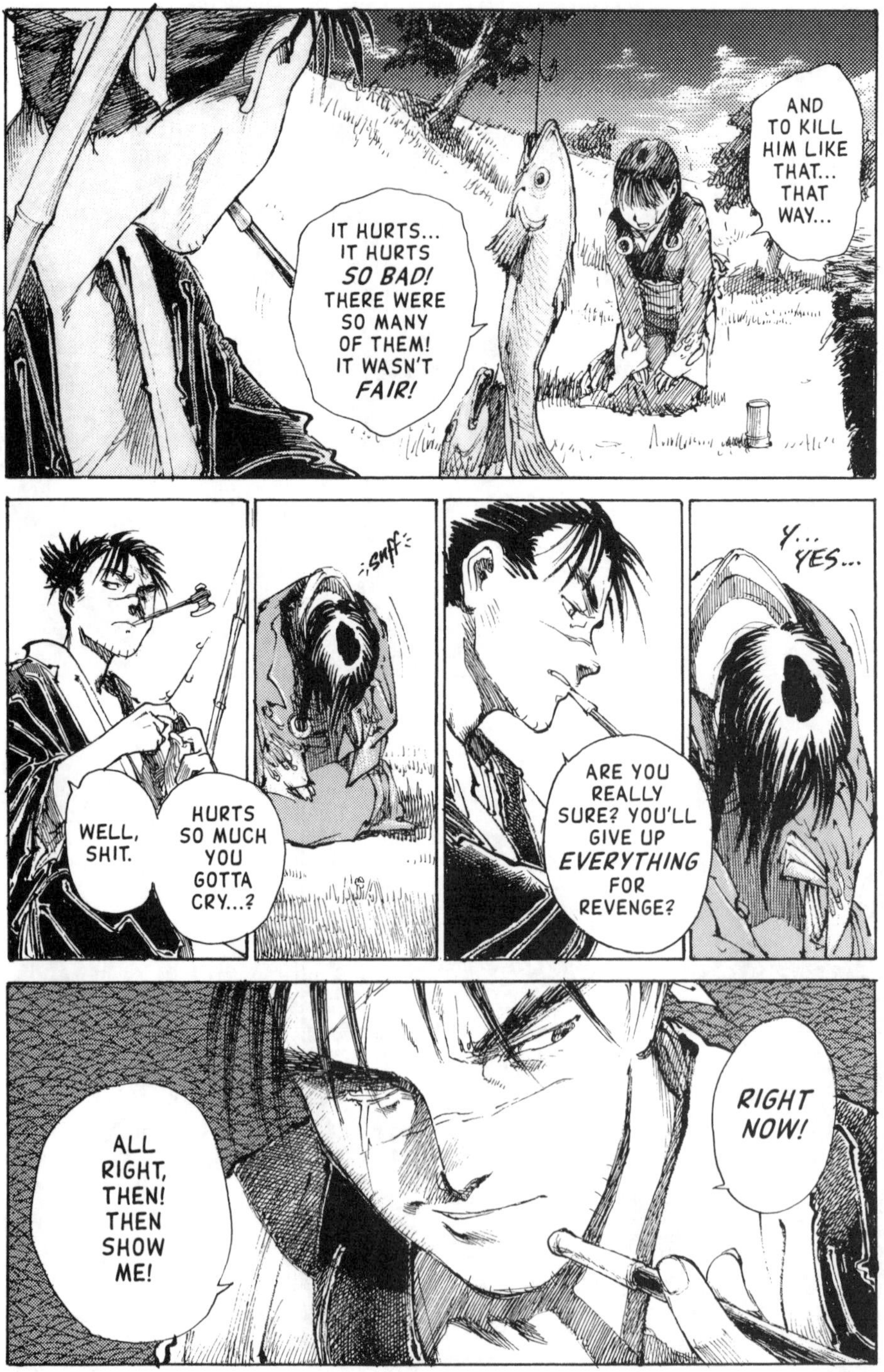
IT HURTS... IT HURTS SO BAD! THERE WERE SO MANY OF THEM! IT WASN'T FAIR!
AND TO KILL HIM LIKE THAT... THAT WAY...
WELL, SHIT.
HURTS SO MUCH YOU GOTTA CRY...?
SNIFF
ARE YOU REALLY SURE? YOU'LL GIVE UP EVERYTHING FOR REVENGE?
Y... YES...
ALL RIGHT, THEN! THEN SHOW ME!
RIGHT NOW!

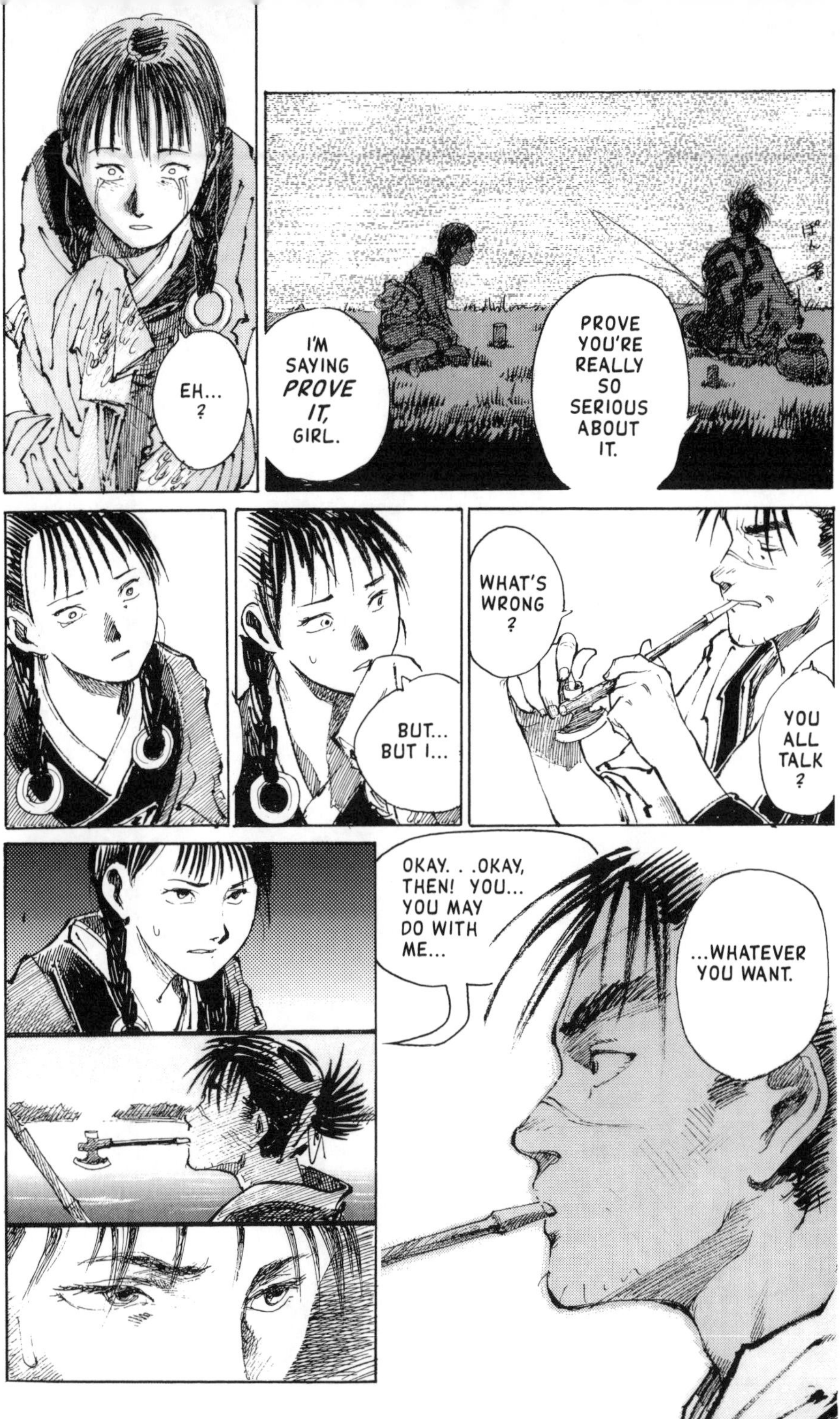
EH...?
I'M SAYING *PROVE IT,* GIRL.
PROVE YOU'RE REALLY SO SERIOUS ABOUT IT.
BUT... BUT I...
WHAT'S WRONG?
YOU ALL TALK?
OKAY. . .OKAY, THEN! YOU... YOU MAY DO WITH ME...
...WHATEVER YOU WANT.

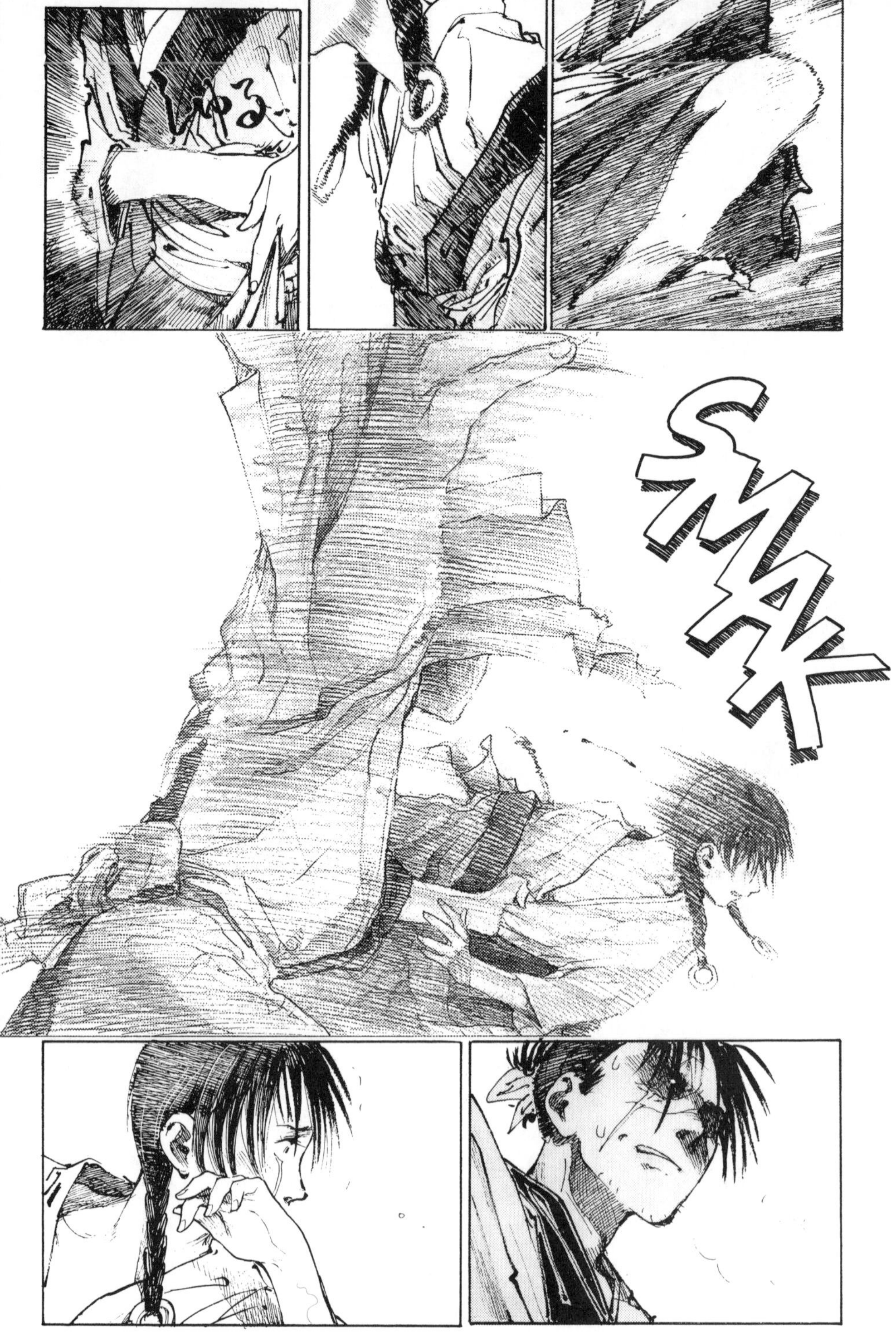
しゅる
SMAK

A KID LIKE YOU SHOULDN'T MAKE A JOKE LIKE THAT!

GET YOUR DAMN CLOTHES BACK ON!

LOOK... I'M SORRY, KID.

IT'S JUST... YOU LOOK LIKE MY LITTLE SISTER.

SO I HIT YOU LIKE I MEANT IT, HEY...?

GOOD-BYE, MANJI.

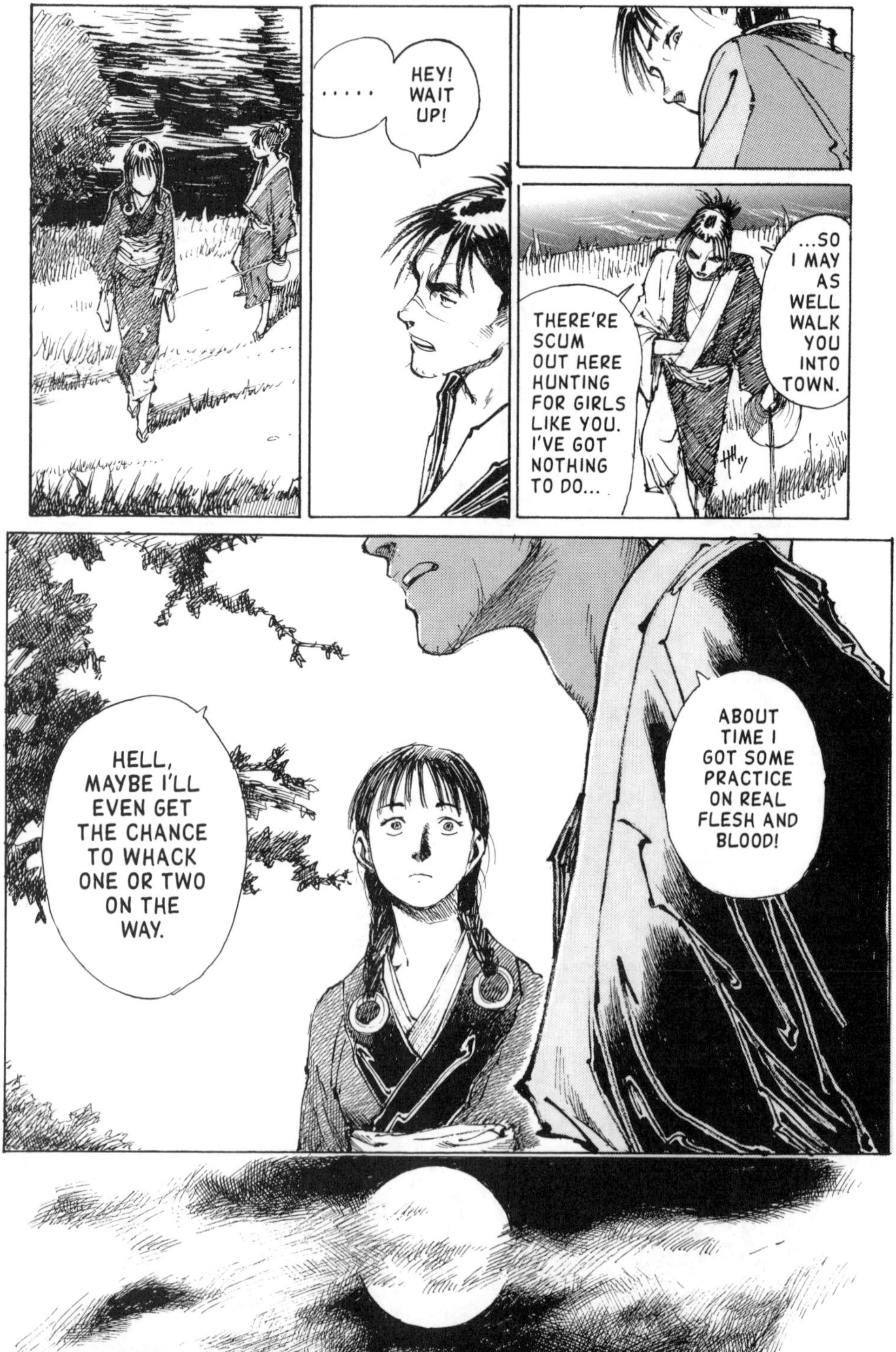

.....
HEY! WAIT UP!
THERE'RE SCUM OUT HERE HUNTING FOR GIRLS LIKE YOU. I'VE GOT NOTHING TO DO...
...SO I MAY AS WELL WALK YOU INTO TOWN.
HELL, MAYBE I'LL EVEN GET THE CHANCE TO WHACK ONE OR TWO ON THE WAY.
ABOUT TIME I GOT SOME PRACTICE ON REAL FLESH AND BLOOD!

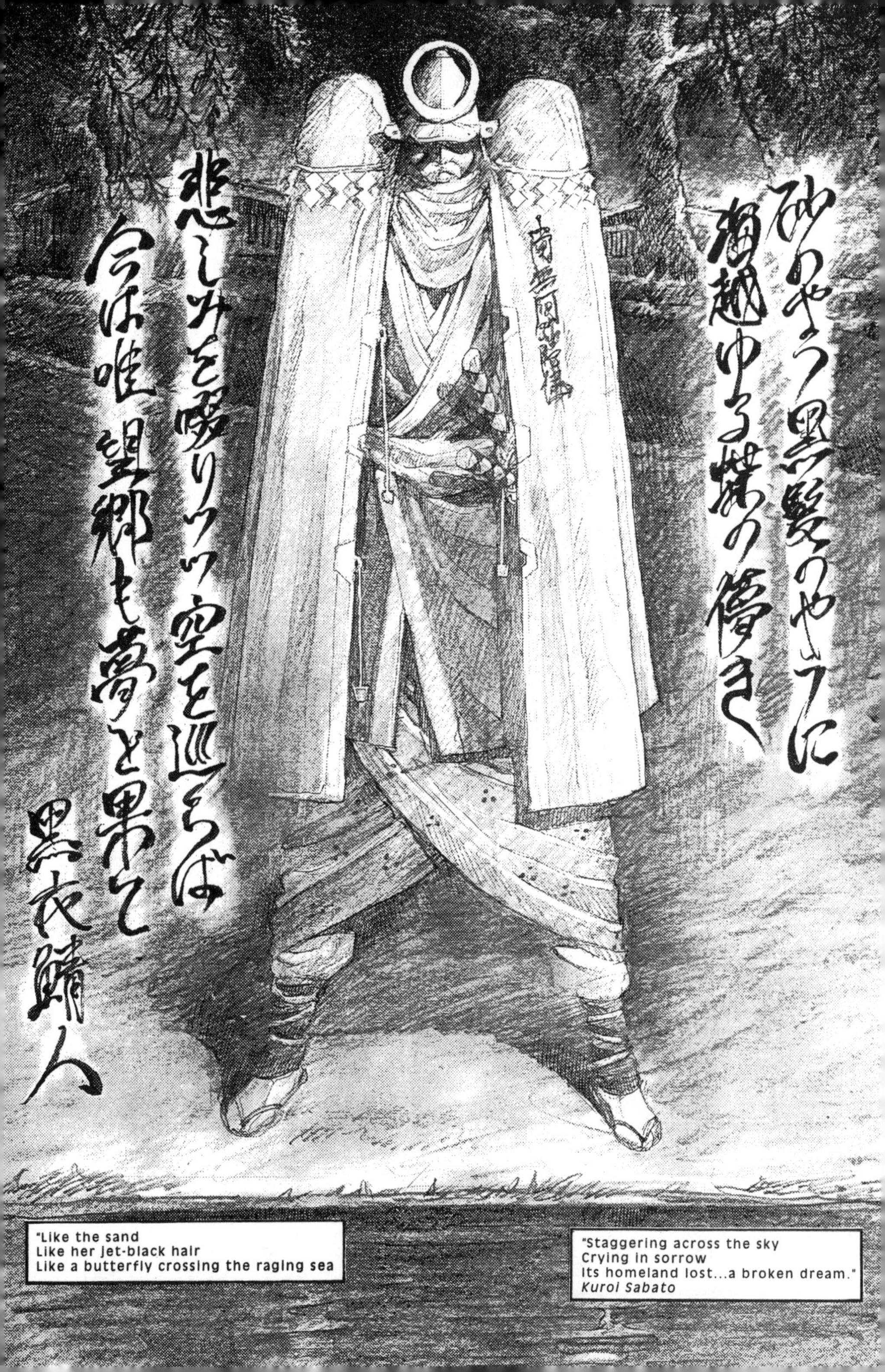
砂のやうに黒髪のやうに
海越ゆる蝶の儚き
悲しみを啼りつつ空を巡らば
今は唯望郷も夢と果て
黒衣鯖人
"Like the sand
Like her jet-black hair
Like a butterfly crossing the raging sea
"Staggering across the sky
Crying in sorrow
Its homeland lost...a broken dream."
Kuroi Sabato

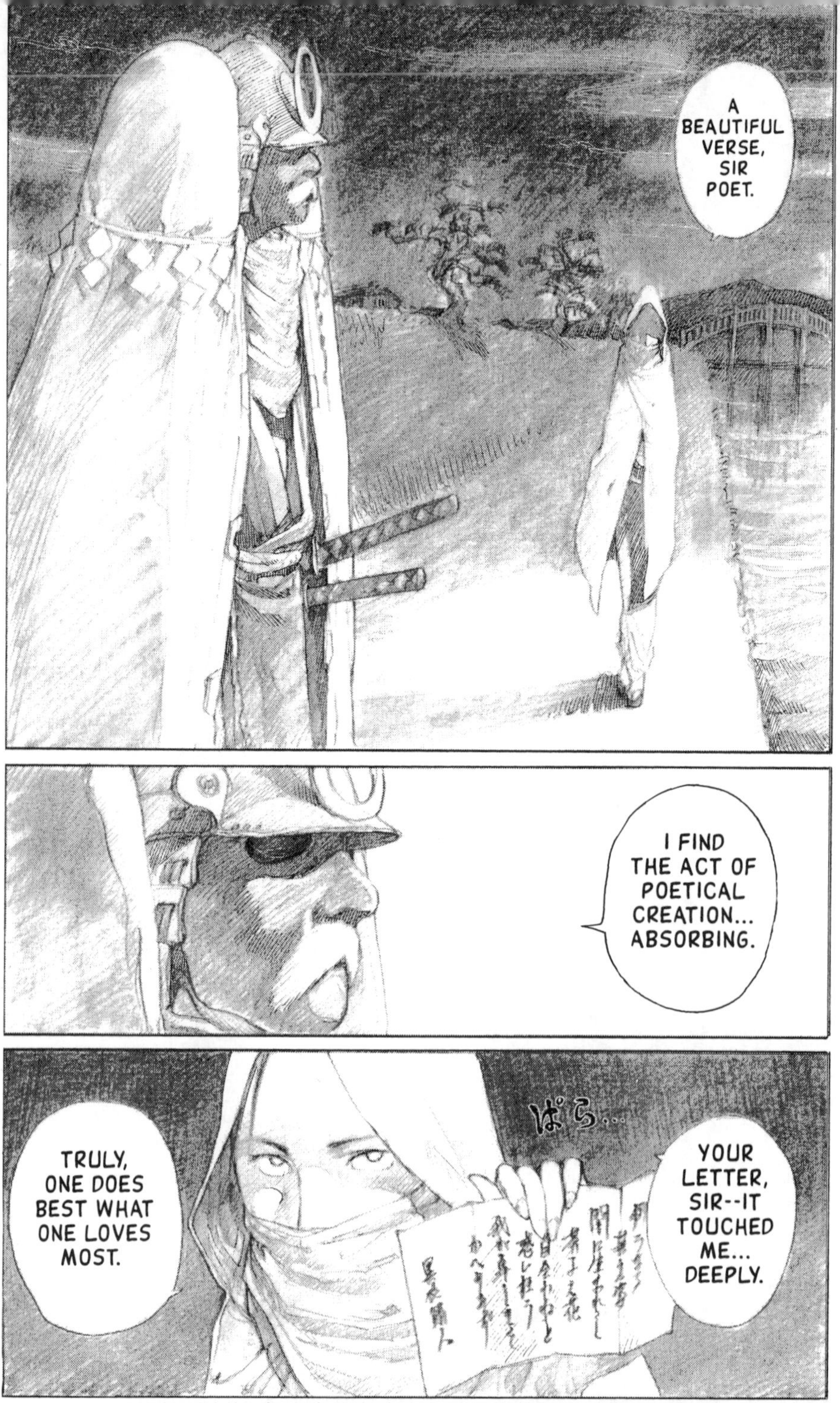
A BEAUTIFUL VERSE, SIR POET.
I FIND THE ACT OF POETICAL CREATION... ABSORBING.
TRULY, ONE DOES BEST WHAT ONE LOVES MOST.
ぱら...
YOUR LETTER, SIR--IT TOUCHED ME... DEEPLY.

"Her pristine form, born in darkness like the tea leaf's flower. If I do not see her, I shall go mad with love: my own path abandoned, without regret." *Kuroi Sabato*

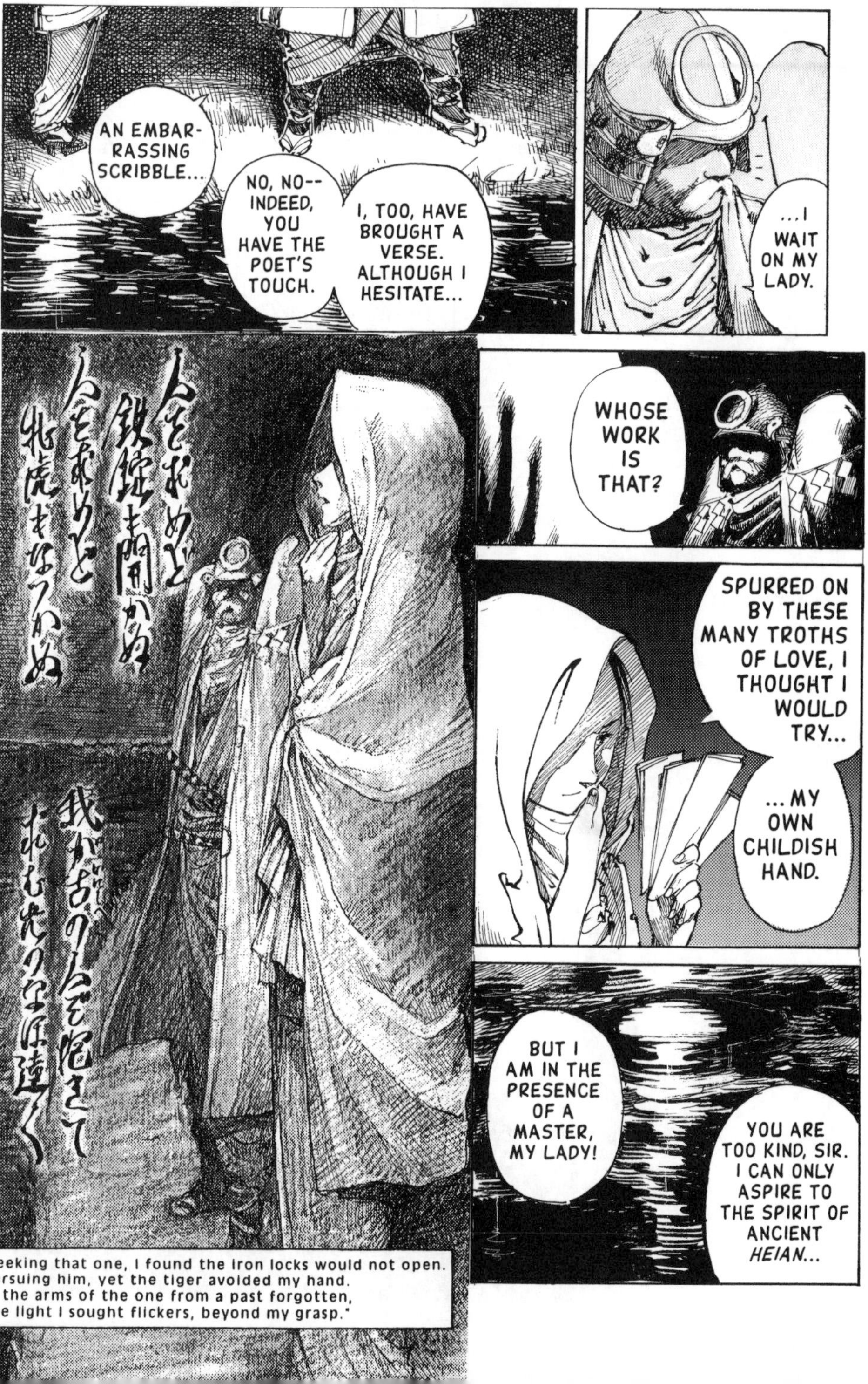
AN EMBARRASSING SCRIBBLE...
NO, NO-- INDEED, YOU HAVE THE POET'S TOUCH.
I, TOO, HAVE BROUGHT A VERSE. ALTHOUGH I HESITATE...
...I WAIT ON MY LADY.
"Seeking that one, I found the iron locks would not open.
Pursuing him, yet the tiger avoided my hand.
In the arms of the one from a past forgotten,
The light I sought flickers, beyond my grasp."
WHOSE WORK IS THAT?
SPURRED ON BY THESE MANY TROTHS OF LOVE, I THOUGHT I WOULD TRY...
...MY OWN CHILDISH HAND.
BUT I AM IN THE PRESENCE OF A MASTER, MY LADY!
YOU ARE TOO KIND, SIR. I CAN ONLY ASPIRE TO THE SPIRIT OF ANCIENT *HEIAN*...

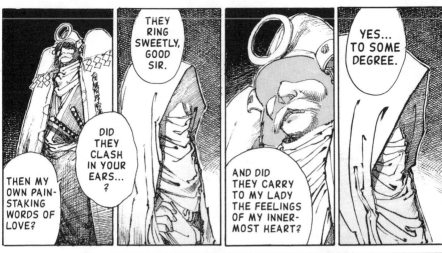

THEN MY OWN PAIN-STAKING WORDS OF LOVE?
DID THEY CLASH IN YOUR EARS...?
THEY RING SWEETLY, GOOD SIR.
AND DID THEY CARRY TO MY LADY THE FEELINGS OF MY INNER-MOST HEART?
YES... TO SOME DEGREE.
I COULD ASK NO GREATER BLESSING. AND NOW, WITH YOUR UNDERSTANDING...
...I SHALL TAKE MY LADY'S LIFE.
IN LOVE, I SEEK PERFECTION. PERFECT LOVE, THY NAME IS... DEATH.
I HAVE LOVED YOU FROM THE MOMENT I SAW YOU, LADY FAIR! FOR ALL ETERNITY NO OTHER SHALL COME BETWEEN US!

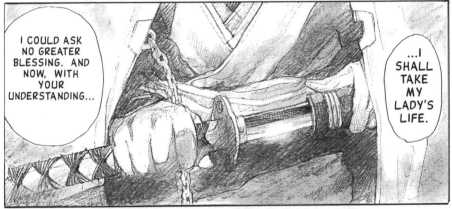

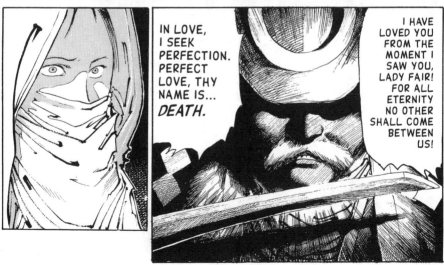

YOUR HAIR... YOUR EYES... ALL THAT IS MOST BEAUTIFUL...

I SHALL MAKE MINE! *MINE ALONE!*

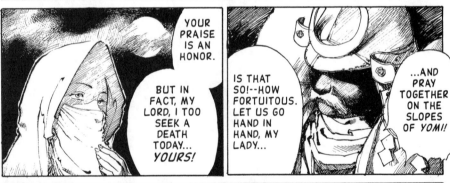

YOUR PRAISE IS AN HONOR.

BUT IN FACT, MY LORD, I TOO SEEK A DEATH TODAY... *YOURS!*

IS THAT SO!--HOW FORTUITOUS. LET US GO HAND IN HAND, MY LADY...

...AND PRAY TOGETHER ON THE SLOPES OF *YOMI!*

THANK YOU FOR THE KIND THOUGHT.

BUT YOU'LL JUST HAVE TO PRAY--

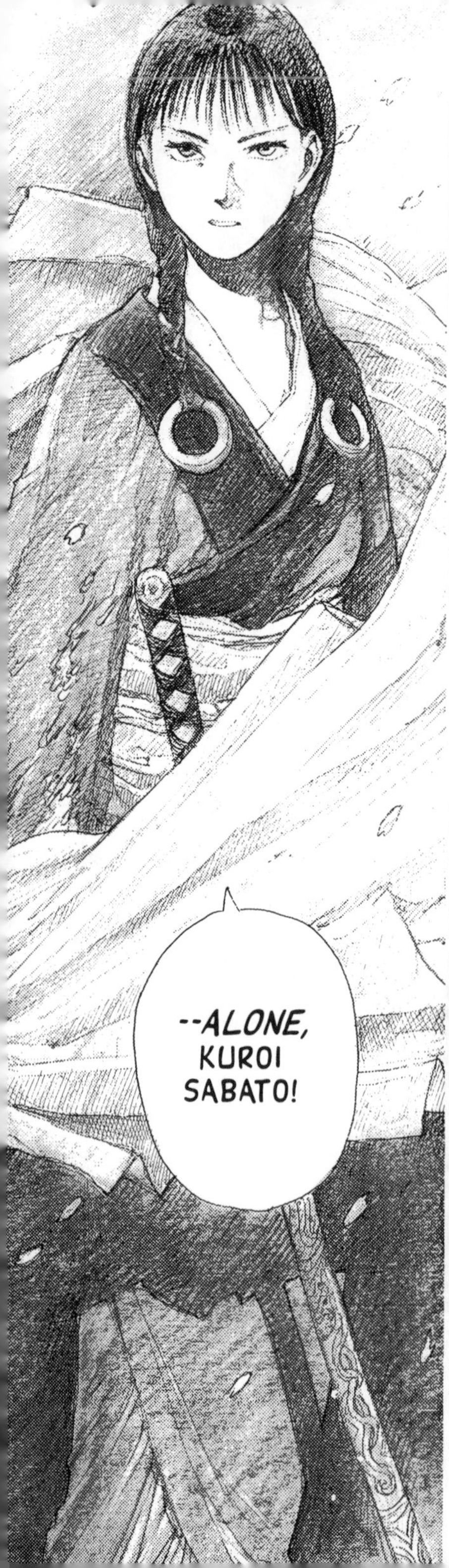
--*ALONE,* KUROI SABATO!

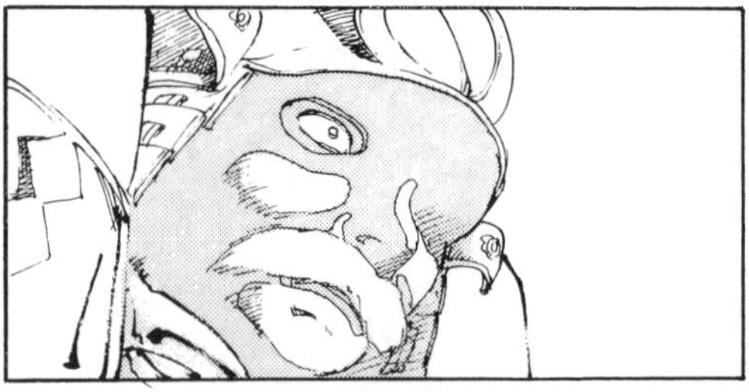

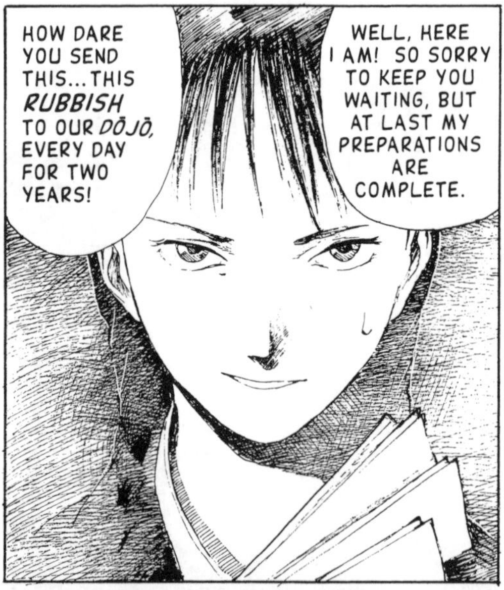
HOW DARE YOU SEND THIS... THIS *RUBBISH* TO OUR *DŌJŌ,* EVERY DAY FOR TWO YEARS!
WELL, HERE I AM! SO SORRY TO KEEP YOU WAITING, BUT AT LAST MY PREPARATIONS ARE COMPLETE.

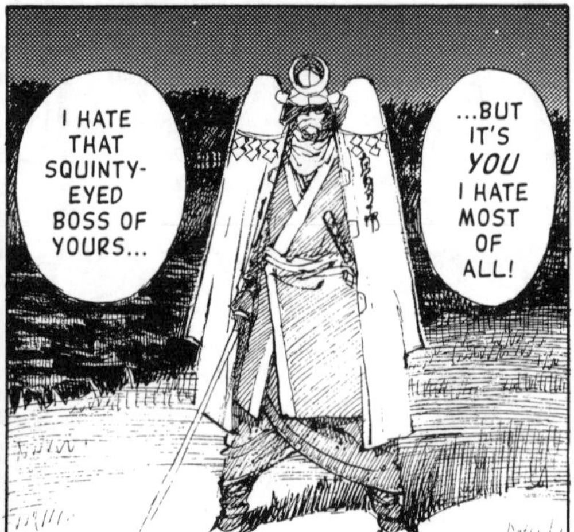
I HATE THAT SQUINTY-EYED BOSS OF YOURS...
...BUT IT'S *YOU* I HATE MOST OF ALL!

FIRST I'LL CUT YOU DOWN, THE MAN WHO KILLED MY FATHER...

...AS THE PROLOGUE TO MY BLOODY DRAMA OF REVENGE!

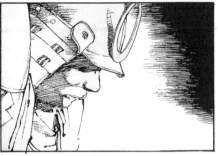

SUCH BEAUTY...

"YOUR FACE IN SUBTLE MOONLIGHT BARED, GLOWS LIKE AN ANGEL COME FROM HEAVEN"...!

SSHH

IT WAS WORTH WAITING TWO YEARS FOR THIS MOMENT.

!

KSSH.

HOW ABOUT THAT, GIRL...

...THOSE LOVE LETTERS REALLY *WERE* FOR YOU.

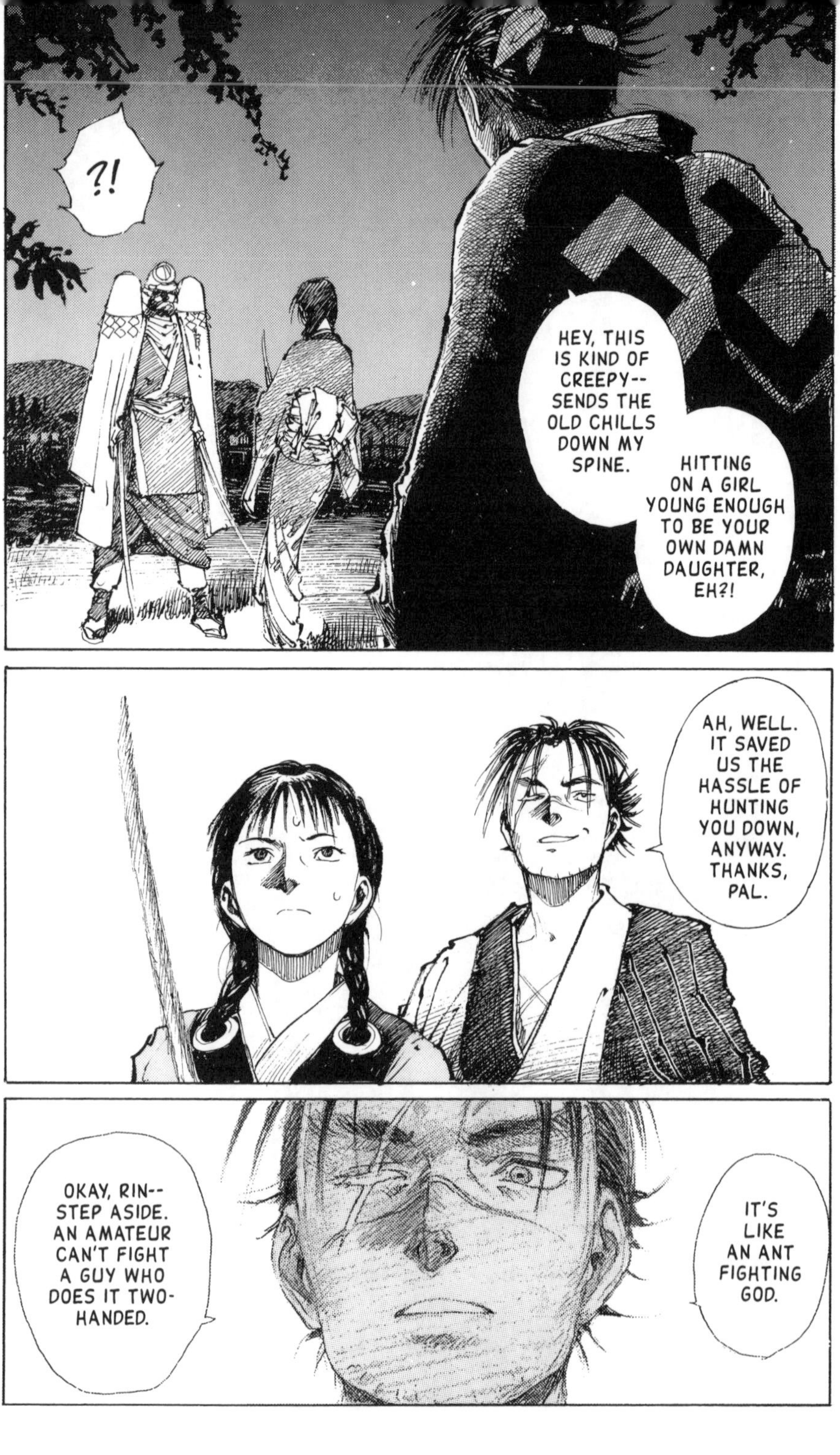
?!
HEY, THIS IS KIND OF CREEPY-- SENDS THE OLD CHILLS DOWN MY SPINE.
HITTING ON A GIRL YOUNG ENOUGH TO BE YOUR OWN DAMN DAUGHTER, EH?!
AH, WELL. IT SAVED US THE HASSLE OF HUNTING YOU DOWN, ANYWAY. THANKS, PAL.
OKAY, RIN-- STEP ASIDE. AN AMATEUR CAN'T FIGHT A GUY WHO DOES IT TWO-HANDED.
IT'S LIKE AN ANT FIGHTING GOD.

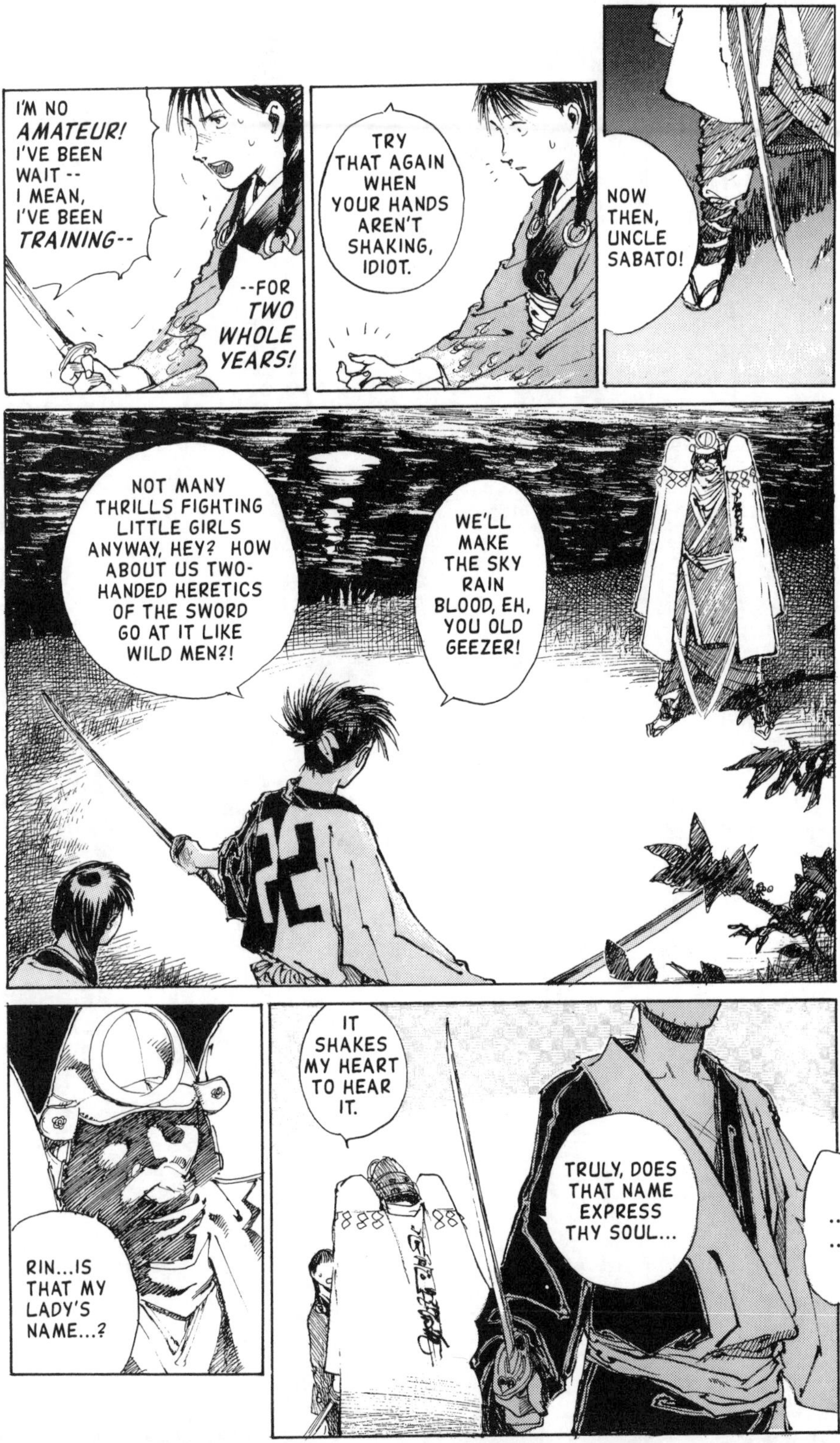
I'M NO AMATEUR! I'VE BEEN WAIT -- I MEAN, I'VE BEEN TRAINING--
--FOR TWO WHOLE YEARS!
TRY THAT AGAIN WHEN YOUR HANDS AREN'T SHAKING, IDIOT.
NOW THEN, UNCLE SABATO!
NOT MANY THRILLS FIGHTING LITTLE GIRLS ANYWAY, HEY? HOW ABOUT US TWO-HANDED HERETICS OF THE SWORD GO AT IT LIKE WILD MEN?!
WE'LL MAKE THE SKY RAIN BLOOD, EH, YOU OLD GEEZER!
RIN...IS THAT MY LADY'S NAME...?
IT SHAKES MY HEART TO HEAR IT.
TRULY, DOES THAT NAME EXPRESS THY SOUL...
....
...!

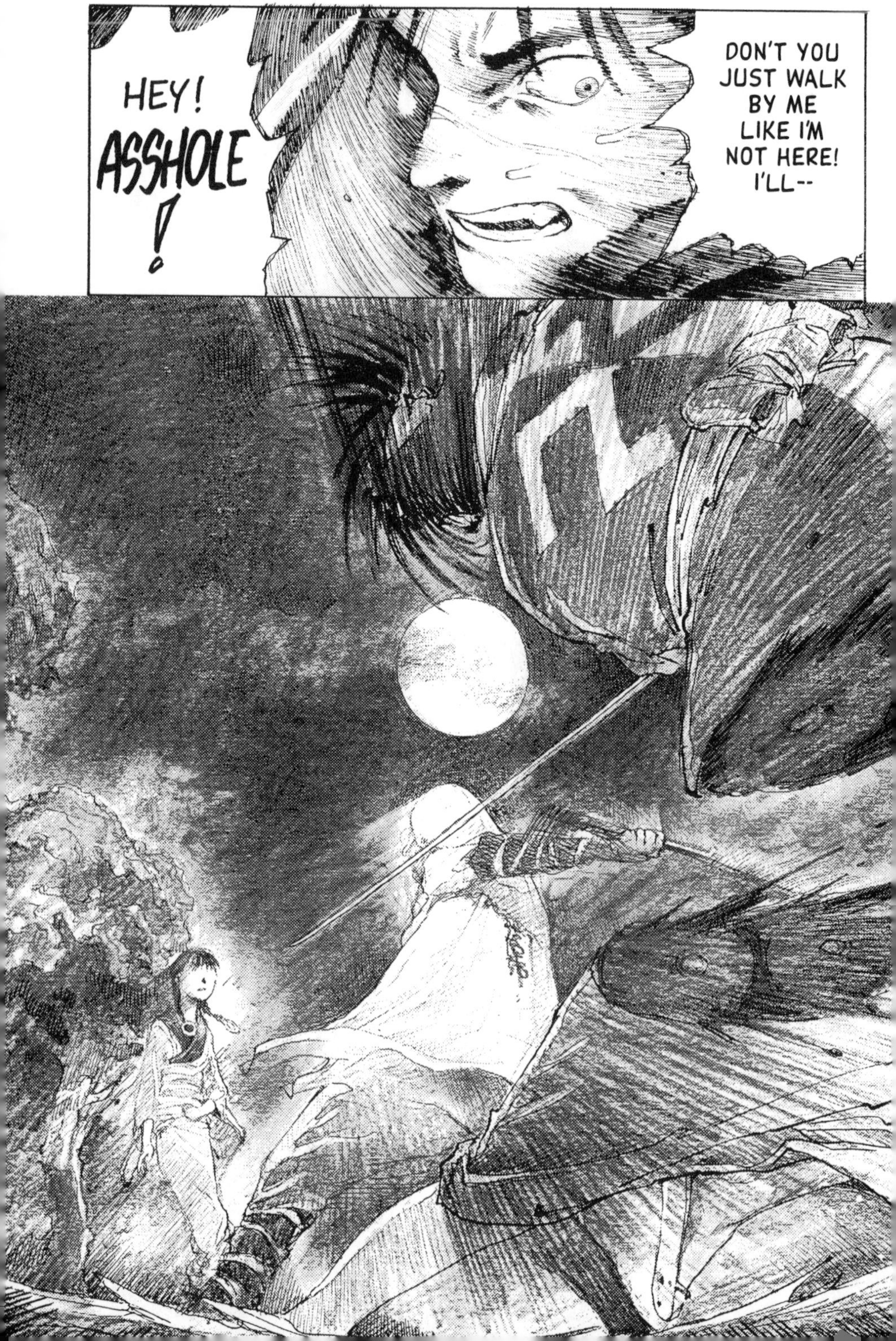
HEY! ASSHOLE!
DON'T YOU JUST WALK BY ME LIKE I'M NOT HERE! I'LL--

....

HUH?

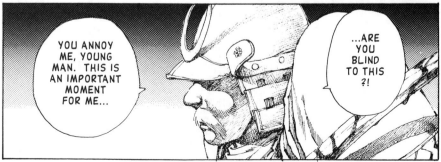

YOU ANNOY ME, YOUNG MAN. THIS IS AN IMPORTANT MOMENT FOR ME...

...ARE YOU BLIND TO THIS ?!

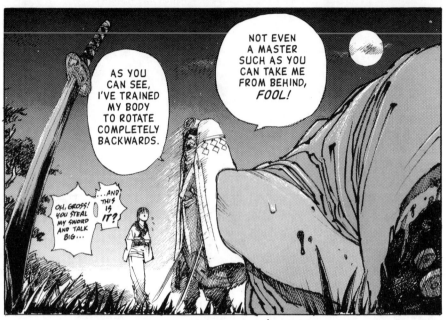

AS YOU CAN SEE, I'VE TRAINED MY BODY TO ROTATE COMPLETELY BACKWARDS.

NOT EVEN A MASTER SUCH AS YOU CAN TAKE ME FROM BEHIND, *FOOL!*

OH, GROSS! YOU STEAL MY SWORD AND TALK BIG...

...AND THIS IS *IT?*

NOW THAT YOU UNDERSTAND, HURRY UP AND DIE.

I'M NOT INTERESTED IN TALKING WITH MEN.

F... FILTHY OLD MAN...

NOW, THEN...

...WITH THAT TEDIOUS EPISODE BEHIND US, LADY RIN...

...SHALL I SHOW YOU THE PROOF OF MY LOVE?

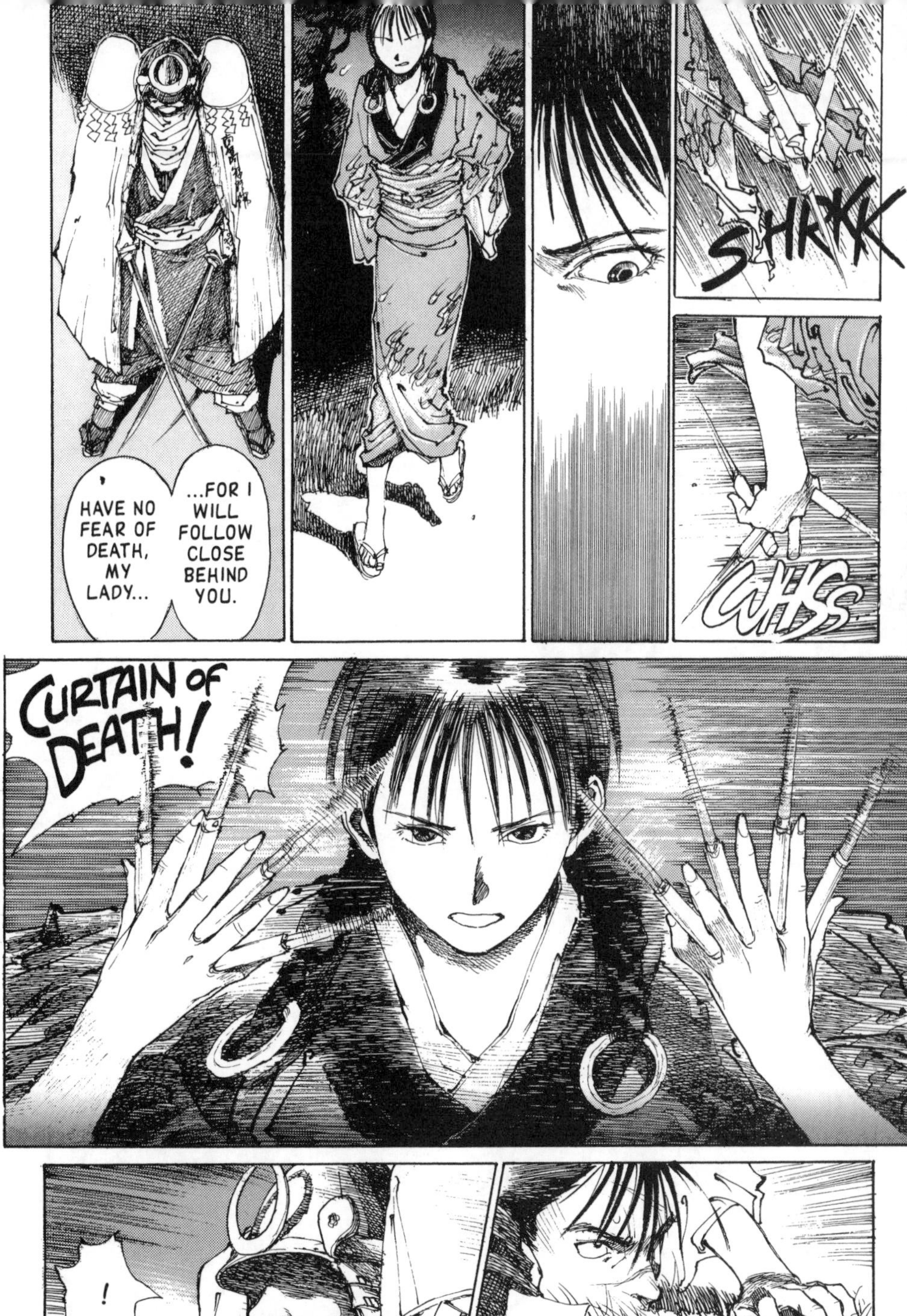
HAVE NO FEAR OF DEATH, MY LADY...
...FOR I WILL FOLLOW CLOSE BEHIND YOU.
SHKKK
WHSS
CURTAIN OF DEATH!
!
?!

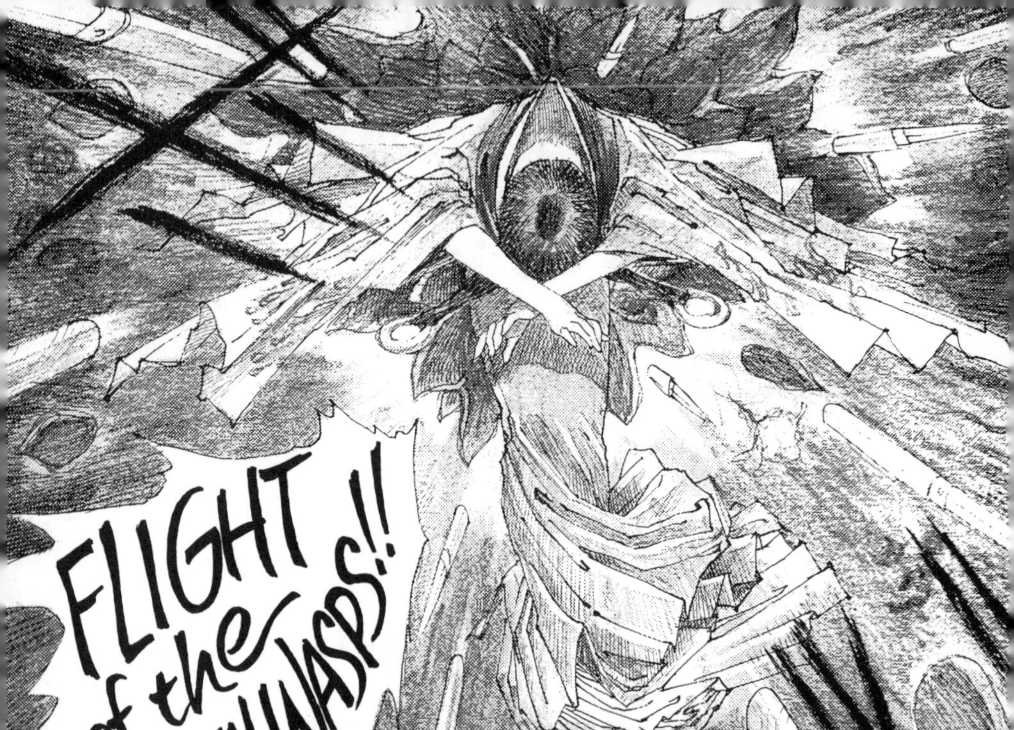
FLIGHT of the GOLDEN WASPS!!
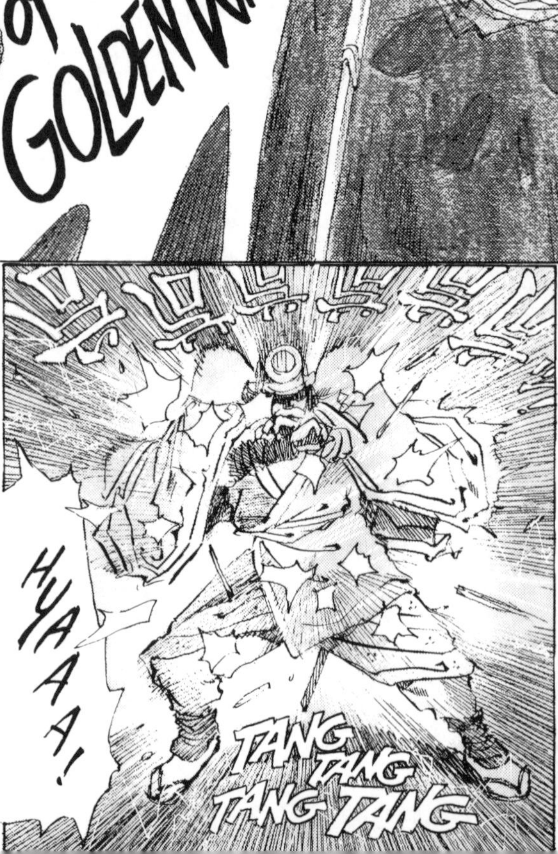
HYAAAA!
TANG TANG TANG TANG
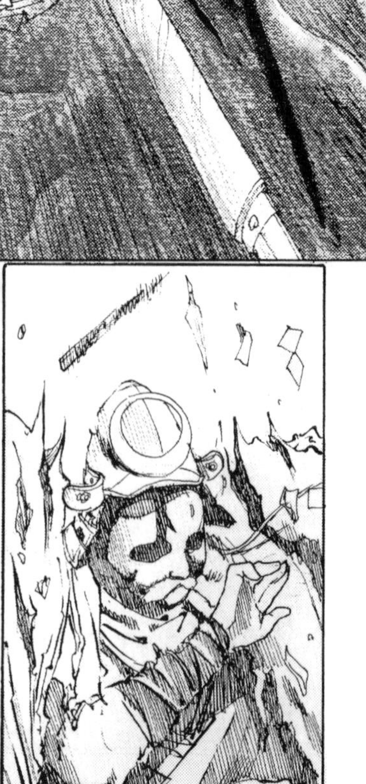

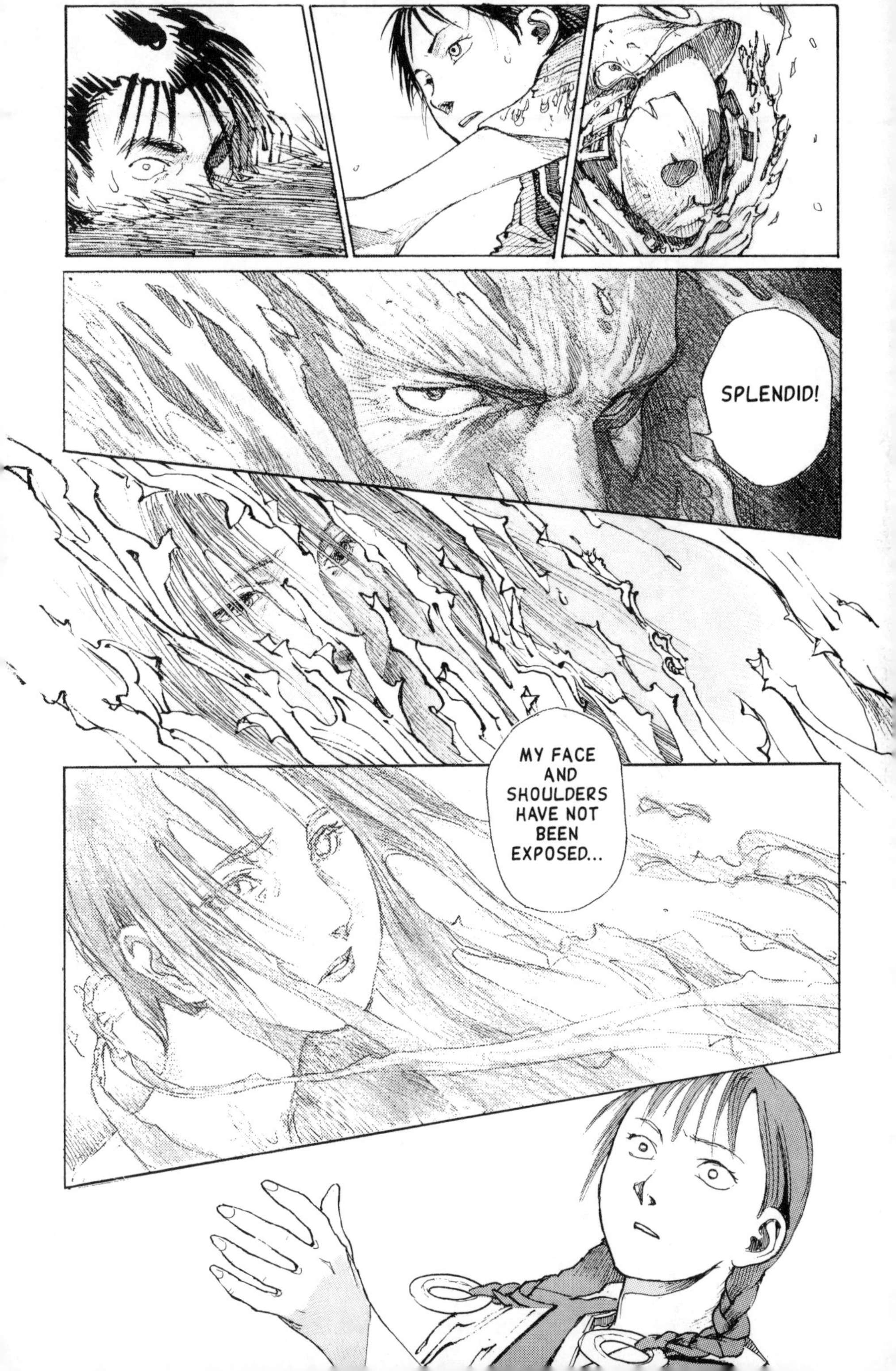
SPLENDID!
MY FACE AND SHOULDERS HAVE NOT BEEN EXPOSED...

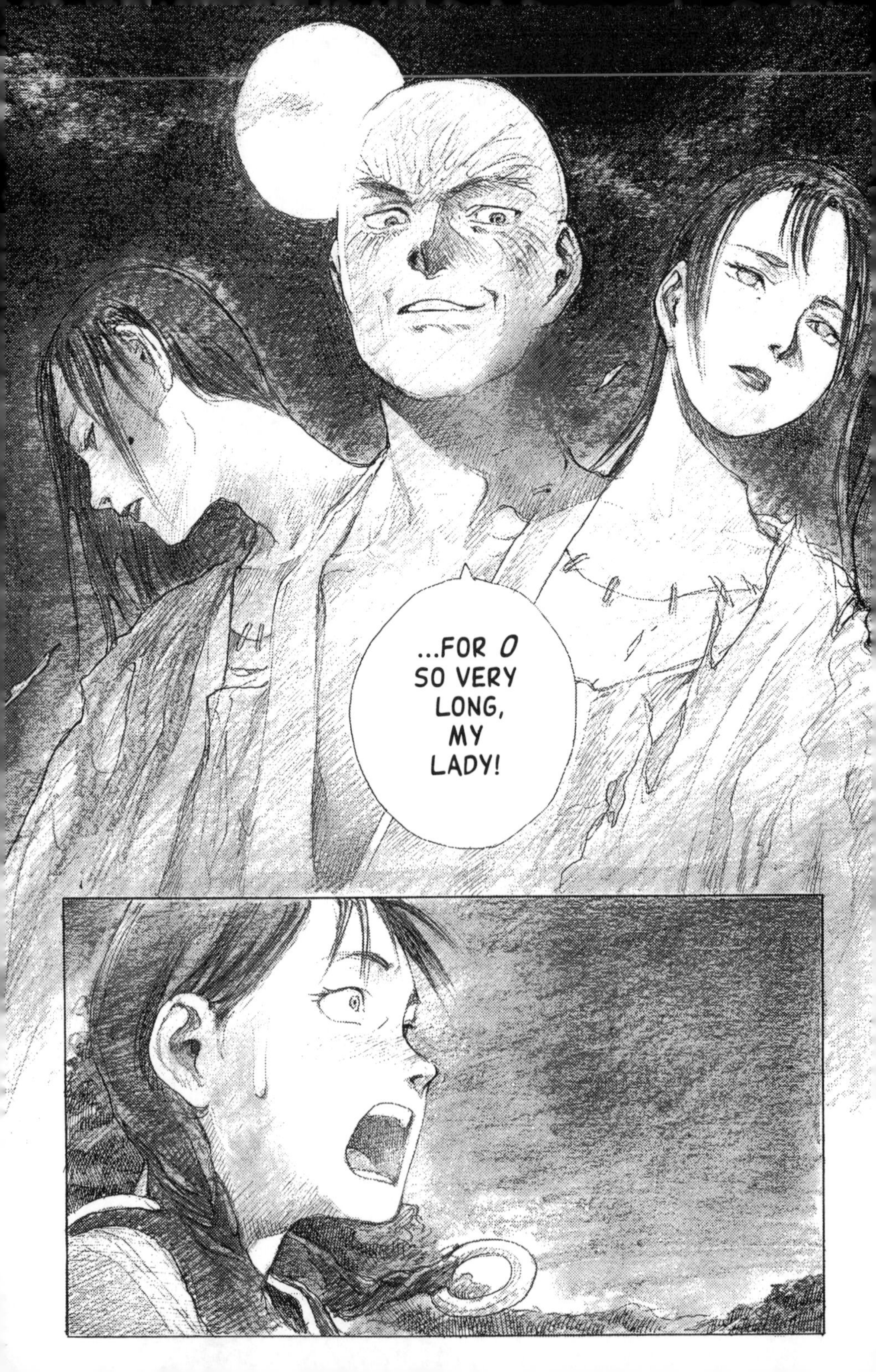
...FOR O SO VERY LONG, MY LADY!

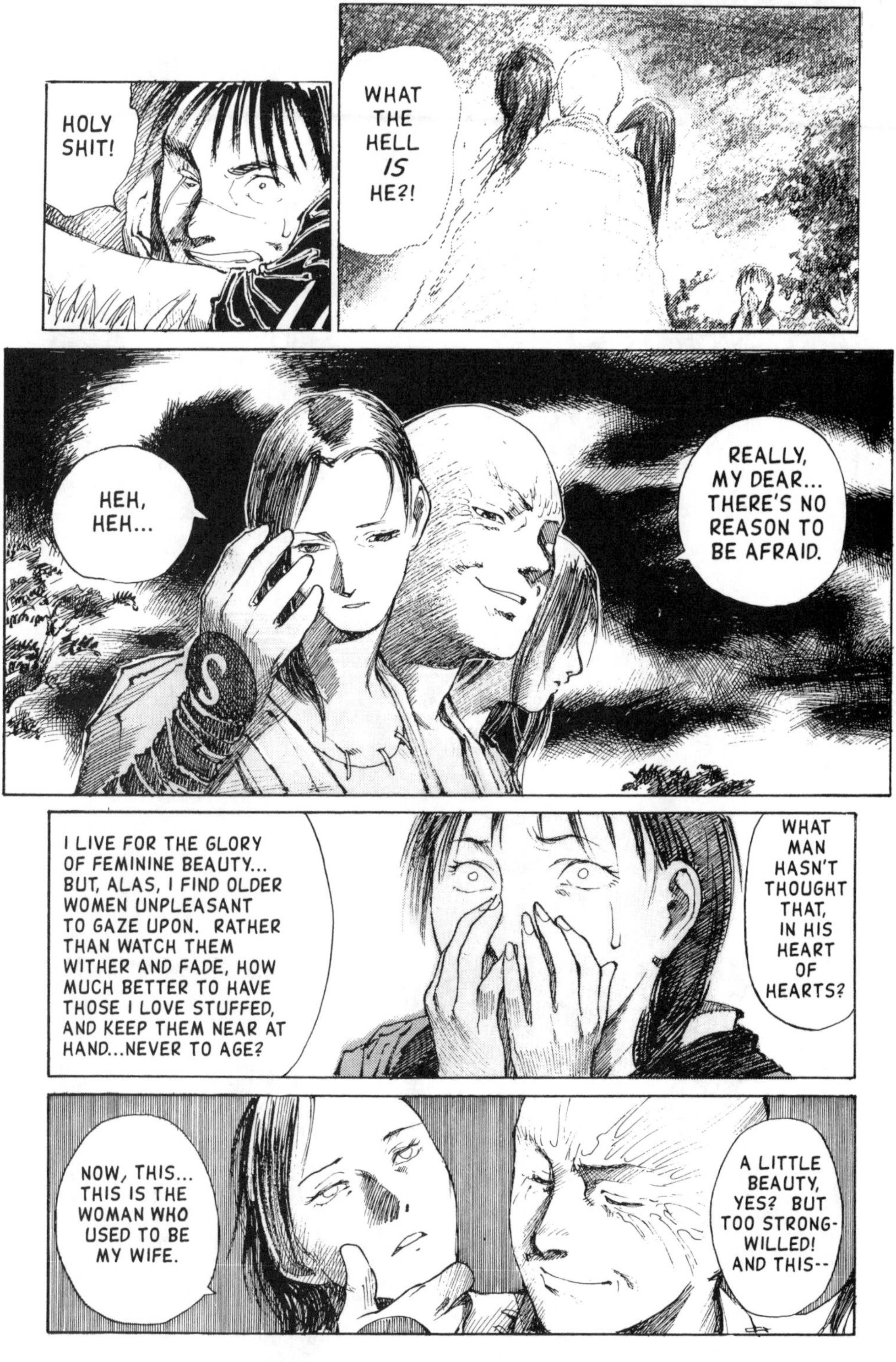
HOLY SHIT!
WHAT THE HELL IS HE?!
HEH, HEH...
REALLY, MY DEAR... THERE'S NO REASON TO BE AFRAID.
I LIVE FOR THE GLORY OF FEMININE BEAUTY... BUT, ALAS, I FIND OLDER WOMEN UNPLEASANT TO GAZE UPON. RATHER THAN WATCH THEM WITHER AND FADE, HOW MUCH BETTER TO HAVE THOSE I LOVE STUFFED, AND KEEP THEM NEAR AT HAND...NEVER TO AGE?
WHAT MAN HASN'T THOUGHT THAT, IN HIS HEART OF HEARTS?
NOW, THIS... THIS IS THE WOMAN WHO USED TO BE MY WIFE.
A LITTLE BEAUTY, YES? BUT TOO STRONG-WILLED! AND THIS--

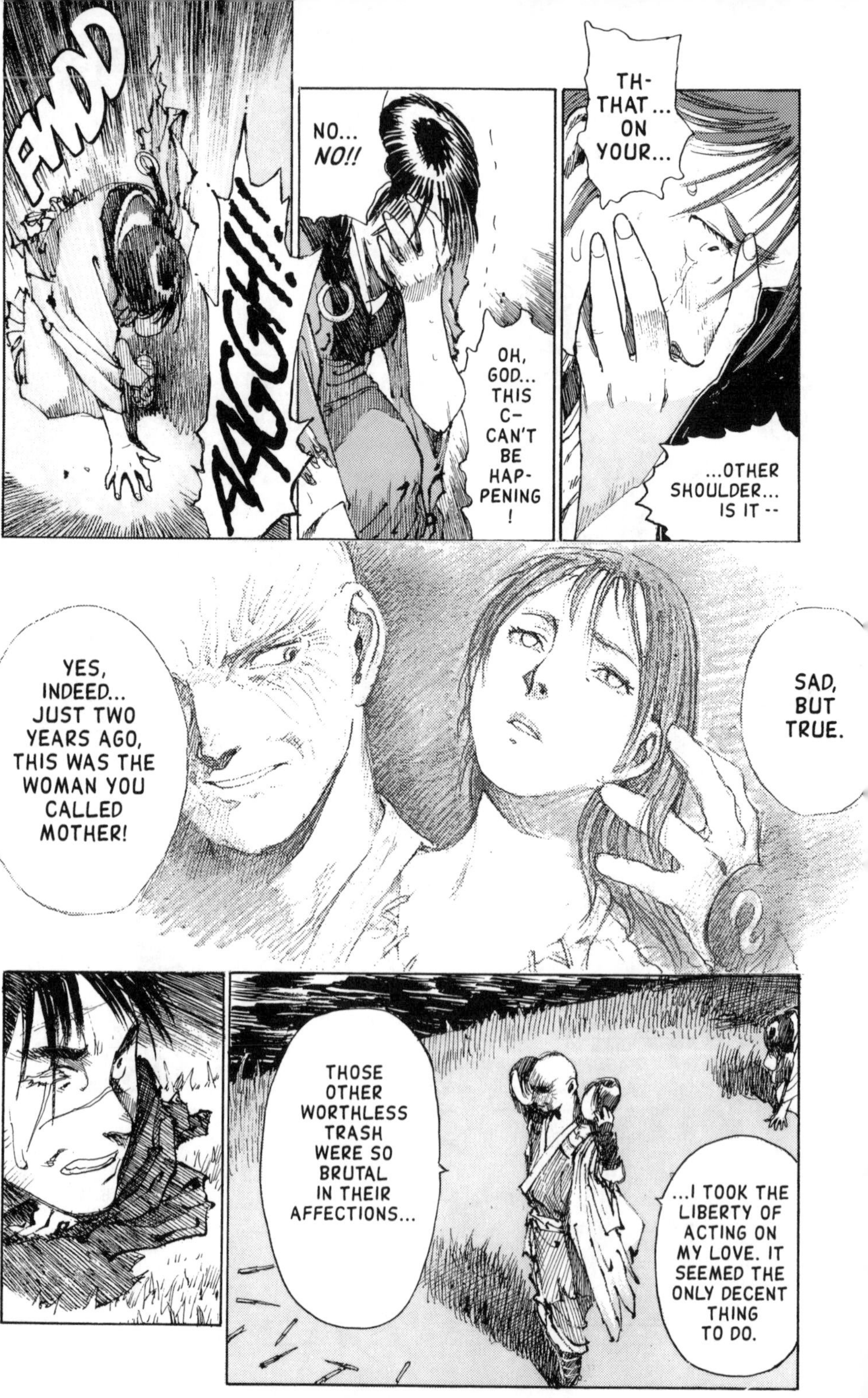
FWOD
AAGH!!!
NO... *NO!!*
OH, GOD... THIS C— CAN'T BE HAP-PENING!
TH-THAT... ON YOUR...
...OTHER SHOULDER... IS IT --
YES, INDEED... JUST TWO YEARS AGO, THIS WAS THE WOMAN YOU CALLED MOTHER!
SAD, BUT TRUE.
THOSE OTHER WORTHLESS TRASH WERE SO BRUTAL IN THEIR AFFECTIONS...
...I TOOK THE LIBERTY OF ACTING ON MY LOVE. IT SEEMED THE ONLY DECENT THING TO DO.

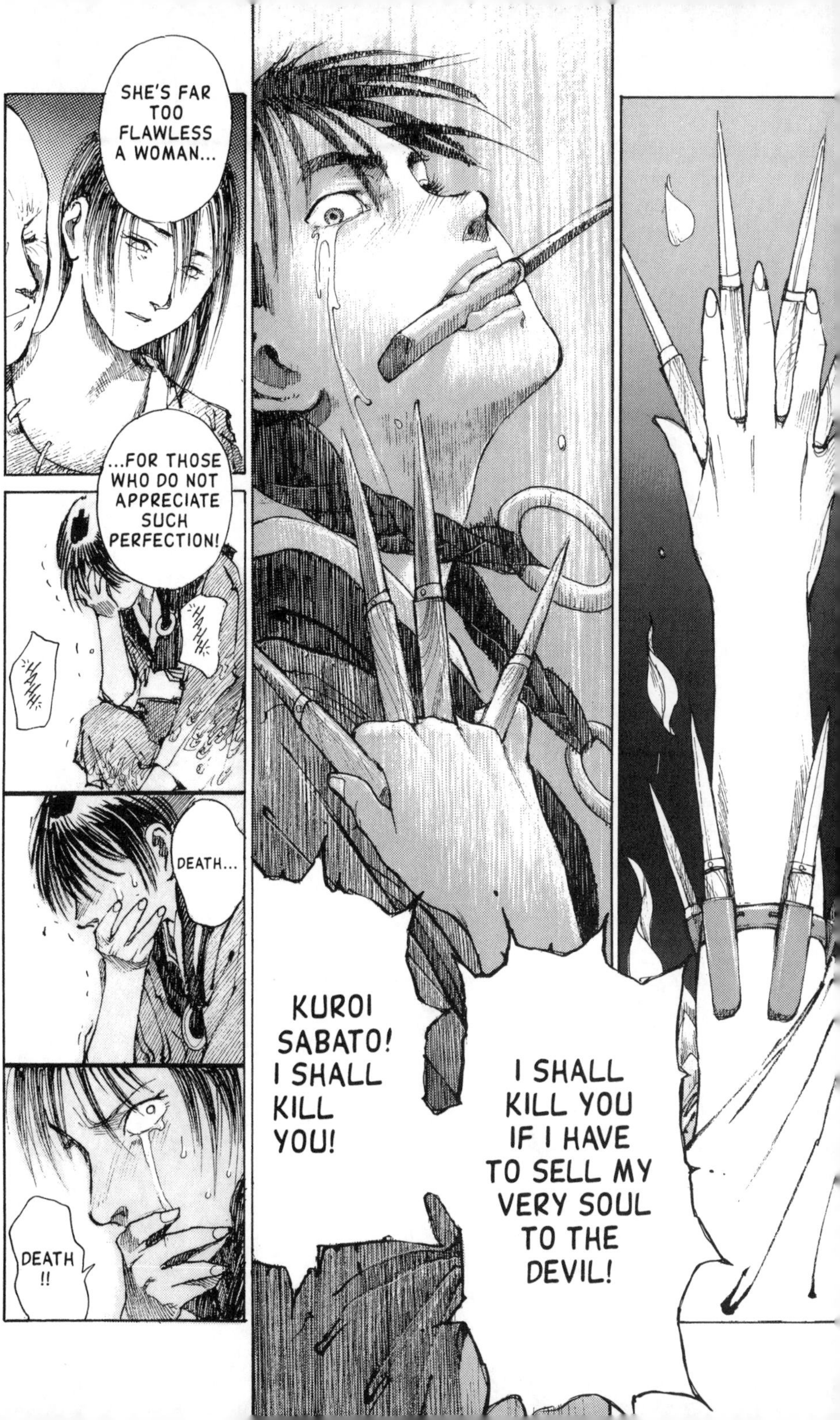
SHE'S FAR TOO FLAWLESS A WOMAN...
...FOR THOSE WHO DO NOT APPRECIATE SUCH PERFECTION!
HAHH
HAHH
DEATH...
DEATH !!
KUROI SABATO! I SHALL KILL YOU!
I SHALL KILL YOU IF I HAVE TO SELL MY VERY SOUL TO THE DEVIL!

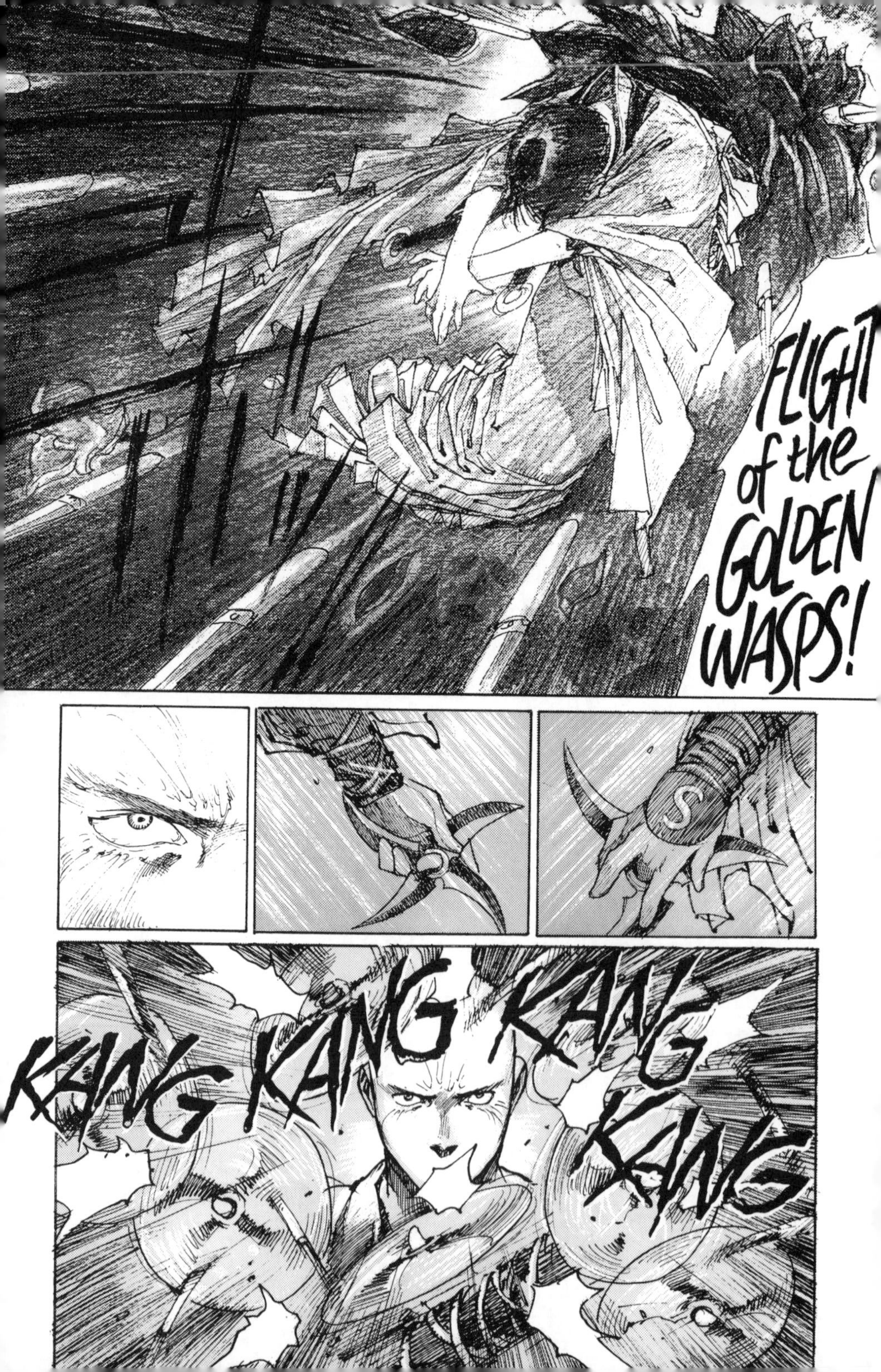
FLIGHT of the GOLDEN WASPS!
KANG KANG KANG KANG
KANG

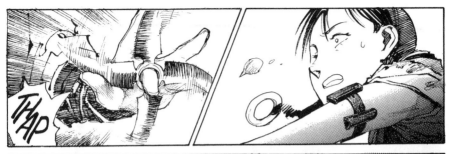

THAP

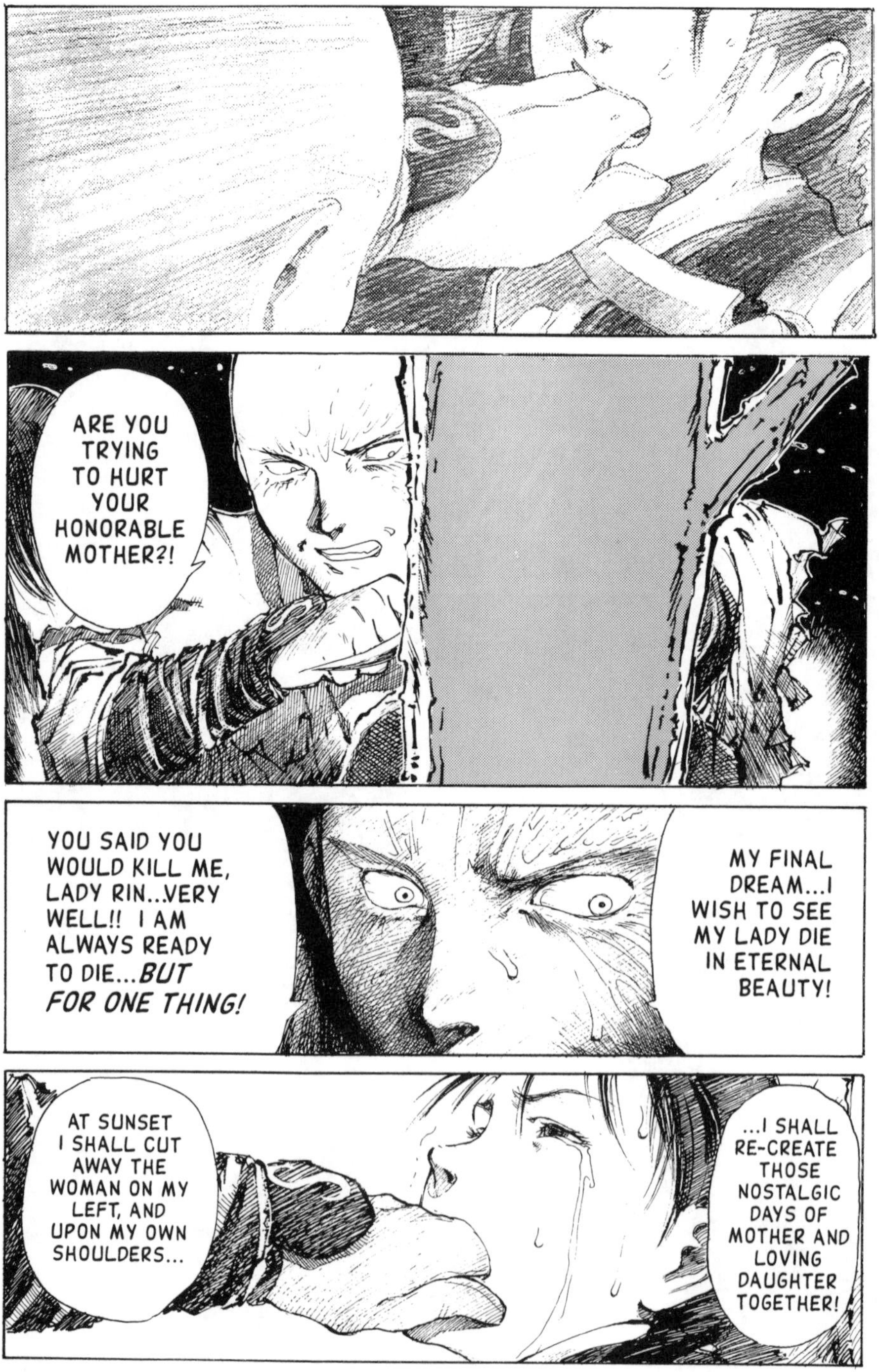
ARE YOU TRYING TO HURT YOUR HONORABLE MOTHER?!
YOU SAID YOU WOULD KILL ME, LADY RIN...VERY WELL!! I AM ALWAYS READY TO DIE...*BUT FOR ONE THING!*
MY FINAL DREAM...I WISH TO SEE MY LADY DIE IN ETERNAL BEAUTY!
AT SUNSET I SHALL CUT AWAY THE WOMAN ON MY LEFT, AND UPON MY OWN SHOULDERS...
...I SHALL RE-CREATE THOSE NOSTALGIC DAYS OF MOTHER AND LOVING DAUGHTER TOGETHER!

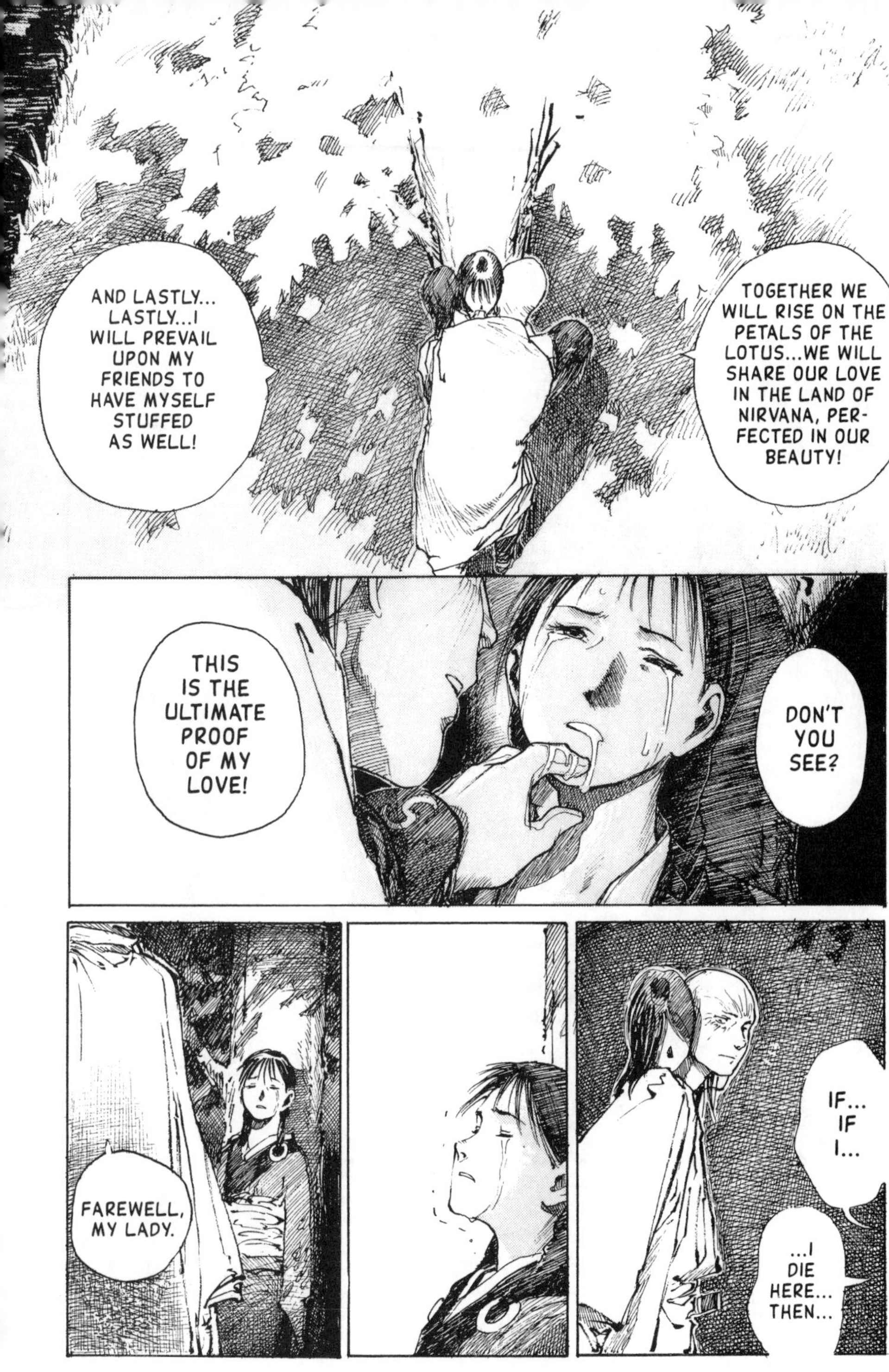
AND LASTLY... LASTLY...I WILL PREVAIL UPON MY FRIENDS TO HAVE MYSELF STUFFED AS WELL!
TOGETHER WE WILL RISE ON THE PETALS OF THE LOTUS...WE WILL SHARE OUR LOVE IN THE LAND OF NIRVANA, PERFECTED IN OUR BEAUTY!
THIS IS THE ULTIMATE PROOF OF MY LOVE!
DON'T YOU SEE?
FAREWELL, MY LADY.
IF... IF I...
...I DIE HERE... THEN...

YES...
THAT IS
CORRECT.
IF YOU
DIE...

...THEN I,
THE ONE
YOU HATE,
SHALL
FOLLOW.

IT SEEMS
AT LAST
YOU
UNDERSTAND.

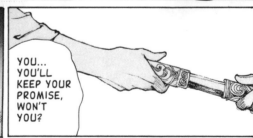

YOU...
YOU'LL
KEEP YOUR
PROMISE,
WON'T
YOU?

IN MY
OWN WAY,
I AM
STILL
SAMURAI,
SO YES...

...AFTER
YOU GO
ON
BEFORE
ME.

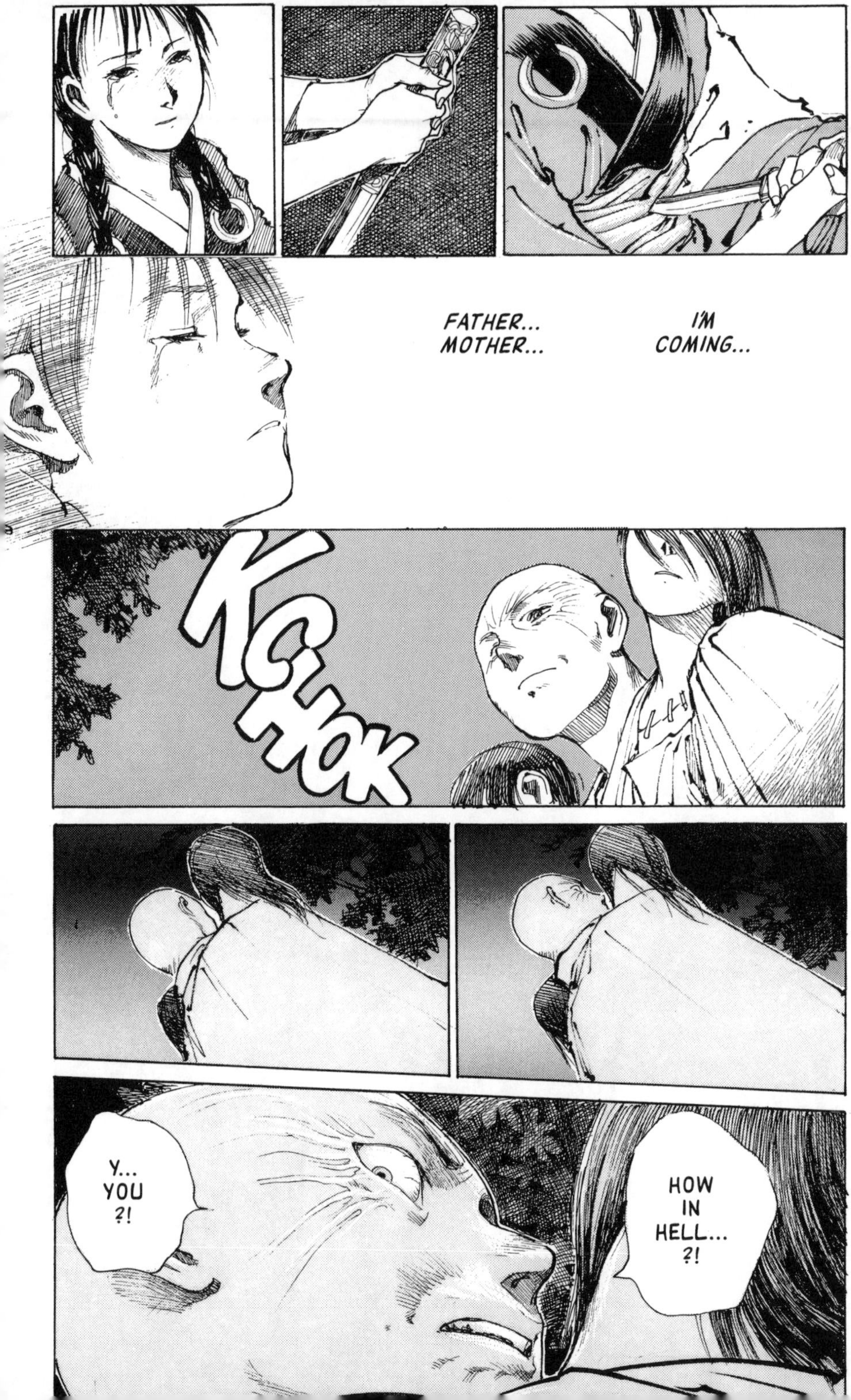
FATHER... MOTHER...
I'M COMING...
KCHOK
Y... YOU ?!
HOW IN HELL... ?!

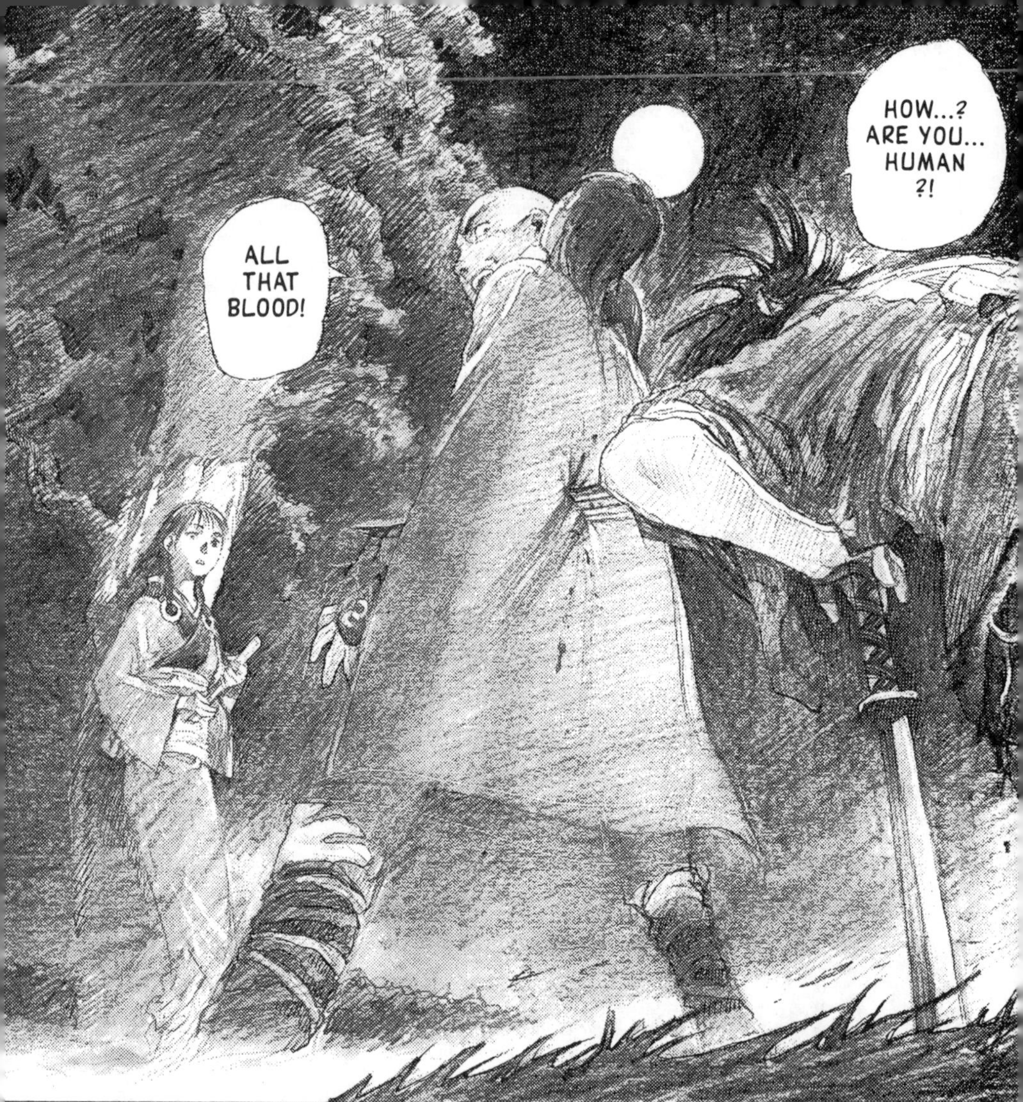
ALL THAT BLOOD!
HOW...? ARE YOU... HUMAN ?!
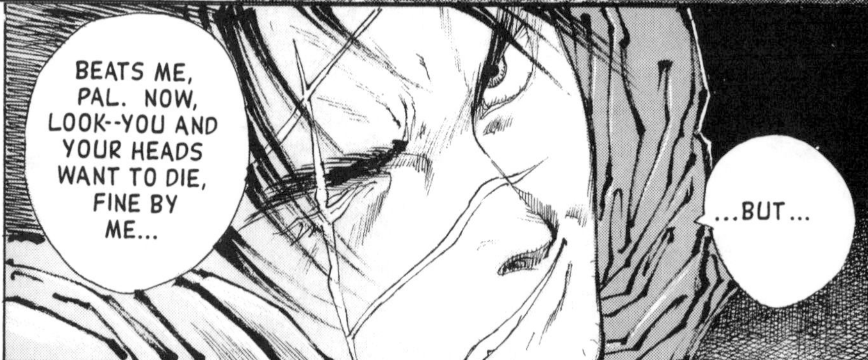
BEATS ME, PAL. NOW, LOOK--YOU AND YOUR HEADS WANT TO DIE, FINE BY ME...
...BUT...

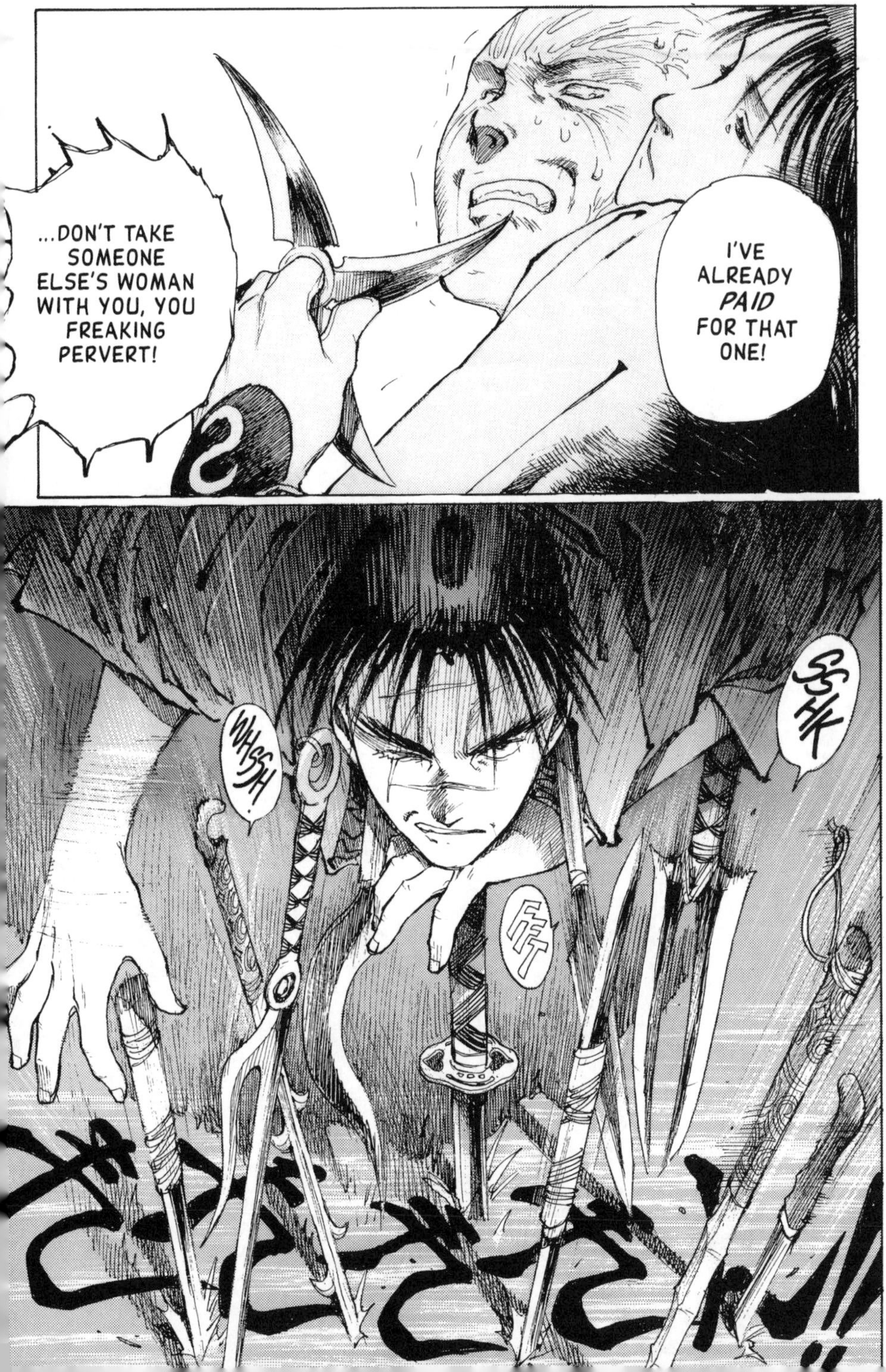

...DON'T TAKE SOMEONE ELSE'S WOMAN WITH YOU, YOU FREAKING PERVERT!
I'VE ALREADY *PAID* FOR THAT ONE!
WHSSH
SSHK
FFT

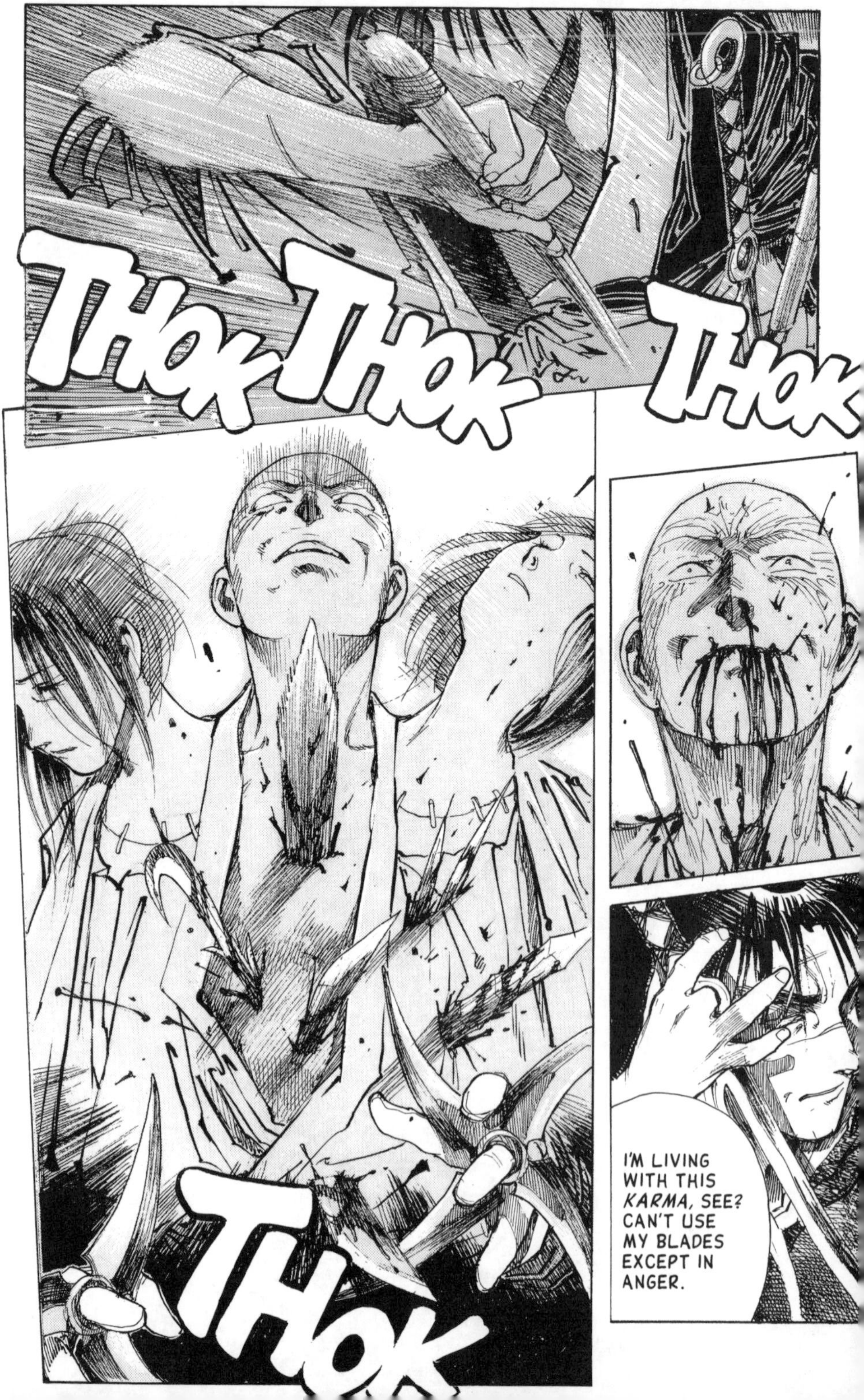
THOK THOK
THOK
THOK
I'M LIVING WITH THIS *KARMA*, SEE? CAN'T USE MY BLADES EXCEPT IN ANGER.

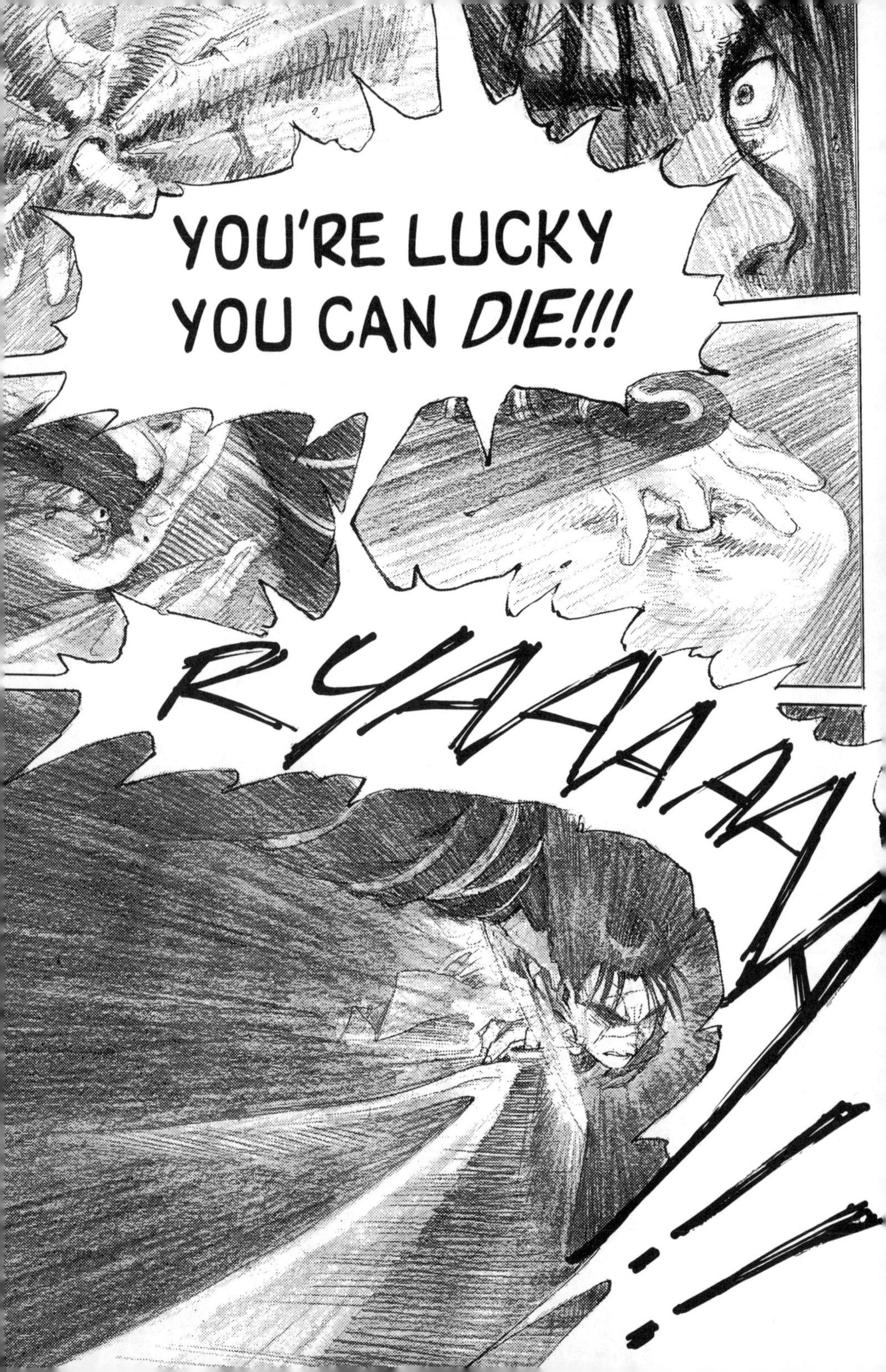
YOU'RE LUCKY YOU CAN *DIE*!!!
RYAAAAAAAH!!!

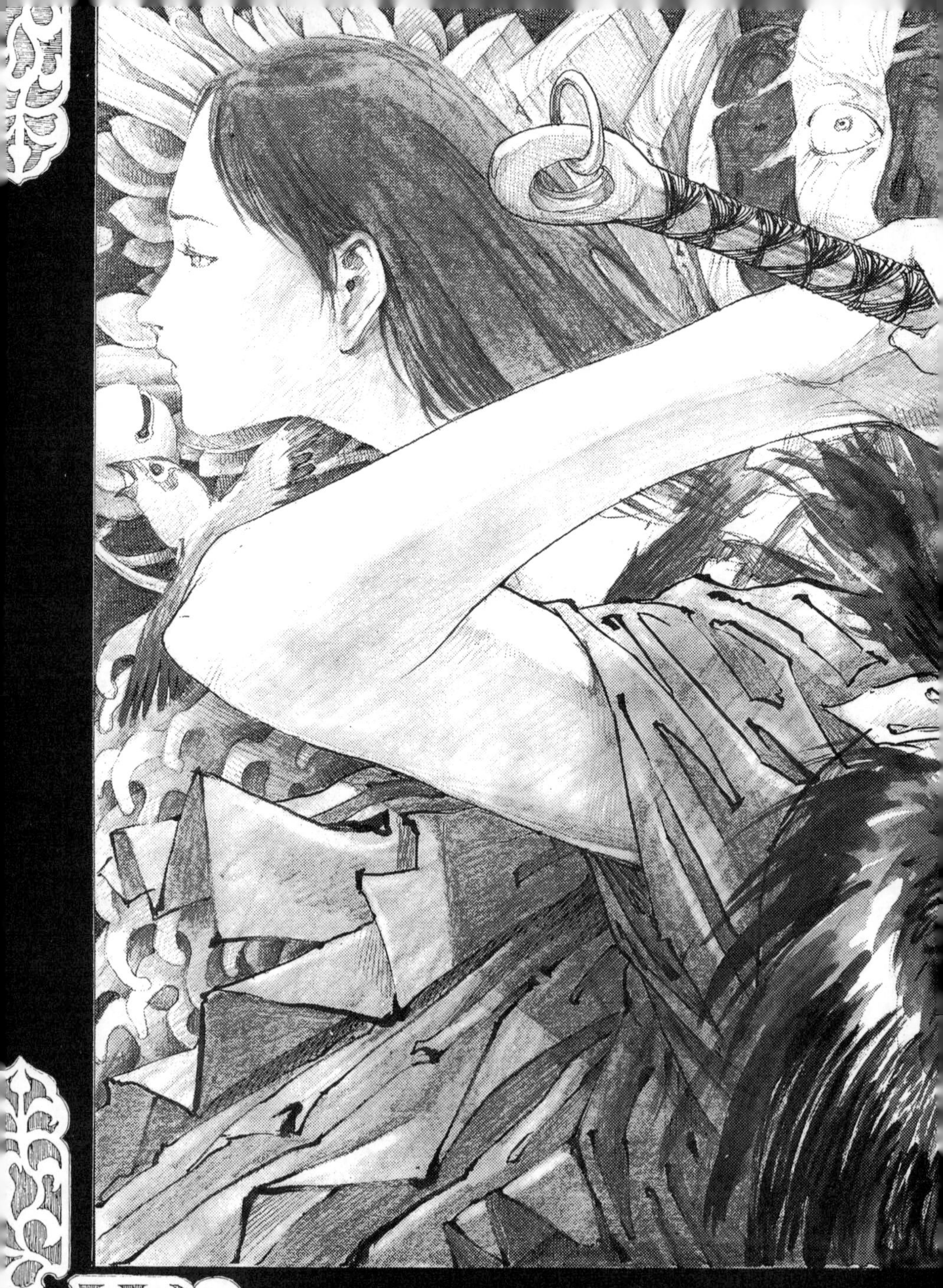

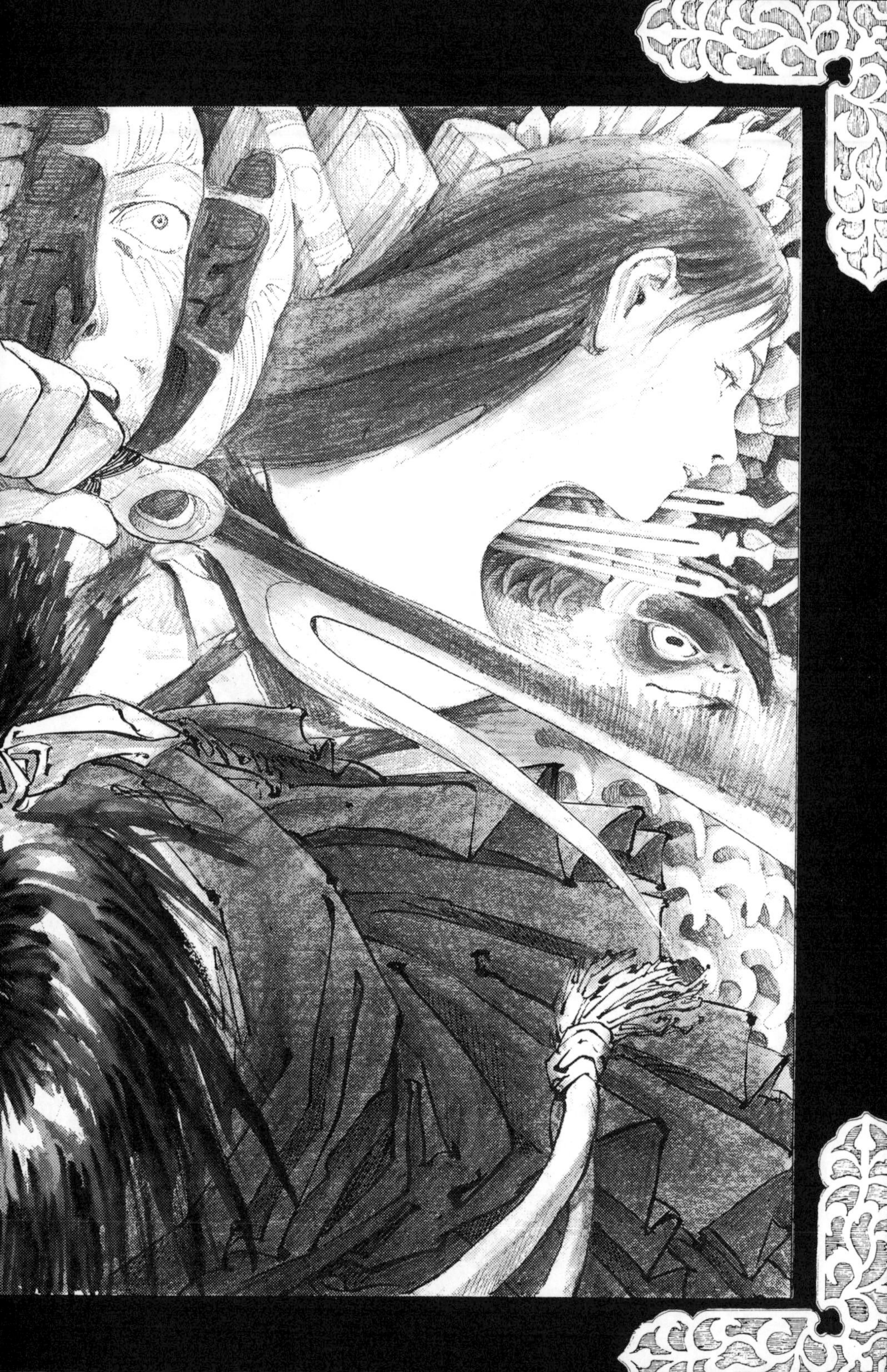

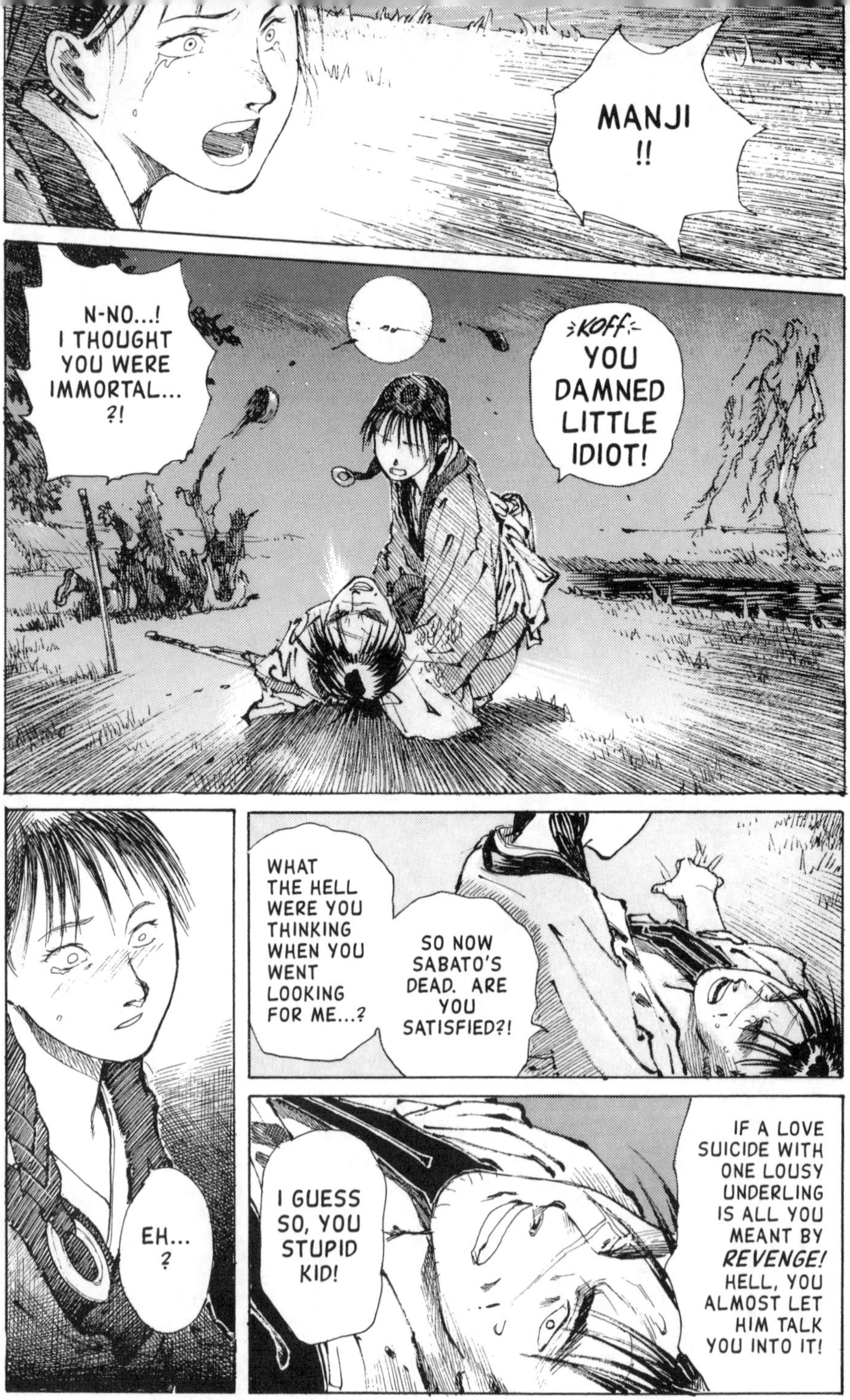
MANJI !!
N-NO...! I THOUGHT YOU WERE IMMORTAL... ?!
KOFF
YOU DAMNED LITTLE IDIOT!
WHAT THE HELL WERE YOU THINKING WHEN YOU WENT LOOKING FOR ME...?
SO NOW SABATO'S DEAD. ARE YOU SATISFIED?!
EH... ?
I GUESS SO, YOU STUPID KID!
IF A LOVE SUICIDE WITH ONE LOUSY UNDERLING IS ALL YOU MEANT BY *REVENGE!* HELL, YOU ALMOST LET HIM TALK YOU INTO IT!

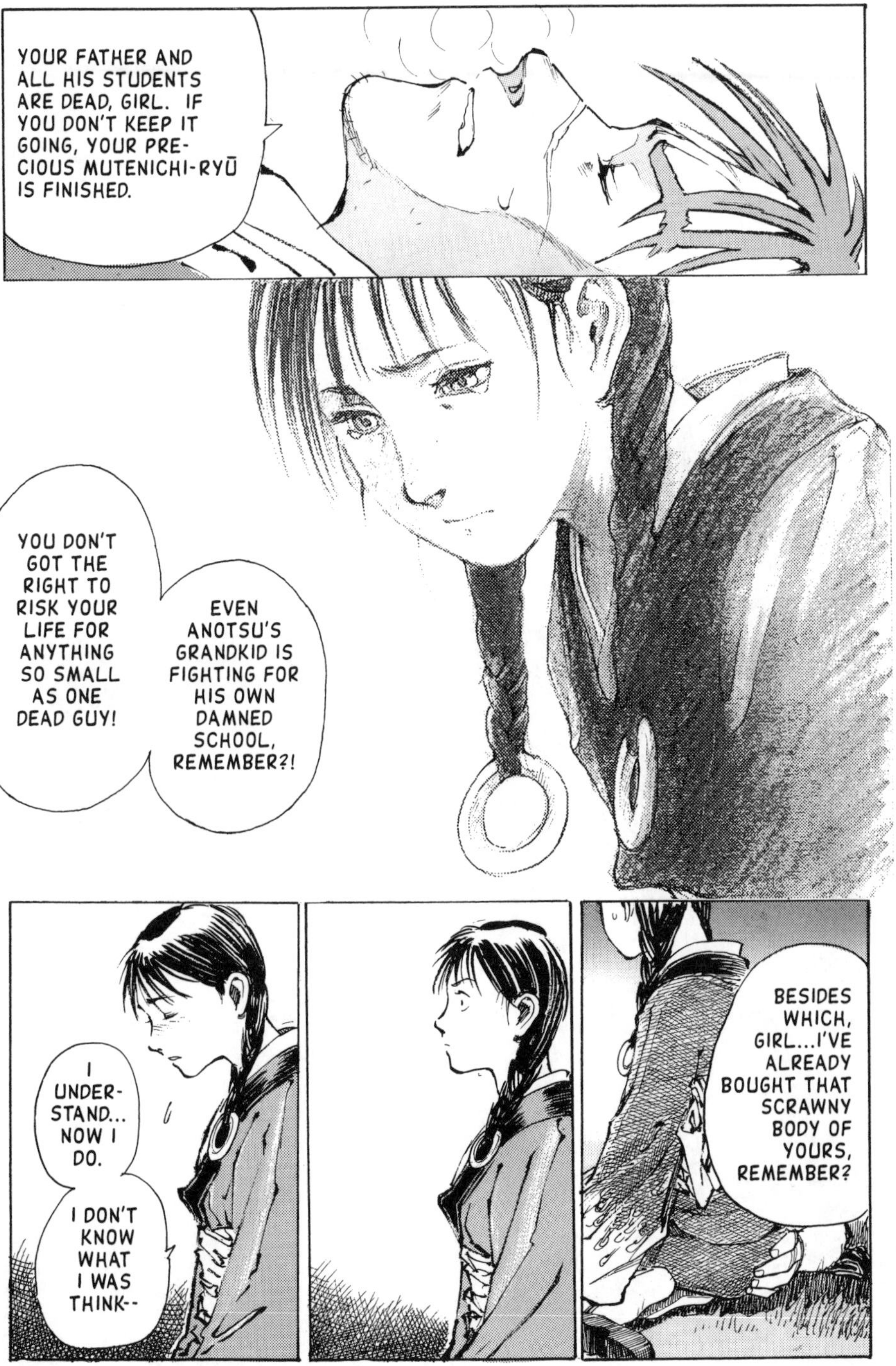
YOUR FATHER AND ALL HIS STUDENTS ARE DEAD, GIRL. IF YOU DON'T KEEP IT GOING, YOUR PRECIOUS MUTENICHI-RYŪ IS FINISHED.
YOU DON'T GOT THE RIGHT TO RISK YOUR LIFE FOR ANYTHING SO SMALL AS ONE DEAD GUY!
EVEN ANOTSU'S GRANDKID IS FIGHTING FOR HIS OWN DAMNED SCHOOL, REMEMBER?!
I UNDERSTAND... NOW I DO.
I DON'T KNOW WHAT I WAS THINK--
BESIDES WHICH, GIRL...I'VE ALREADY BOUGHT THAT SCRAWNY BODY OF YOURS, REMEMBER?

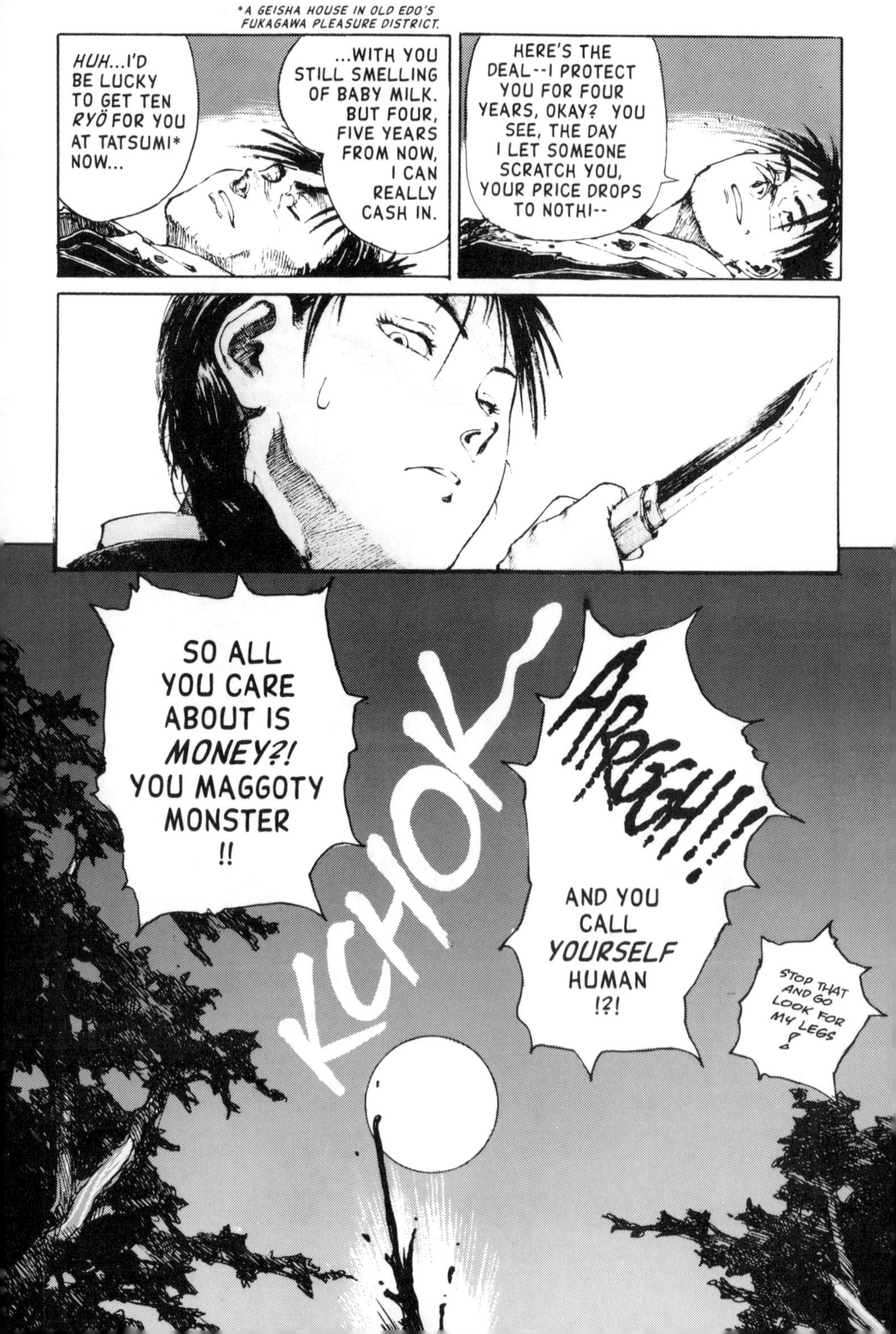
*A GEISHA HOUSE IN OLD EDO'S FUKAGAWA PLEASURE DISTRICT.
HUH...I'D BE LUCKY TO GET TEN RYÖ FOR YOU AT TATSUMI* NOW...
...WITH YOU STILL SMELLING OF BABY MILK. BUT FOUR, FIVE YEARS FROM NOW, I CAN REALLY CASH IN.
HERE'S THE DEAL--I PROTECT YOU FOR FOUR YEARS, OKAY? YOU SEE, THE DAY I LET SOMEONE SCRATCH YOU, YOUR PRICE DROPS TO NOTHI--
SO ALL YOU CARE ABOUT IS MONEY?! YOU MAGGOTY MONSTER !!
KCHOK
ARRGH!!!
AND YOU CALL YOURSELF HUMAN !?!
STOP THAT AND GO LOOK FOR MY LEGS !

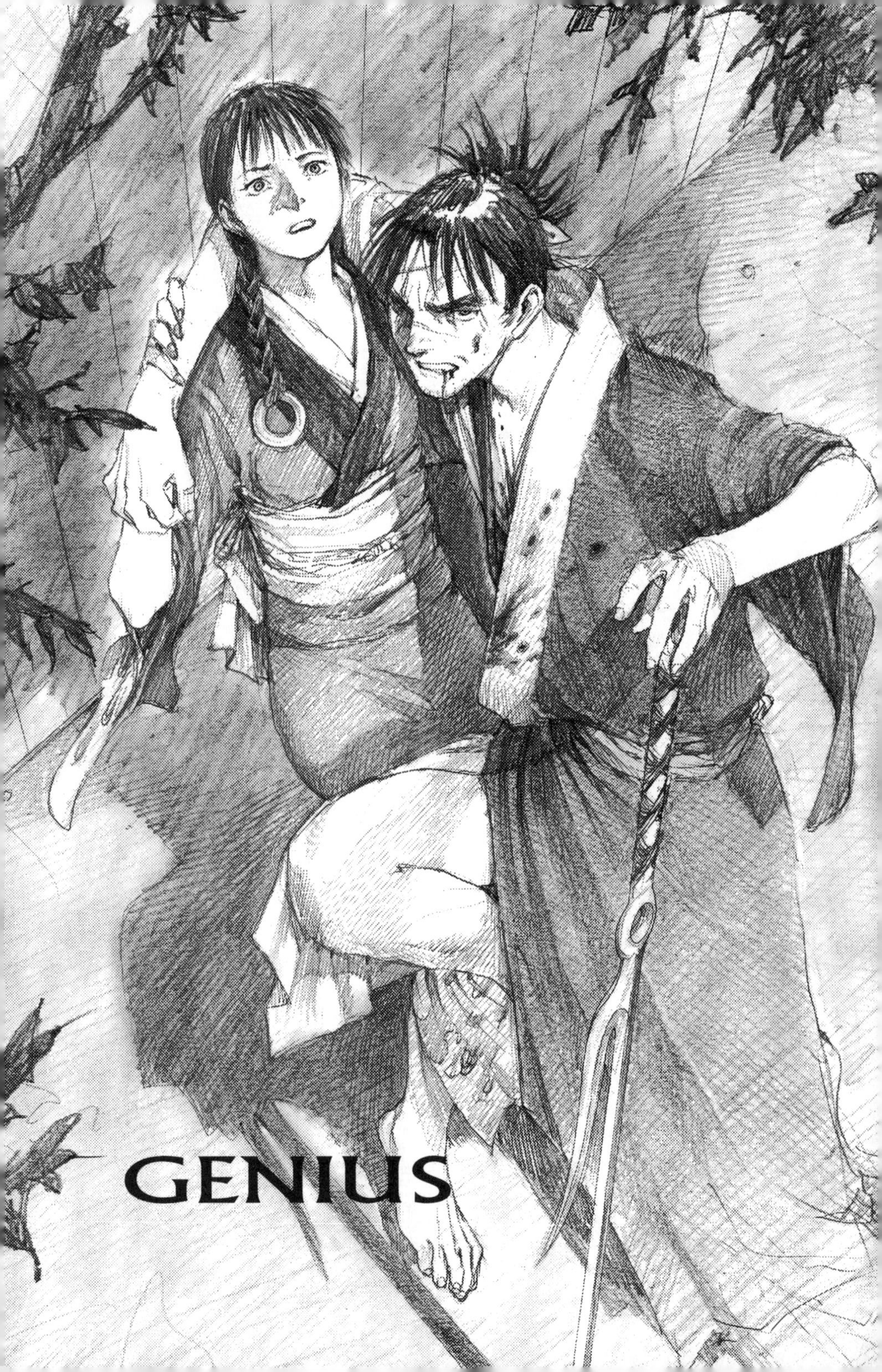

GENIUS

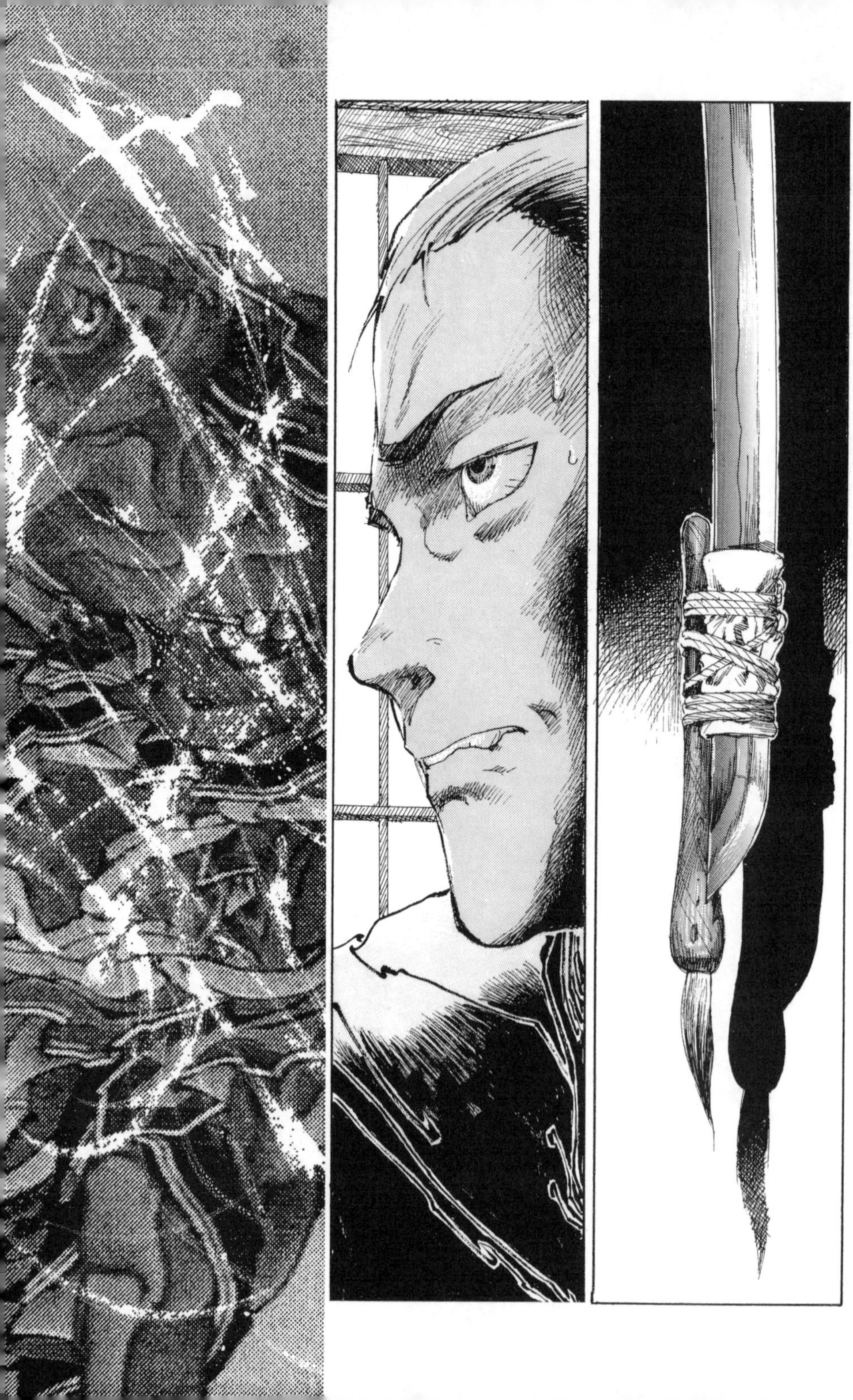

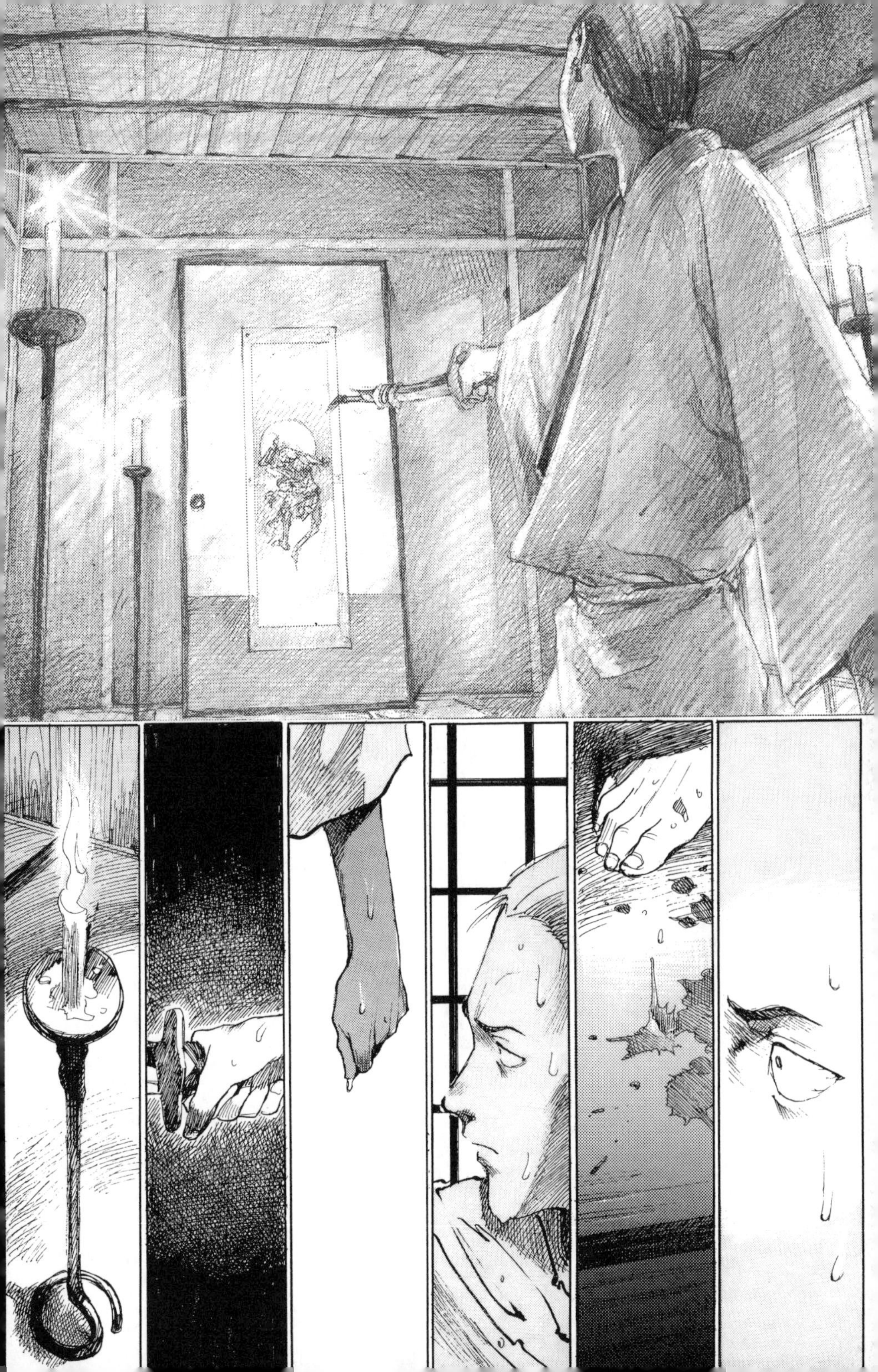

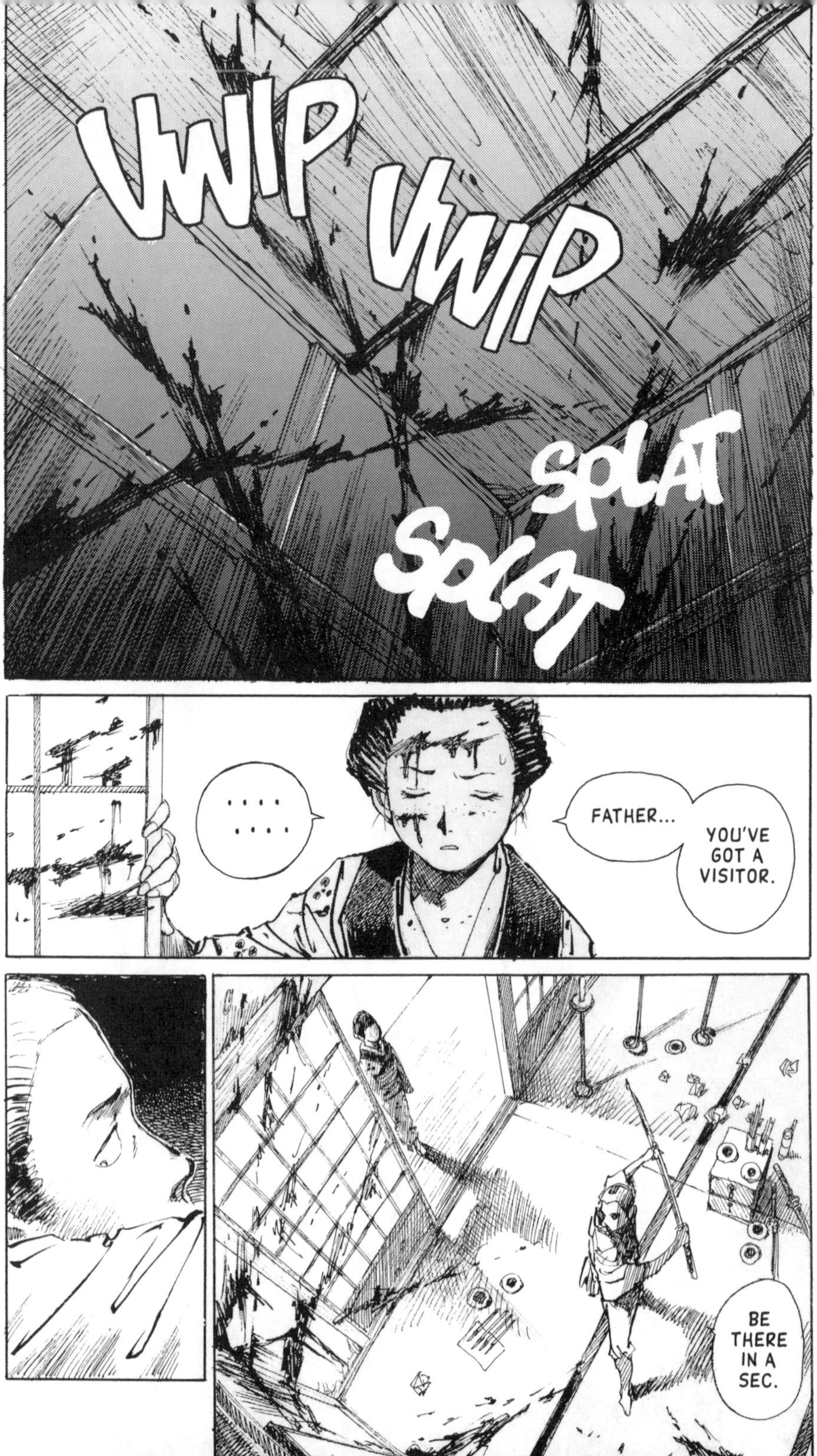
VWIP
VWIP
SPLAT
SPLAT
....
FATHER...
YOU'VE GOT A VISITOR.
BE THERE IN A SEC.

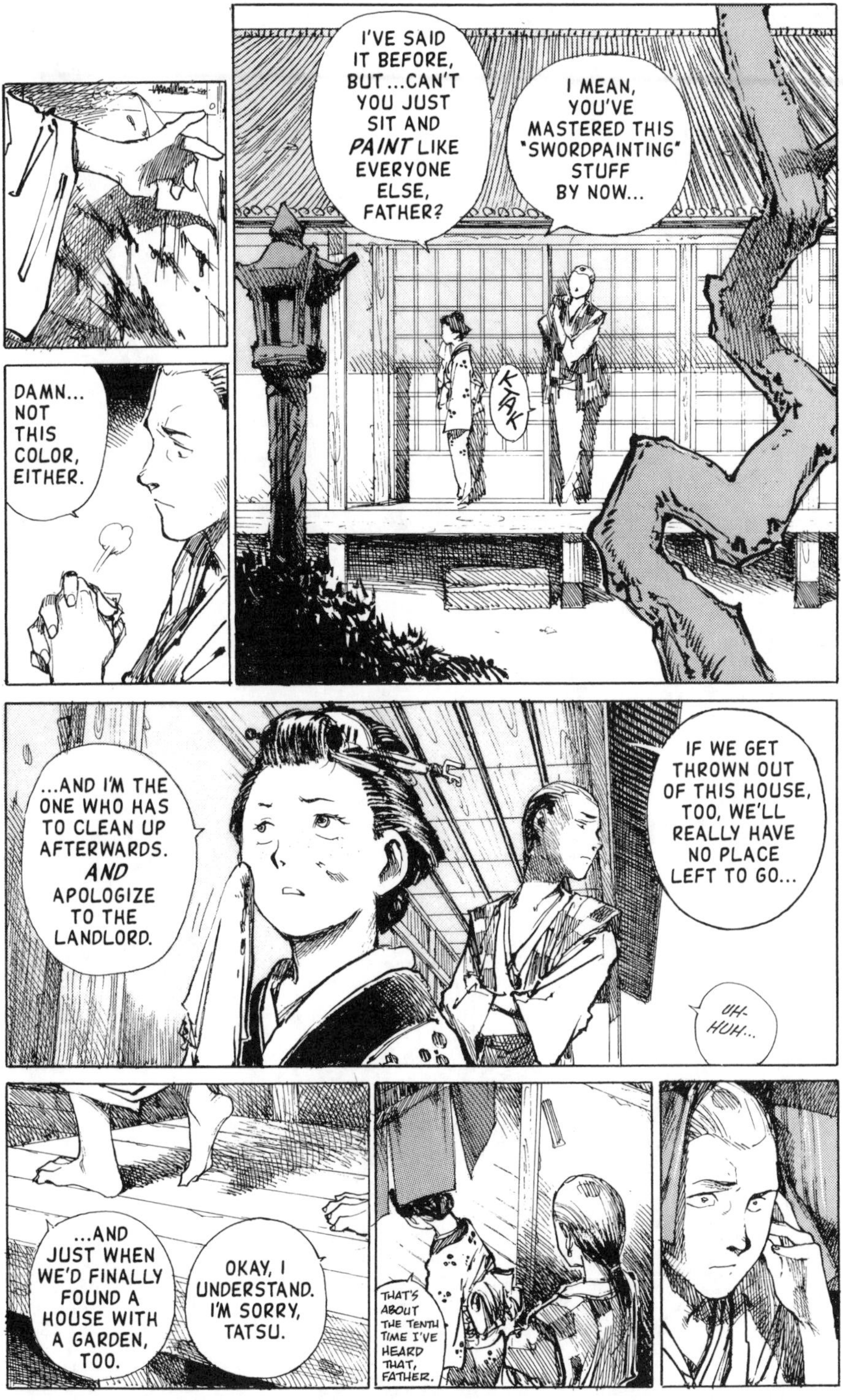
DAMN... NOT THIS COLOR, EITHER.
I'VE SAID IT BEFORE, BUT...CAN'T YOU JUST SIT AND *PAINT* LIKE EVERYONE ELSE, FATHER?
I MEAN, YOU'VE MASTERED THIS "SWORDPAINTING" STUFF BY NOW...
KAK
...AND I'M THE ONE WHO HAS TO CLEAN UP AFTERWARDS. *AND* APOLOGIZE TO THE LANDLORD.
IF WE GET THROWN OUT OF THIS HOUSE, TOO, WE'LL REALLY HAVE NO PLACE LEFT TO GO...
UH-HUH...
...AND JUST WHEN WE'D FINALLY FOUND A HOUSE WITH A GARDEN, TOO.
OKAY, I UNDERSTAND. I'M SORRY, TATSU.
THAT'S ABOUT THE TENTH TIME I'VE HEARD THAT, FATHER.

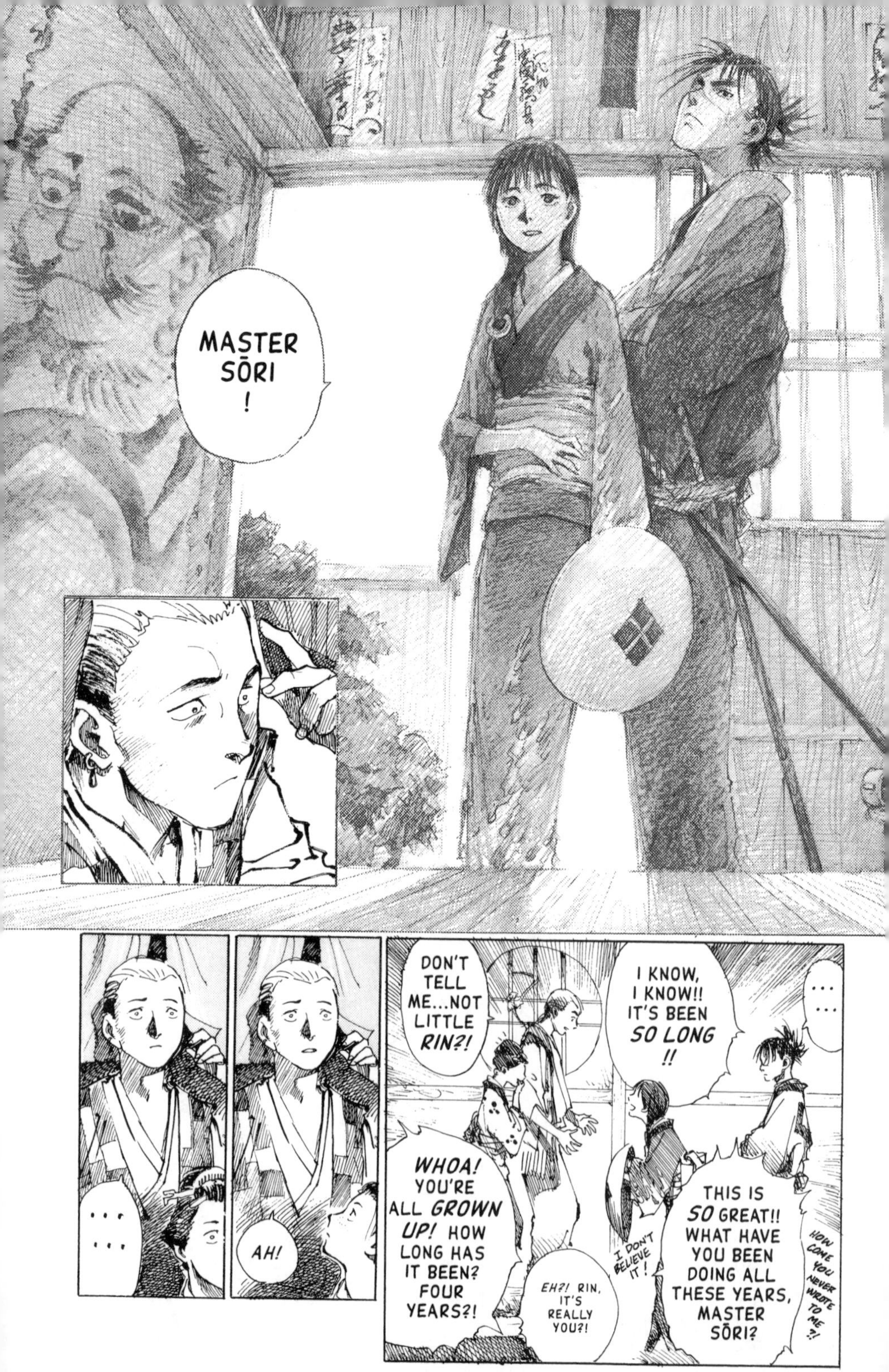
MASTER SŌRI !
......
AH!
DON'T TELL ME...NOT LITTLE RIN?!
I KNOW, I KNOW!! IT'S BEEN SO LONG !!
......
WHOA! YOU'RE ALL GROWN UP! HOW LONG HAS IT BEEN? FOUR YEARS?!
EH?! RIN, IT'S REALLY YOU?!
I DON'T BELIEVE IT!
THIS IS SO GREAT!! WHAT HAVE YOU BEEN DOING ALL THESE YEARS, MASTER SŌRI?
HOW COME YOU NEVER WROTE TO ME?!

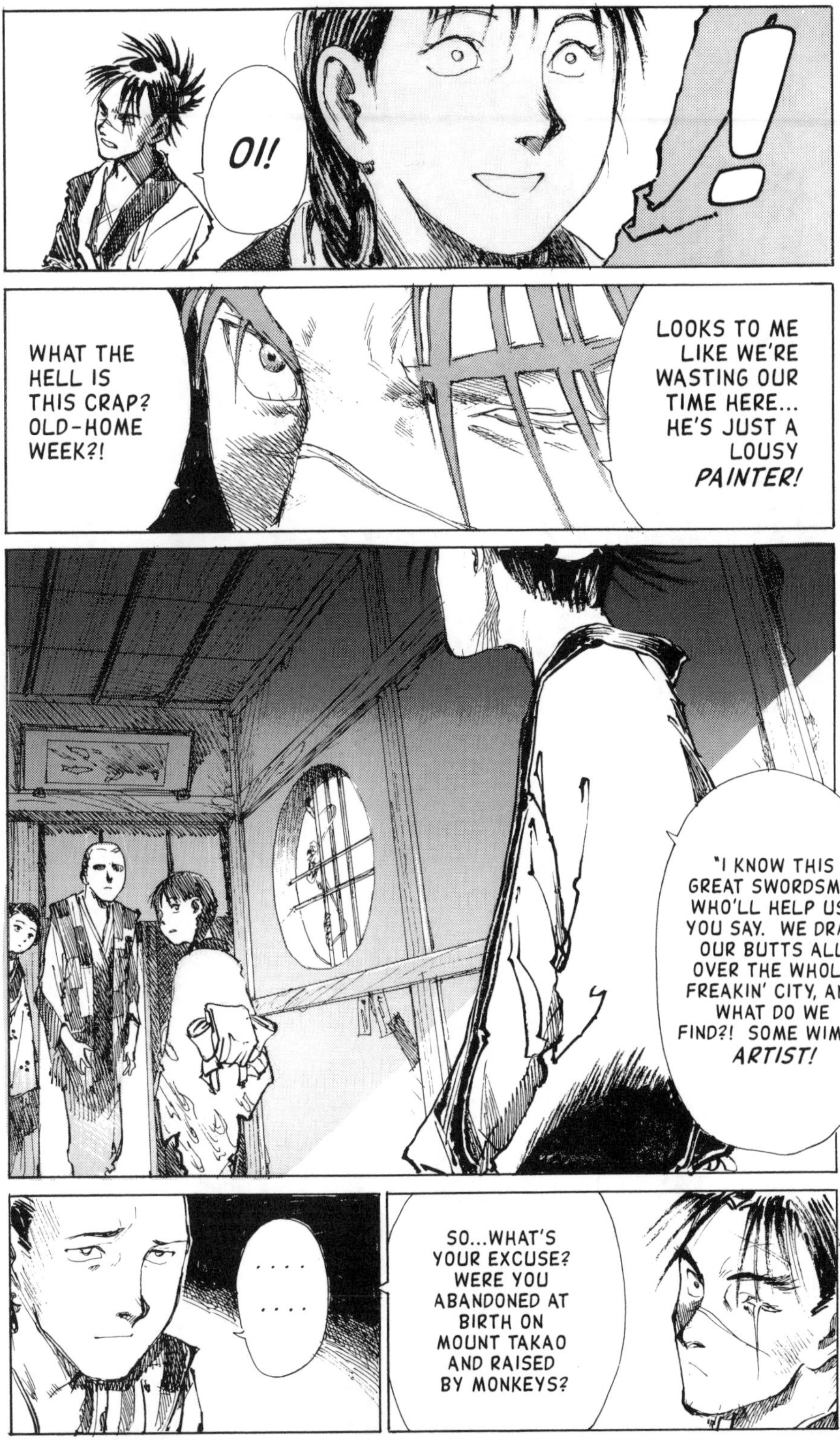
OI!
WHAT THE HELL IS THIS CRAP? OLD-HOME WEEK?!
LOOKS TO ME LIKE WE'RE WASTING OUR TIME HERE... HE'S JUST A LOUSY *PAINTER!*
"I KNOW THIS GREAT SWORDSMAN WHO'LL HELP US," YOU SAY. WE DRAG OUR BUTTS ALL OVER THE WHOLE FREAKIN' CITY, AND WHAT DO WE FIND?! SOME WIMPY *ARTIST!*
. . . .
. . . .
SO...WHAT'S YOUR EXCUSE? WERE YOU ABANDONED AT BIRTH ON MOUNT TAKAO AND RAISED BY MONKEYS?

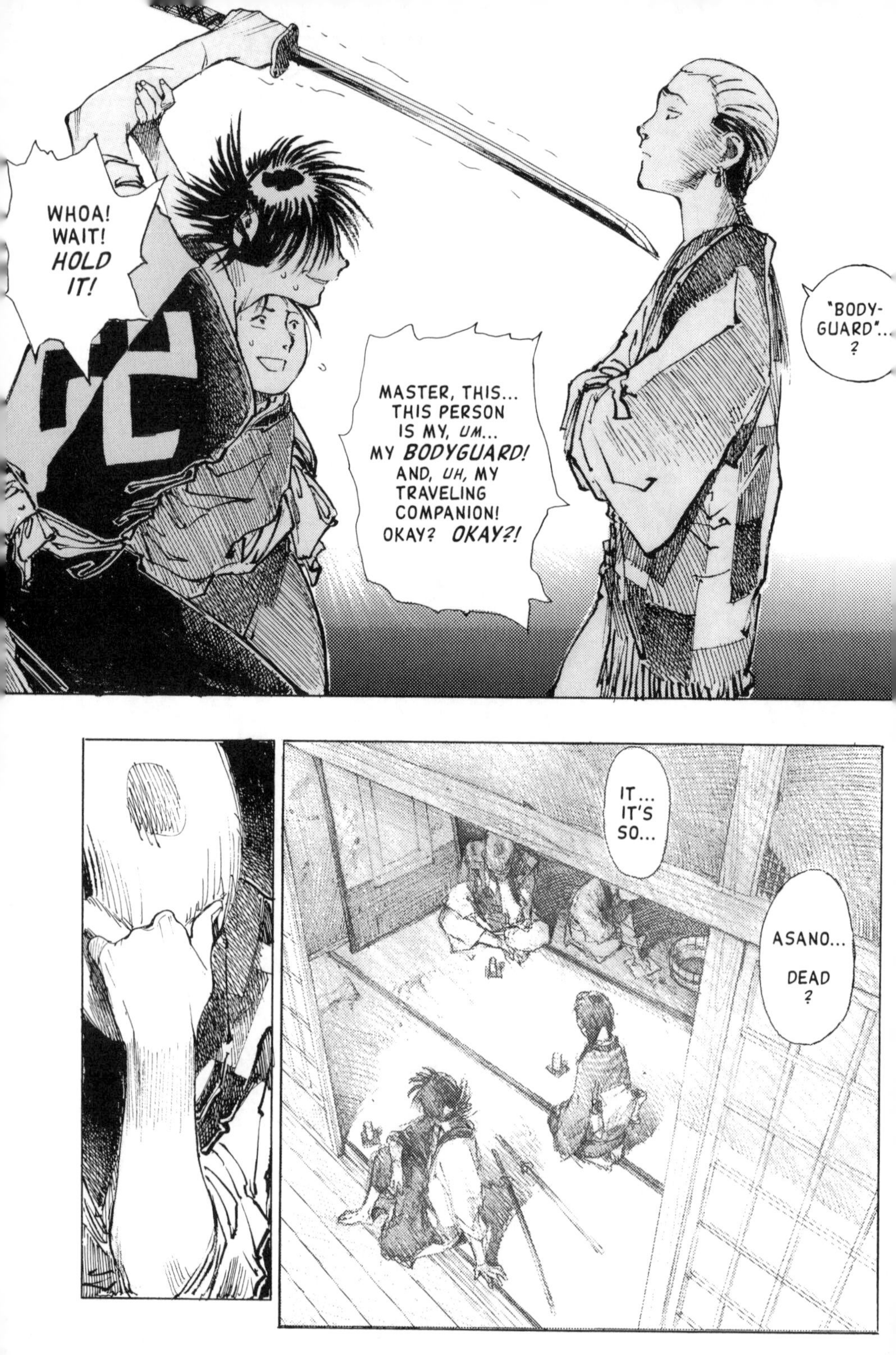
WHOA! WAIT! HOLD IT!
MASTER, THIS... THIS PERSON IS MY, UM... MY BODYGUARD! AND, UH, MY TRAVELING COMPANION! OKAY? OKAY?!
"BODY-GUARD"...?
IT... IT'S SO...
ASANO... DEAD?

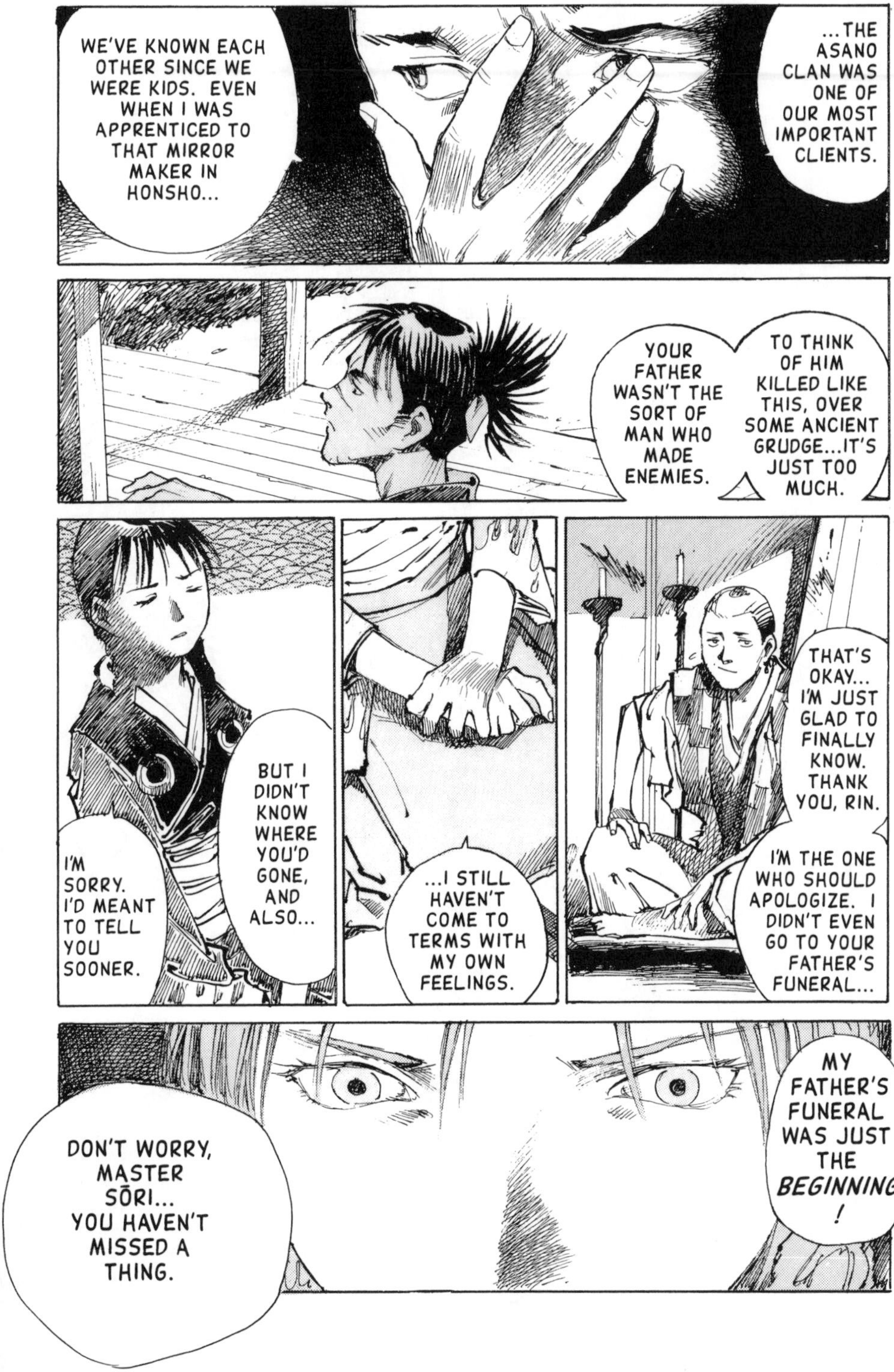
WE'VE KNOWN EACH OTHER SINCE WE WERE KIDS. EVEN WHEN I WAS APPRENTICED TO THAT MIRROR MAKER IN HONSHO...
...THE ASANO CLAN WAS ONE OF OUR MOST IMPORTANT CLIENTS.
YOUR FATHER WASN'T THE SORT OF MAN WHO MADE ENEMIES.
TO THINK OF HIM KILLED LIKE THIS, OVER SOME ANCIENT GRUDGE...IT'S JUST TOO MUCH.
I'M SORRY. I'D MEANT TO TELL YOU SOONER.
BUT I DIDN'T KNOW WHERE YOU'D GONE, AND ALSO...
...I STILL HAVEN'T COME TO TERMS WITH MY OWN FEELINGS.
THAT'S OKAY... I'M JUST GLAD TO FINALLY KNOW. THANK YOU, RIN.
I'M THE ONE WHO SHOULD APOLOGIZE. I DIDN'T EVEN GO TO YOUR FATHER'S FUNERAL...
DON'T WORRY, MASTER SŌRI... YOU HAVEN'T MISSED A THING.
MY FATHER'S FUNERAL WAS JUST THE *BEGINNING*!

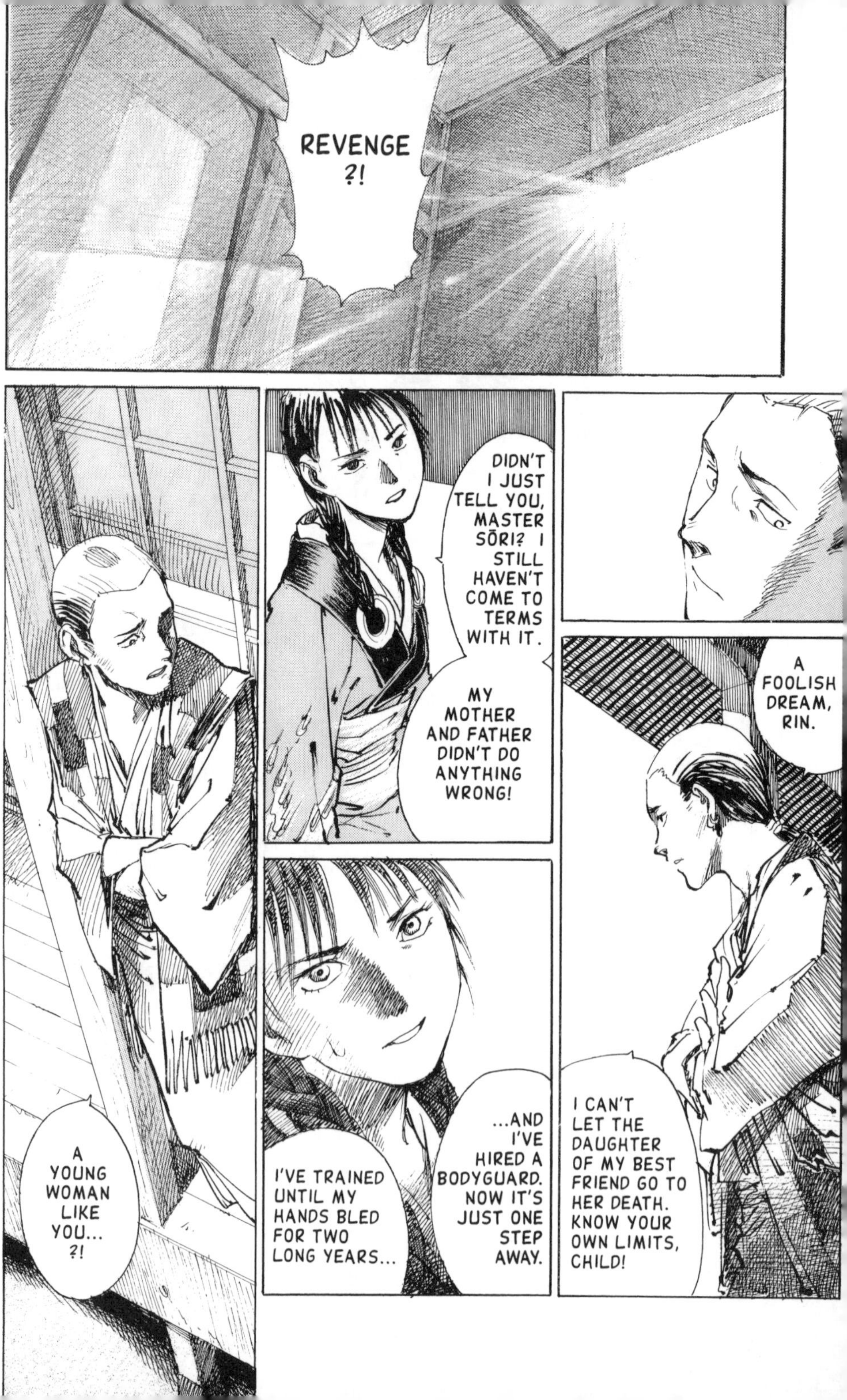
REVENGE ?!
A YOUNG WOMAN LIKE YOU... ?!
DIDN'T I JUST TELL YOU, MASTER SŌRI? I STILL HAVEN'T COME TO TERMS WITH IT.
MY MOTHER AND FATHER DIDN'T DO ANYTHING WRONG!
I'VE TRAINED UNTIL MY HANDS BLED FOR TWO LONG YEARS...
...AND I'VE HIRED A BODYGUARD. NOW IT'S JUST ONE STEP AWAY.
A FOOLISH DREAM, RIN.
I CAN'T LET THE DAUGHTER OF MY BEST FRIEND GO TO HER DEATH. KNOW YOUR OWN LIMITS, CHILD!

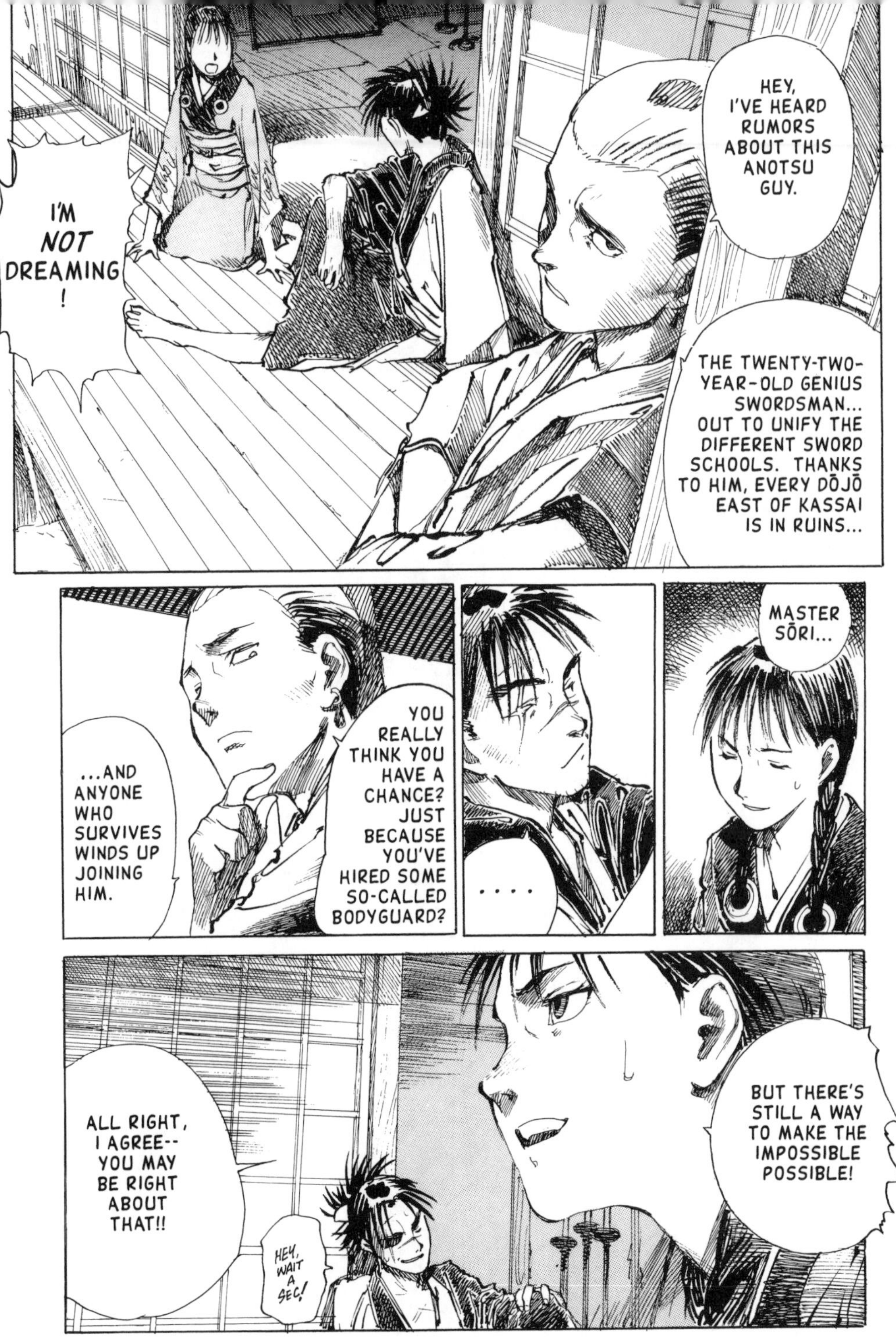
I'M NOT DREAMING!
HEY, I'VE HEARD RUMORS ABOUT THIS ANOTSU GUY.
THE TWENTY-TWO-YEAR-OLD GENIUS SWORDSMAN... OUT TO UNIFY THE DIFFERENT SWORD SCHOOLS. THANKS TO HIM, EVERY DŌJŌ EAST OF KASSAI IS IN RUINS...
...AND ANYONE WHO SURVIVES WINDS UP JOINING HIM.
YOU REALLY THINK YOU HAVE A CHANCE? JUST BECAUSE YOU'VE HIRED SOME SO-CALLED BODYGUARD?
....
MASTER SŌRI...
ALL RIGHT, I AGREE-- YOU MAY BE RIGHT ABOUT THAT!!
HEY, WAIT A SEC!
BUT THERE'S STILL A WAY TO MAKE THE IMPOSSIBLE POSSIBLE!

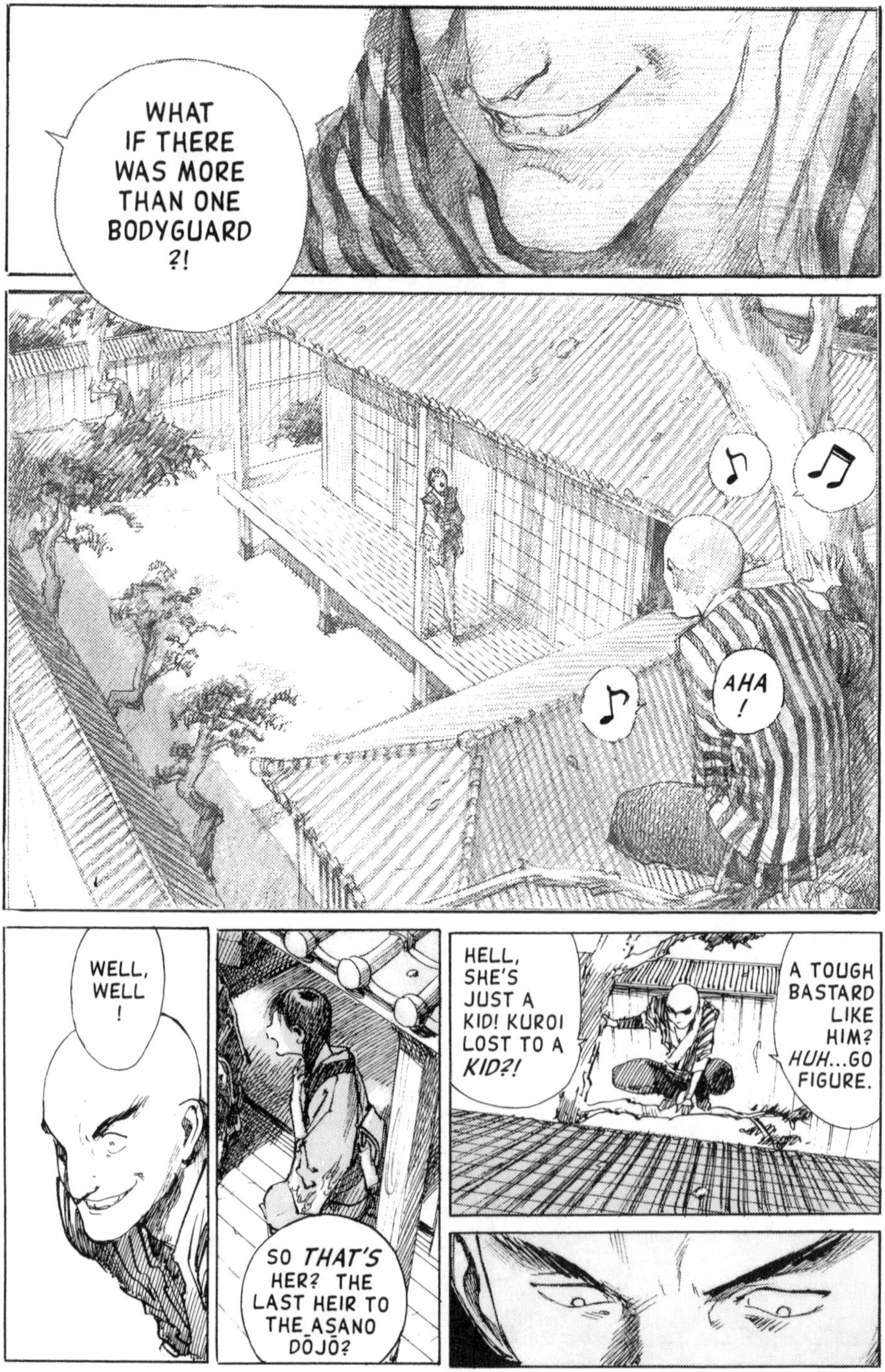
WHAT IF THERE WAS MORE THAN ONE BODYGUARD ?!
♪
♫
♪
AHA !
WELL, WELL !
SO *THAT'S* HER? THE LAST HEIR TO THE ASANO DŌJŌ?
HELL, SHE'S JUST A KID! KUROI LOST TO A *KID?!*
A TOUGH BASTARD LIKE HIM? *HUH*...GO FIGURE.

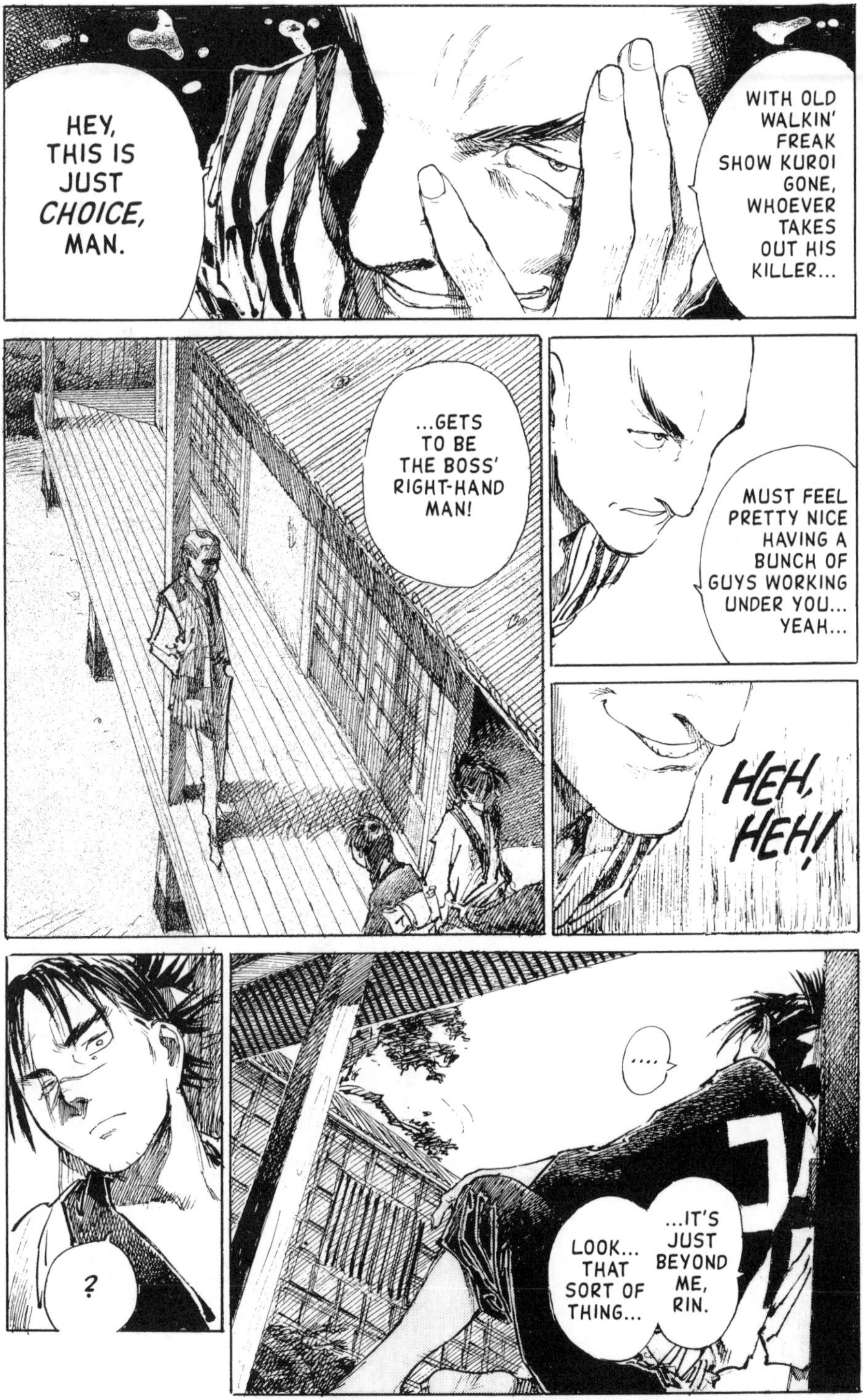
HEY, THIS IS JUST *CHOICE,* MAN.
WITH OLD WALKIN' FREAK SHOW KUROI GONE, WHOEVER TAKES OUT HIS KILLER...
...GETS TO BE THE BOSS' RIGHT-HAND MAN!
MUST FEEL PRETTY NICE HAVING A BUNCH OF GUYS WORKING UNDER YOU... YEAH...
HEH, HEH!
?
....
LOOK... THAT SORT OF THING...
...IT'S JUST BEYOND ME, RIN.

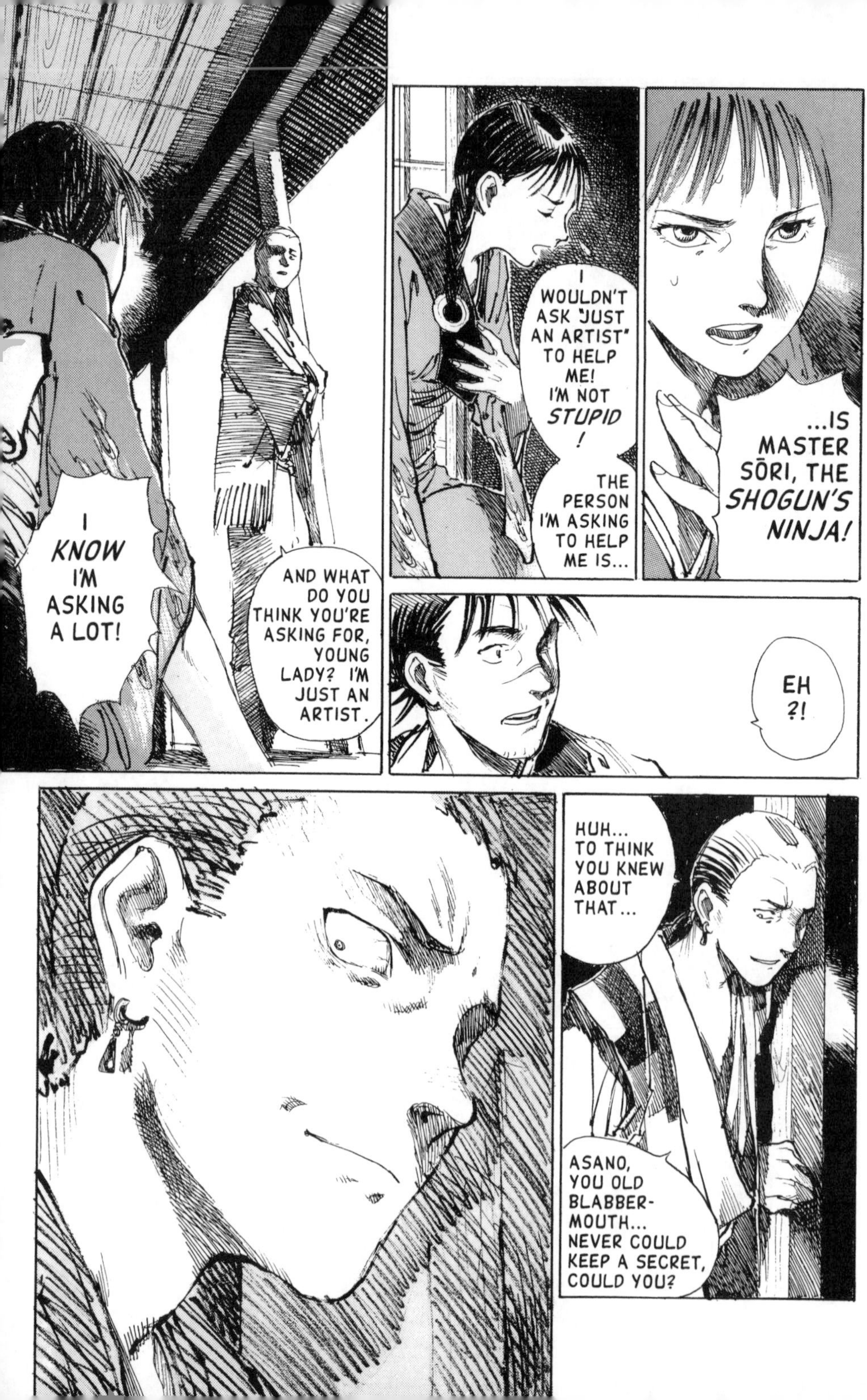
I KNOW I'M ASKING A LOT!
AND WHAT DO YOU THINK YOU'RE ASKING FOR, YOUNG LADY? I'M JUST AN ARTIST.
I WOULDN'T ASK "JUST AN ARTIST" TO HELP ME! I'M NOT STUPID!
THE PERSON I'M ASKING TO HELP ME IS...
...IS MASTER SŌRI, THE SHOGUN'S NINJA!
EH ?!
HUH... TO THINK YOU KNEW ABOUT THAT...
ASANO, YOU OLD BLABBER-MOUTH... NEVER COULD KEEP A SECRET, COULD YOU?

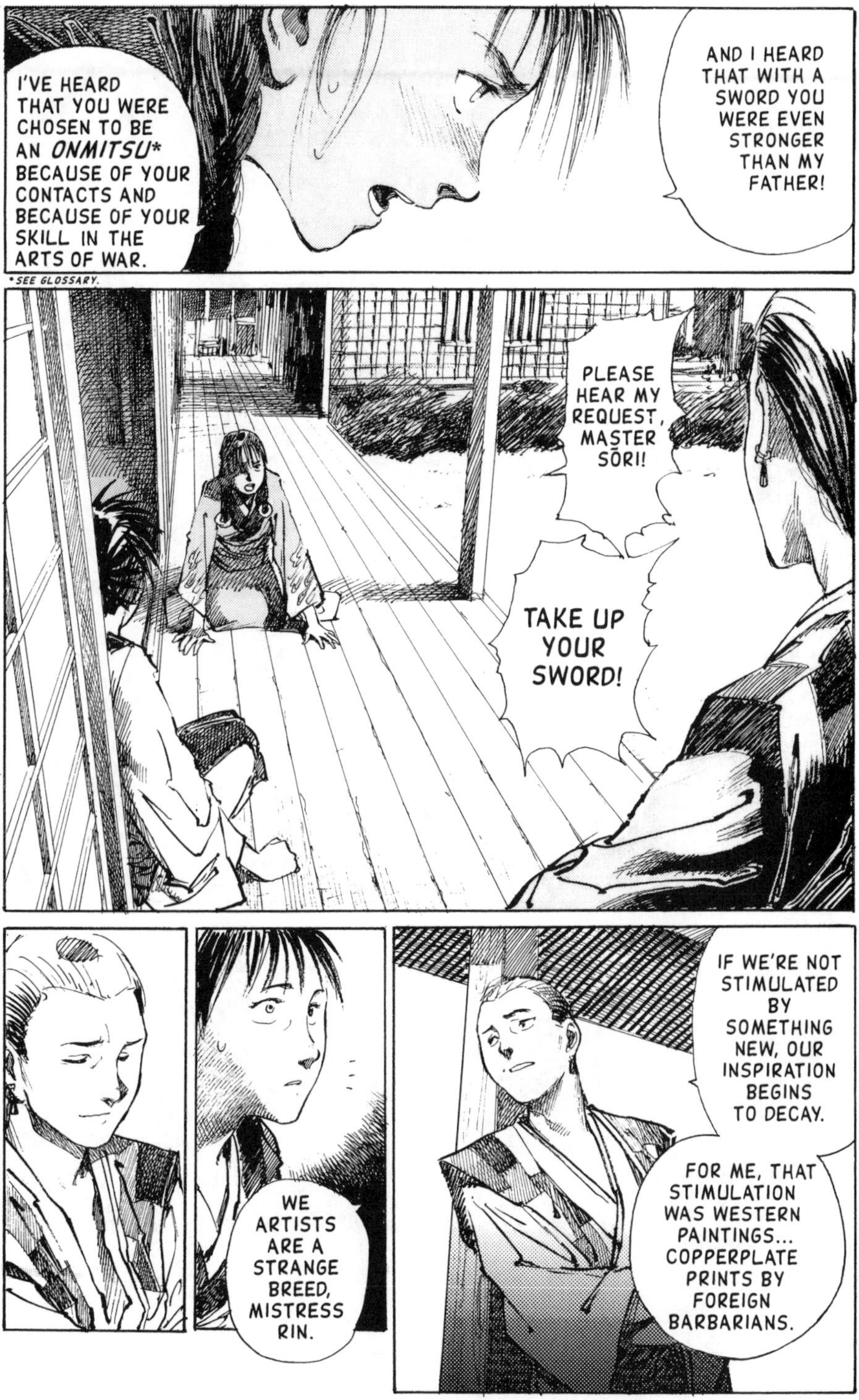
I'VE HEARD THAT YOU WERE CHOSEN TO BE AN *ONMITSU** BECAUSE OF YOUR CONTACTS AND BECAUSE OF YOUR SKILL IN THE ARTS OF WAR.
AND I HEARD THAT WITH A SWORD YOU WERE EVEN STRONGER THAN MY FATHER!
*SEE GLOSSARY.
PLEASE HEAR MY REQUEST, MASTER SŌRI!
TAKE UP YOUR SWORD!
WE ARTISTS ARE A STRANGE BREED, MISTRESS RIN.
IF WE'RE NOT STIMULATED BY SOMETHING NEW, OUR INSPIRATION BEGINS TO DECAY.
FOR ME, THAT STIMULATION WAS WESTERN PAINTINGS... COPPERPLATE PRINTS BY FOREIGN BARBARIANS.

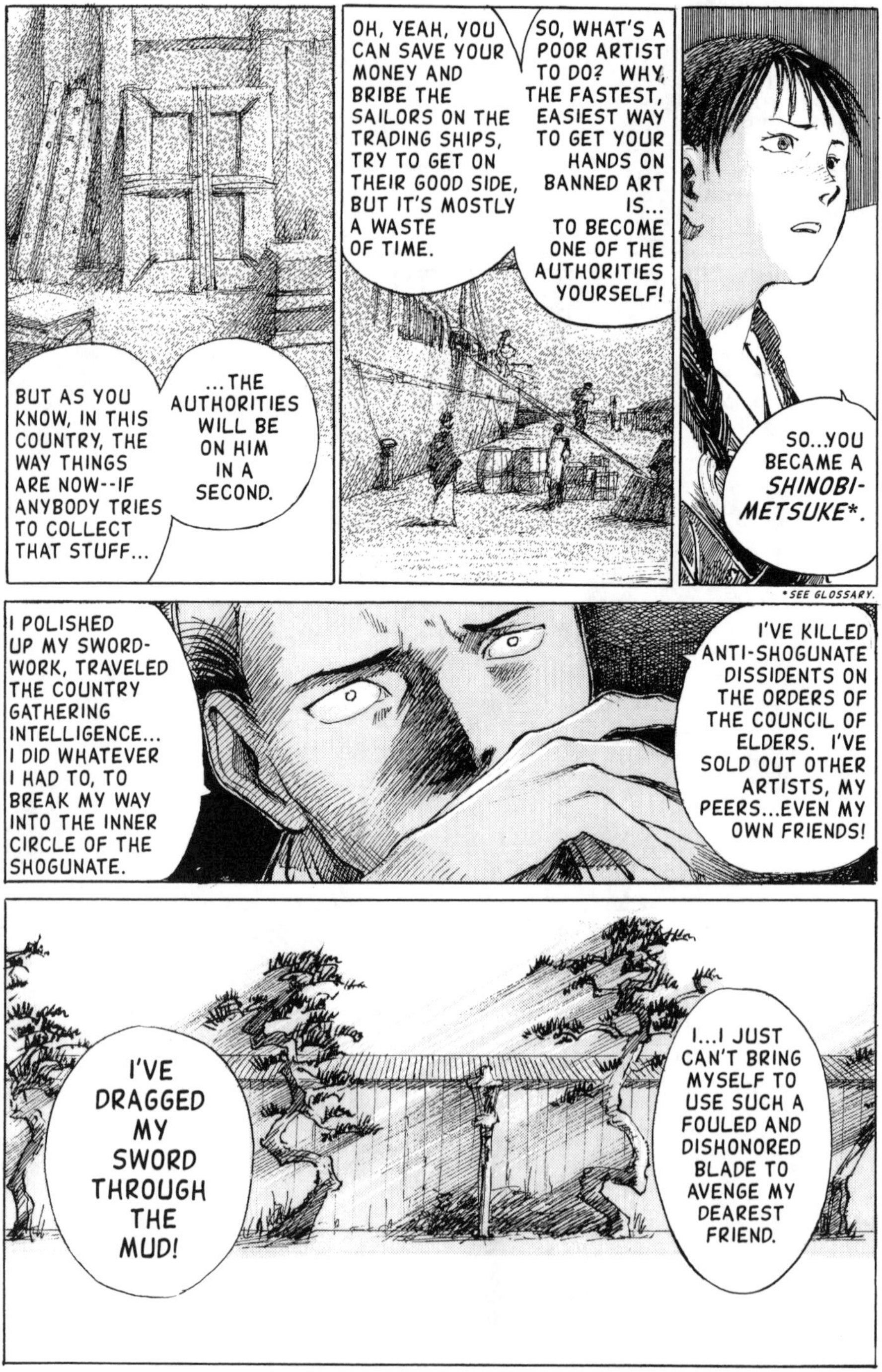

BUT AS YOU KNOW, IN THIS COUNTRY, THE WAY THINGS ARE NOW--IF ANYBODY TRIES TO COLLECT THAT STUFF...
...THE AUTHORITIES WILL BE ON HIM IN A SECOND.
OH, YEAH, YOU CAN SAVE YOUR MONEY AND BRIBE THE SAILORS ON THE TRADING SHIPS, TRY TO GET ON THEIR GOOD SIDE, BUT IT'S MOSTLY A WASTE OF TIME.
SO, WHAT'S A POOR ARTIST TO DO? WHY, THE FASTEST, EASIEST WAY TO GET YOUR HANDS ON BANNED ART IS... TO BECOME ONE OF THE AUTHORITIES YOURSELF!
SO...YOU BECAME A *SHINOBI-METSUKE**.
*SEE GLOSSARY.
I POLISHED UP MY SWORD-WORK, TRAVELED THE COUNTRY GATHERING INTELLIGENCE... I DID WHATEVER I HAD TO, TO BREAK MY WAY INTO THE INNER CIRCLE OF THE SHOGUNATE.
I'VE KILLED ANTI-SHOGUNATE DISSIDENTS ON THE ORDERS OF THE COUNCIL OF ELDERS. I'VE SOLD OUT OTHER ARTISTS, MY PEERS...EVEN MY OWN FRIENDS!
I'VE DRAGGED MY SWORD THROUGH THE MUD!
I...I JUST CAN'T BRING MYSELF TO USE SUCH A FOULED AND DISHONORED BLADE TO AVENGE MY DEAREST FRIEND.

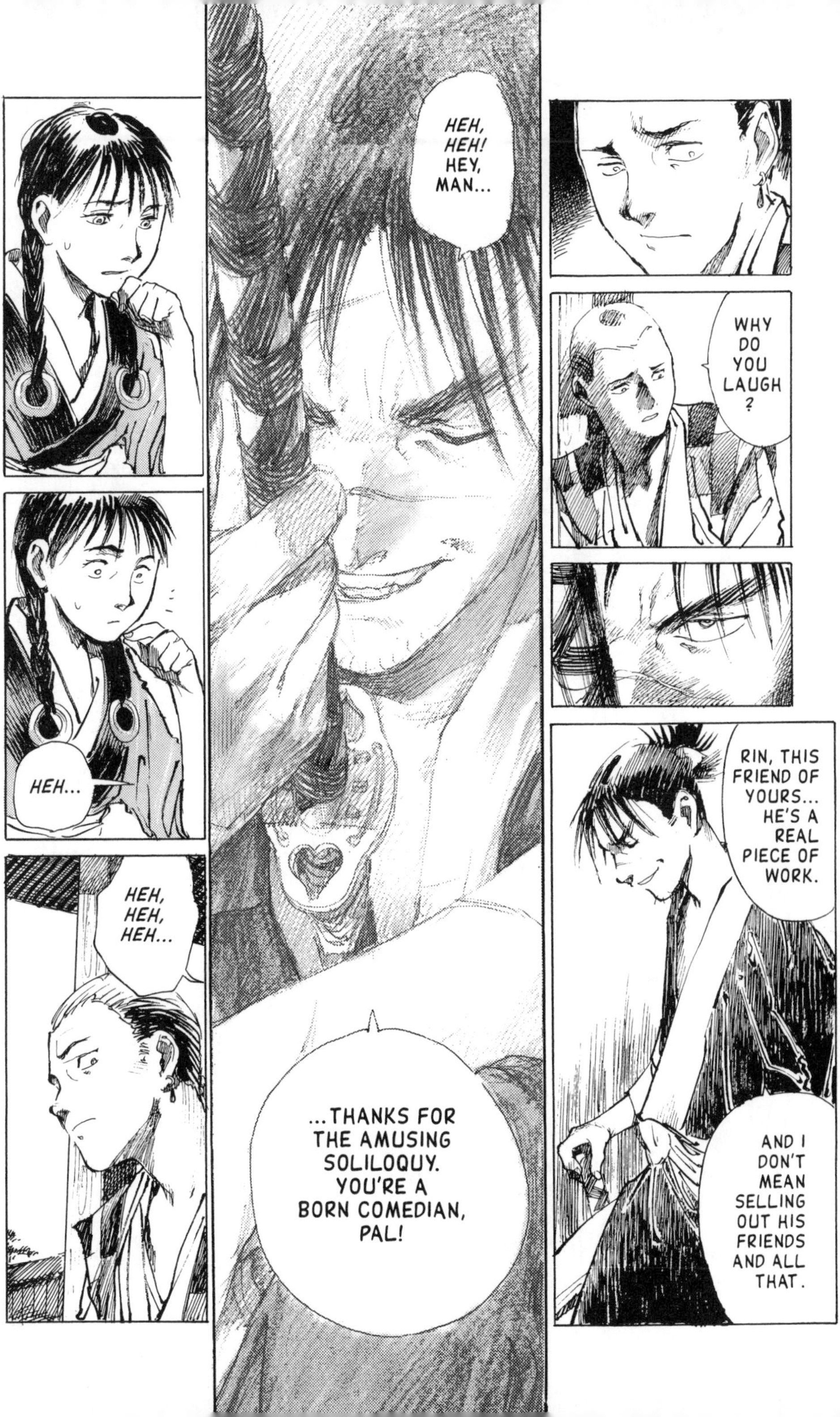
HEH...
HEH, HEH, HEH...
HEH, HEH! HEY, MAN...
...THANKS FOR THE AMUSING SOLILOQUY. YOU'RE A BORN COMEDIAN, PAL!
WHY DO YOU LAUGH?
RIN, THIS FRIEND OF YOURS... HE'S A REAL PIECE OF WORK.
AND I DON'T MEAN SELLING OUT HIS FRIENDS AND ALL THAT.

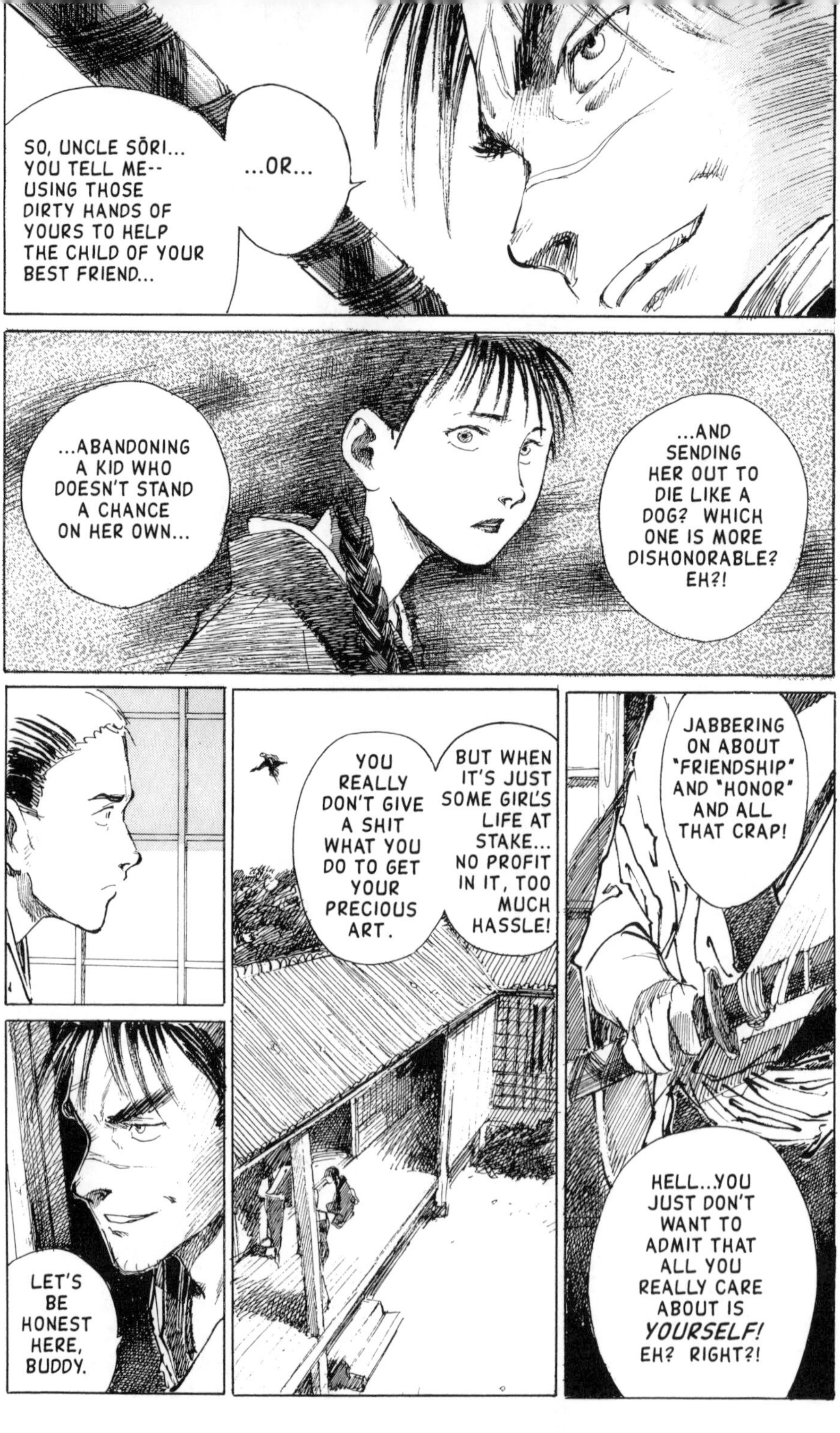
SO, UNCLE SŌRI... YOU TELL ME-- USING THOSE DIRTY HANDS OF YOURS TO HELP THE CHILD OF YOUR BEST FRIEND...
...OR...
...ABANDONING A KID WHO DOESN'T STAND A CHANCE ON HER OWN...
...AND SENDING HER OUT TO DIE LIKE A DOG? WHICH ONE IS MORE DISHONORABLE? EH?!
LET'S BE HONEST HERE, BUDDY.
YOU REALLY DON'T GIVE A SHIT WHAT YOU DO TO GET YOUR PRECIOUS ART.
BUT WHEN IT'S JUST SOME GIRL'S LIFE AT STAKE... NO PROFIT IN IT, TOO MUCH HASSLE!
JABBERING ON ABOUT "FRIENDSHIP" AND "HONOR" AND ALL THAT CRAP!
HELL...YOU JUST DON'T WANT TO ADMIT THAT ALL YOU REALLY CARE ABOUT IS *YOURSELF!* EH? RIGHT?!

SO WHAT AM I LAUGHING AT? I'M LAUGHING AT YOUR WINNING PERSONALITY! MAKING ALL THESE LAME EXCUSES WHEN ALL YOU GOTTA DO IS SAY, "HEY, THIS IS WHO I AM--YOU DON'T LIKE IT, TOUGH LUCK!"

RIGHT?

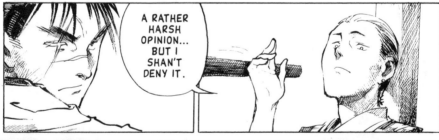

A RATHER HARSH OPINION... BUT I SHAN'T DENY IT.

I'M JUST NOT READY TO DIE. I'VE GOT A MOUNTAIN OF THINGS LEFT TO PAINT.

AND I'M NOT ASHAMED. IT'S JUST HOW WE ARTISTS ARE, HEY?

DON'T GIVE ME THAT CRAP! *ARTISTS!* BAH!!

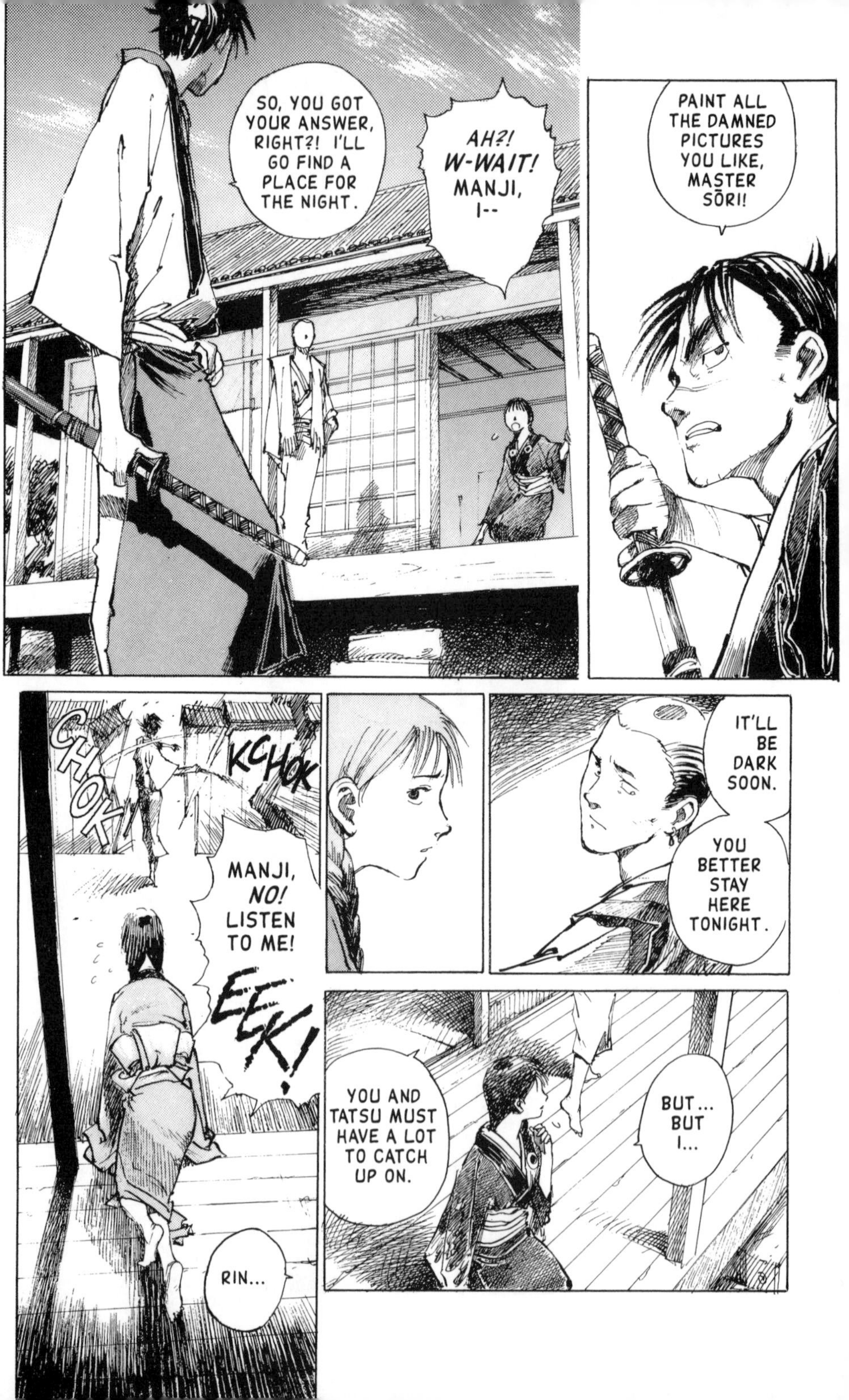
SO, YOU GOT YOUR ANSWER, RIGHT?! I'LL GO FIND A PLACE FOR THE NIGHT.
AH?! W-WAIT! MANJI, I--
PAINT ALL THE DAMNED PICTURES YOU LIKE, MASTER SŌRI!
CHOK
KCHOK
MANJI, NO! LISTEN TO ME!
EEK!
RIN...
IT'LL BE DARK SOON.
YOU BETTER STAY HERE TONIGHT.
YOU AND TATSU MUST HAVE A LOT TO CATCH UP ON.
BUT... BUT I...

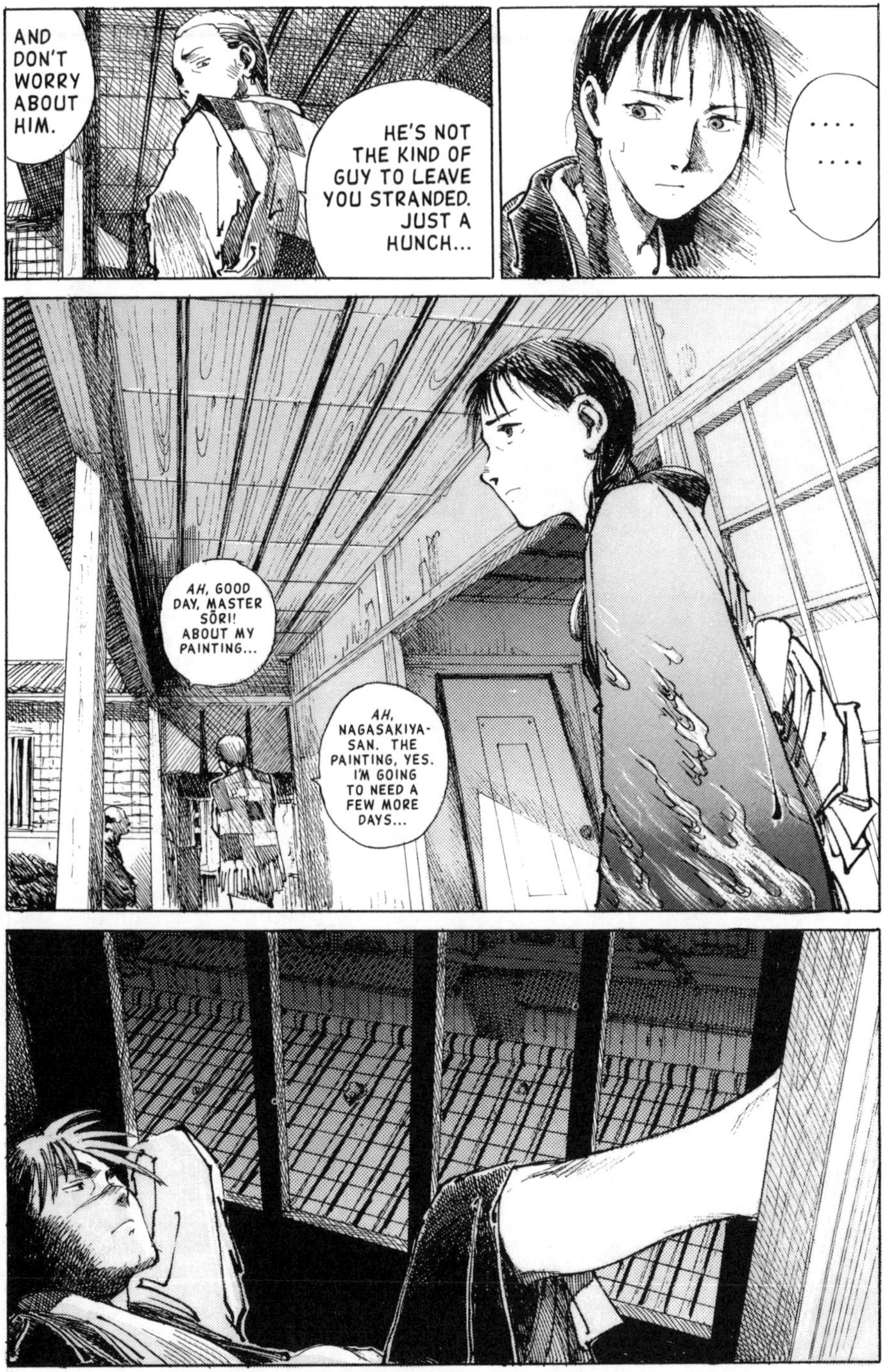
AND DON'T WORRY ABOUT HIM.
HE'S NOT THE KIND OF GUY TO LEAVE YOU STRANDED. JUST A HUNCH...
....
....
AH, GOOD DAY, MASTER SŌRI! ABOUT MY PAINTING...
AH, NAGASAKIYA-SAN. THE PAINTING, YES. I'M GOING TO NEED A FEW MORE DAYS...

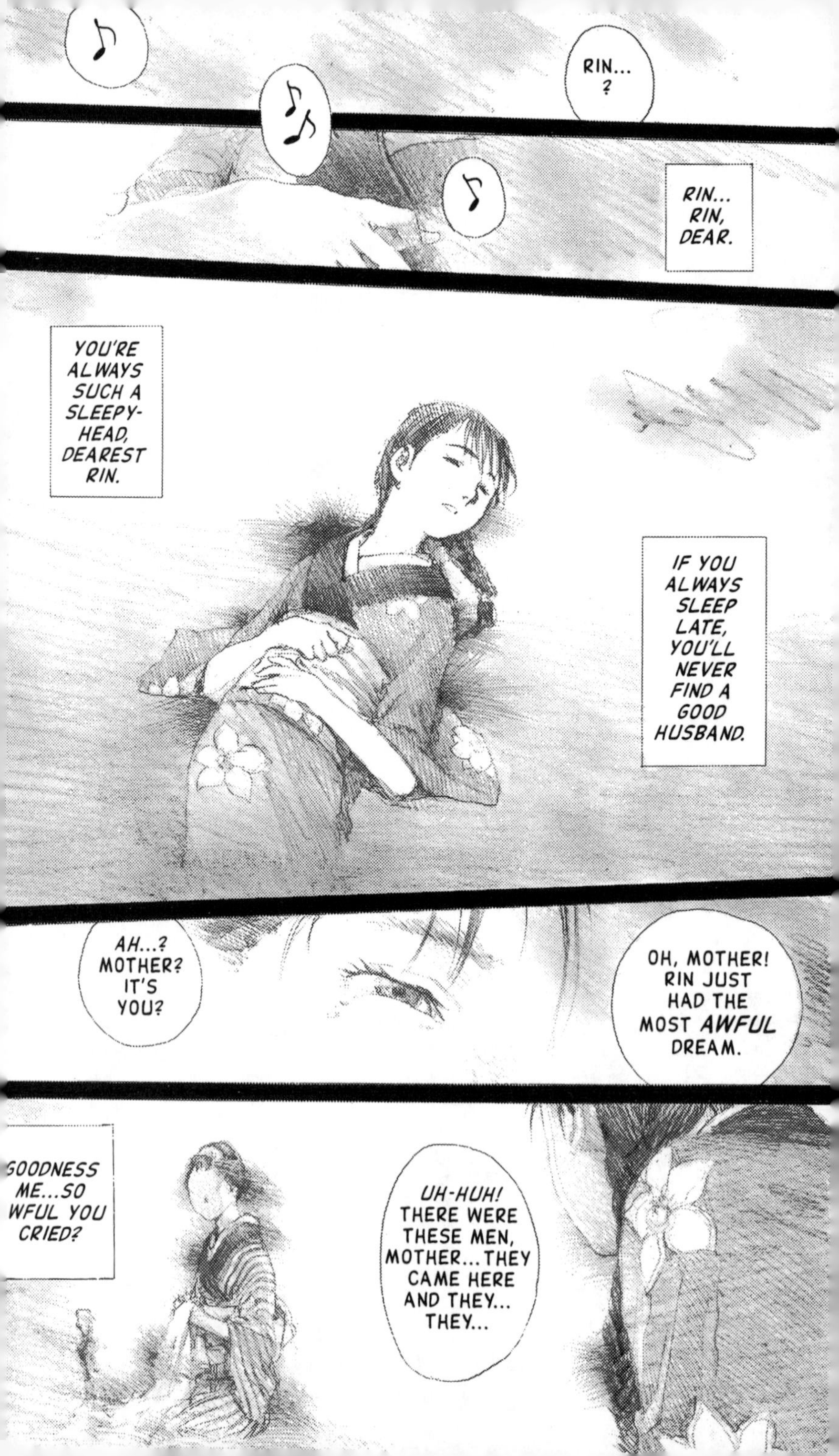
RIN... ?
RIN... RIN, DEAR.
YOU'RE ALWAYS SUCH A SLEEPY-HEAD, DEAREST RIN.
IF YOU ALWAYS SLEEP LATE, YOU'LL NEVER FIND A GOOD HUSBAND.
AH...? MOTHER? IT'S YOU?
OH, MOTHER! RIN JUST HAD THE MOST AWFUL DREAM.
GOODNESS ME...SO WFUL YOU CRIED?
UH-HUH! THERE WERE THESE MEN, MOTHER... THEY CAME HERE AND THEY... THEY...

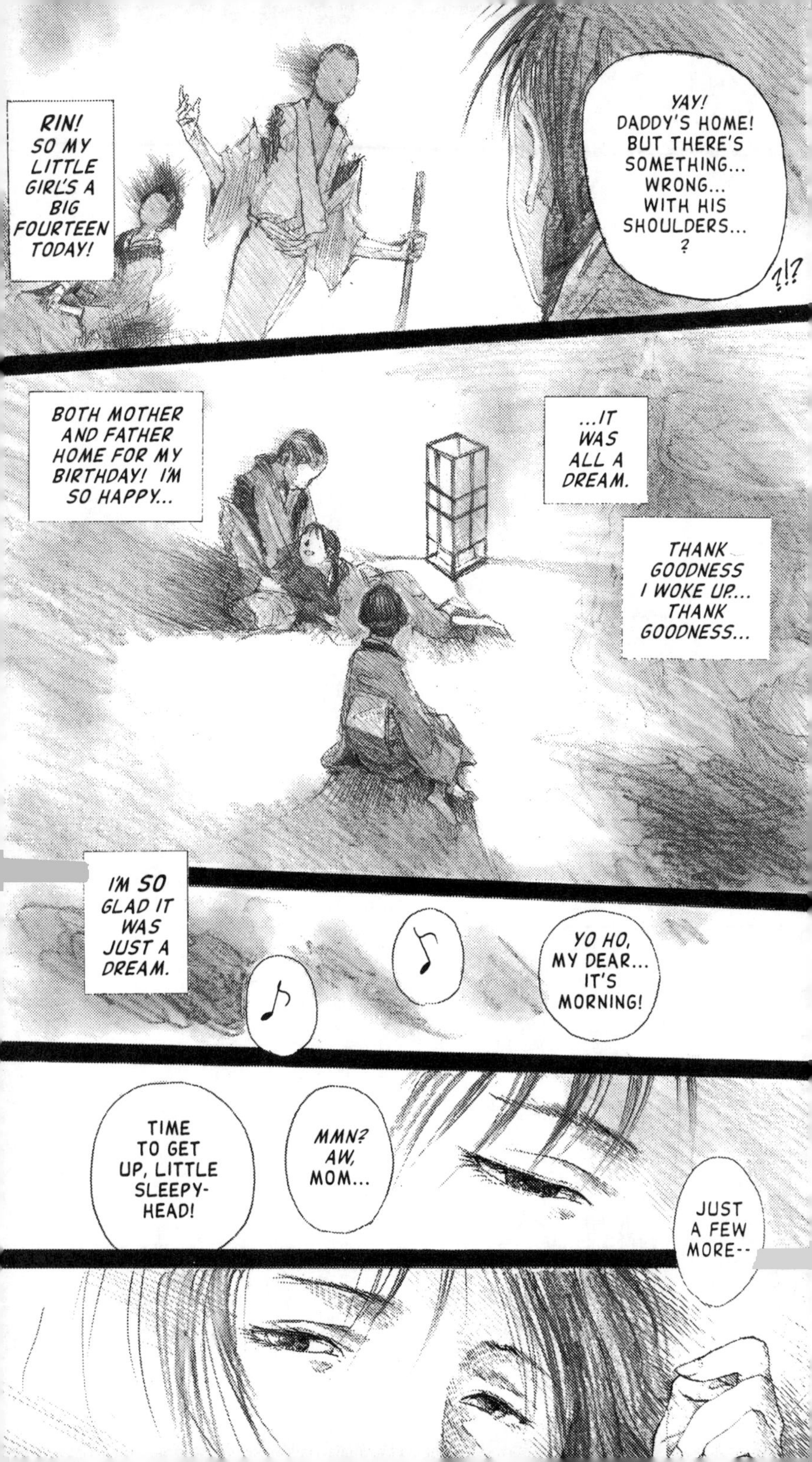
RIN! SO MY LITTLE GIRL'S A BIG FOURTEEN TODAY!
YAY! DADDY'S HOME! BUT THERE'S SOMETHING... WRONG... WITH HIS SHOULDERS... ?
?!?
BOTH MOTHER AND FATHER HOME FOR MY BIRTHDAY! I'M SO HAPPY...
...IT WAS ALL A DREAM.
THANK GOODNESS I WOKE UP... THANK GOODNESS...
I'M SO GLAD IT WAS JUST A DREAM.
♪
♪
YO HO, MY DEAR... IT'S MORNING!
TIME TO GET UP, LITTLE SLEEPY-HEAD!
MMN? AW, MOM...
JUST A FEW MORE--

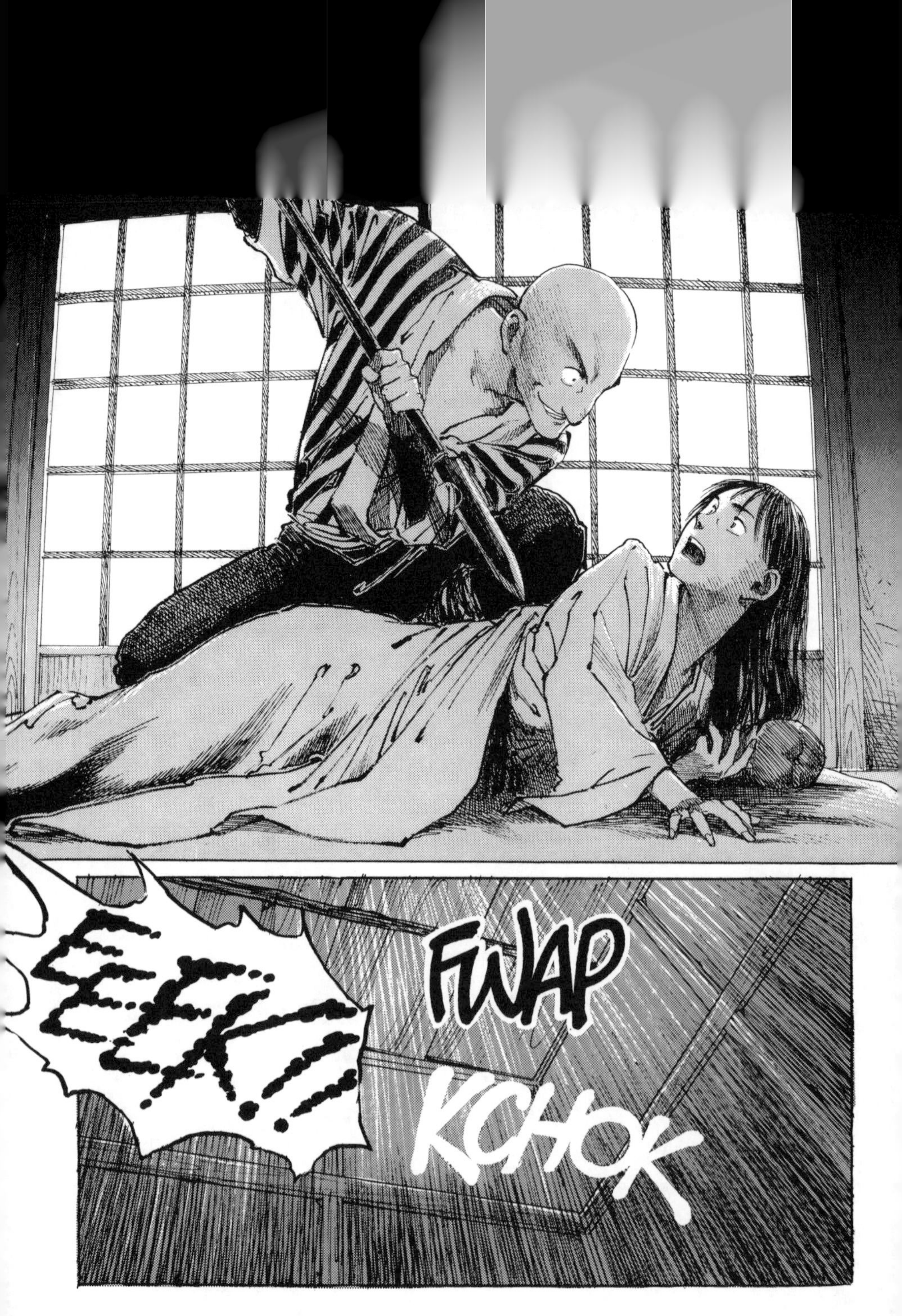
EEEK!!
FWAP
KCHOK

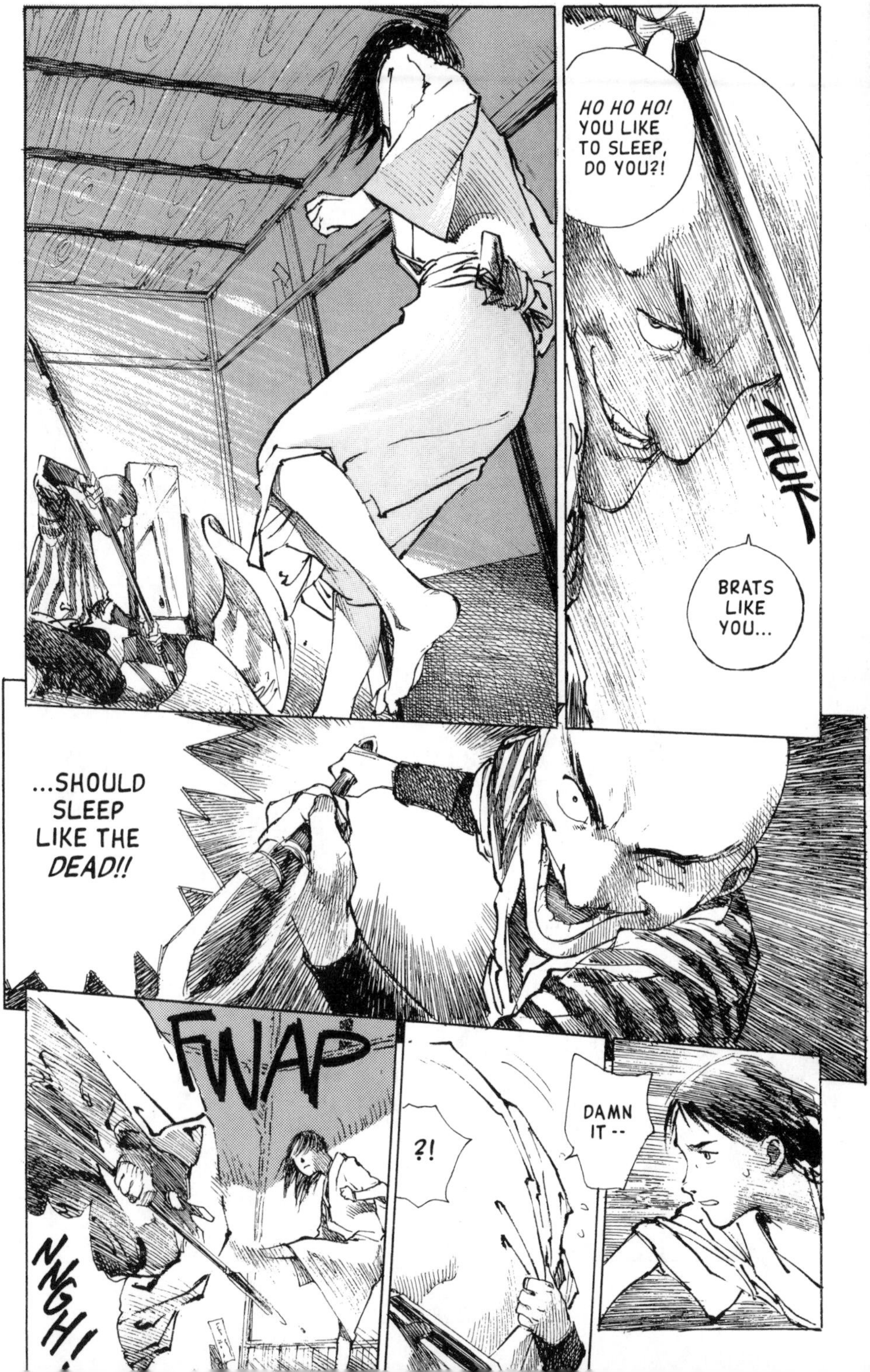
HO HO HO! YOU LIKE TO SLEEP, DO YOU?!
THUK
BRATS LIKE YOU...
...SHOULD SLEEP LIKE THE DEAD!!
FWAP
NNGH!
?!
DAMN IT --

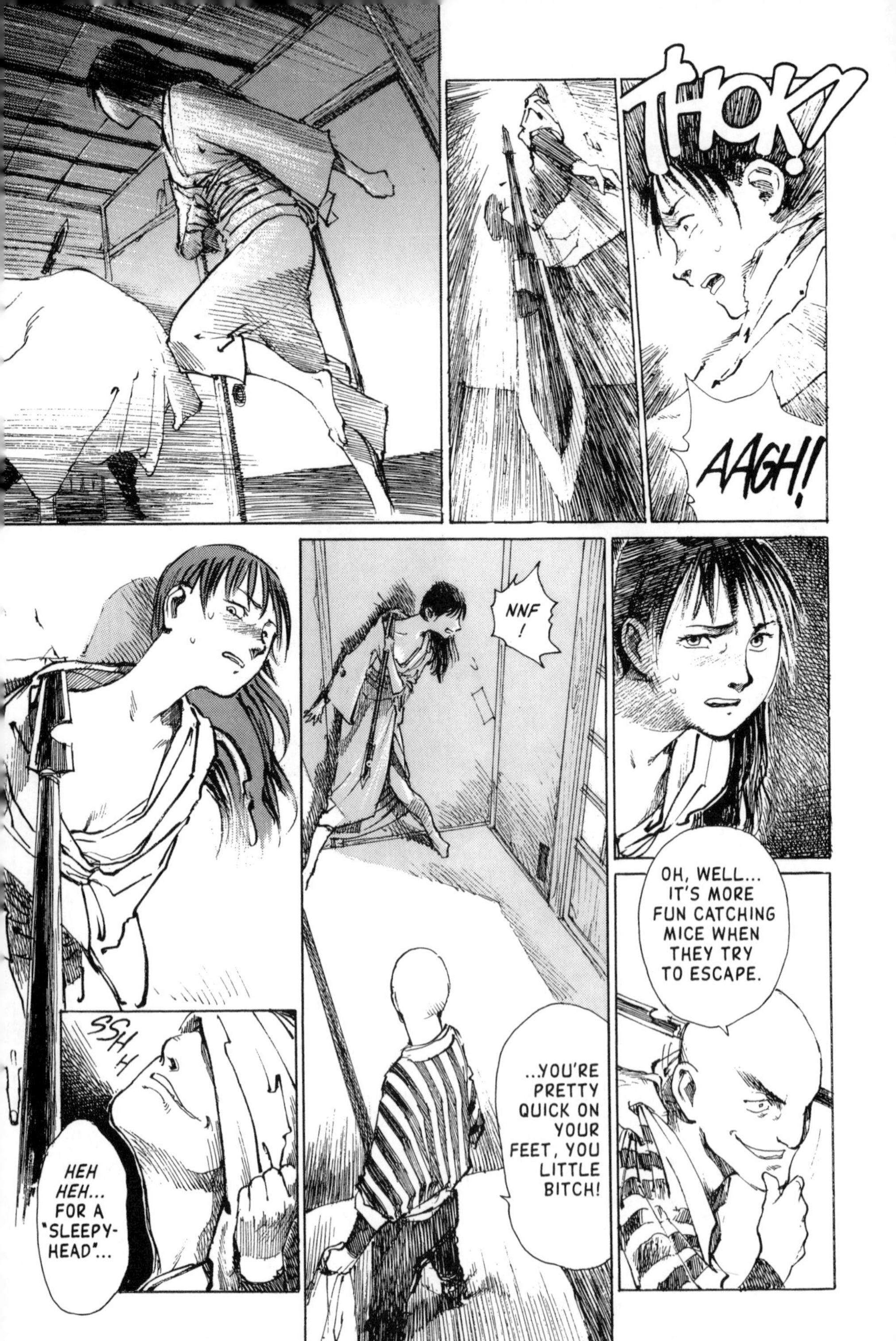
THOK!
AAGH!
SSHH
HEH HEH... FOR A "SLEEPY-HEAD"...
NNF!
...YOU'RE PRETTY QUICK ON YOUR FEET, YOU LITTLE BITCH!
OH, WELL... IT'S MORE FUN CATCHING MICE WHEN THEY TRY TO ESCAPE.

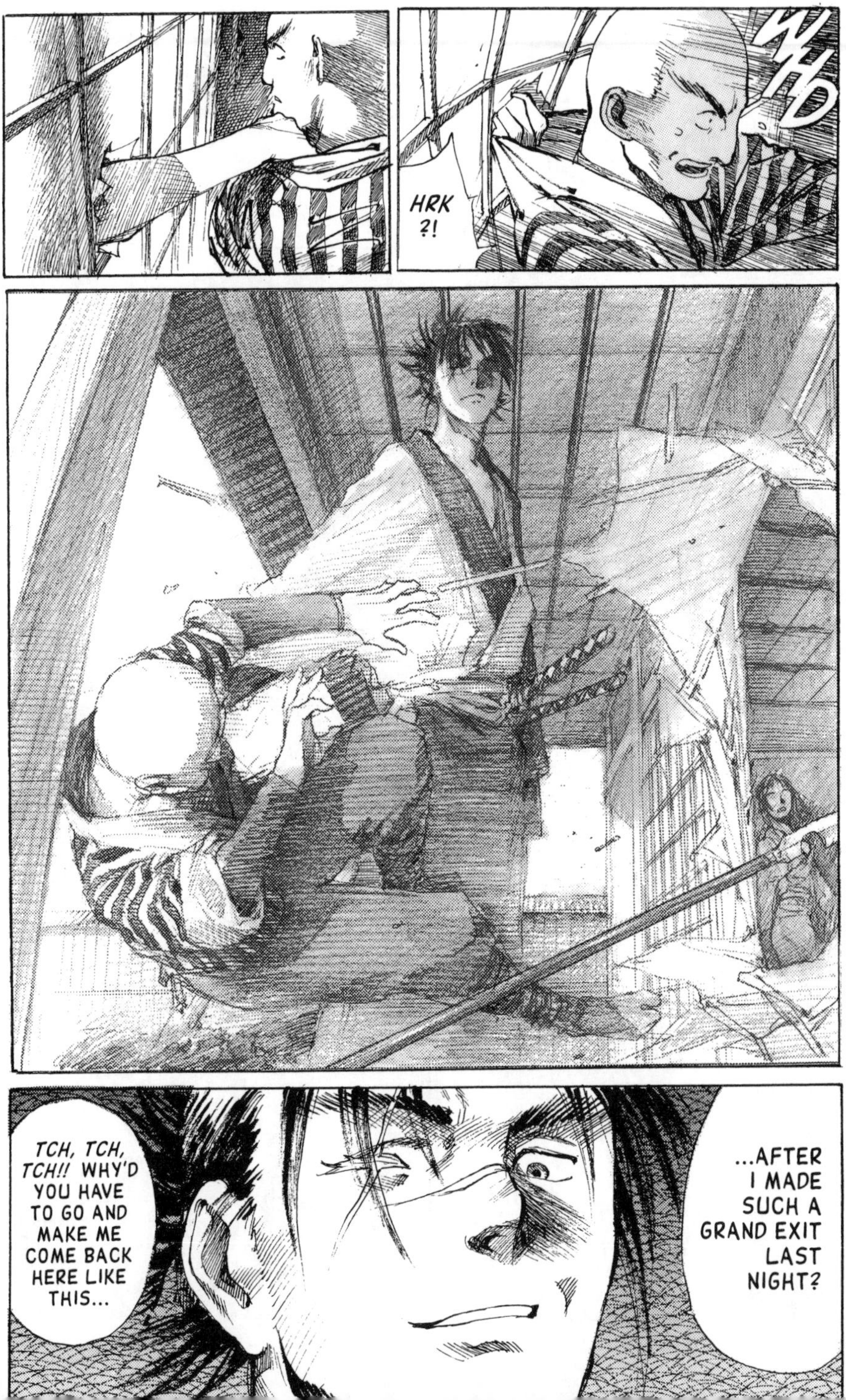
HRK ?!
WHD
TCH, TCH, TCH!! WHY'D YOU HAVE TO GO AND MAKE ME COME BACK HERE LIKE THIS...
...AFTER I MADE SUCH A GRAND EXIT LAST NIGHT?

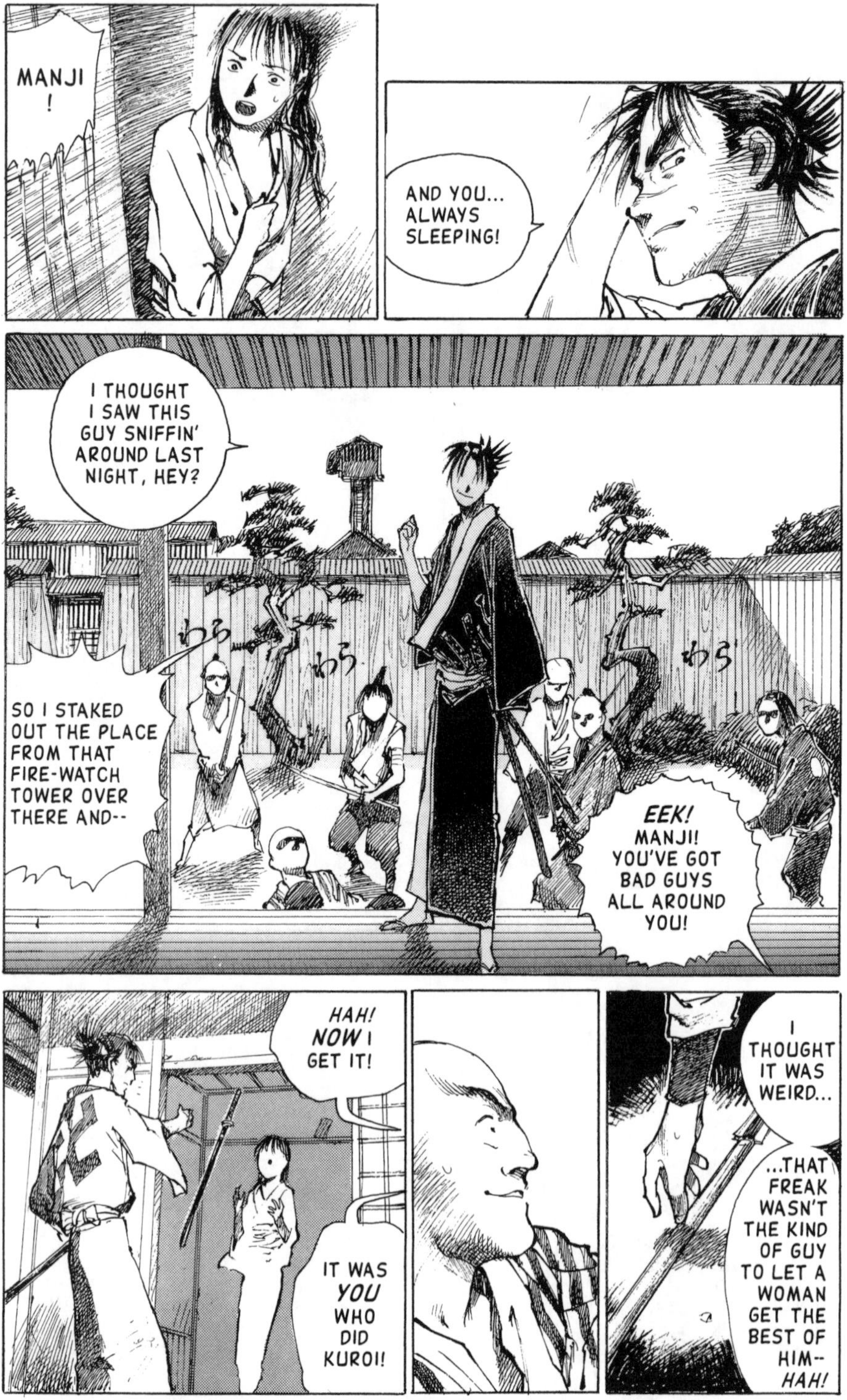
MANJI!
AND YOU... ALWAYS SLEEPING!
I THOUGHT I SAW THIS GUY SNIFFIN' AROUND LAST NIGHT, HEY?
わら
わら
わら
SO I STAKED OUT THE PLACE FROM THAT FIRE-WATCH TOWER OVER THERE AND--
EEK! MANJI! YOU'VE GOT BAD GUYS ALL AROUND YOU!
HAH! NOW I GET IT!
IT WAS YOU WHO DID KUROI!
I THOUGHT IT WAS WEIRD...
...THAT FREAK WASN'T THE KIND OF GUY TO LET A WOMAN GET THE BEST OF HIM--HAH!

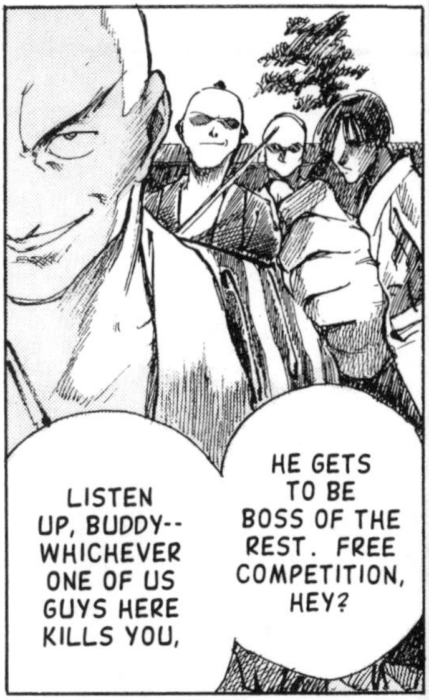
LISTEN UP, BUDDY-- WHICHEVER ONE OF US GUYS HERE KILLS YOU,
HE GETS TO BE BOSS OF THE REST. FREE COMPETITION, HEY?

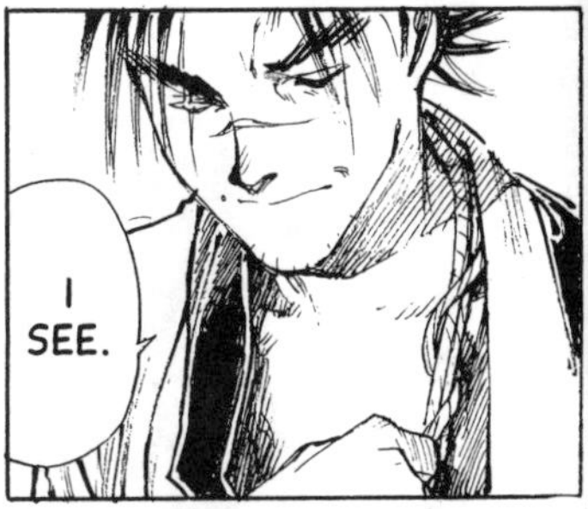
I SEE.

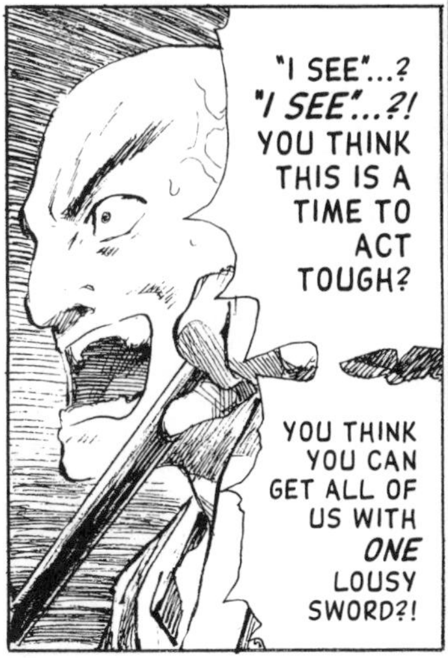
"I SEE"...? *"I SEE"*...?! YOU THINK THIS IS A TIME TO ACT TOUGH?
YOU THINK YOU CAN GET ALL OF US WITH *ONE* LOUSY SWORD?!

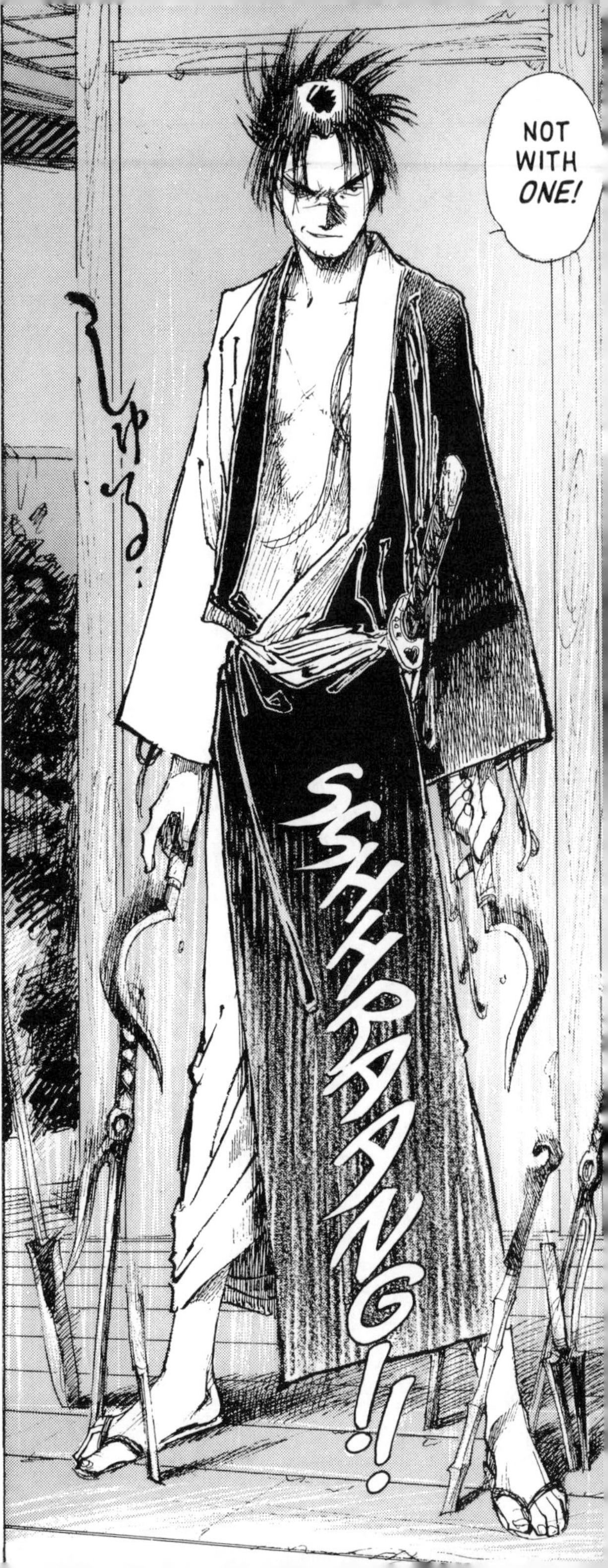
NOT WITH *ONE!*
しゅる…
SHHRAANG!!

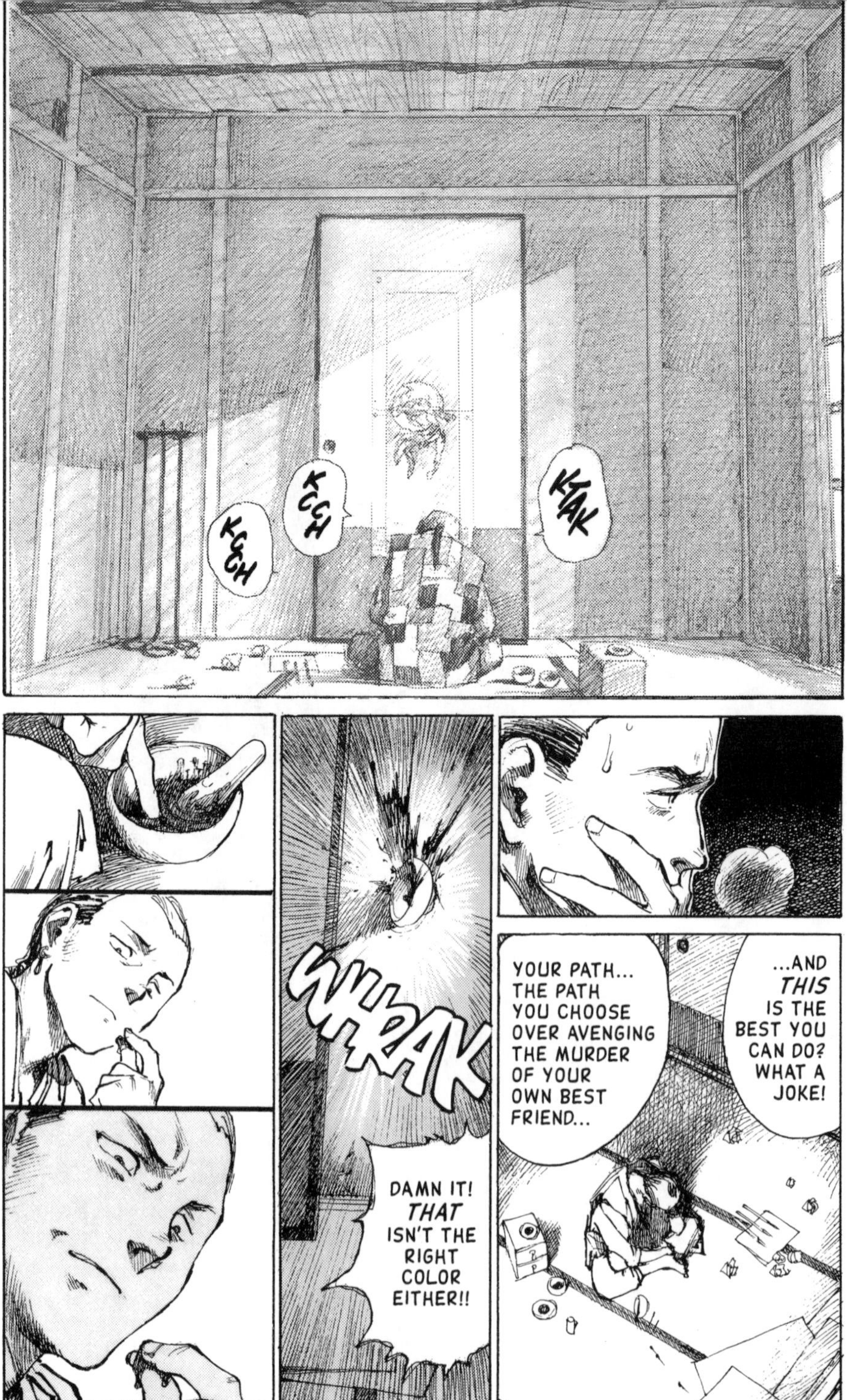
KCCH
KCCH
KTAK
WHRAK
DAMN IT! *THAT* ISN'T THE RIGHT COLOR EITHER!!
YOUR PATH... THE PATH YOU CHOOSE OVER AVENGING THE MURDER OF YOUR OWN BEST FRIEND...
...AND *THIS* IS THE BEST YOU CAN DO? WHAT A JOKE!

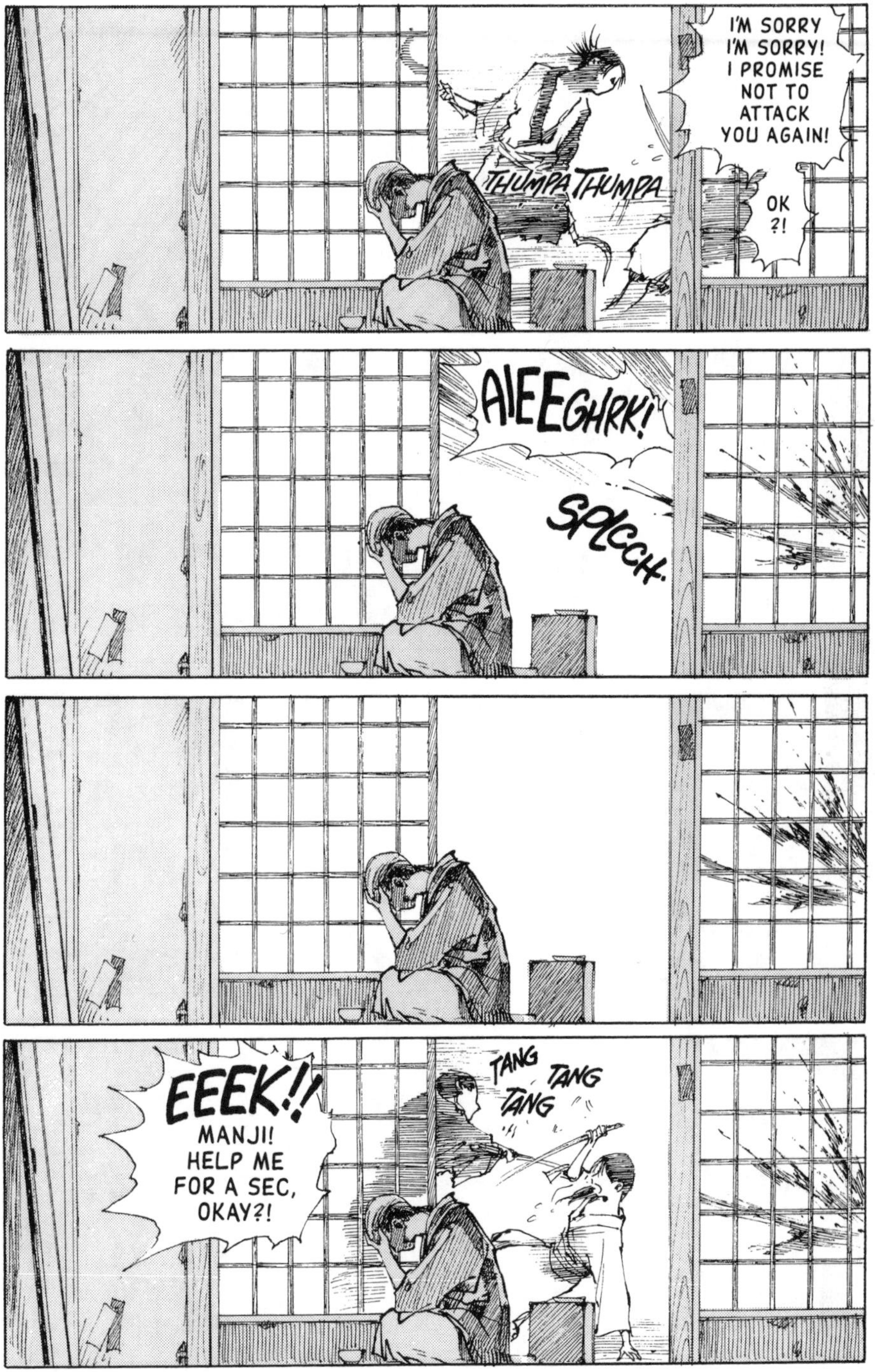
THUMPA THUMPA
I'M SORRY I'M SORRY! I PROMISE NOT TO ATTACK YOU AGAIN!
OK ?!
AIEEGHRK!
SPLCCH.
EEEK!! MANJI! HELP ME FOR A SEC, OKAY?!
TANG
TANG
TANG

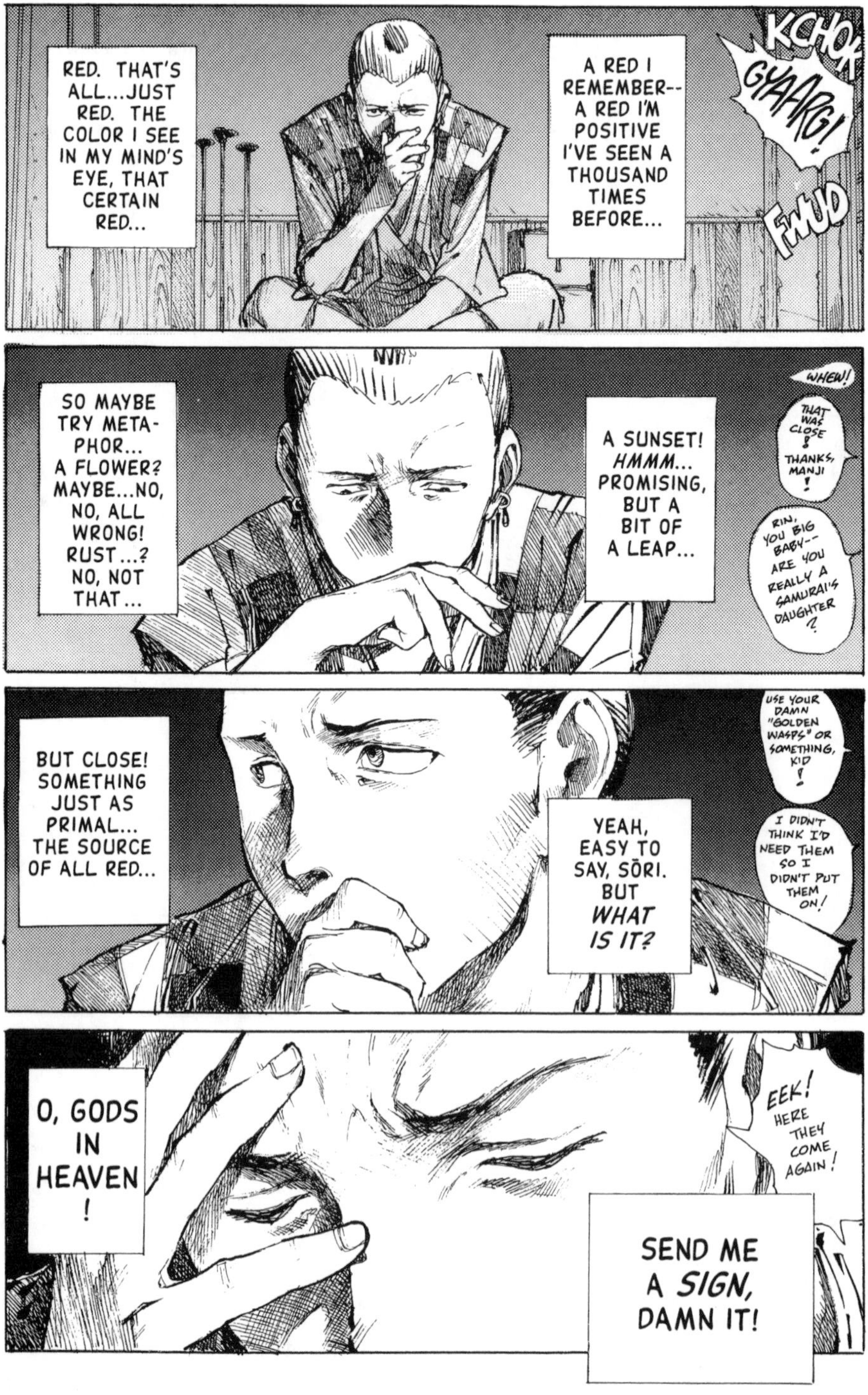
RED. THAT'S ALL...JUST RED. THE COLOR I SEE IN MY MIND'S EYE, THAT CERTAIN RED...
A RED I REMEMBER-- A RED I'M POSITIVE I'VE SEEN A THOUSAND TIMES BEFORE...
KCHOK
GYAARG!
FWUD
SO MAYBE TRY METAPHOR... A FLOWER? MAYBE...NO, NO, ALL WRONG! RUST...? NO, NOT THAT...
A SUNSET! *HMMM...* PROMISING, BUT A BIT OF A LEAP...
WHEW!
THAT WAS CLOSE! THANKS, MANJI!
RIN, YOU BIG BABY-- ARE YOU REALLY A SAMURAI'S DAUGHTER?
BUT CLOSE! SOMETHING JUST AS PRIMAL... THE SOURCE OF ALL RED...
YEAH, EASY TO SAY, SŌRI. BUT *WHAT IS IT?*
USE YOUR DAMN "GOLDEN WASPS" OR SOMETHING, KID!
I DIDN'T THINK I'D NEED THEM SO I DIDN'T PUT THEM ON!
O, GODS IN HEAVEN!
EEK! HERE THEY COME AGAIN!
SEND ME A *SIGN,* DAMN IT!

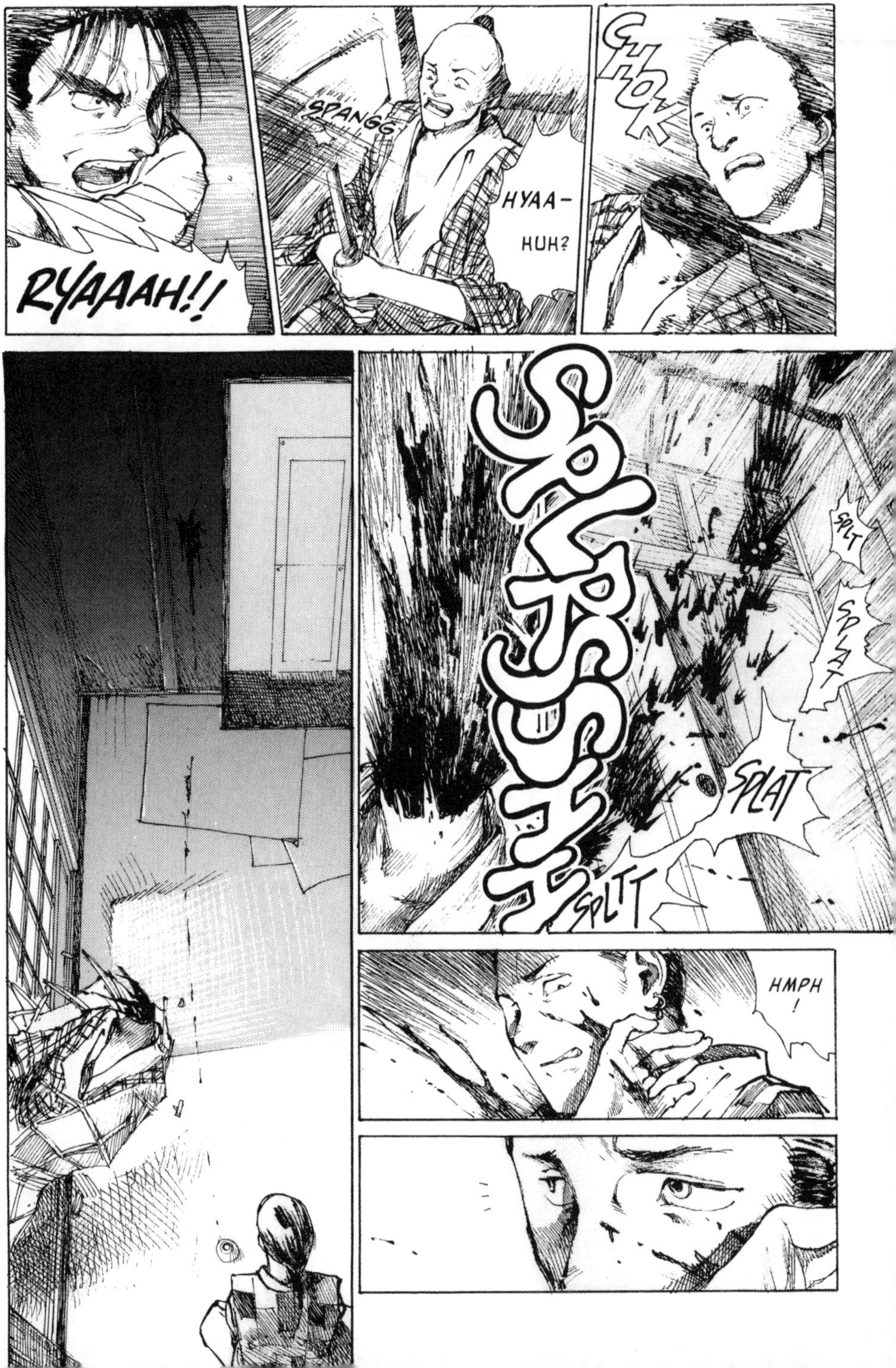
RYAAAH!!
SPANGG
HYAA-
HUH?
CHOK
SPLRSSHH
SPLT
SPLAT
SPLAT
SPLTT
HMPH
!

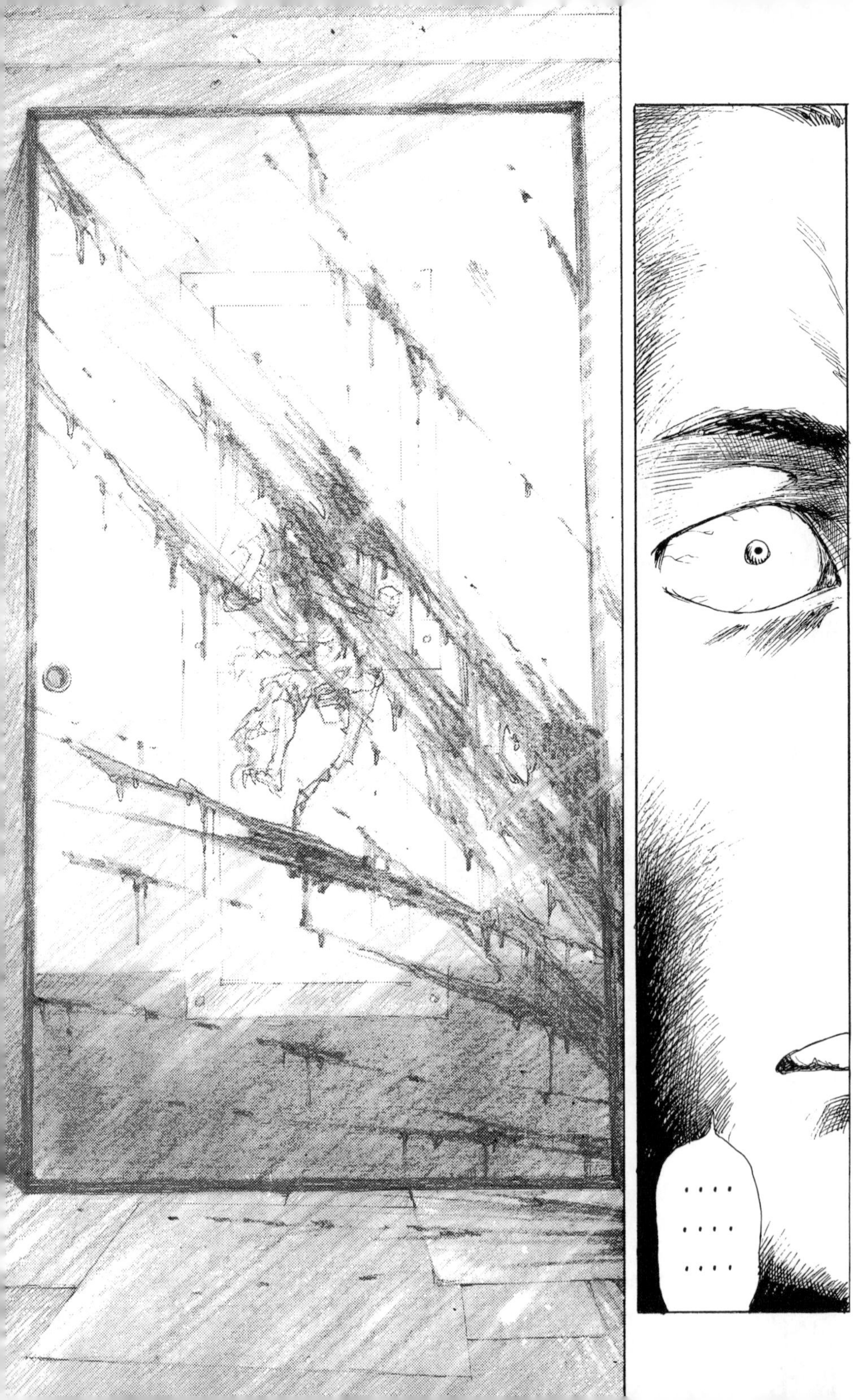
....

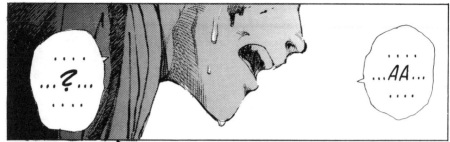

...?...

...AA...

TH...**THAT'S IT!!!**

HAHA

HAHA

...HEH.

HEH, HEH, HEH...

YES! THIS IS IT!

THIS IS *EXACTLY* WHAT I'VE BEEN LOOKING FOR!

--PRIMAL RED !!

THAT COLOR YOU CAN'T GET FROM ALL THE DYES AND PAINT IN THE WORLD--

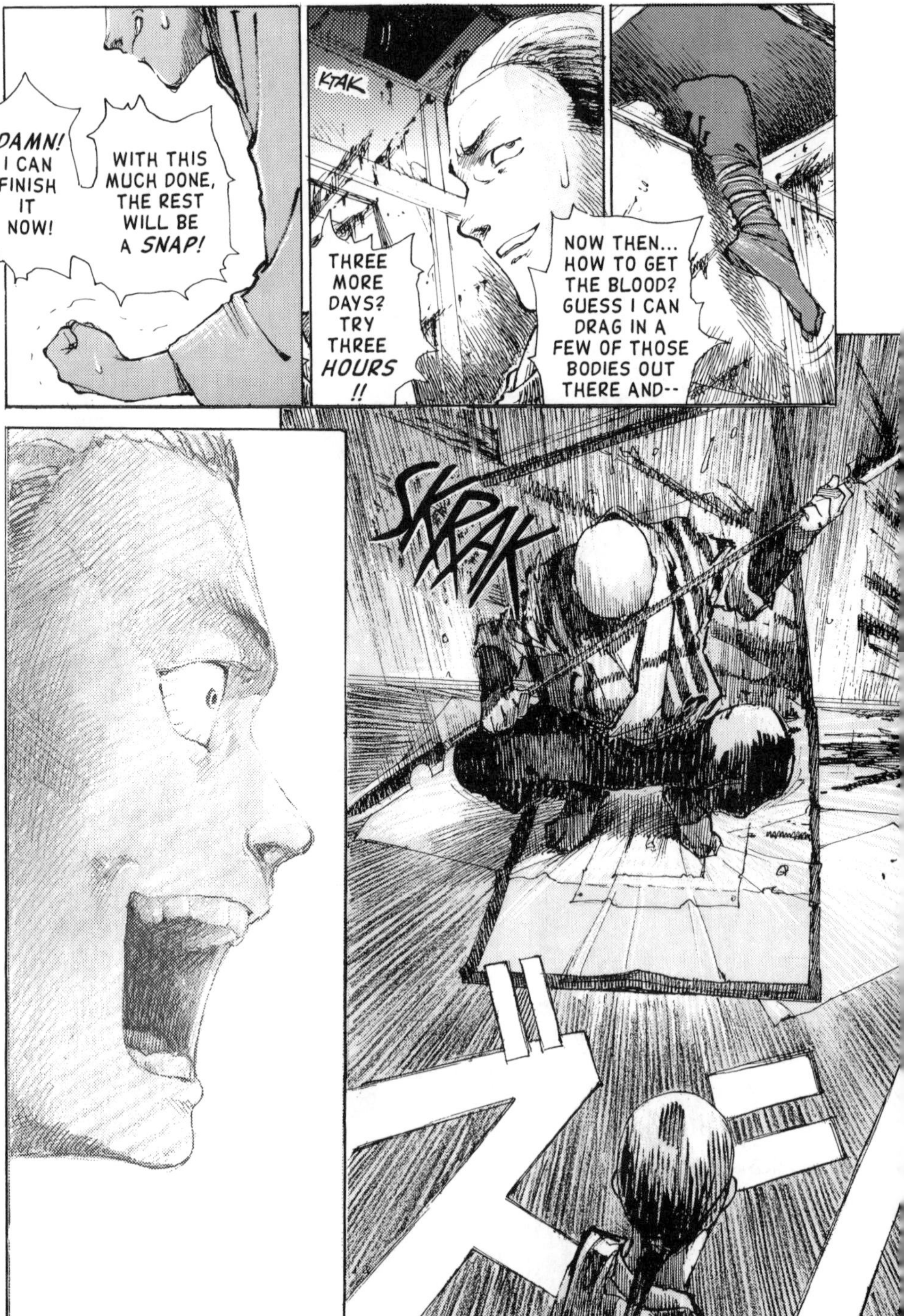
DAMN! I CAN FINISH IT NOW!
WITH THIS MUCH DONE, THE REST WILL BE A SNAP!
KTAK
THREE MORE DAYS? TRY THREE HOURS !!
NOW THEN... HOW TO GET THE BLOOD? GUESS I CAN DRAG IN A FEW OF THOSE BODIES OUT THERE AND--
SKRAK

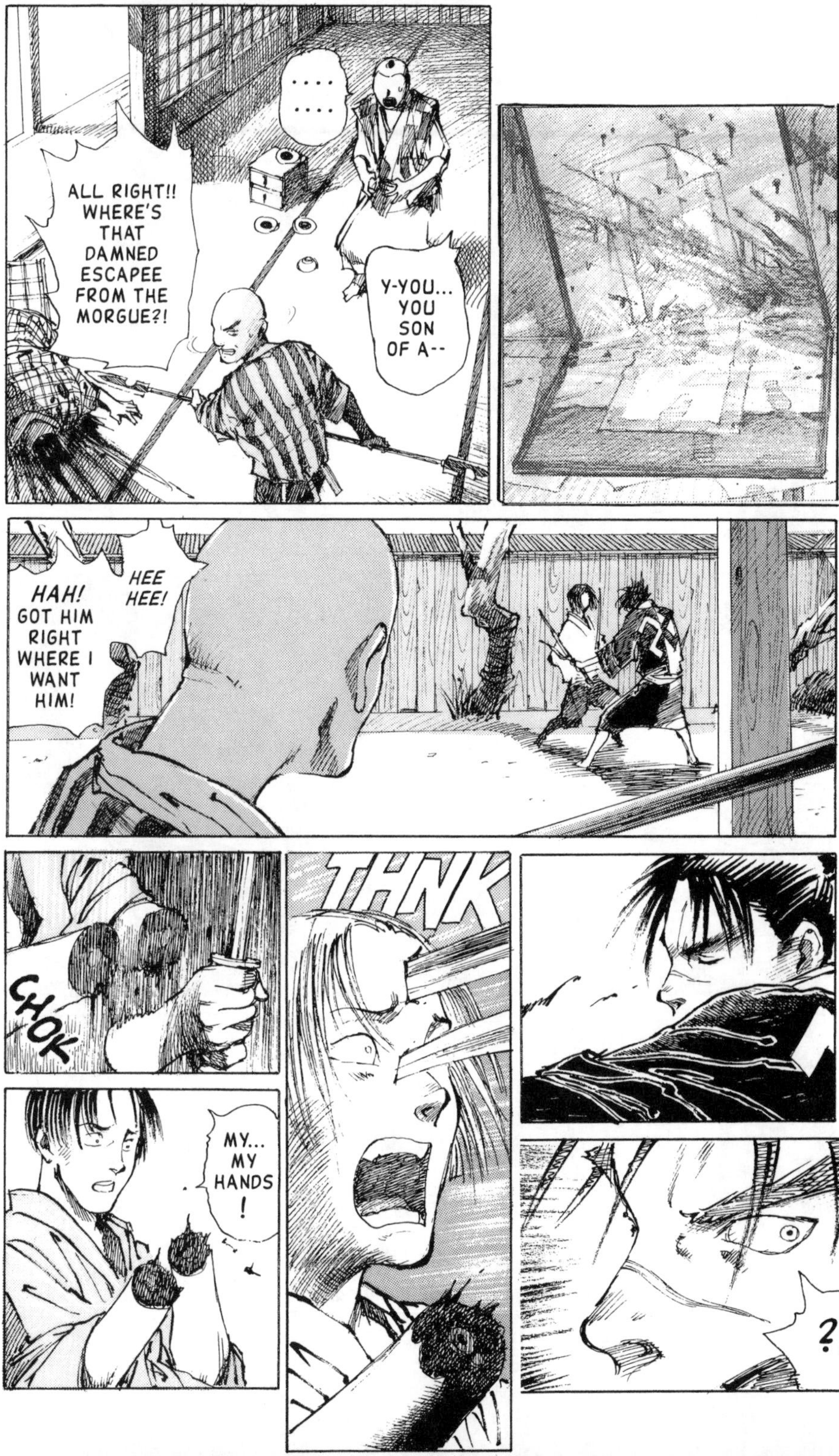
ALL RIGHT!! WHERE'S THAT DAMNED ESCAPEE FROM THE MORGUE?!
. . . .
. . . .
Y-YOU... YOU SON OF A--
HAH! GOT HIM RIGHT WHERE I WANT HIM!
HEE HEE!
CHOK
THNK
MY... MY HANDS !
?!

HYAH!

HAYEE!

WHSST

HA!

WHSSH
VNHIP

HO!

HYAH!

HAH!

hahh
hahh
hahh

WHEW... LOOK HERE, PAL...

...THE WAY YOU KEEP HOLLERING LIKE THAT EVERY TIME YOU TAKE A SWING AT ME, NO WONDER YOU'RE OUTTA BREATH.

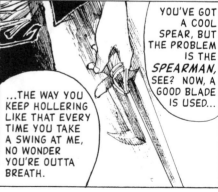

YOU'VE GOT A COOL SPEAR, BUT THE PROBLEM IS THE SPEARMAN, SEE? NOW, A GOOD BLADE IS USED...

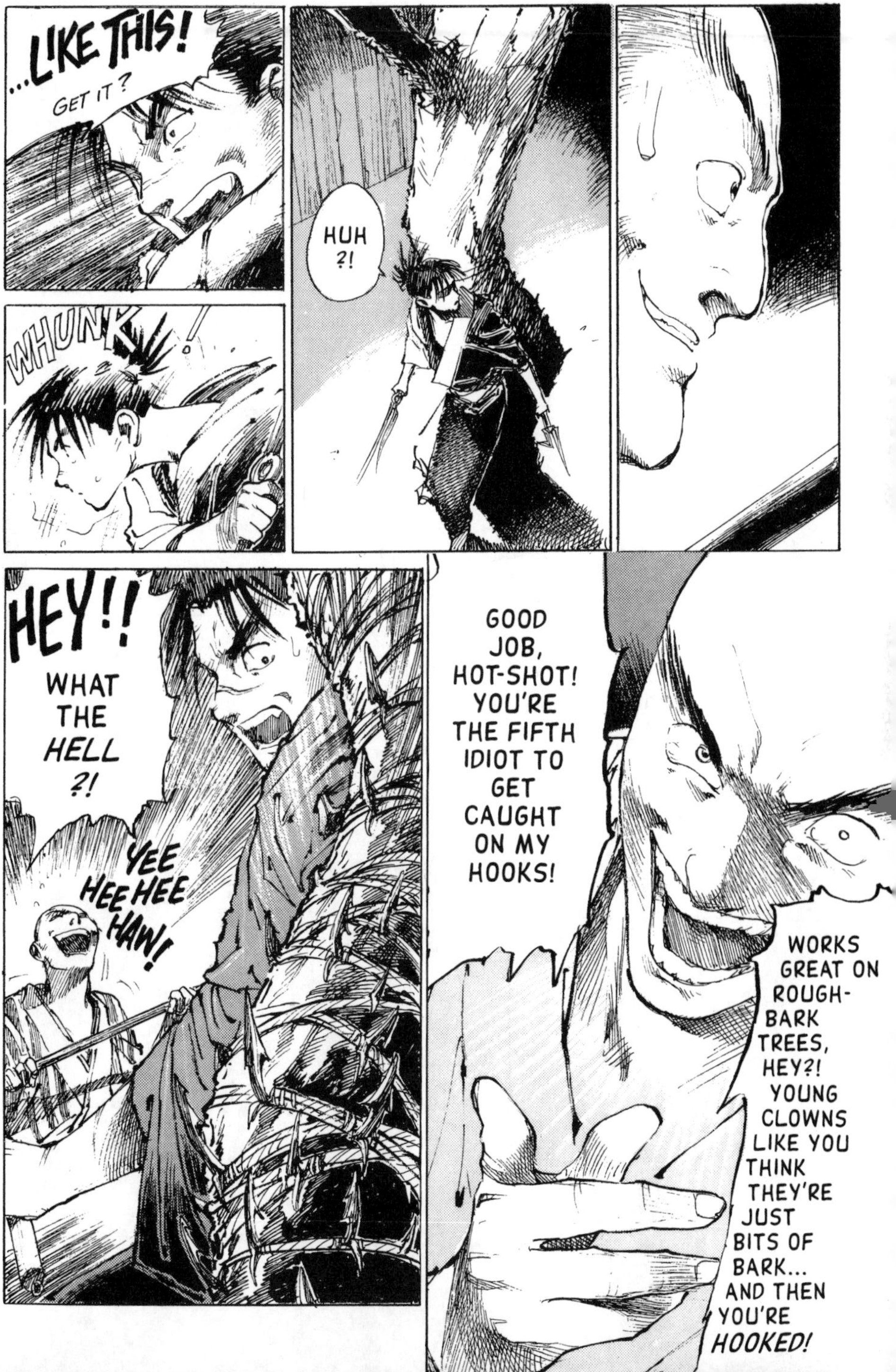
...LIKE THIS!
GET IT?
WHUNK
HUH ?!
HEY!!
WHAT THE HELL ?!
YEE HEE HEE HEE HAW!
GOOD JOB, HOT-SHOT! YOU'RE THE FIFTH IDIOT TO GET CAUGHT ON MY HOOKS!
WORKS GREAT ON ROUGH-BARK TREES, HEY?! YOUNG CLOWNS LIKE YOU THINK THEY'RE JUST BITS OF BARK... AND THEN YOU'RE HOOKED!

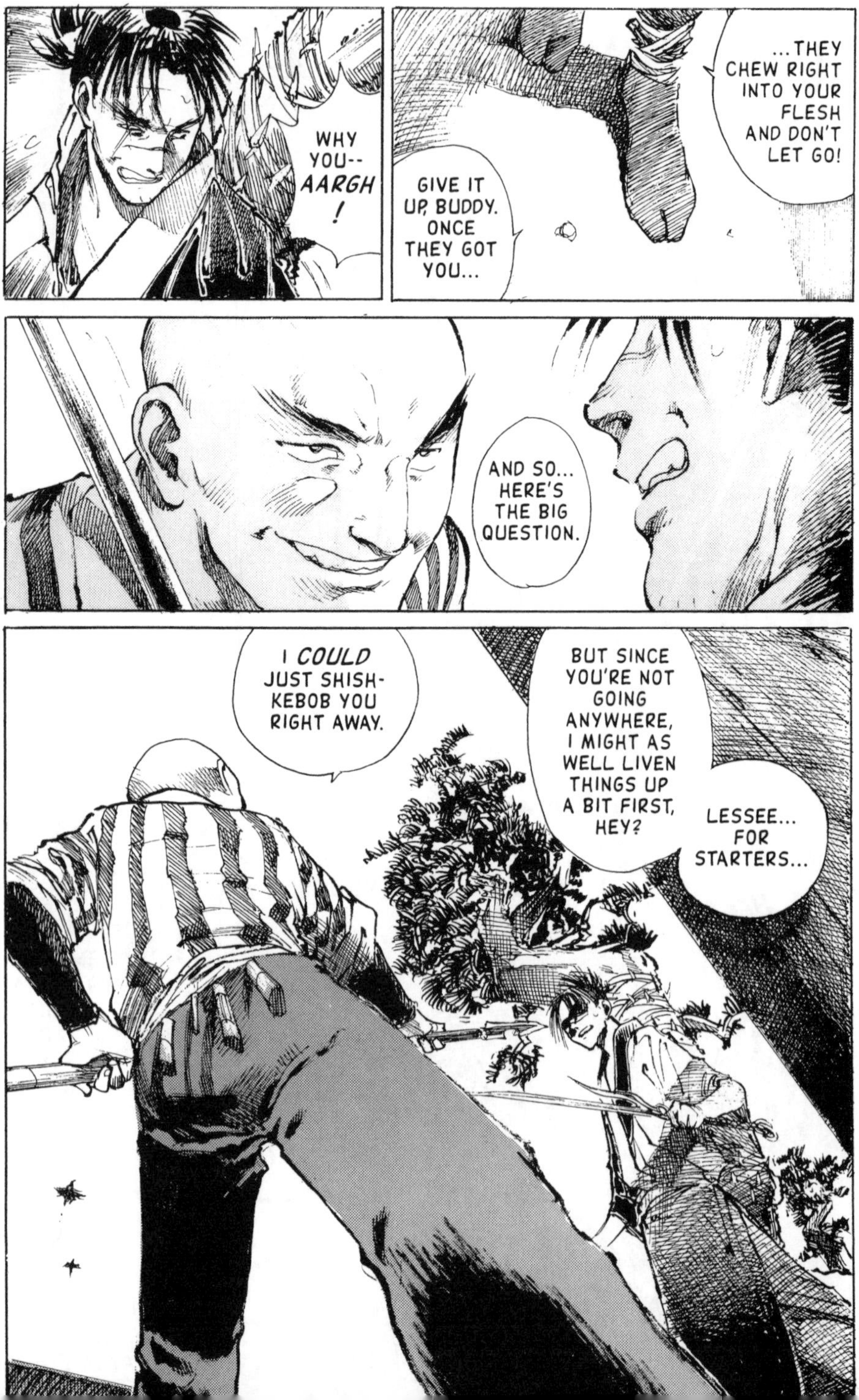
WHY YOU-- AARGH!
GIVE IT UP, BUDDY. ONCE THEY GOT YOU...
...THEY CHEW RIGHT INTO YOUR FLESH AND DON'T LET GO!
AND SO... HERE'S THE BIG QUESTION.
I COULD JUST SHISH-KEBOB YOU RIGHT AWAY.
BUT SINCE YOU'RE NOT GOING ANYWHERE, I MIGHT AS WELL LIVEN THINGS UP A BIT FIRST, HEY?
LESSEE... FOR STARTERS...

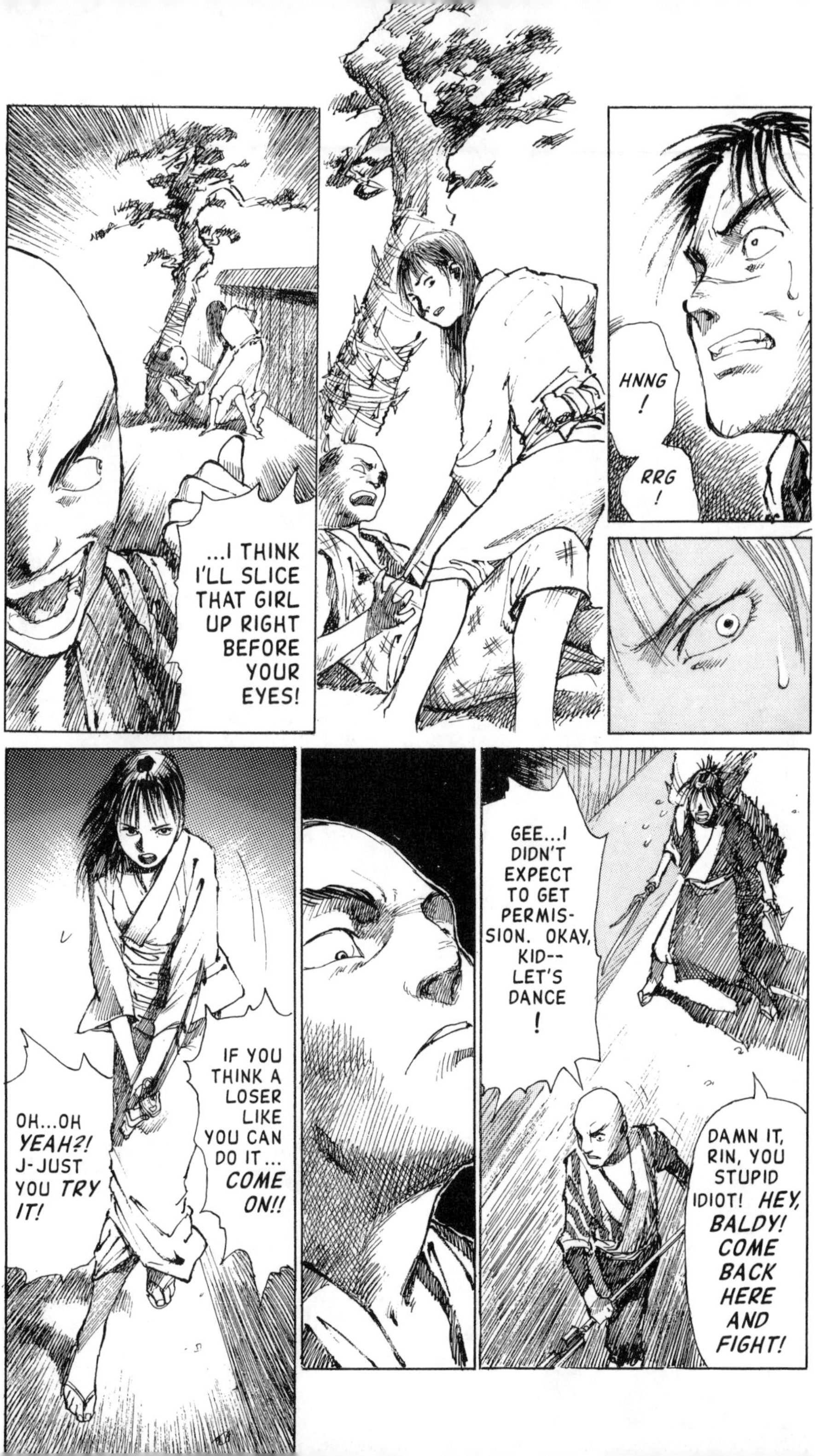
...I THINK I'LL SLICE THAT GIRL UP RIGHT BEFORE YOUR EYES!
HNNG!
RRG!
IF YOU THINK A LOSER LIKE YOU CAN DO IT... COME ON!!
OH...OH YEAH?! J-JUST YOU TRY IT!
GEE...I DIDN'T EXPECT TO GET PERMISSION. OKAY, KID-- LET'S DANCE!
DAMN IT, RIN, YOU STUPID IDIOT! HEY, BALDY! COME BACK HERE AND FIGHT!

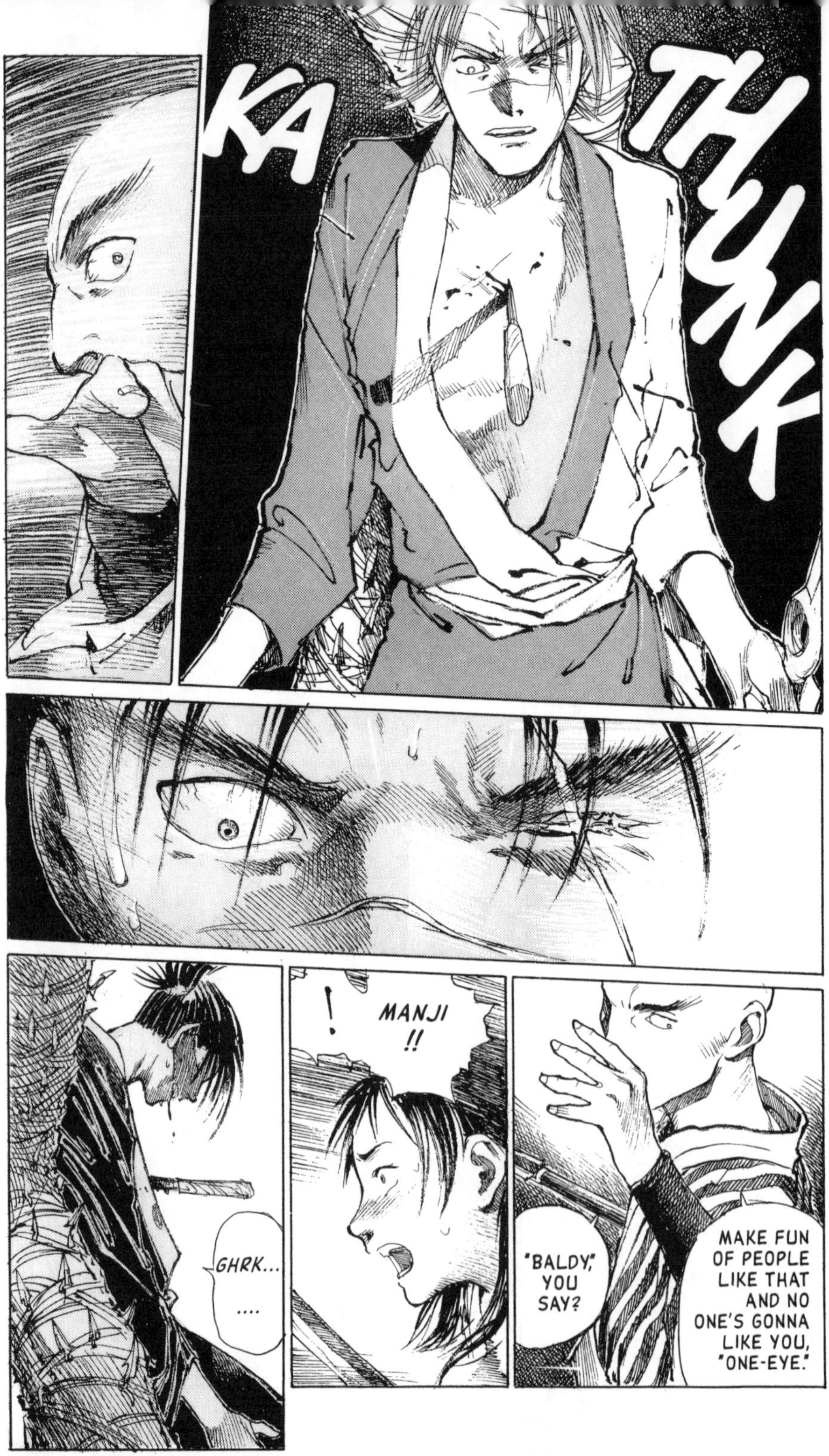
KA
THUNK
GHRK...
....
!
MANJI !!
"BALDY," YOU SAY?
MAKE FUN OF PEOPLE LIKE THAT AND NO ONE'S GONNA LIKE YOU, "ONE-EYE."

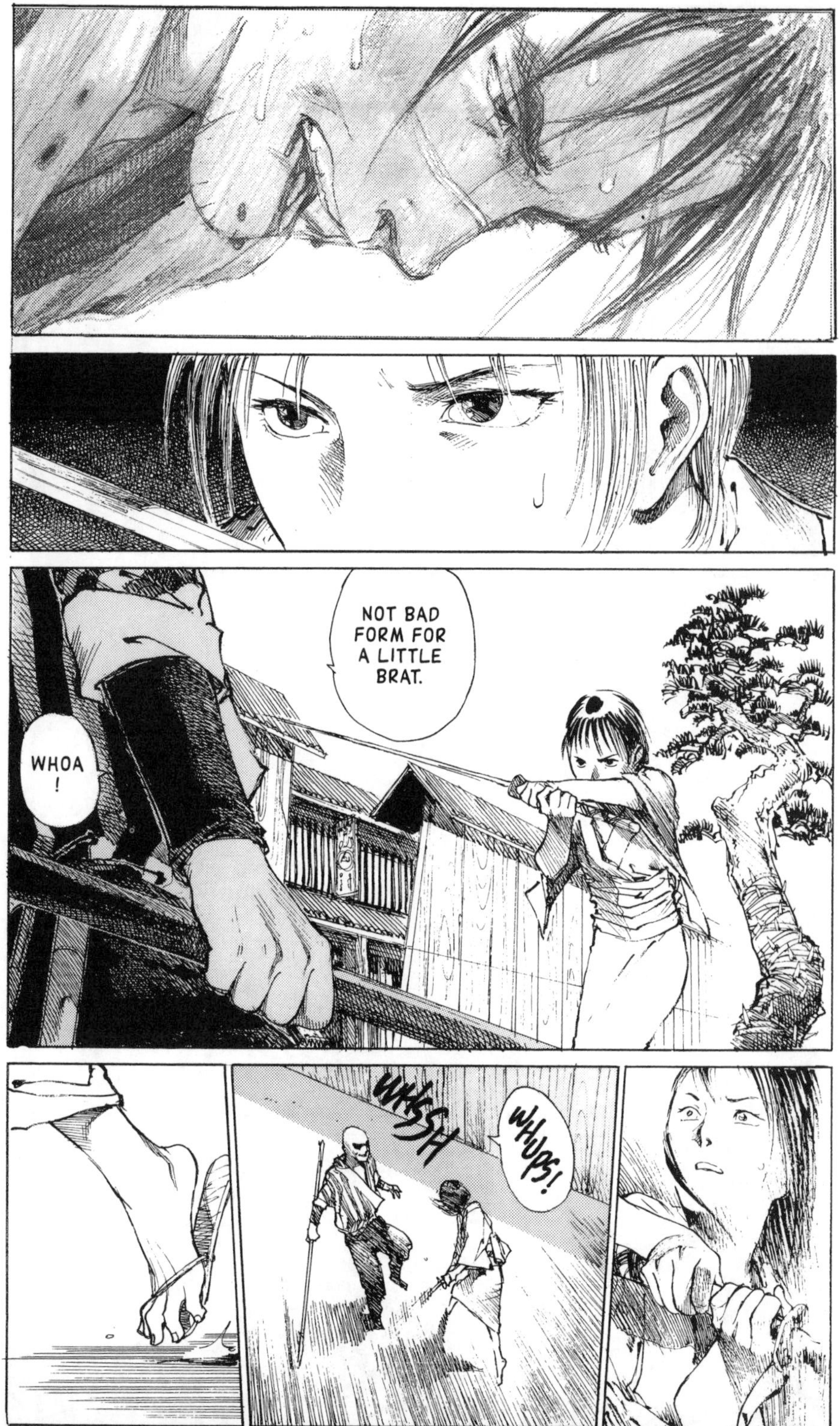
WHOA!
NOT BAD FORM FOR A LITTLE BRAT.
WHSSH
WHUPS!

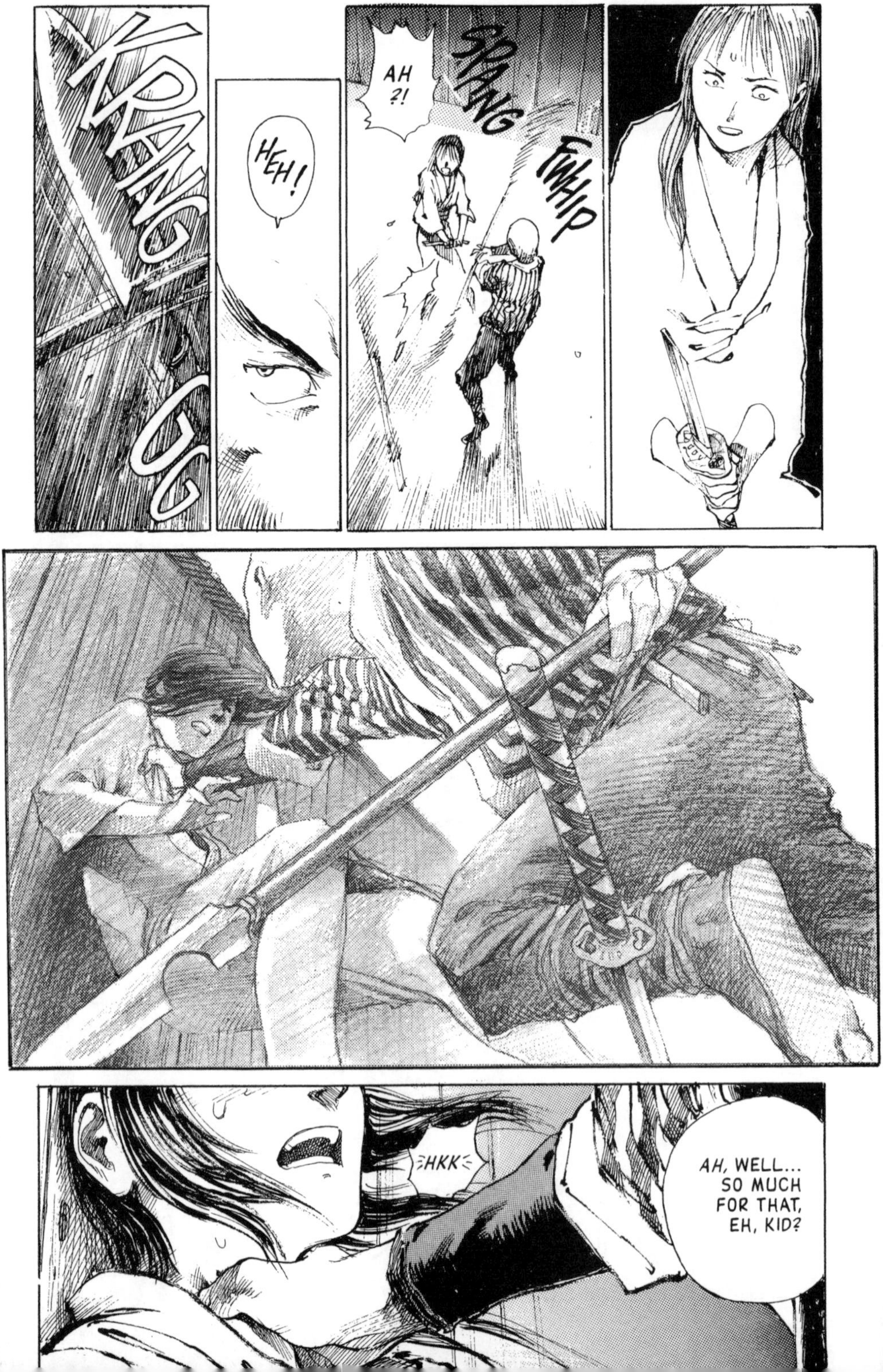
KRANG
GIG
HEH!
AH ?!
SPRANG
FWHIP
HKK
AH, WELL... SO MUCH FOR THAT, EH, KID?

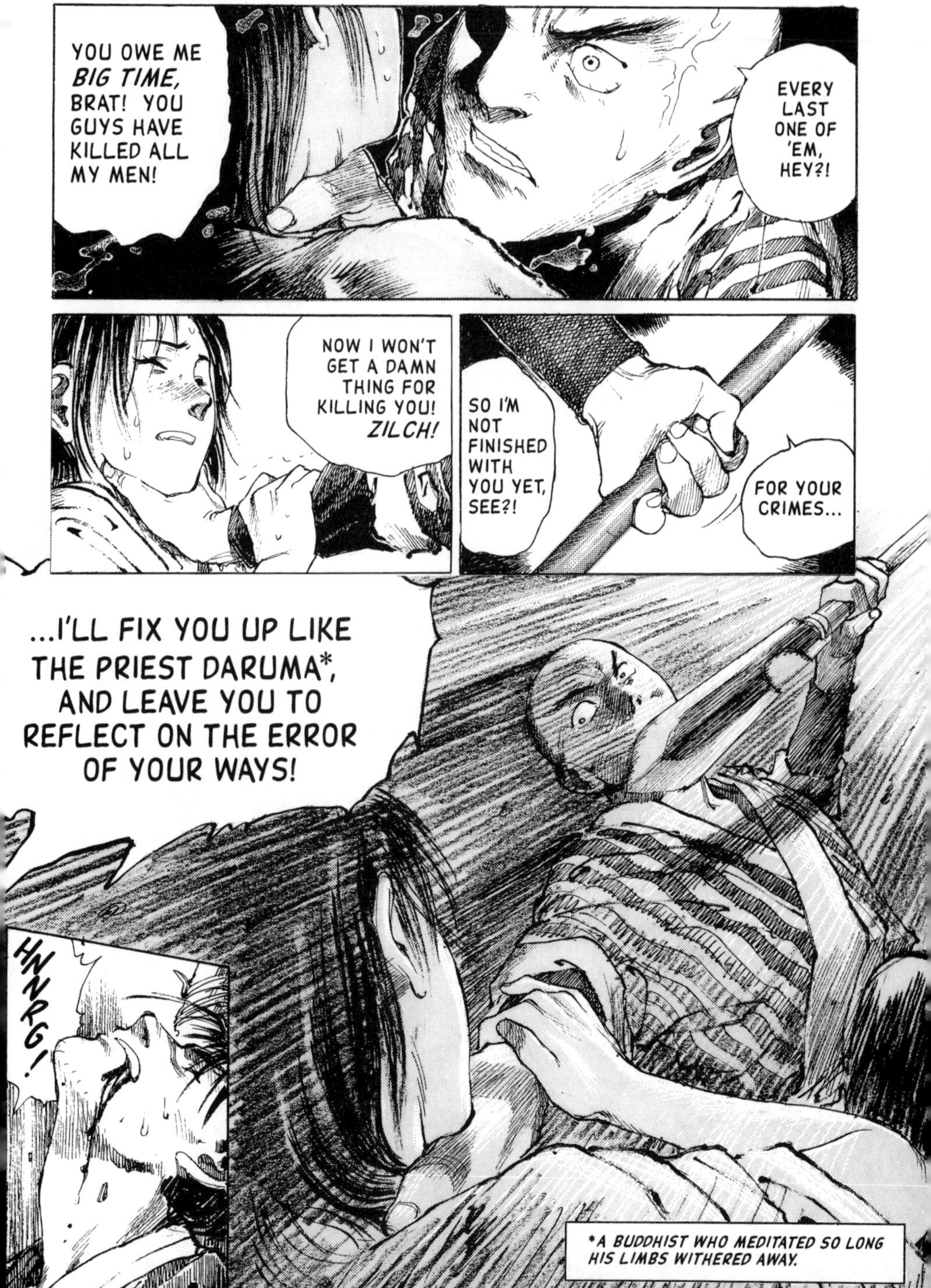
YOU OWE ME BIG TIME, BRAT! YOU GUYS HAVE KILLED ALL MY MEN!
EVERY LAST ONE OF 'EM, HEY?!
NOW I WON'T GET A DAMN THING FOR KILLING YOU! ZILCH!
SO I'M NOT FINISHED WITH YOU YET, SEE?!
FOR YOUR CRIMES...
...I'LL FIX YOU UP LIKE THE PRIEST DARUMA*, AND LEAVE YOU TO REFLECT ON THE ERROR OF YOUR WAYS!
HNNRG!
*A BUDDHIST WHO MEDITATED SO LONG HIS LIMBS WITHERED AWAY.

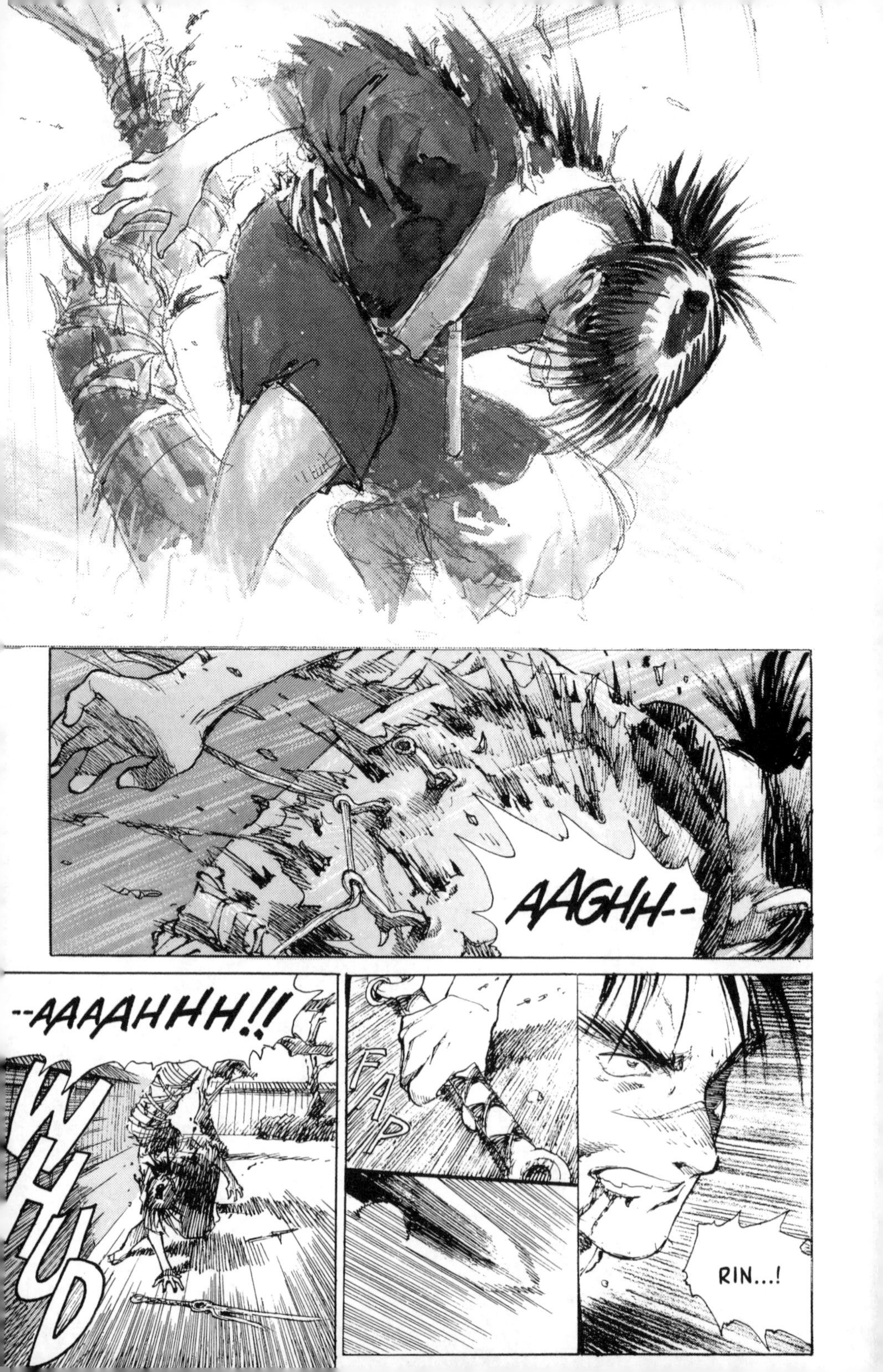
AAGHH--
--AAAAHHH!!
WHUD
FAP
RIN...!

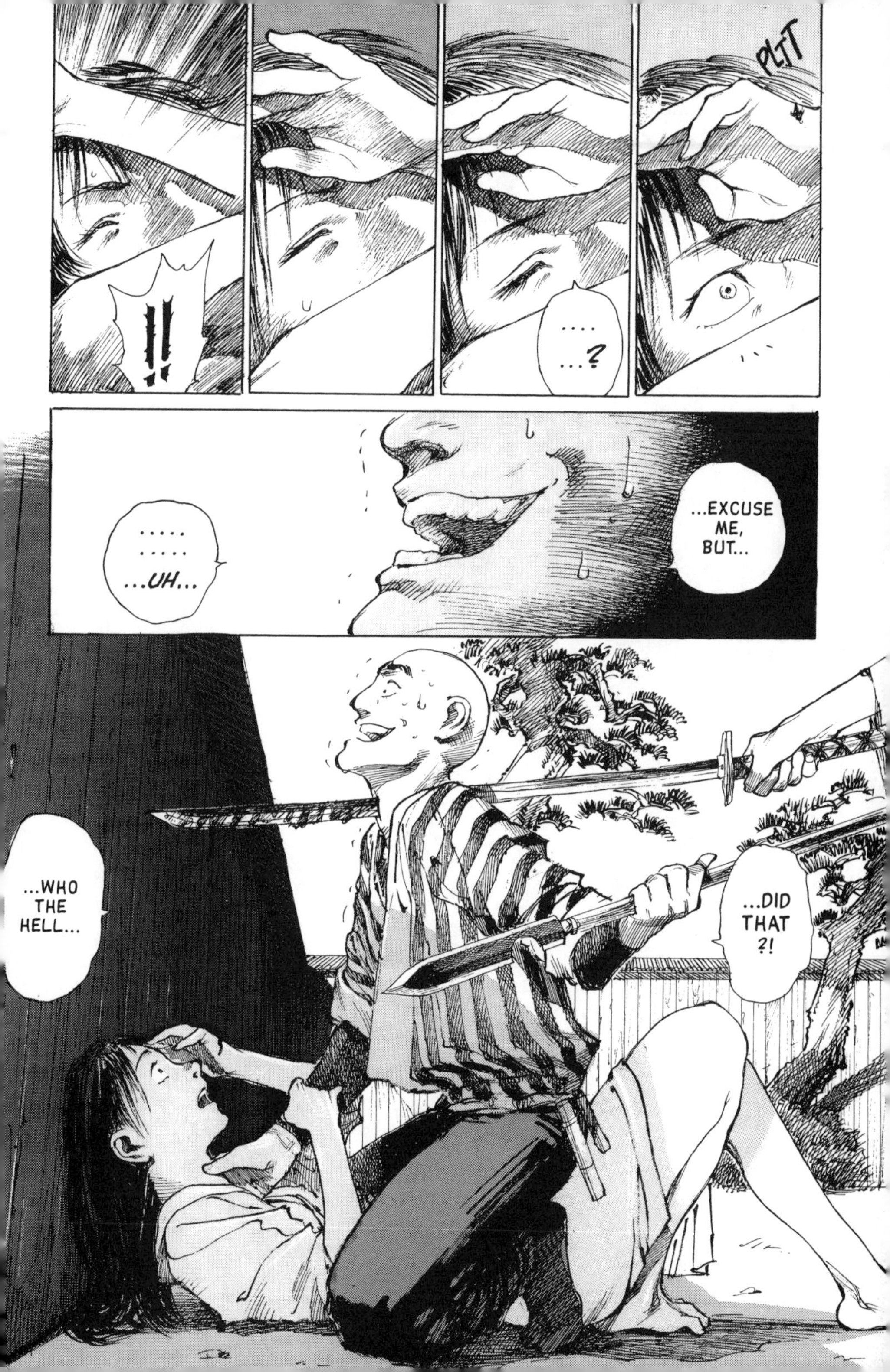
!!
....
...?
PLTT
.....
.....
...UH...
...EXCUSE ME, BUT...
...WHO THE HELL...
...DID THAT?!

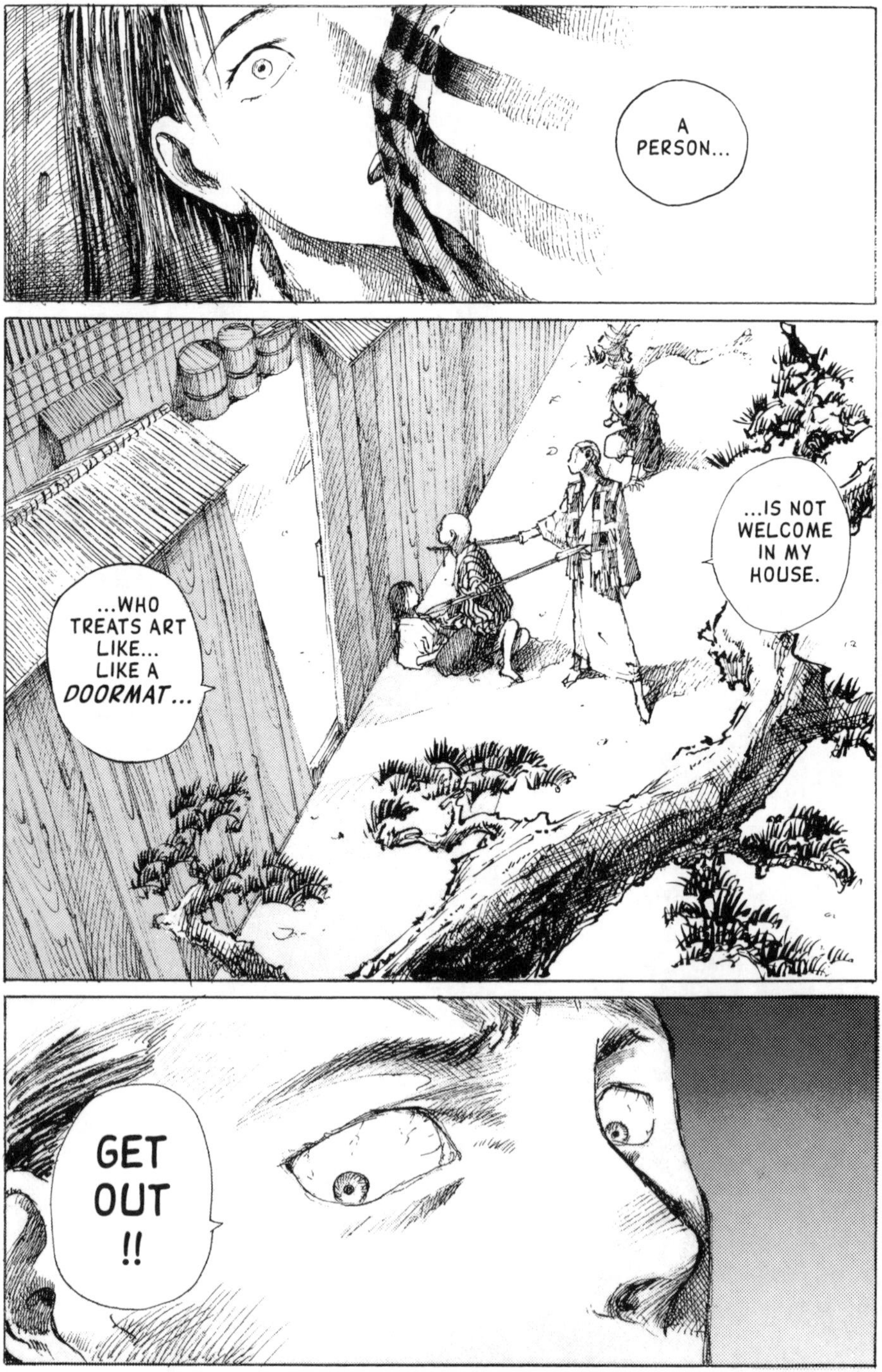
A PERSON...
...WHO TREATS ART LIKE... LIKE A *DOORMAT*...
...IS NOT WELCOME IN MY HOUSE.
GET OUT !!

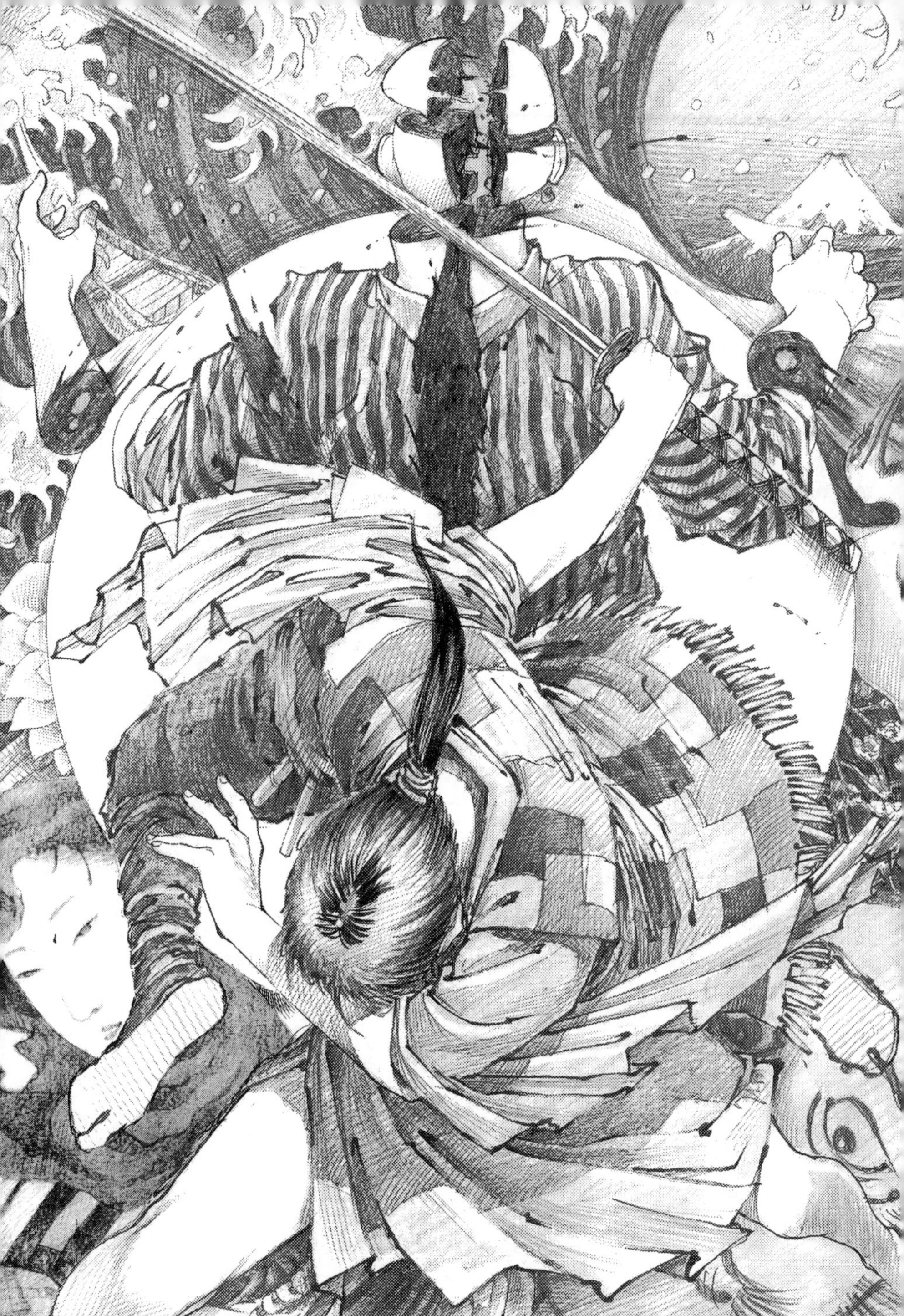

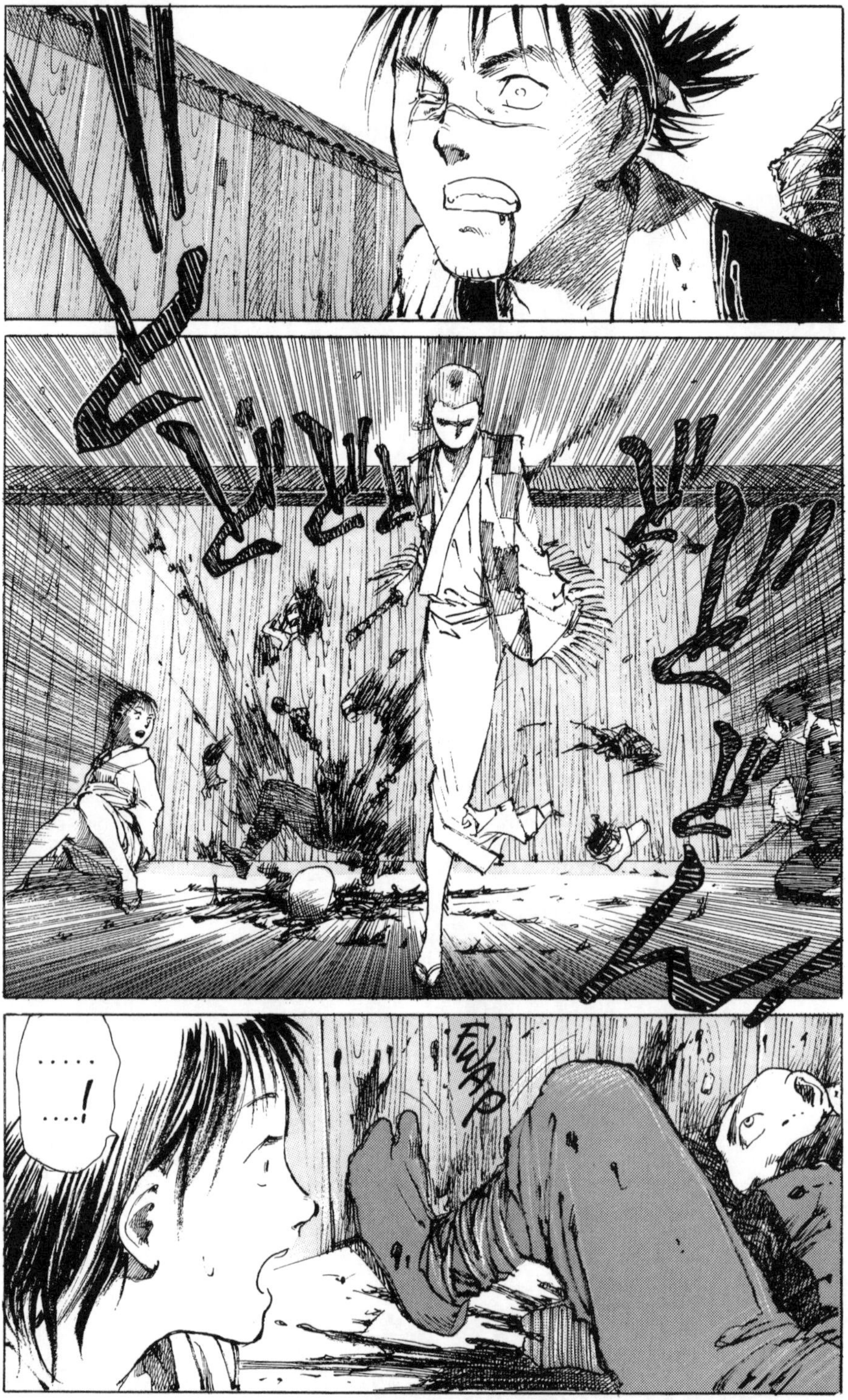
.....
....!
FLUMP

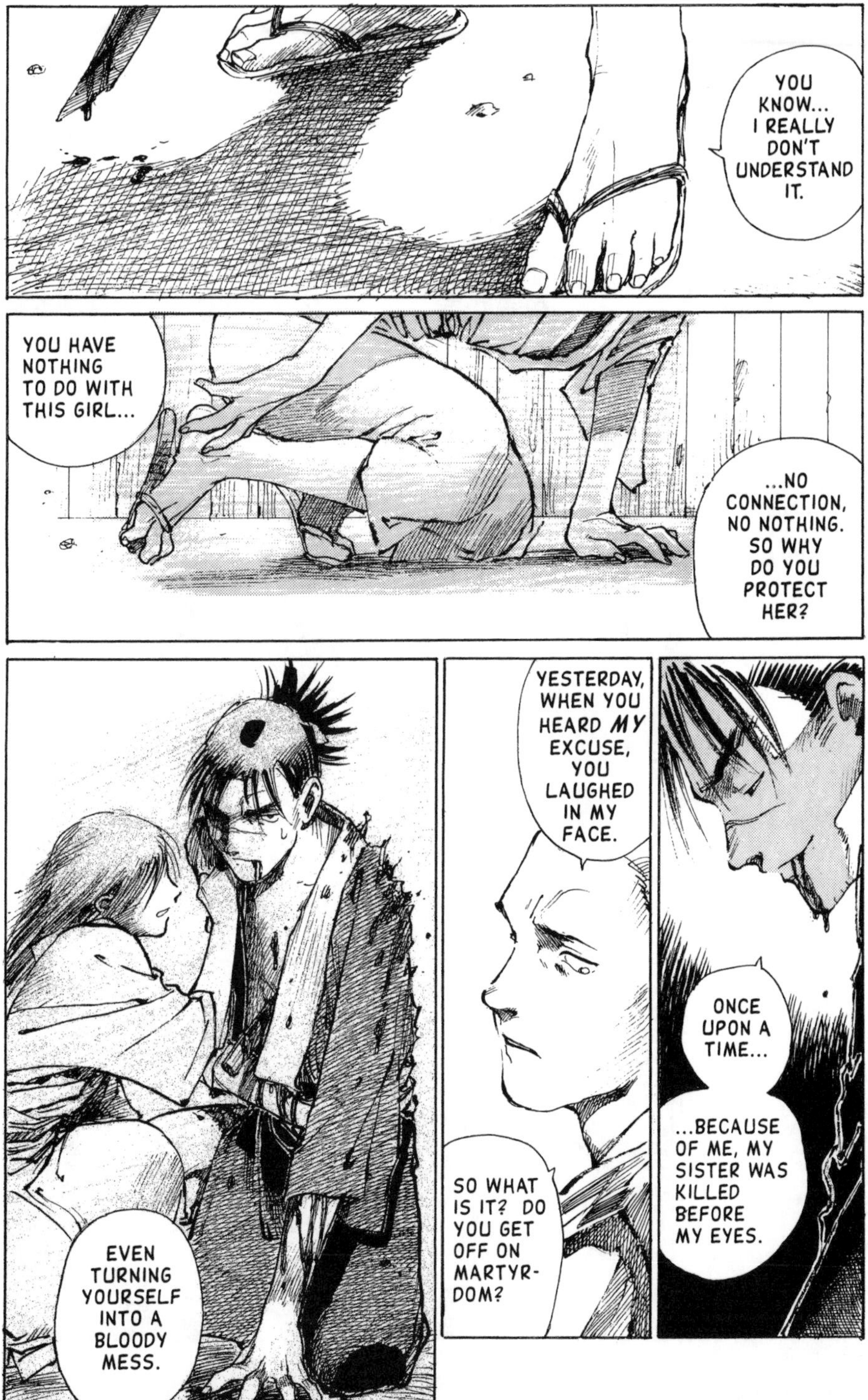
YOU KNOW... I REALLY DON'T UNDERSTAND IT.
YOU HAVE NOTHING TO DO WITH THIS GIRL...
...NO CONNECTION, NO NOTHING. SO WHY DO YOU PROTECT HER?
EVEN TURNING YOURSELF INTO A BLOODY MESS.
YESTERDAY, WHEN YOU HEARD *MY* EXCUSE, YOU LAUGHED IN MY FACE.
SO WHAT IS IT? DO YOU GET OFF ON MARTYR-DOM?
ONCE UPON A TIME...
...BECAUSE OF ME, MY SISTER WAS KILLED BEFORE MY EYES.

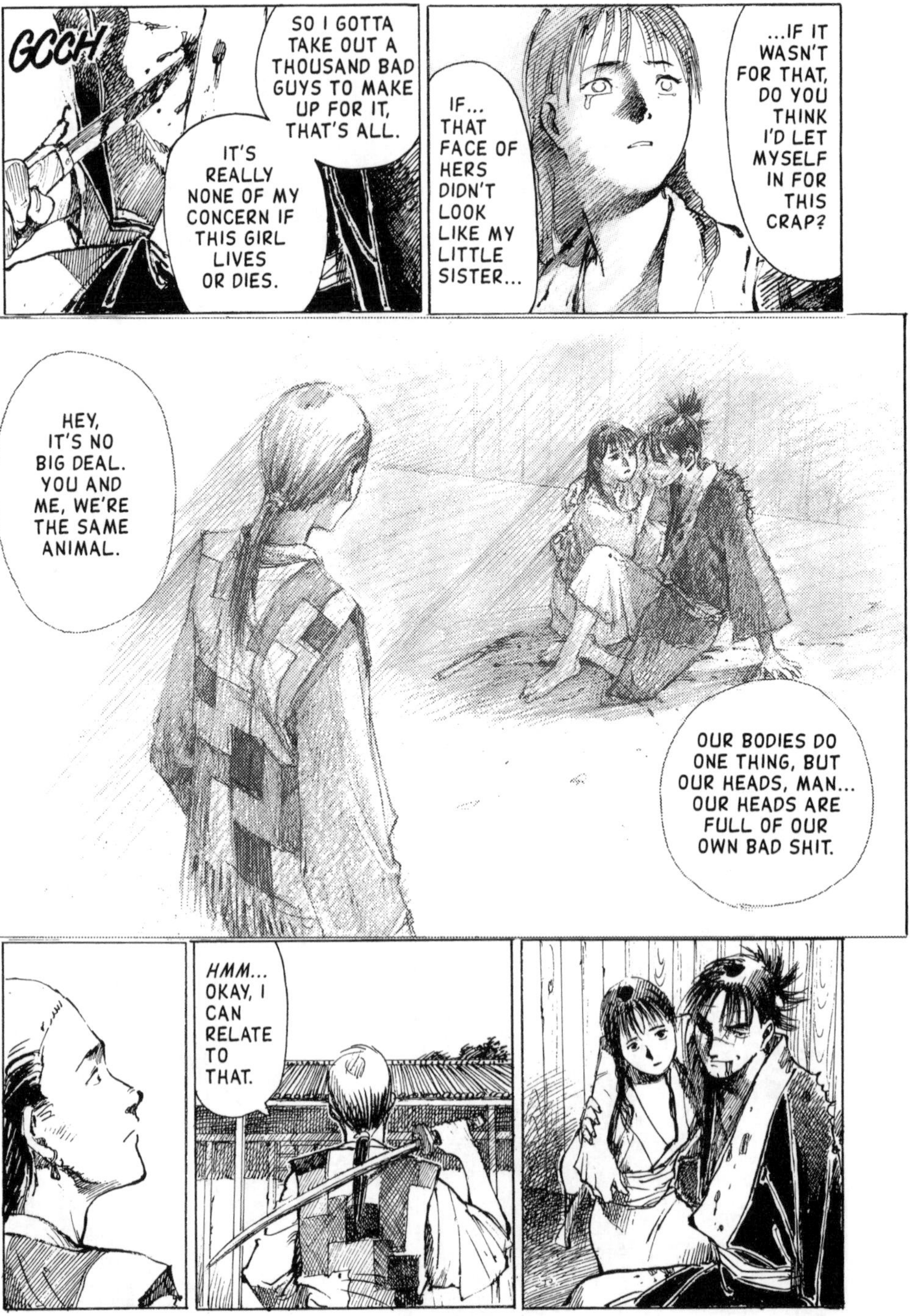
GCCH
SO I GOTTA TAKE OUT A THOUSAND BAD GUYS TO MAKE UP FOR IT, THAT'S ALL.
IT'S REALLY NONE OF MY CONCERN IF THIS GIRL LIVES OR DIES.
IF... THAT FACE OF HERS DIDN'T LOOK LIKE MY LITTLE SISTER...
...IF IT WASN'T FOR THAT, DO YOU THINK I'D LET MYSELF IN FOR THIS CRAP?
HEY, IT'S NO BIG DEAL. YOU AND ME, WE'RE THE SAME ANIMAL.
OUR BODIES DO ONE THING, BUT OUR HEADS, MAN... OUR HEADS ARE FULL OF OUR OWN BAD SHIT.
HMM... OKAY, I CAN RELATE TO THAT.

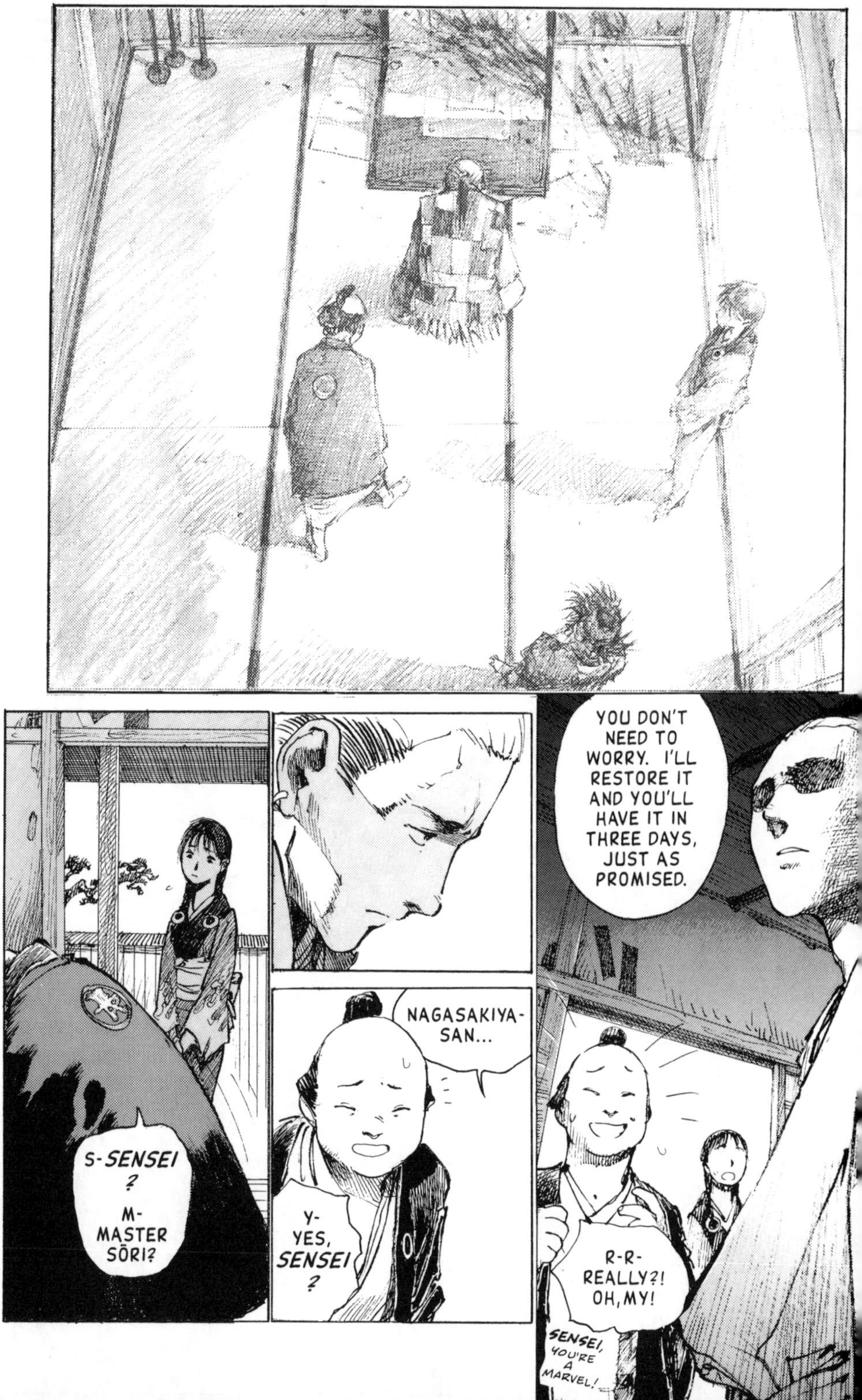
S-SENSEI?
M-MASTER SŌRI?
NAGASAKIYA-SAN...
Y-YES, SENSEI?
YOU DON'T NEED TO WORRY. I'LL RESTORE IT AND YOU'LL HAVE IT IN THREE DAYS, JUST AS PROMISED.
R-R-REALLY?! OH, MY!
SENSEI, YOU'RE A MARVEL!

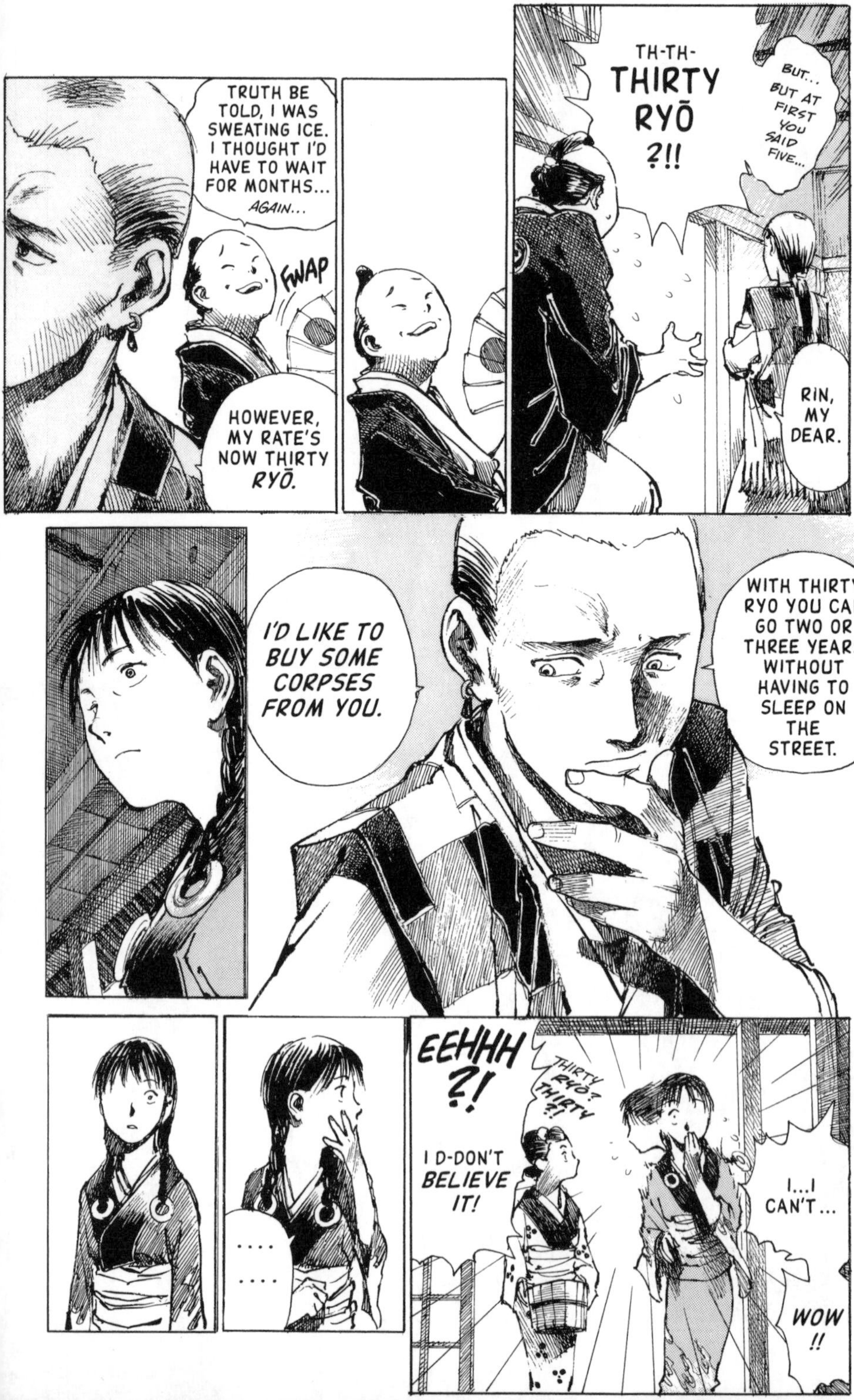
TRUTH BE TOLD, I WAS SWEATING ICE. I THOUGHT I'D HAVE TO WAIT FOR MONTHS... AGAIN...
FWAP
HOWEVER, MY RATE'S NOW THIRTY RYŌ.
TH-TH- THIRTY RYŌ ?!!
BUT... BUT AT FIRST YOU SAID FIVE...
RIN, MY DEAR.
I'D LIKE TO BUY SOME CORPSES FROM YOU.
WITH THIRTY RYO YOU CAN GO TWO OR THREE YEARS WITHOUT HAVING TO SLEEP ON THE STREET.
....
EEHHH ?!
THIRTY RYŌ? THIRTY ?!
I D-DON'T BELIEVE IT!
I...I CAN'T...
WOW !!

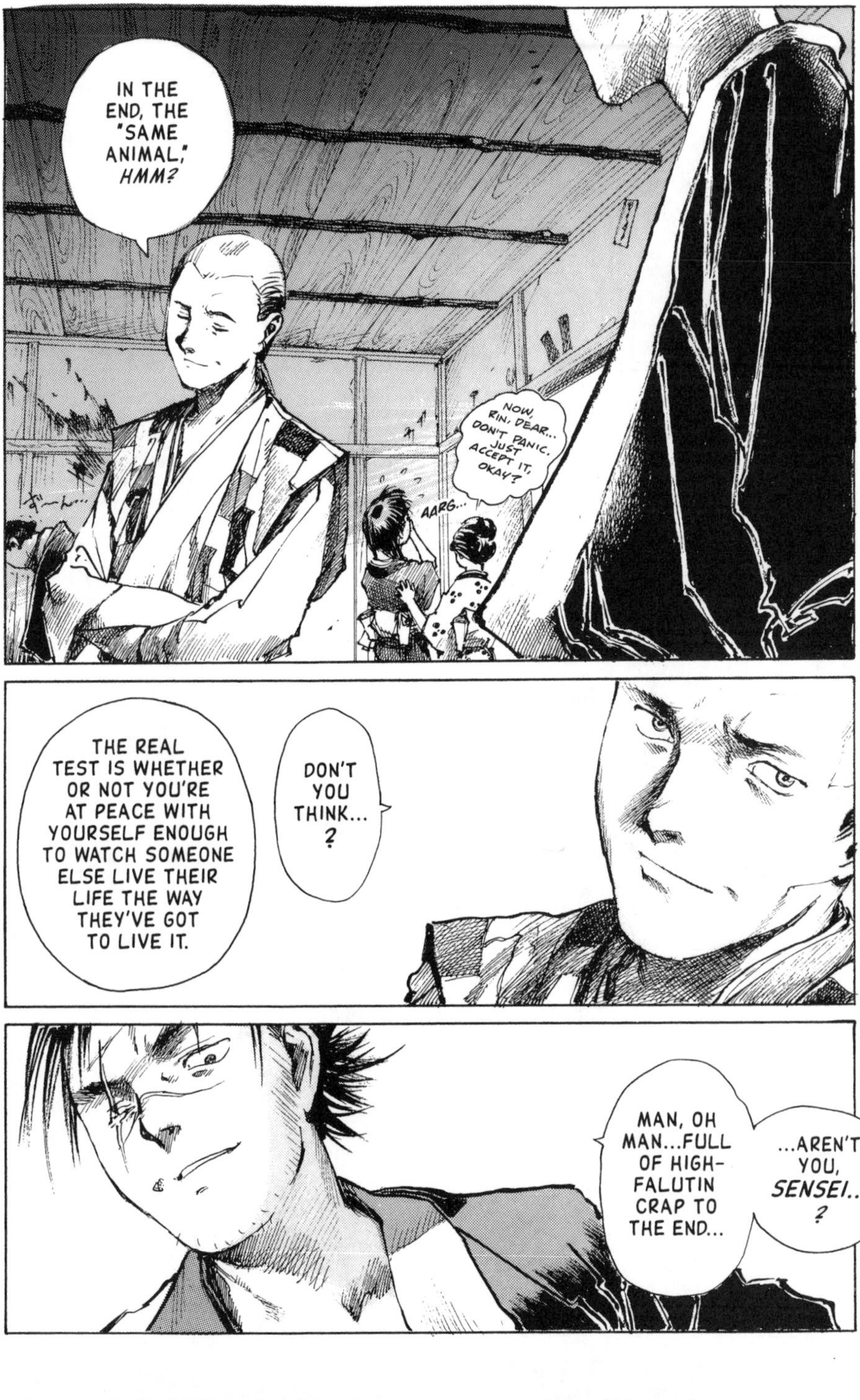
IN THE END, THE "SAME ANIMAL," *HMM?*
AARG...
NOW, RIN, DEAR... DON'T PANIC. JUST ACCEPT IT, OKAY?
THE REAL TEST IS WHETHER OR NOT YOU'RE AT PEACE WITH YOURSELF ENOUGH TO WATCH SOMEONE ELSE LIVE THEIR LIFE THE WAY THEY'VE GOT TO LIVE IT.
DON'T YOU THINK...?
MAN, OH MAN...FULL OF HIGH-FALUTIN CRAP TO THE END...
...AREN'T YOU, *SENSEI...*?

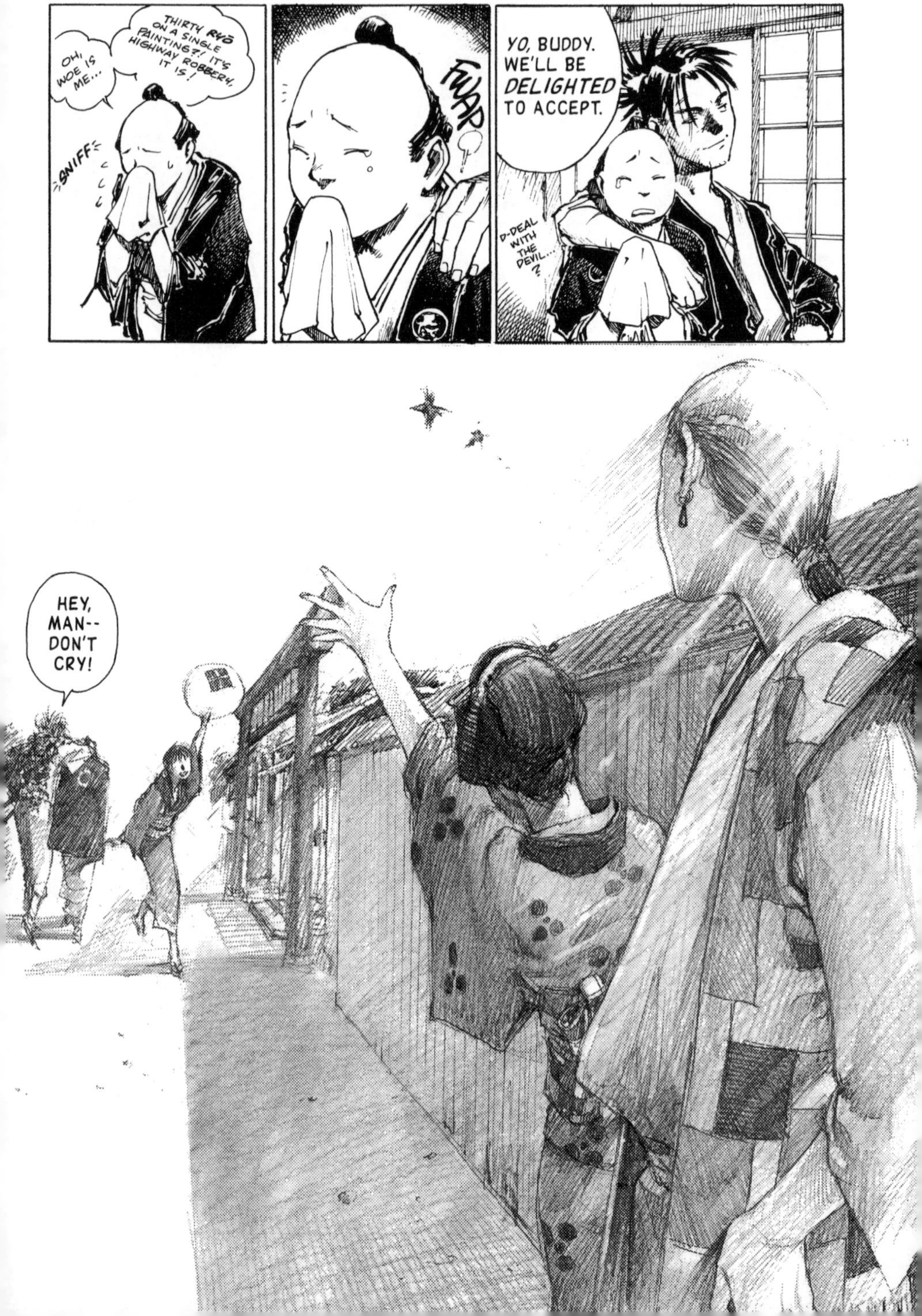
OH, WOE IS ME...
THIRTY RYŌ ON A SINGLE PAINTING?! IT'S HIGHWAY ROBBERY, IT IS!
SNIFF
FWAP
YO, BUDDY. WE'LL BE DELIGHTED TO ACCEPT.
D-DEAL WITH THE DEVIL...?
HEY, MAN-- DON'T CRY!

AN INTERVIEW WITH

HIROAKI SAMURA

Samurai stories are as old as the history of manga in Japan. But when Hiroaki Samura released Blade of the Immortal *in the pages of* Afternoon *comics, it sent a shock wave through the industry. Samura's nihilistic-punk sensibility, masterful artwork, and science-fiction edge turns the old chestnut of "the lone swordsman steeped in Bushido" on its head. The immortal Manji is looking for a way to die, and he doesn't much care who gets in the way of his arsenal of exotic weapons. It's the aspiring swordswoman Rin, seeking to avenge her father's murder, who finally leads Manji to the only samurai in Japan who cares even less about Bushido than he does — the road-warrior swordsmen of Itto-ryu. The lesson is life, but it's written in blood.*

Studio Proteus: *Where did* Blade of the Immortal *come from?*

Samura: I set out with the idea of trying to create a new genre of manga . . . But even before that, back when I first started into comics, I told myself that I would make the problem of living in this world my lifelong theme. For that, I figured that *jidai-geki* (period samurai dramas) would be better than something with a modern setting; death was a bigger part of life in Samurai times. But if I tried to make it totally real, I knew I'd get all kinds of complaints about accuracy from the samurai freaks. So I chose a style right from the beginning that said, "don't obsess about the details. Look at the story."

SP: *And the characters and storytelling?*

S: On the visual side, my biggest model has been *Tange Sazen*. I was blown away by the illustrations Tatsumi Shimura drew of Sazen, so I took the liberty of trying it myself. On the character side, in the protagonist Manji I've drawn a totally straight, unvarnished version of my own ideal hero — a person who never reveals his or her own weaknesses to others but who, at the same time, is not as unassailably

powerful as he or she may seem. I didn't have a model for Rin herself, but after I drew her, my family started saying she looks like my younger sister.

SP: *How did you become a manga artist?*

S: There's no story to tell, really. After I finished college, I submitted some of my work to *Afternoon's* new talent contest, and I was in. It's not as if I came up with my pencil work on my own. In my circle of manga friends at school, there was an upperclassman who used pencil, and I learned a lot from him.

SP: Blade of the Immortal *features all kinds of exotic swords and other weapons . . .*

S: Almost all of the weapons and combat techniques are my own creations. The Itto-ryu school of swordfighting is a play on the name of another, real school of swordsmanship, but the content is totally different. The Itto-ryu swordsmen and swordswomen reject all notions of "schools" of fighting and ritualistic formula. That's where they came up with all those crazy techniques they use. And by the way, I can't do any martial arts myself.

SP: *Every episode features a climactic duel, which you recreate in an almost mandala-like, full-page illustration. It seems like a lot of work.*

S: I spend a full day on a two-page spread like that. It's not so much the actual drawing . . . What's really hard is finding the right pose. I chose black and white because, frankly, I don't like painting colors over art. I've never once thought I'd like to work in color.

SP: *Like Masamune Shirow, you refuse to be photographed or to make public appearances. Can you tell us something about your personal life?*

S: Came into the world on February 17, 1970. Born in Chiba prefecture (near Tokyo), never married. I don't appear in public because I believe there's no reason for readers to know that much about the cartoonist. What matters is the art. As for hobbies, I don't really have one. But I have been drawing some erotic pictures of women, all kinds of variations. If enough of them pile up, I may put out a collection — on my own dime, of course.

COVER GALLERY

While this collected edition features Hiroaki Samura's cover art to *Blade of the Immortal* issue five, here and on the following three pages are the covers, in order, of issues one, two, three, and six.

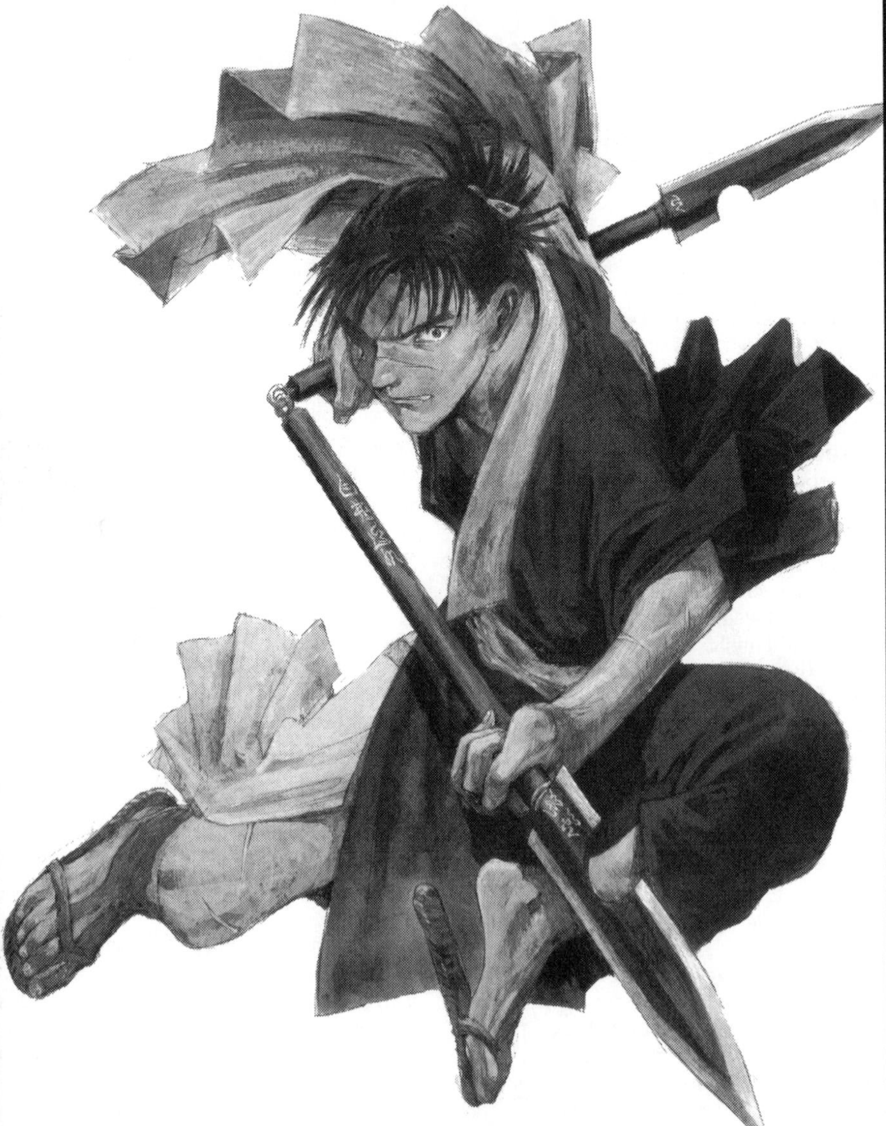

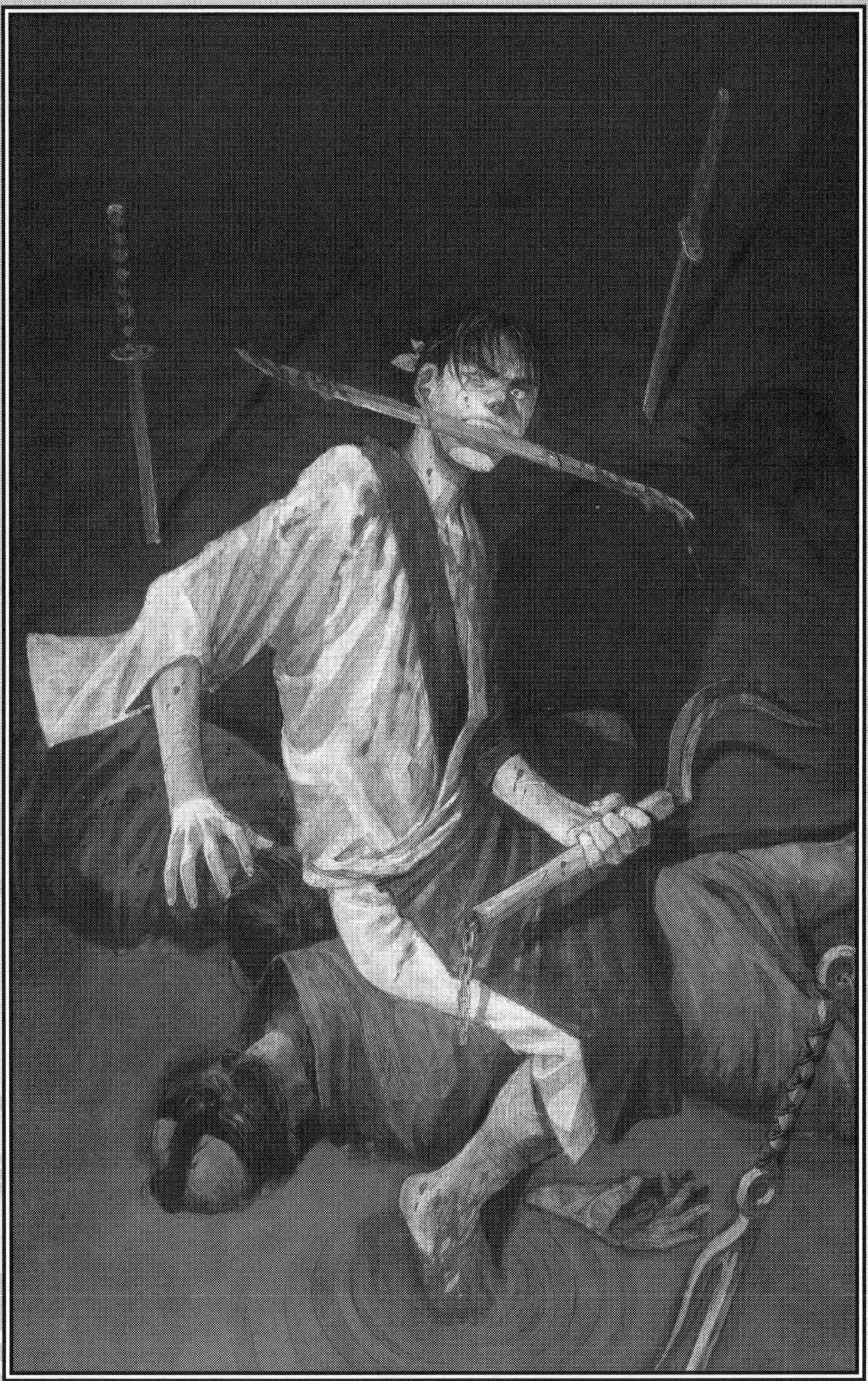

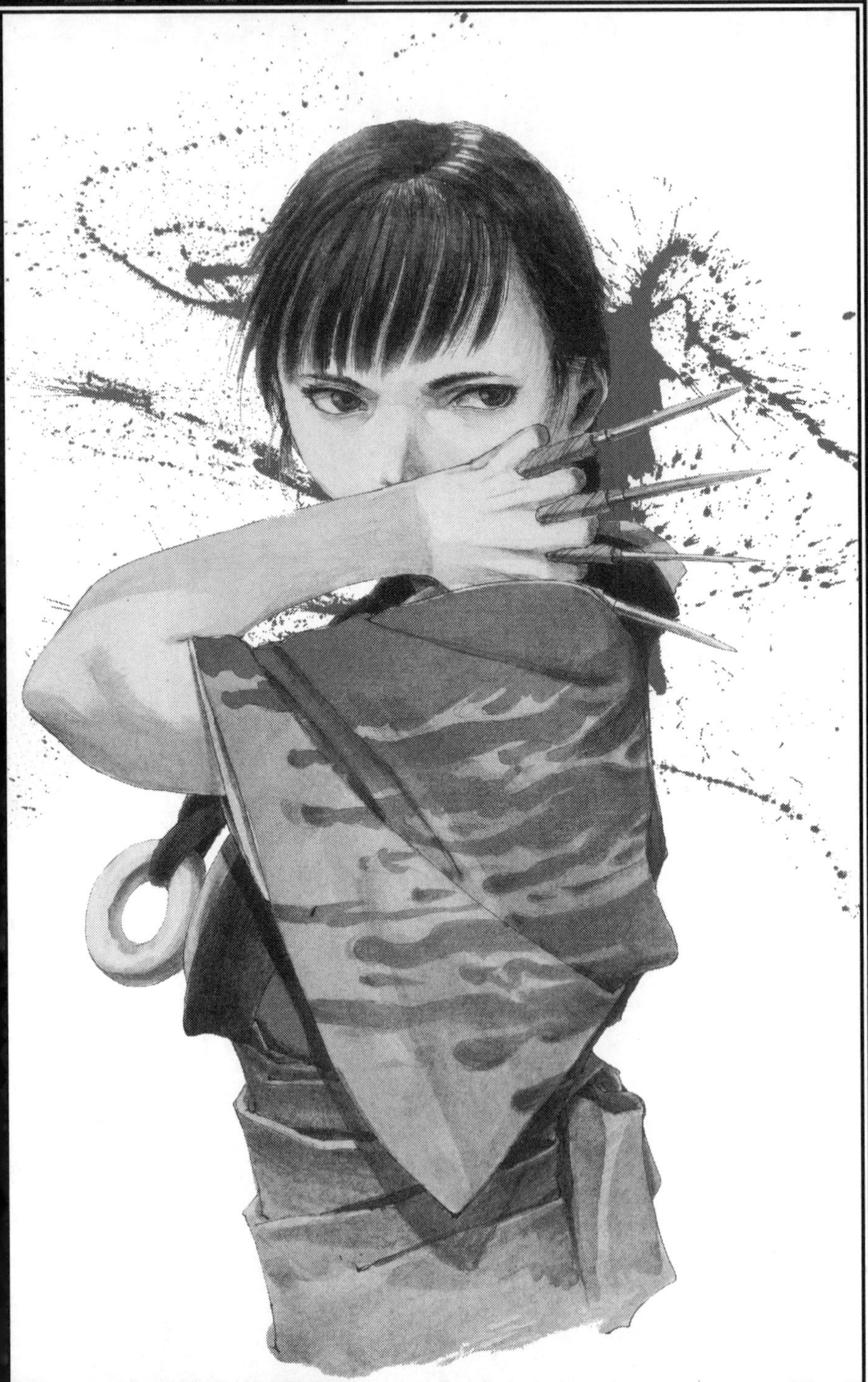